Change in SMEs

Change in SMEs

Towards a New European Capitalism?

Edited by

Katharina Bluhm
*Assistant Professor, Friedrich-Schiller-University Jena,
Germany*

and

Rudi Schmidt
Emeritus Professor, Friedrich-Schiller-University Jena, Germany

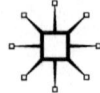

First published 2008 by
PALGRAVE MACMILLAN
Houndmills, Basingstoke, Hampshire RG21 6XS and
175 Fifth Avenue, New York, N.Y. 10010
Companies and representatives throughout the world

PALGRAVE MACMILLAN is the global academic imprint of the
Palgrave Macmillan division of St. Martin's Press, LLC and of
Palgrave Macmillan Ltd. Macmillan® is a registered trademark
in the United States, United Kingdom and other countries.
Palgrave is a registered trademark in the European Union
and other countries.

ISBN-13: 978–0–230–51589–5   hardback
ISBN-10: 0–230–51589–4   hardback

This book is printed on paper suitable for recycling and made
from fully managed and sustained forest sources. Logging,
pulping and manufacturing processes are expected to conform
to the environmental regulations of the country of origin.

A catalogue record for this book is available from the British Library.

Library of Congress Cataloging-in-Publication Data

Change in SMEs : towards a new European capitalism? / edited by
    Katharina Bluhm and Rudi Schmidt.
        p. cm.
    Based on a conference of the Collaborative Research Center 580,
    German Research Association that took place at the Friedrich–
    Schiller–University of Jena in 2007.
    Includes bibliographical references and index.
    ISBN 0–230–51589–4 (alk. paper)
    1. Small business—Europe—Management—Congresses.   2. Small
    business—Europe—Finance—Congresses.   3. Capitalism—Europe-
    Congresses.   I. Bluhm, Katharina.   II. Schmidt, Rudi.
    HD62.7.C452 2008
    338.6'42094—dc22
                                                        2008016154

10   9   8   7   6   5   4   3   2   1
17   16   15   14   13   12   11   10   09   08

Printed and bound in Great Britain by
CPI Antony Rowe, Chippenham and Eastbourne

Contents

List of Tables   *vii*

List of Figures   *viii*

Acknowledgements   *ix*

Notes on the Contributors   *x*

1. Why Should the Varieties Literature Grant Smaller
   Firms More Attention? An Introduction   1
   Katharina Bluhm and Rudi Schmidt

Part I   Changing Financing, Ownership and
Firm Management   15

2. The Power of Financial Markets – What Does that
   Mean and How Does it Work for Different Categories
   of Companies?   17
   Jürgen Kädtler and Michael Faust

3. Change within Traditional Channels: German SMEs,
   the Restructuring of the Banking Sector, and the
   Growing Shareholder-Value Orientation   39
   Katharina Bluhm and Bernd Martens

4. Corporate Financing, Management and Organization
   in SMEs: An Anglo-German Comparison   58
   Mike Geppert and Bernd Martens

5. Stakeholder or Shareholder Orientation? Entrepreneurial
   Careers and Value Preferences of Entrepreneurs in
   East Germany   77
   Rainhart Lang

6. SMEs in France: New Perspectives and New Generation
   of Small-Business Owners   99
   Alain Fayolle and Salma Fattoum

7. Family Business and Family Change: The End of Patriarchalism 118
Hermann Kotthoff

Part II   SMEs in Globalized Production Networks   133

8. SMEs in the Global Economy: A Comparison of the Global Production Networks of German and British Clothing Firms 135
Christel Lane and Jocelyn Probert

9. Flexibility and Formalization: Rethinking Space and Governance in Corporations and Manufacturing Regions 152
Gary Herrigel

10. Innovation Strategies of Non-Research-Intensive SMEs 171
Hartmut Hirsch-Kreinsen

11. From the 'Wild West' Towards Europe: Change and Challenges in SMEs in Poland 185
Tadeusz Borkowski and Aleksander Marcinkowski

Part III   Labour Relations in Change   201

12. Structural Changes and New Forms of Social Regulation in the 'Third Italy' – the Case of the Emilia-Romagna Region 203
Volker Telljohann

13. Polish SMEs at a Crossroads: Market Strategies and Labour Relations in Global Competition 228
Ralph-Elmar Lungwitz, Manfred Wannöffel and Yvonne Rückert

14. Unravelling Regulation: How Production Relocation to the East Impacts the German Model of Labour Relations at the Workplace 243
Michael Fichter

15. Irregular Forms of Employee Interest Representation in SMEs: A German-French Comparison 258
Ingrid Artus

16. Social Relationships in German SMEs: An East-West Comparison 274
Rudi Schmidt

Index 291

List of Tables

Table 1.1	Year of implementation according to company's size	9
Table 3.1	Result of two logistic regressions with the German 2002 and 2005 data sets	47
Table 3.2	Distribution of succession planned or carried out in per cent	50
Table 4.1	Distributions of the three above-mentioned surveys	61
Table 5.1	CSR value preferences in critical decisions	87
Table 5.2	CSR value preferences in critical decision clusters	88
Table 5.3	Differences in leadership dimensions between owner-managers and employed managers	92
Table 6.1	Distribution of French companies (1 January 2005) by number of employees and activity sector	101
Table 8.1	Structure of the German and UK clothing industries, 2001–02	138
Table 13.1	The existence of TU organizations in firms and the enforcement of workers' rights (in per cent)	231
Table 15.1	German companies without a works council according to company size, 2003 (in per cent)	262
Table 15.2	German employees in workplaces without a works council according to company size, 2003 (in per cent)	262
Table 15.3	French companies and employees without any workplace structures of employee representation (IRPs), according to company size, 1998–99 (in per cent)	263
Table 15.4	French companies and workers with the complete system of workplace interest-representation	263
Table 16.1	Enterprises with works council in East- and West-German manufacturing SMEs	277
Table 16.2	Assessment of worker co-determination and union influence	279
Table 16.3	Management's relationship to the works council	280

List of Figures

Figure 5.1   Value preferences of owner-managers and employed managers in critical management decisions   85

Figure 5.2   Value preferences of all CEOs and immediate subordinates in critical management decisions   86

Figure 6.1   Possible paths   110

Figure 6.2   Positioning of the various types of entrepreneurs   113

Figure 8.1   Steps in the clothing value chain   139

Figure 13.1   Factors crucial for competitiveness according to entrepreneurs (2003–2005)   233

Acknowledgements

This book is the result of a conference of the Collaborative Research Center 580 – a chapter of the German Research Foundation (Deutsche Forschungsgemeinschaft or DFG) – that took place at the Friedrich-Schiller-University of Jena in 2007. We would like to thank the DFG and the state of Thuringia for their financial assistance as well as the Friedrich-Schiller-University for their logistical support. Many thanks also to Heather Fuchs and Franz Zurbrugg, who were a tremendous help during the editing process.

Notes on the Contributors

Ingrid Artus is Assistant Professor of Sociology at the Technical University of Munich. She publishes on collective bargaining systems in Germany, France and at European level. Her publications include *Krise des deutschen Tarifsystems. Die Erosion des Flächentarifvertrags in Ost und West* (2001), *Betriebe ohne Betriebsrat* (2006, co-editor), and 'Strike Action to Save the Live of a Plant is Followed by Its 'Honourable Death': The Conflict at AEG in Nuremberg,' *Transfer* (2006). She is currently writing a book on informal interest representation in French and German firms. For this research she received a grant from the Maison de Sciences de l'Homme (MSH) in Paris.

Katharina Bluhm is Assistant Professor for Sociology at the Friedrich-Schiller-University of Jena and currently fellow at the Wissenschaftszentrum in Berlin (WZB). She has been a Research Fellow at the Center for European Studies at Harvard. Her research focuses on varieties of capitalism in east-central Europe, relocation of production, economic and management sociology. Among her recent publications are 'Dealing with the Regulation Gap. Labour Relations in Polish and Czech Subsidiaries of German Companies', in A.-M. Legloannec (ed.): *Non-State Actors in International Relations: The Case of Germany* (2007), *Experimentierfeld Ostmitteleuropa? Deutsche Unternehmen in Polen und der Tschechischen Republik* (2007) and 'The Dilemma of Labour-Relations Liberalisation in East-Central Europe before and after EU Enlargement' in M. A. Moreau and M. E. Blas López (eds): *Restructuring in the New EU Member States* (2008).

Tadeusz Borkowski is Professor at the Jagiellonian University in Krakow (Institute of Economics and Management) and President of Hermes Organization. He researched and/or lectured at Stanford University, Harvard University, Rochester University, University of Wisconsin at Stevens Point, University of Padova, Lithuanian Academy of Science, and the University of Messina. The contribution for this chapter is related to the EU-project PILOT 'Policy and Innovation in Low Tech' (2002–2004). His research interests include: social and psychological aspects of innovation, policy of small- and medium-sized enterprises, relations between regional business and regional administration, and business ethics. Among others he is co-author of the book *Modernization Crises. The Transformation of Poland*, ed. by W. D. Perdue (1995).

Salma Fattoum is a PhD Student at the University of Lyon 3 and EM Lyon and a part-time Pedagogical Assistant at EM Lyon Business School. She is also working at the Entrepreneurship Research Centre 'Entrepreneurial Process Dynamics'. Her research interests include entrepreneurship, family business and small- and medium-sized enterprises.

Alain Fayolle is Professor and Director of the Entrepreneurship Research Centre at EM Lyon, Senior Researcher at CERAG at the University Pierre Mendès France of Grenoble and Visiting Professor at Solvay Business School (Belgium) and HEC Montréal (Canada). His current research focuses on the dynamics of entrepreneurial processes and the social effects of entrepreneurship education programmes. He is author and editor of *Entrepreneurship Research in Europe: Outcomes and Perspectives* (with P. Kyrö J. and Ulijn, 2004) *International Entrepreneurship Education. Issues and Newness* (with H. Klandt, 2006), *Handbook of Research in Entrepreneurship Education* (2007) and *Entrepreneurship and New Value Creation: The Dynamic of the Entrepreneurial Process* (2007).

Michael Faust is a Senior Researcher at the Sociological Research Institute (SOFI) at the Georg-August-University in Göttingen and lecturer at the University. His fields of interest cover the sociology of work and organizations and economic sociology. His main research areas include the sociology of management and business consulting and the field of comparative political economy. He is co-author of the book *Befreit und entwurzelt; Führungskräfte auf dem Weg zum internen Unternehmer* (2000) and co-editor of *Organisation der Arbeit* (2005).

Michael Fichter is a Senior Lecturer and Researcher at the Otto-Suhr-Institute for Political Science, Free University Berlin, His research interests include trade unions and labour relations in Germany and Europe, production relocation and the transformation of labour relations in east-central Europe. Among his recent publications are: 'The German Way. Still Treading the Path of Institutionalized Labor Relations?' in St. Beck, F. Klobes and Ch. Scherrer (eds) *Surviving Globalization? Perspectives for the German Economic Model* (2005), 'Industrial Relations and European Integration', in *Industrielle Beziehungen*' (2006), and 'German Trade Unions and Right Extremism: Understanding Membership Attitudes' in *European Journal of Industrial Relations* (2008).

Mike Geppert is Professor of Comparative International Management and Organization Studies at the School of Management at the University of Surrey, UK. His research is on comparative organization studies, management and organization of MNCs, and institutional change. His research has been published in various academic journals, and led to the editorship of two Special Issues, with Human Relations and the Journal of International Management. Mike has also edited two books with Palgrave, *Challenges for European Management in a Global Context* (2002) and *Global, National and Local Practices in MNCs* (2006).

Gary Herrigel is Professor at the Department of Political Science, University of Chicago and author of numerous works on industrial transformation in the US and Europe, including, most recently: 'Roles and Rules: Ambiguity, Experimentation and Institutional Reform in Germany', in *Industrielle Beziehungen* (2007), 'Varieties of Vertical Disintegration: The Global Trend Toward Heterogeneous Supply Relations and the Reproduction of Difference in US and German Manufacturing', in G. Morgan, E. Moen and R. Whitley (eds) *Changing Capitalisms: Internationalization, Institutional Change and Systems of Economic Organization* (2005) and 'Emerging Strategies and Forms of Governance in the Components Industry in High Wage Regions', in *Industry and Innovation* (2004).

Hartmut Hirsch-Kreinsen is Professor of Economic and Industrial Sociology at the University of Dortmund. He has researched at the Institute for Social Research in Munich (ISF), at the University of Wisconsin/Madison and at the Arbetsmiljöinstitutet in Stockholm. His research focuses on internationalization of companies and company networks, sectoral changes, development of work; and innovation and development of new technologies. Recent publications: *Wirtschafts- und Industriesoziologie* (2005), *Low-tech Innovation in the Knowledge Economy* (co-editor, 2005), and "Low-Tech' Industries: Innovativeness and Development Perspectives – A Summary of a European Research Project', in *Prometheus* (with D. Jacobson und P. L. Robertson, 2006).

Jürgen Kädtler is Senior Researcher and Director of Sociological Research Institute (SOFI) at the Georg-August-University in Göttingen. His research interests include industrial relations, organization theory and social framing of economic action. His most recent publications focus on the impacts of 'financialization' of corporate governance and its impacts on labour relations (*Sozialpartnerschaft im Umbruch*, 2006). His publications also include 'The Power of Financial Markets and the Resilience of

Operations. Arguments and Evidence from the German Car Industry' in *Competition and Change* (with H. J. Sperling, 2002).

Herrmann Kotthoff is Professor of Industrial and Organizational Sociology at the Technical University of Darmstadt and was Director of the Institute for Social Research and Social Economy (ISO) in Saarbrücken. His research interests include: industrial relations (especially works councils), corporate culture, the sociology of management and SMEs. Publications include: *Die soziale Welt kleiner Betriebe* (1990) and author of 'Local Social Spaces in Global Operating German Companies', in L. Pries (eds) *The Emergence of Transnational Social Spaces. International Migration and Transnational Companies* (2001).

Christel Lane is Professor of Economic Sociology in the Faculty of Social and Political Sciences, Senior Research Associate at the Centre for Business Research and Fellow of St John's College, all in the University of Cambridge. She is the author of *Industry and Society in Europe* (1995) and the co-editor of *Trust Within and Between Organizations* (1998). She has published numerous articles in a range of journals. Her current research is a comparative study of how companies reorganize their value chains in response to the pressures of intensified global competition.

Rainhart Lang is Professor of Organization Studies at the Chemnitz University of Technology. His research focuses on cultural changes and organizational transformations in east-central Europe, transfer of management knowledge and practices, values, attitudes and leadership behaviour of managers, and transformation theories. He was Country-Co-Investigator for Germany within the intercultural GLOBE – Leadership project. His publications include: 'The Transfer of Human Resource Management Techniques in International Joint Ventures: An Institutionalist Approach', in *International Journal of Applied Human Resource Management* (with D. J. Pollard and E. Weick, 2002), 'Career Path of the Elite of Former GDR Combinates During the Post Socialist Transformation Process,' in *Journal of World Business* (with T. Steger, 2003) and 'Transformation Research in East Germany: Institutions, Knowledge and Power', in E. Clark and S. Michailova (eds) *Fieldwork in Transforming Societies* (with R. Alt, 2004).

Aleksander Marcinkowski is Senior Lecturer at Institute of Economics and Management, Jagiellonian University. He worked in the Institutional Development Project devoted to excelling strategic planning skills in the area of regional development and sponsored by the World's Bank and Polish Ministry of Internal Affaires and Administration (2002–2004). His recent publications include 'Dilemmas of Policy on LMT Industries. The Polish Case', in G. Bender, D. Jacobson, and P. L. Robertson (eds), *Non-Research-Intensive Industries in the Knowledge Economy*. Special Edition of *Perspectives of Economic Political and Social Integration* (with T. Borkowski, 2005).

Bernd Martens is Senior Researcher in the Collaborative Research Centre 580 at the Friedrich-Schiller-University of Jena as well as a member of the Institute for Sociology at the University of Tübingen. He has research experience in different fields of sociology and with qualitative, as well as quantitative, research methods. His current research focuses on the sociology of management and the transformation process of East-German companies. His recent publications include: 'Still on the Tracks of the Nineties: East-German Management and Enterprises in the Perspective of Managerial Elites,' in R. Kollmorgen, J. Kopstein and A. Port (eds) *Between Past and Future: East Germany before and after 1989* (2008).

Jocelyn Probert is a Lecturer in International Management and Organization at the Birmingham Business School, University of Birmingham. Previously she was a Research Fellow in the Centre for Business Research, University of Cambridge, conducting comparative research on global value chains and the organizational reconfiguration of firms. She has a PhD from Judge Business School at the University of Cambridge in which she explores the organizational restructuring of Japanese firms.

Ralph-Elmar Lungwitz is Director of the Institute of Social and Economic Research in Chemnitz (WISOC). His research topics include: networks and co-operations, labour relations and transition in Central and Eastern Europe, especially in Poland and East Germany. Among his publications are 'Privatization in Eastern Germany and the Chance of Worker's Participation,' in T. Clarke (ed.) *International Privatization: Strategies and Practices* (with V. Kreißig, 1994) and 'Co-ordination Media in Cross National Networks of Small and Medium Sized Enterprises', in *Journal for East European Management Studies* (with P. Le and S. Campagna, 2006).

Yvonne Rückert worked as Scientific Researcher at the Ruhr University of Bochum. Since 2006, she has studied at the University of Oviedo, Spain and participating on the doctoral programme 'Economics and Sociology of Globalization'.

Rudi Schmidt is Emeritus Professor of Sociology and has held university and research posts at the universities of Berlin, Erlangen and Jena. His research interests include the sociology of work and management, industrial relations, the modernization of industry and production systems and transition in east-central Europe. Recent publications include 'Eastern Germany's Incorporation into the Federal Republic', in D. Lane, M. Myant (eds), *Varieties of Capitalism in Post-Communist Countries* (2007) and 'The Integration of the GDR into the Federal Republic: Challenges and Constraints' in D. Lane *The Transformation of State Socialism* (2007).

Volker Telljohann is Senior Researcher at the Institute for Labour Foundation in Bologna. He is the Secretary General of the international network 'Regional and Local Development of Work and Labour' and an active member of the network 'Europeanization of Labour Relations' organized by the German Hans-Böckler-Foundation. Most recently he is doing research on new tendencies in regional, national and European industrial relations, working conditions, as well as the role of Social Dialogue for local development policies. His publications include *New Forms of Work Organisation and Industrial Relations in Southern Europe* (co-editor, 2007) and 'Interest Representation and European Identity – a Twofold Challenge for European Works Councils,' in H. Knudsen, M. Whittall, F. Huijgen (eds) *European Works Councils and the Problem of European Identity* (2007).

Manfred Wannöffel is Head of the Office of the Cooperation between the Ruhr-University Bochum and Industrial Metal Union (IG Metall), he also lectures Sociology of Organizations and Participation Studies at the Ruhr-University Bochum and at the Centre for Further Education at the Ruhr-University Bochum. He conducted research projects on industrial relations in international comparison (international participation research), reorganization and company strategies in the context of globalization in Germany and Mexico. Between 1995–1998 he was Professor for Sociology of Work and Economics at the Universidad Autonoma Mexico (UAM) in Mexico-City. He is co-editor of the book *Transnacionalidad del Trabajo* (2007).

1
Why Should the Varieties Literature Grant Smaller Firms More Attention? An Introduction

Katharina Bluhm and Rudi Schmidt

1.1 Introduction

Small- and medium-sized enterprises (SMEs) are still a disregarded species in social science. This may be explained by the 'long shadow' of Fordism, which raised the expectation that large vertically integrated conglomerates would eliminate the SME sector, especially in manufacturing. In contrast to large firms, SMEs have little power to shape the institutional and market environment. The lack of scholarly interest might also be caused by the cultural distance to the patriarchal-authoritarian leadership style that used to be widespread in family firms, as well as by the difficult access for academic researchers to this type of enterprise. The latter has partly to do with the limited available time of small management staffs in SMEs, and partly with owner desires to control the information flow going outside the firm.

The situation has slightly changed with the rediscovery of the concept of entrepreneurship, the disintegration of large firms and the rise of the 'New Economy'. Still, fairly little attention is given to the distinctiveness of this firm type. This is also true for the Varieties-of-Capitalism approach (VoC) that has triggered a fruitful stream of interdisciplinary research and debate in recent years. One cannot say, though, that the VoC approach completely ignores smaller firms. Many assumptions about the macro-micro-conjunction between institutional frameworks and firm strategies can be applied to firms of different size (cf. Hall and Soskice 2001). Moreover, based on historical institutionalism, the approach focuses rather on collective behaviour and coalitions, which may include smaller firms instead of isolated actors (for a good example see Molina and Rhodes 2007). Yet there has been no systematic treatment of the differences between large and small- and medium-sized firms with regard to the influence of institutional frameworks on firm strategies and vice versa. All the more astonishing is that in the thorough critiques of the VoC approach, the issue of firm size is hardly raised anymore, while the limits of the dichotomy between coordinated and liberal market economy, the underestimated role of the state, and the concept of path dependency are intensively disputed (for an overview see Hancké, Rhodes, and Thatcher 2007). Firm size does play a significant role when critics come to the 'within-system' diversity that refers to regional variations within countries, making a country-based typology even more difficult (Crouch 2005; cf. Locke 1995; Herrigel 1996; Sorge 2005). The different regional production systems in Italy and, to lesser extent, in Germany are often taken as an argument against the view of Hall and Soskice that the national level is still the most decisive for institution-building and, therefore, also for the constitution of varieties of capitalism and production regimes (cf. Soskice 1999, 2000).

With this book we want to shed light on SMEs in the changing European market economies from different disciplinary angles. We argue that SMEs have empirical and theoretical relevance for a better understanding of this change and its probable direction. Large firms and SMEs are affected differently by institutional and economic change and respond to this change differently. This book goes beyond the regional-cluster approach that contests the national focus of VoC and in which SMEs play a prominent role. The cluster approach not only fails to grasp the decoupling of region and industrial community (cf. Herrigel in this volume) but also has too narrow a focus on SMEs as social actors.

In three ways we see size differences as a crucial factor in further investigations of the linkages between institutional change and firm behaviour:

1. First, size has an impact on how firms are 'embedded' in the institutional framework of the political economy. Organizational features like ownership structure, strategic capacities, the degree of formality of their organization, and their resource dependency influence which institutional spheres firms are involved in and to what extent they are shaped by them. Size also correlates quite often with the magnitude of the societal attention a firm's behaviour is given, which is relevant for rule enforcement by actors who are not part of the relationship ('third parties'). While owner-led SMEs are traditionally bound to local communities, large firms attract more often attention of unions, NGOs and react sensitively to the media, for example.

Due to the differences in 'institutional embeddedness' the impacts and outcomes of institutional change diverge according to size, too.

2. Second, SMEs often rely on relationships to large firms in the value chain and in broader 'organizational fields', which influences the strategies and structures of SMEs (cf. DiMaggio and Powell 1991). Large firms contribute to the rules by which SMEs play and are an important vector for the diffusion of new management practices, methods and concepts that often trickle down from large to small. Hence, the relationship between large and smaller firms is not only important for networks but also for institutional analyses that focus on the linkages between framework and strategies and the way institutional change is triggered by changing actors' behaviour and expectations.

3. Third, the role of owner-managers or -families in their businesses and the traditionally high informality of organization mean similar social features of SMEs across countries and regions. They constitute the special advantages of small-firm size in terms of quick and flexible decision-making. Hence, nation-specific institutional effects might be modified or weakened by social features similar among countries, such as organizational forms and the crucial role of entrepreneur-owners. Moreover, as long as owners are people or a group of people who also run the business, the change in ownership structure and corporate governance cannot be explained only by institutional and economic change. They may also express social change caused by changing relationships within the families, the values and orientations of the owners and the like. Thus for SMEs – in contrast to large firms – succession is one of the most crucial events in their life cycle. Putting SMEs onto the agenda of institutional analysis means to include the social changes that affect SME strategies, governance structures and firm prospects.

1.2 Variations in institutional 'embeddedness'

Size correlates with the resources, strategic capacities, and societal expectations of 'stakeholder groups', which are greater for large firms; size is often linked to different ownership structures and determines the degree of formalization in organizations and employment relationships. This implies that the institutional 'embeddedness' of large and smaller firms diverges in most of the spheres of the political economy, especially with regard to the financial system and the system of labour relations.

The advantages firms can capitalize on in certain institutional contexts, therefore, differ as well.

The analysis of finance and corporate governance systems usually focuses on large firms. Peter Hall and David Soskice (2001) discriminate here mainly between market-based coordination, which encourages firms to be attentive to current earnings and the price of the share on equity markets, and non-market coordination with its 'patient capital'. This distinction is often equated with 'market-based' and 'bank-based' that reflect whether firms are mostly externally financed by capital markets or by bank loans (cf. Amable 2003; Vitols 2004). Most of the Continental European financial systems are bank-based, while Anglo-Saxon financial systems are market-based. Which mode of financing dominates has to do with the welfare state, the traditional capital-market regulation and the tax system. Yet for SMEs the 'market-based' and 'bank-based'-distinction is less striking. In spite of increasing interest in alternative forms of financing, most European SMEs rely on banks when seeking external funding (Observatory European Network of European SMEs 2003). This holds true for France, Germany and Poland, for example, but also for the UK (cf. Geppert and Martens in this volume; Cosh and Hughes 2003; Observatory European Network of European SMEs 2003). Hence one could argue that SMEs' external financing is always 'bank-based'.

Systemic differences become clearer if one considers in what way SMEs use banks. Here we find that in some European countries overdraft is the most preferred relationship with banks, which is flexible but expensive (as in the UK and Italy), while in other countries bank loans play the major role (Germany, Austria, Belgium, Denmark, Spain, France, Finland and the Netherlands; see Observatory European Network of European SMEs 2003: 20–2). Overdrafting establishes short-term, arm's-length relationships between firms and banks, indicating that firms strongly prefer their own equity financing. Bank loans, in contrast, especially longer-term lending, lead to closer and more complex communication between the two sides. In the UK problems of access to banks for SMEs are considered one factor that has contributed to the decline of the manufacturing sector (cf. Mullineux 1994; Lane and Quack 2002; Mullineux and Terberger 2006; Geppert and Martens in this volume). In Italy, where traditionally most banks have been state-owned and detached from the corporate governance of the country's private sector, firms rely often on family and intergroup sources by cross-shareholding for long-lasting financing (Molina and Rhodes 2007). In short, a closer look at firm size is necessary in order to complete the institutional analysis: it reveals the flipside of a market-based finance system and allows detecting various forms of non-market coordination. In 'marked-based' systems the way large firms solve the financing problem appears still more distant from the mode in which SMEs act.

The differences in bank-financing of European SMEs are also relevant to understanding the impacts of institutional change. It explains, for instance, why for British SMEs the Second Capital Accord (Basel II) that promotes the standardization of credit products has not become a big issue, while in Germany and in other European countries the EU banking reform has been accompanied by strong fears of a deterioration of lending conditions for SMEs (cf. more Bluhm and Martens; Geppert and Martens, Kädtler and Faust, all in this volume).

Investigations of labour-relations systems, as well, have a large-firm bias. The German labour-relation system is a good example, for it has mostly been portrayed as highly formalized, standardized and regulated. The system works, in spite of the fact that small firms do not share all the institutional features (cf. Schmidt in this volume), because of the existence of a critical mass of firms with co-determination and membership in employers' associations, and because unions and employers' associations (in which large firms determine policy) are powerful enough for standard-setting and rule enforcement. Thus, these standards have become guidelines even for those firms not obliged to follow the agreements of collective bargaining. With the ongoing weakening of the two pillars of the German system – works councils and industry-wide collective bargaining – the erosion of collective and even labour-code standards in SMEs is progressing much faster than in large firms, which are still more under control of works councils, unions and the public. Consequently the results of collective bargaining are losing their guiding function for those firms not covered by collective bargaining agreements.

Ingrid Artus shows in this volume that weaker regulation in French labour relations produces even less deviation from institutional forms than in Germany. However, this does not mean that the practices within the firms are so much different in the two countries. On the contrary, the informality of smaller firms produces striking similarities in labour relationships in the French and German SMEs investigated, consisting mainly of direct but unbalanced interest-reconciliation between employees and superiors.

Artus and Schmidt (in this volume) point to the tension between formal institutions and actual practice that is not only important to different degrees in 'institutional embeddedness', but also relevant for the actors' interpretation of the institutions. This becomes especially clear in

Rudi Schmidt's East-West-German comparison that reveals, first, a cautious acceptance of co-determination by managements in East and West and, secondly, remarkable differences in how the actors interpret the institutions crucial to their functioning. In the Polish case, the acceptance of works councils among SMEs as well as the role of 'third parties' is so weak, as Ralph Lungwitz et al. point out in this volume, that the institutionalization of works councils, which were introduced in the wake of EU accession as a new legal form, is severely constrained. Though in Poland, as in East Germany, firm size and market position are causing extreme cost-cutting pressure, these are not the only reasons behind the phenomenon there. Yet there is a notable difference between East Germany and Poland: the weakness of collective and legal enforcement in Poland leads to a widespread disobeying of the labour code, especially in the SME sector, something unknown in East Germany on this scale.

1.3   The influence of large firms within globalized production networks

Large firms play a crucial role in shaping the economic and institutional environment of SMEs. They do this in different ways: their market power directly creates pressure on and incentives for SMEs to adjust strategies and organization, relocate operations and take on new practices, methods and concepts. They influence SMEs more indirectly as actor in broader 'organizational fields' of an industry in countries and regions in which the diffusion not only occurs by coercion and normative pressure but also due to mimetic processes. Large firms contribute to general institutional standard-setting, as in the German collective bargaining system that also applies to the SME sector and thus influences the strategic behaviour of those firms.

Christel Lane and Jocelyn Probert in this volume raise the question of how the globalization of production networks and commodity chains, dominated by large firms, intertwine with national institutional influences on SMEs. In accordance with the VoC approach, they show that in the textile and clothing industry in the UK and Germany institutions 'shape both the competences that firms develop and the product strategies they adopt' (see also Geppert and Martens in this volume). Facing similar challenges – the cost pressure of large retailers controlling the global commodity chain – manufacturers in the two countries still behave differently. The stronger German 'Mittelstand' have been better able to develop some countervailing powers with their paradigm of a 'diversified quality' production, which British firms, as 'diversified mass' producer, miss out on. Yet, for quality German producers, too, cost-cutting pressure and 'market-type' contracting have tremendously intensified. This development underlines how large multinational firm strategies and networks set limits on the VoC approach to explaining SME strategies in globalized commodity chains.

Gary Herrigel (in this volume) goes a step further. With respect to the relationships between supplier and globally-acting final producer ('original equipment manufacturer' – OEM), he reveals how the traditional distinction of 'arm's-length' relationships related to liberal market economies and long-term and trust-based relational contracting, traditionally identified with coordinated market economies, do not work anymore. Large OEMs establish relationships to their suppliers marked by close and much more demanding collaboration and great uncertainty over its time horizon and continuity. For the suppliers this combination creates the incentive and even the need to upgrade and innovate, but also puts them under huge cost constraints, making their specific investments more risky. The new mixture of market relation and direct coordination between OEMs and suppliers is accompanied by an increase in formalization of the relationship that reduces the reliance on informality and tacit forms of knowledge typical of SMEs. It also produces a new borderline of differentiation among SMEs that runs between those firms who manage to meet the new demands and grow within the globalized production networks and commodity chains and those who remain restricted to their local economies.

Herrigel also explores in this volume consequences for regional policy, adjustment strategies in industrial regional governance, and their limits. As under the more volatile conditions of vertical disintegration, the character of local ties is constantly changing and the content of useful public services and public goods must be continuously revised. It becomes a major assignment for regional actors to support smaller firms constantly redefining their roles according to the demands of the OEMs. In this respect traditional SME clusters with their established institutional infrastructure might (but not necessarily) have a competitive advantage as Hartmut Hirsch-Kreinsen and Volker Telljohann point out – an advantage SMEs in Poland and in other east-central European countries still lack, representing a serious obstacle to their upgrading within the transnational production networks (cf. Borkowski and Marcinkowski; Lungwitz et al., all in this volume).

Telljohann states that globalization does not destroy the regional clusters or 'industrial districts' in Italy. Rather, they undergo a radical transformation including relocation and outsourcing, while locally rooted production factors, skills and knowledge recombine and generate new innovation paths. For the automotive cluster in Emilia-Romagna he observes that this transformation is accompanied with a shift towards a new flexible work organization at the micro-level that intensifies work, increases precarious forms of labour contracts and threatens the existing collective bargaining structure. To this finding, Michael Fichter adds for Germany that the structural changes due to relocation lead to an increase in white-collar employment that contributes to further erosion of collective interest representation in SMEs (in this volume).

Telljohanns in-depth study strengthens Herrigels argumentation in another way by bringing the increased formalization of the relationships between OEMs and suppliers into connection with the diffusion of management practices, methods and concepts from large firms to small. The dissemination of new human-resource management techniques, in which 'direct employee participation' in team-work is a key element, is directly and indirectly imposed by OEMs. Large multinationals aim, thereby, to prepare their suppliers for collaboration within global production networks. The application of these management practices to Italian SMEs has caused a formalization of relationships between managers and employees within the organizations, which were much more informal in the past.

The automobile industry is a suitable object not only for an examination of how strong the influence of large firms may become, but it also illustrates that direct and indirect, coercive and less coercive influences of large firms on SMEs are often close to each other. However, indirect impacts of large firms in 'organizational fields' are less well investigated, although they are indispensable to a better understanding of how new rules, management practices and methods become general standards (by cohesion, normative or mimetic processes; cf. DiMaggio and Powell 1991).

The economic historian Harm G. Schröter (2004; 2005) has investigated processes of longitudinal 'trickle-down' of new management concepts like marketing and market research from large to small firms. Even more obvious are 'trickle-down' effects with respect to successive quality standards like ISO 9000 and others, which suppliers are obliged to use. Such examples also illustrate the importance of other actors in the organizational fields of standard-setting such as consultancies, business schools and the media. In the course of our project on changing management concepts in East- and West-German SMEs at the Friedrich-Schiller-University Jena[1] we found similar longitudinal effects regarding accounting. In a survey for the International Controller Verein (ICV),

Table 1.1 Year of implementation according to company's size

Number of employees	Mean	Number of firms	Standard deviation	Median
up to 100	1995	46	8.2	1998
101–500	1994	82	6.5	1996
501–1000	1992	46	7.2	1992
more than 1000	1985	103	9.8	1987

Source: Marten and Schmidt 2003: 32

a German-based accounting association, Bernd Martens and Rudi Schmidt (2003: 32) found that the implementation of management accounting systems correlates with firm size. While 80 per cent of the questioned firms with fewer than 100 employees (all ICV members) implemented their accounting systems in the late 1990s, large firms had done it much earlier (see Table 1.1)

In Germany large firms play an indirect role in the diffusion of professional management accounting systems, while banks directly promoted the introduction of new accounting standards in preparation for Basel II, which came into effect in 2007. This usually takes place when SMEs are experiencing an economic crisis. Therefore, it strengthens the cost- and financial-orientation in the firms, although owner-managers display strong antipathy towards the shareholder-value concept that large German corporations have embraced in recent years (cf. Bluhm and Martens in this volume).

The professionalization of the corporate governance of SMEs, described by Katharina Bluhm and Bernd Martens in this volume, has neither caused an immediate and drastic alteration in the style of decision-making within firms, nor automatically implied, as a consequence, the subsequent reorganization in other areas (see also Becker, Bluhm and Martens 2008). Otherwise, they found a reliable statistical correlation between accounting-related reorganization activities and the existence of 'management-by-objective' procedures,[2] which also flows from large to smaller firms and indicates indirect 'organizational-field' effects.[3]

1.4 The changing social background of SMEs

Despite great market dependence and organizational changes, direct intervention of managing directors continues to play a crucial role for

SMEs' flexibility and success, especially when they (entrepreneurs or more neutrally: owner-managers) hold shares in the firm. This has to do with the smaller degree of formalization – in spite of the observed increase – as well as with the greater vulnerability of SMEs on markets and the greater risk owner-managers bear compared to employed managers. Consequently, personal change in management has a greater impact here on firm strategies, structure and corporate culture than in large firms.

Rainhart Lang (in this volume) stresses the relevance of values and attitudes of managing directors of East-German SMEs and relates them to experiences, social and educational background. He argues that the transition period from planned to market economy created a situation where rules and norms were weakly institutionalized, providing the heads of the firms with even more room to follow their own notions of leadership. His exploratory study reveals that, in spite of remarkable differences between owner-managers and employed managers, there is no general trend towards a mere shareholder-value orientation among East-German managing directors.

Alain Fayolle and Salma Fattoum question deterministic relationships between SME strategies and the changing educational background of their leaders and point to the relevance of market positions, structural effects and institutions (in this volume). They discuss this issue with regard to the problem of innovativeness of French SMEs, which is perceived as dramatic. Yet, Fayolle and Fattoum observe a general trend on French labour markets in favour of academic graduates, which is of great relevance to the traditional elite-centred network coordination in the French political economy. In the post-war political economy a strong connection emerged between elite reproduction in state administration and big (often state-owned) business, offering graduates from the 'Grand Ecoles' safe entry tickets into one or both spheres. As the SME sector has not been capable of attracting this clientele, an early social segmentation occurred similar to that in the UK (but for different reasons) but unknown on this scale in Germany or Italy. In Germany the recruiting circles of large firms and the 'Mittelstand' fall apart *after* graduates have decided on one sector.

While in the UK the expanding finance industry, a magnet for highly qualified graduates, has solidified the lack of interest in SMEs and especially in the manufacturing sector, in France the situation is changing. The authors trace this back to institutional changes within the educational system and to the globalization of the French multinationals. As a consequence, graduates of French 'Grandes Ecoles' do not find it as easy to enter into large French firms as they used to and have, therefore, turned their attention to the SME sector. This development is fostered by the demographic change in the sector caused by a retirement wave. Fayolle and Fattoum observe the emergence of a new type of entrepreneur who, in helping erode the traditionally strong patriarchalism of French owner-managers, is contributing to changing the qualification structure in SME management.

Hermann Kotthoff discusses in this volume the linkage between family business and social change in owner families that one can observe in several countries. He seizes, thereby, on a widely ignored topic in the research on European SMEs. Kotthoff explains not only that business families pass through a generational cycle full of risks and conflicts for the firms alone. He also detects a general tendency in the western world crucial to the persistence of family firms and, therefore, to the future ownership structure and management culture of SMEs in Europe: the ongoing individualization and the rise of patchwork families as new family models make it more difficult to transmit businesses along traditional father-son lines – the basic idea of dynasties. This lack of suitable or interested sons and sons-in-law is filled by daughters, firm-internal successors or external actors who take over the businesses instead. This leads to the erosion of the dynastic and patriarchal pattern that has been a common feature of traditional SMEs across Europe.

While Kotthoff bases his argumentation on findings regarding SMEs of different size and in various industries and countries, we looked at a sample of nearly 800 medium-sized manufacturing firms (of 50 to 1,000 employees) from the already-mentioned Jena DFG-project and found that succession within the family is still the dominant pattern in Germany (in 44 per cent of the relevant cases), followed by firm-internal solutions (employees or managers as successors), while external solutions still play only a minor role (cf. Bluhm and Martens in this volume). Yet, our findings support Kotthoff's conclusion that SMEs are moving away from the traditional dynastic pattern. This even holds true for the role of daughters, although the medium-sized manufacturing SMEs we questioned are not the best place to study an increase of takeovers by daughters. While in the total sample only 5 per cent of the founders and 7 per cent of the employed managers are female, their share is more than twice as great if we consider the heirs who run the business: here, 17 per cent of the interviewees who inherited firms are women. In short, as in other European countries, German SMEs have changed their mode of succession to an extended insider model when the preferred recruiting within the family fails. Except for prominent examples among large family firms, the succession problem in family business is still far from being the crucial point of entry for the new finance-driven investors, who are expected to radically alter the social character of SMEs (see also Martens and Michailow 2006).

1.5   Conclusions

SMEs in Europe, although they are not powerful players shaping market and institutional conditions, are crucial to the analysis and differentiation of political economies and varieties of capitalism. Their mere number and the industries populated by SMEs indicate to what extent, and with what strategies, SMEs can survive in certain institutional settings. As we can see in the case of UK and Germany, former strategic adjustments to the institutional settings of SMEs still shape their strategic capacities and opportunities to cope with new challenges.

Yet the study of size differences in a more systematic way is also significant, because the degree and mode of 'institutional embeddedness' of large and smaller firms vary. SMEs are important to understanding to what extent formal institutions and firm practices are concordant; institutions are, therefore, generally adopted in business. International comparison reveals that not only do national institutional differences still matter, but also that differences among countries in the mode and degree of firms' 'embeddedness' have a strong impact on how SMEs are affected by institutional and economic changes.

In addition, the analysis needs to include the relationship between large and smaller firms in a broader sense. On the one hand, this is necessary to understand power relationships in a political economy undergoing institutional change. On the other hand, large firms are important actors (though not the only ones) in the 'organizational fields' of SMEs, as they create, transmit and alter rules, methods and concepts in business. This goes beyond the reach of national contexts. In the course of globalization, the role of OEMs is ambivalent: while large firms pass much of the risk and costs along their value chain, exerting high pressure on employment and labour conditions in European SMEs, they do give SMEs more room to grow and contribute to the professionalization of their management methods and concepts. Under this influence the external and internal relationships of SMEs become, to some extent, more formalized and professional. They are, therefore, similar to those of large firms, who in turn, copying organizational features of SMEs, have reorganized into more flexible, market-oriented units. However, a levelling of the organizational features of the two types is unlikely, since size effects and differences in ownership structure still constitute decisive differences.

Finally, although entrepreneurship has gained more interest in the last few decades, it is often limited to newly founded firms and a few high-tech sectors and clusters. Yet, the social figure of the owner-manager and the concept of entrepreneurship underlie social changes that take place in a wider society that go beyond national institutional frameworks. The consequences of these changes for the future of the European business landscape will need to be explored further.

Notes

1. This project is part of a larger research group at the universities of Jena and Halle (Saale) and is financed by the German Research Foundation (Deutsche Forschungsgesellschaft – DFG). Bluhm and Martens, Geppert and Martens and Schmidt in this volume refer to the data of this project.
2. 'Management by objective' is a procedure in which management and employees agree to objectives (for the employees) that often, but not necessarily always, are combined with variable payment.
3. The sample consists of two survey waves from 2002 and 2005. In both panel waves there was a significant statistical correlation between the two variables. For more details about the panels see Bluhm and Martens in this volume.

References

Amable, B. (2003) Diversity of Modern Capitalism (Oxford: Oxford University Press).
Becker, K., K. Bluhm and B. Martens (2008) 'Unternehmensführung in den Zeiten des "Shareholder Value": Zum Wandel des industriellen Mittelstands', in R. Benthin and U. Brinkmann (eds), Unternehmenskultur und Mitbestimmung (Frankfurt/Main, New York: Campus), 215–244.
Cosh, A. and A. Hughes (2003) 'Enterprise Challenged: Policy and Performance in the British SME Sector 1999–2003', CBR Small Business Survey Research Report (Cambridge: Centre for Business Research).
Crouch, C. (2005) Capitalist Diversity and Change (Oxford: Oxford University Press).
DiMaggio, P. J. and W. W. Powell (1991) 'The Iron Cage Revisited: Institutional Isomorphism and Collective Rationality', in W. W. Powell and P. J. DiMaggio (eds), The New Institutionalism and Organizational Analysis (Chicago: University of Chicago), 63–8.
Hancké, B., M. Rhodes and M. Thachter (2007) 'Introduction: Beyond Varieties of Capitalism', in Hancké, B., .M. Rhodes and M. Thachter (eds), Beyond Varieties of Capitalism. Conflict, Contradictions, and Complementarities in European Economy, (Oxford: Oxford University Press), 3–38.

Hall, P. A. and D. Soskice (2001) 'An Introduction to Varieties of Capitalism', in P. A. Hall and D. Soskice (eds), *Varieties of Capitalism. The Institutional Foundations of Comparative Advantage* (Oxford: Oxford University Press), 1–70.

Herrigel, G. (1996) *Industrial Constructions. The Sources of German Industrial Power.* (Cambridge: Cambridge University Press).

Lane, C. and S. Quack (2002) 'How Banks Construct and Manage Risk: A Sociological Study of Small Firm Lending in Britain and Germany, *WZB Discussion Paper*, FS I 02–101 (Berlin: Social Science Research Center Berlin).

Locke, R. (1995) *Remaking the Italian Economy Work* (New York: Cornell University Press).

Martens, B. and R. Schmidt (2003) 'Aufgaben zwischen Betriebswirtschaftlichem Service und Strategischer Unternehmensteuerung', Ergebnisse einer Mitgliederbefragung des Internationalen Controller Vereins, Jena.

Martens, B. and Michailow, M. (2006) 'Wandel und Kontinuität Mittelständischer Unternehmen – Eine Untersuchung zu Differenzen zwischen und Gemeinsamkeiten von Unternehmensleitern', *Zeitschrift für KMU & Entrepreneurship*, 54, 221–42.

Molina, Ó. and M. Rhodes (2007) 'The Political Economy of Adjustment in Mixed Market Economies: A Study of Spain and Italy', in B. Hancké, M. Rhodes and M. Thachter (eds), *Beyond Varieties of Capitalism. Conflict, Contradictions, and Complementarities in European Economy* (Oxford: Oxford University Press), 223–52.

Mullineux, A. (1994) 'Small and Medium Sized Enterprise (SME) Financing in the UK: Lessons from Germany', *Discussion Paper* (London: Anglo-German Foundation for the Study of Industrial Society).

Mullineux, A. and E. Terberger (2006) *The British Bank Sector a Good Role Model for Germany?* (London: Anglo-German Foundation of the Study of Industrial Society).

Observatory Network of European SMEs (2003) 'SME and Access to Finance', no. 2, European Commission, <http://www.insme.org/documenti/smes_observatory_ 2003_report2_en.pdf>.

Schröter, H. G. (2004) 'Zur Geschichte der Marktforschung in Europa im 20. Jahrhundert', in R. Walter (ed.), *Geschichte des Konsums* (Stuttgart: Steiner), 319–41.

Schröter, H. G. (2005) *Americanization of the European Economy. A Compact Survey of American Economic Influence in Europe since the 1880s* (Dordrecht: Springer).

Sorge, A. (2005) *The Global and the Local. Understanding the Dialectics of Business Systems* (Oxford: Oxford University Press).

Soskice, D. (1999) 'Divergent Production Regimes. Coordinated and Uncoordinated Market Economies in the 1980s and 1990s', in H. Kitschelt, P. Lange, G. Marks and J. D. Stephens (eds), *Continuity and Change in Contemporary Capitalism* (Cambridge: Cambridge University Press), 101–34.

Soskice, D. (2000) 'Explaining Changes in Institutional Frameworks. Societal Patterns of Business Coordination', in M. Maurice and A. Sorge (eds), *Embedding Organizations. Societal Analysis of Actors, Organizations and Socio-Economic Context* (Amsterdam: John Benjamin's Publishing), 167–84.

Vitols, S. (2004) 'Changes in Germany's Bank-Based Financial System: A Varieties of Capitalism Perspective', *WZB Discussion Paper*, SP II 2004 – 03 (Berlin: WZB).

Part I
Changing Financing, Ownership and Firm Management

2
The Power of Financial Markets – What Does that Mean and How Does it Work for Different Categories of Companies?

Jürgen Kädtler and Michael Faust

2.1 Introduction

In business today, referring to financial markets to justify economic (and non-economic) actions has become exceptionally significant, thus marking a change that proves to be the most momentous transformation within capitalism since the 1990s. Arguing from the perspective of regulation theory, Robert Boyer (1999) identified the core development of economies in the fact that the monetary and financial system as an organizational centre has replaced the 'productionist' compromise of capital and labour that used to form the basis of the Fordist accumulation regime. The 'maid of production' in times of Fordism – the financial market – now seems to have become the lord of the process, dictating the direction and aims of the real economy.[1] Like recent references to 'globalization', the blanket reference to the power and demands of financial markets and financial-market players now provides sufficient justification for the basic reorientation of corporate strategies, almost without alternative. Following the example of authors such as Boyer (1999, 2000) and Cutler (2001), Froud et al. (Froud, Haslam, Johal and Williams 1999, 2000; Froud, Sukhdev, Leaver and Williams 2006) and Orléan (1999), we are speaking here of 'financialization'.

However, the origin of the power of financial markets and the mechanisms on which it is based, or through which it becomes effective, remain oddly vague and inconsistent. In this chapter, we question the supposed unambiguity of the power shift focusing on the relationship between financial markets and enterprises.[2] It holds that it is not so much the direct economic dependency that confers the power granted by reference to financial markets today, but rather the fundamental paradigm shift at the level of economic models, rationality criteria and ideas about legitimacy.

2.2   The power of financial markets – what power?

Before we can decide what the power of financial markets means for different categories of companies, we first need to clarify how it makes sense to talk about the power of those markets. Within the framework of Max Weber's classic definition, we go along with Crozier and Friedberg (Crozier and Friedberg 1977; Friedberg 1993) by assuming that the category of power relates to players' options for action or self-assertion in social contexts but not to the qualities of social structures as such. Such structures only bestow power when parties bring them into play effectively against other parties in certain situations and, thus, influence the options for action of these parties.

The power of the financial markets is not market power – which may sound paradoxical at first. It is also not due to a shortage of investment capital or because of a growing demand for investable resources. On the contrary, the shift of power in favour of financial markets and financial-market players goes hand in hand with a dramatic increase in the worldwide supply of capital that is seeking investment objects and a comparatively moderate increase in the corresponding demand. Financialization results rather from a rearrangement of the hierarchy of reasons that are (or can be) given for economic activity. At the same time, it denotes a rearrangement in the order of economic players behind each of these reasons. The relationship between these two aspects is not deterministic: is it the players who, as a result of possessing power resources elsewhere, are in a position to impose 'their' reasons onto others? Or is it the credit of the reasons themselves that makes those people particularly influential who can exploit that credit more effectively than others? We aim to show that this is not a question of strict alternatives but of relative weightings. To be more precise, we understand financial markets along the same lines as Bourdieu; that is, as a social field that acts first and foremost as 'a sparring ground and a battlefield to change power relations' (Bourdieu 2001: 41, 49). On this social field it is never eternally decided to what extent structural positions and cultural interpretations support or conflict with one another, or, in the latter case, which of the two retains the upper hand.

Some aspects of our discussion are strongly focused on UK/US developments, which is purely due to their outstanding influence on global financial markets in general. Anglo-Saxon institutional investors are the big players in these markets. Anglo-Saxon financial markets have been the point of reference for institutional restructuring and generalized models of corporate governance worldwide.

The increased importance of organized financial investment companies – for which 'institutional investors' has become the established international term[3] – indicates the relevance of powerful players. This results, first, from the concentration of widespread shareholdings in listed companies by (collective) investors, such as pension and investment funds, insurance companies and so on in the US and UK (Froud et al. 2006: 40; Windolf 2005b: 23). There was also the far-reaching lifting of investment restrictions which, until 1974, stipulated that US pension funds were to invest in US government bonds and selected blue chips that, though not necessarily regarded as particularly profitable, were considered to be secure (Montagne 2000; Lavigne 2002).

Finally, in the early 1980s the strengthened funds largely succeeded in abolishing the strict conditions set in the early 1930s as a consequence of the financial market crash and worldwide economic crisis – an event that had largely restricted financial investors' options for intervention against enterprises and, in particular, categorically ruled out coordinated action (Davis and Thompson 1994). If one sees the financial markets as being an organizational field in Bourdieu's sense, including all the players involved in some way in financial investments and their mutual relations, it is apparent that the combined concentration of capital investments in the hands of organized, collective players who are able to act strategically, and the political granting of far-reaching room for manoeuvre, give financial investors considerable power resources among economic players. While the domination of managers referred to by Berle and Means (1950 [1932]) was largely due to the powerlessness of isolated small shareholders, this situation definitely no longer applies today.

Yet, the blank reference to institutional investors as 'the new owners', as found in a number of recent publications on the subject of 'financial market capitalism' (Windolf 2005b, 2005a; Zugehör 2000), is too simple. It ignores the fact that ownership is only one of the connections between investors and enterprises, and that even ownership can signify very different things depending on whether it takes the form of shares or private equity. Institutional investors place their eggs in very different baskets. Accordingly, these investors ultimately stand behind share investments, capital market loans, private equity funds and risk capital investments – forms of investment that function in accordance to strongly contrasting principles and that relate differently to corporate action. To take the admittedly extreme example of the 'New Economy', many of the companies whose shares the fund managers were literally scrambling to get hold of were at the bottom of the pile in terms of the credit rating hierarchy. In addition, the reference to 'the new owners' is unable to fully explain the orientation of financial markets, when the owners in fact are actually not very new. In Germany, for example, insurance companies have been some of the cornerstones of 'Germany Inc.' – a prime example of coordinated capitalism. It is not their importance as financial investors, but rather their altered investment practices that now allow them to them promote the financial market driven restructuring of German capitalism (Streeck and Höpner 2003). Likewise in the US, pension funds – traditionally significant investors – acted differently in the past than they do today. Contrarily, there are enough examples of companies that have consistently set out on course for the financial markets without 'new owners' (Kädtler 2006). Reference to the increased significance of a certain category of organized financial investors alone, important as these players may be, cannot explain the new quality of the power of 'the financial markets'. In addition, other fundamental questions relating to the hierarchy of reasons underlying economic practice come into play: ideas about rationality and legitimacy that are (or may be) taken as the basis of economic practice.

This second aspect of the readjustment of power relations referred to by the term financialization – that is, the restructuring of the hierarchy of reasons for economic practice – concerns the mutual influence of economic science, economic practice and political regulation. Michel Callon (1998) analysed this connection generally as the 'embeddedness of economy in economics'. MacKenzie (2004, 2005, 2006) demonstrated the 'performative' character of financial theory specifically for the financial markets. The focus here is on the advancement of microeconomically-founded financial science based on mathematical models – having led a shadowy academic existence for decades – to a leading economic discipline and the basis for evaluating managerial action. The key impetus for this reweighting came not from academia but from the wider socio-political sphere. The main issues here are lawmaking and legal decisions in the field of trustee legislation – the basis of pension fund regulation in the Anglo-Saxon countries. Paradigmatic in this perspective is the development of the Employment Retirement Investment Security Act (ERISA) since 1974[4]. The central changes here include: a) the obligation of the trustee to adhere to the rules of the 'prudent expert', that is, to those of a professionalism typical for business people, instead of, as previously, to the virtues and judgement of the domestic 'prudent man'; b) the transition from a substantial regulation based on permissible investment objects to one based solely on adherence to procedural rules (diversification, transparent and sequential decision-making processes); and c) the definition of these obligations as claims of the individual claimant on the pension fund since ERISA was adopted for private pension funds in 1974 (typically the provisions have also been taken over in the articles of public pension funds). This last change is the consequence of the transition from pension funds with guaranteed payments (by the enterprise) to ones that have fixed contributions, whereby it is the benefiting employees alone who bear the profit risk. In the financial sector, this new interpretation of trustee law corresponds to the establishment of modern portfolio theory, which no longer focuses its assessment on the yield perspectives of the respective individual investment objects, but rather on the relationship between yield prospects and risk in the context of a portfolio that is widely diversified in this respect. With a view to economic practice in (non-financial) enterprises and their assessment, this gives rise to the demand for consistent evaluation criteria based on financial science by which real economic practice is guided, managed and judged. A central evaluation criterion here is whether the yield of an economic unit or measure is above an assumed rate of return on equity, that is, above a yield that would have been achievable with a risk-free investment (typically government bonds). Only in this case is the unit or measure concerned regarded as value-creating or at least value-maintaining in the case of a break-even result. If not, according to this logic, it is corporate-value destroying, even if operations are making a profit (Jensen and Meckling 1976; Jensen 1998; Ehrbar 1998; Stewart 1999). Frédéric Lordon (2000) demonstrated the extent to which the establishment of such assessment standards relied less on scientific debate than on the campaign-like creation of acceptance in public opinion influenced by the media, by using the case of the establishment of Economic Value Added (EVA) as the state-of-the-art concept. The outcome of being guided by 'corporate value' in this way is not simply a technical redefinition or a more precise definition of profitability measures, but a fundamentally new definition of the criterion for profitability in order to popularize a new economic model. Lordon refers to this as an *idée simple*.[5] This general claim to validity, which goes beyond simply making a claim to validity to justify shareholders' demands, also finds expression in terms such as economic value added, 'value creation' and 'value-based management', which are increasingly used in defining shareholder-value orientation.

The corresponding German terms *Unternehmenswert* and *Wertorientierung* are used in a similar manner. From a purely linguistic point of view, these suggest that there is a substantial concept of value that contains no trace of external demands. Decontextualizing this model semantically is an important step towards generalizing it beyond the original context of listed companies and shareholder requirements.

While the profitability claim based on these arguments may, in itself, be unambiguously and stringently substantiated, its practical consequences are vague. An evaluation model intended to provide conclusive and compelling evidence for minimum yield with reference to assumed costs of capital using simple mathematical formulae forms the hard core of value orientation and value-based management. This is *claimed* to provide for a stringent management and evaluation process covering fund administrators and investment managers, strategic and operative management, down to individual employees. However, there is little evidence for this. Apart from the plethora of more or less academically embellished propaganda in the form of case studies from the field of management consultancy (cf. Ittner and Larcker 2001), there is little empirical evidence for the broad application of value-oriented management in any sense that does justice to this theory. Empirical studies (Malmi and Ikaheimo 2003), as well as our own observations (Kädtler, 2006), suggest rather that relevant instruments are only introduced sporadically, are often limited to incentive systems in the remuneration of top management, and are frequently mere rhetoric. Moreover, the detailed evaluation of the long-term development of relevant performance indicators for the top league of listed companies in the US and UK – S&P 500 and FTSE 100 (Froud et al. 2000; Froud et al. 2006: 74–98) does not provide any evidence for the influence of value-based management. While Total Shareholder Return (TSR) from dividends and share price appreciation between 1983 and 2003 rose by more than 20 per cent per annum, this was largely due to share price appreciation having nothing to do with whether enterprises created or destroyed corporate value in the sense of value-based management. Apart from extraordinary temporary developments, such as the 'New Economy bubble' of 1995–2000, the simple mechanism of supply and demand was in operation here. Low interest rates and a strong increase in capital-seeking investments drove up share prices without any special contribution by management. In contrast, the management-influenced parameters showed very little dynamism over the same period. The Return on Capital Employed (ROCE) in both S&P 500 and FTSE 100 companies in 2003 was significantly lower than the level in 1983, a comparable year in economic terms. Other parameters, such as turnover and pre-tax profits, too, were extremely static. Some ten years after the arrival of the shareholder-value movement in Europe, the financial-market reorientation of the top companies in the Anglo-Saxon trailblazer economies still does not show any effect in terms of improved economic performance – the focus of financial management theories. A fundamental dilemma underlies this striking discrepancy between claim and reality. In order to be effective in practice, the entitlement to returns based on stringent financial mathematics must be translated into practical, real economic strategy. If this does not occur, the indicators on their own are, at best, good for penalizing failure, but poor for providing (non-financial) enterprises with positive orientation.

Here, the problem of strategically dealing with real uncertainty that Frank H. Knight (1921) saw as the key to entrepreneurial action arises with a new quality. As Ortmann (1995) correctly observed, 'red figures don't say anything about how they will get black again'; that applies similarly to black figures, or ones that are supposed to become even 'blacker'. No one can know for certain what practical measures will actually lead to an abstract profit target being reached in the future. That applies in principle to every entrepreneurial action and all the more to acting according to the demands of the financial markets, which, in principle, do not provide any justification for making assumptions about their application to real economic strategies. The fact that corporate reality lags behind these demands results from the gap between real economic players, who act on the basis of given resources, specific competencies and certain product strategies, and the demands of the financial markets for which these conditions are only variables that, in principle, are all open to question.

It remains open at this point whether, as in our opinion, there is a fundamental conflict that cannot be resolved, or whether enterprises' inadequate performances are merely due to their (still) inadequate application of value-oriented management principles, as assumed by the relevant management theory. Here too, it is not a problem of technical application, but a clash between different models, ideas or fictions about rationality and their representatives.

We conclude that the new power granted by the financial markets is not primarily due to real economic undertakings being directly dependent on financial resources in a previously unknown manner. It is also not due to financial-market players offering a generally implementable and applicable set of instruments for increasing enterprises' profitability. Rather, it is due to the institutionalization of a specific public sphere consisting of pension funds and investment companies, interpretational authorities, such as economists, management scientists, analysts and rating agencies, the media and the financial investing public, by which a *volonté générale* of the financial community emerges and is reproduced, and against whose criteria companies and management behaviour are measured. Just like any public opinion, the concerned financial markets must, likewise, be understood as a mixture of long- and short-term behaviour indications of the players. The principles of *corporate governance*, accounting standards and publicity regulations, for example as communicated and to some extent legally approved by the financial community, tend to be long-term orientations. As a result of the essential significance of conflicts of interest and interpretation for the social field of financial markets, 'long-term' is, of course, a relative term. For example, the submission of quarterly reports, which was taken over in Germany as an unshakeable principle of shareholder-value orientation in the early 1990s, is meanwhile being questioned in the US. Short-term indications are basically ad-hoc theories, such as the 'New Economy', the 'Asian Miracle', 'Life Sciences', certain business models and the like, which of course – by changing structures – usually also have long-term effects.

This gives rise to the question as to what effect this financial-market public sphere has on enterprises. That is, by whom, or the situations in which the priorities are thus justified, are (or can be) made to override other aspects more or less effectively. We will proceed to discuss two general constellations that are of particular significance in the pertinent scholarly debate: listed companies under the influence of shareholder value; and the position of different companies on the global credit markets. What is the basis of the frequently cited dictate of shareholder value and how far-reaching is it? And what is the basis of a real or presumed 'dictatorship of lenders' (Chesnais 1997) and whom does it affect?

2.3   The listed company and the influence of shareholders

Since the 1990s, listed companies have been changing their corporate governance, strategic orientation and business profile, even in Germany. Key points in this process are: the dilution of cross- and interconnections and a withdrawal of the banks from entrepreneurial responsibility; a transition from bank-oriented to investor-oriented accounting pursuant to US or international standards (US GAAP and IFRS); a shift from internal growth to portfolio management with a concentration on frequently changing core business areas; re-evaluation of previous synergies as cross-subsidies to be combated; and management of all business processes according to capital-market-oriented keys, such as EVA, EBITDA and others.

The most noticeable changes in operative company structures in the course of this development are:

- business decentralization or segmentation: the organization of the company as a portfolio of investments in separate operating areas, each of which can be viewed, managed, evaluated and integrated or separated;
- a policy of concentration on a few frequently changing 'core competencies', which would be better termed 'core business areas' (Becker and Sablowski 1998), since these are actually not the specific competencies that are developed and extended in the course of the longer-term operation of complex businesses, but rather short-term, changing business-area orientations;
- the more or less permanent restructuring of companies, whereby the focus here is not on operative problems and perspectives of real economic business but rather are prescribed, blanket economic indicators substantiated by financial market figures, often linked with the assumption of new business models popularized by consultants (Faust 2006, 2002);
- in connection with the widespread trend towards quarterly reporting, there is a trend towards continually cultivating indicators in the short term, with the consequence that strategic decisions that have a long-term effect are often taken with a short-term perspective on numbers.

The common denominator of these developments is that corporate structures are made more fluid, resulting in the normal state of companies being transitory rather than stable.

Two, not mutually exclusive explanations are offered for this reorientation towards shareholder value: the need to take better into account the interests of shareholders as financial backers with a view to corporate financing; and the market for corporate control, where underperformance is penalized by hostile takeovers and the replacement of management staff. When subjected to closer examination, neither of these explanations is very convincing.

As regards the first point – the demands of corporate financing – it must be stated that listed companies have never financed their activities primarily via the stock market and that they now do so less than ever before. In the US, where stock exchange capitalization has always played a much greater role than, for example, in Germany, the proportion of stock flotations in the financing of listed companies was never more than 18 per cent in the late 1920s immediately before 'Black Friday' and since then has always been considerably lower. In the first half of the 1990s, the proportion of the financing of all companies in the US was 1 per cent; in Germany it was 2 per cent (O'Sullivan 2000: 79; Huff-schmid 2002: 27). The situation of 'New Economy' companies in the second half of the 1990s, most of which actually were financed by stock-market flotation, was a quite exceptional case; one that ended abruptly with the bursting of the New Economy bubble. New issues by estab-lished companies constitute a marginal phenomenon compared with the opposite practice of share buy-back programmes. In pursuing this pol-icy of distributing 'surplus' capital through share buy-back programmes, referred to as 'downsize and distribute' by Mary O'Sullivan (2000), the companies are indeed responding to the norms of the financial mar-kets. This is because, in the logic of value-oriented management, this practice represents the compelling alternative to investing in business that destroys corporate value, resulting in a return on investment below supposed capital costs.

A more complicated picture emerges with regard to the sanctioning power of the market for corporate control: the threat of a hostile takeover as punishment for inadequate management, which can be replaced with this process. Even authors who view this as the central mechanism of the financial markets, or of 'the new owners' (see Windolf 2005b), admit that, in practice, this mechanism rarely 'goes all the way' and point to the constant presence of the virtual hostile takeover. This argument would be more convincing if the empirical reality of actual hostile takeovers did not point in a clearly different direction. In real life, it is mostly companies that the financial sphere regards as paradigms of good busi-ness management that are the objects of hostile takeovers. In Germany this has happened to Mannesmann, Aventis, and Schering. The manage-ment of the Bayer Group, on the other hand, which clung to its profile as an integrated chemicals and pharmaceutical company in the 1990s, was confronted with split-up proposals by fund management companies, and the company's stock-market value indeed suffered seriously from the fact that financial markets are unsupportive toward large conglomer-ates. However, the firm remained unscathed by takeover attempts, even though the interventions of organized shareholders were consistently ignored. And that is where the situation remained when the conglomer-ate had to take its strategic pharmaceuticals-sector blockbuster off the market in 2001, causing its share value to plummet by a third as a result.

Examples such as these certainly do not definitely disprove the thesis of the disciplinary impact of the market for corporate control. It can, after all, be plausibly claimed that in the sense of anticipatory obedience, the thesis is commonly borne out far in advance. At the same time, it should be pointed out that substantial objections are to be made to the presumption of a rigid penalty mechanism:

- If the market for corporate control functions as a penalty mechanism, it does not do so unambiguously and directly, but rather diffusely and ambiguously. Its impact can be likened to that of the Inspector General in Gogol's comedy: everybody expects that Inspector General's arrival, but nobody knows exactly when he will come, what precisely he will require, and whether he will come at all.

- Even where it is sufficiently clear as to what 'the financial markets' or the players in the financial markets want, it is apparently common for management to have considerable room for manoeuvre in resisting their demands, not lock, stock and barrel to be sure, but in significant points. As long as the yields are in order, the replacement of a management team on the grounds of insufficient attention to share price is unlikely. And where they are not in order, as is notoriously the case in the US automotive industry, the management is replaced, but internally. Whether or not a company is subjected to a hostile takeover depends less on the management's financial-market conformity than on whether or not at least one other company is pursuing an industrial strategy within which precisely this takeover seems to make sense. In this sense, the US automotive companies are protected by their underperformance, while firms such as Porsche and BMW would be taken over regardless of their high share price if the ownership structure did not prevent such a takeover. The French pharmaceutical company Sanofi Syntélab did not attack and ultimately take over its significantly larger German-French competitor Aventis because of any poor management that might have taken place at Aventis, but because Aventis could be of good use within Sanofi's own strategy (Kädtler 2006). To what extent a hostile takeover functions as a penalty or as a reward for good management is then not least a question of the price and the amount of golden handshakes involved. The two hostile takeovers that have taken place clearly suggest the reward variant.

- At this level of companies, the increased power of the financial markets against this background represents, indeed, an increase in the power of strategic management. The only corporate indicator that has changed greatly and permanently as a result of financialization – the level of top management pay, which has increased drastically – may be regarded as a not entirely insignificant symptom here. Portraying oneself to other players and groups of players within and outside of the enterprise as a party merely driven by the financial markets is an instrument of power par excellence, regardless of whether it is deployed tactically or believed by oneself to be true. Due to a supposed lack of alternatives, the management's own strategy thus becomes unquestionable, although management itself has a great deal of freedom in determining it. This applies to an especially high degree when one understands financialization, as discussed above, not as the subjugation of the real economy by the financial markets, but as the rearrangement of aspects within the framework of what is, according to currently prevailing opinion, economically advantageous: as a change to the economics in which the economy is embedded.

- This is supported by the fact that we find central aspects of management oriented to financial-market principles also in companies that are dominated by strategic shareholders, or companies that are not listed at all. And amongst the large companies, we find hardly any to which these principles do not apply, at least in significant aspects.

Then again, though, ownership structure and openness to the capital market are not epiphenomenal; they do play a role in corporate governance. Enterprises that are not in spread holdings deviate from capital market imperatives in their strategic decisions more often than others, but there are equally significant instances of such deviating behaviour among other companies as well. Therefore ownership structure does not fully predict company behaviour. Thus, John Child's old (1992) dictum still holds that framework conditions may change the preconditions for strategic choice, but they change nothing about the possibility and necessity of strategic choice.

At this point it is important to make one observation: what seems to be a result of strategic choice at the level of listed companies often manifests itself in the form of rigid cost and margin pressure on arrival downstream at the level of sub-contractors and service enterprises. The large listed companies' complex relation to financial markets is passed on via very simple product-market dependence to companies that have nothing to do with the stock market but all the more with the credit-market sector of the financial markets.

2.4   Companies and the 'dictatorship of lenders'

Whilst, as a rule, the purchase or sale of shares affects companies only indirectly, changes in the conditions of access to credit have direct consequences for their operative business. From the investors' perspective, it is not the increase in corporate value that takes centre stage here but rather a company's reliable ability to pay combined with comprehensive safeguarding against possible risks. The keywords in this context are: continual and prompt evaluation of risks, autonomy for action at short notice in the event of changes, and strict monetization of risks entered into.

Financialization here means that financial markets become dominant (not only) for companies in comparison with other external sources of funds for capital investments, which consist mainly of banks. It seems problematic to interpret this as being the creation of a new 'dictatorship of lenders' (Chesnais 1997) regarding the fact that the new dependence is largely not forced upon companies, but rather has been perceived and sought out by them as a new option. After all, access to the financial markets, which have undergone a gradual process of globalization since the 1970s, gives many companies broader access to investment capital. To a significant extent, companies are not the passive objects of this development but have actively contributed to it.

However, while room for manoeuvre is extended on the one hand, new dependencies are created on the other. While the globalization of financial markets results from deregulation in the form of dismantling national restrictions, it is also accompanied by new forms of regulation within a global framework. Credit ratings of the private firms Moody's and Standard & Poor's have gained the status of *de facto* public standards, enjoying worldwide acceptance. Under some aspects this *de facto* status is even transformed to public law status by the reformed guidelines of the Basel Committee on Banking Supervision of the Bank for International Settlements (Basel II) (Sinclair 2000; 1994).[6] Such systems provide investors and financial managers with the necessary indications for involvement in enterprises anywhere in the world – that is, normalized and standardized risk assessment and calculability of conditions for resale. A market for standardized credit products is created that is transparent worldwide. Through this, investment decisions become independent of personal acquaintance of certain borrowers and their conditions; access to loans for enterprises whose creditworthiness is dependent on such individual assessments becomes more difficult. However, these schematic evaluation instruments are not neutral. They reflect the interpretation routines and fictions of rationality on which those responsible for the ratings, and all other economic players, depend. Thus, unofficially their ideas about good corporate management become globally effective criteria for creditworthiness and credit costs.

For the various categories of companies, this globalization of the credit markets has varying consequences: It increases the room for manoeuvre of *large, financially sound enterprises* that primarily finance themselves, and that are in a position to steer clear of the expensive borrowing terms of the banks by floating loans. This also has its price, since with regard to the costs of loans, the ratings and the evaluation criteria on which they are based must be observed.

On the other hand, the globalization of loans markets reduces the room for manoeuvre of such enterprises that are, first and foremost, dependent on loans to finance their operative business, and that until now have been able to rely above all on credit relations rooted in the locality. These consist primarily of small- and medium-sized enterprises (SMEs) with limited own equity resources. The consequence would be a tendency towards the blanket establishment of the Anglo-Saxon circumstances characterized by Doug Henwood's observation: 'In sum, big corporations, the ones with easy access to the (non-bank) capital markets, have more money than they know what to do with; small ones, who invest most of what they earn, don't find a generous reception in the capital markets' (Henwood 1997: 65).

In Germany, such a development would not only affect marginal economic areas but an economic sector that is of key significance for the economy as a whole with regard to the number of people it employs, its innovative energy for the economy and the level of qualification of its employees: the *Mittelstand*[7]. Engineering, a central sector of the German export industry and the technological basis of other key sectors such as the automotive industry (Kädtler and Sperling 2001, 2002), for example, largely comprises small- and medium-sized enterprises. Characteristic of SMEs is their basic economic orientation, which may be understood as epitomizing the maxim 'retain and reinvest' – the strategic approach Mary O'Sullivan (2000) attributed to large US companies before the turn towards financialization. 'Distribution' is a fundamentally foreign concept to the management of SMEs beyond the remuneration of owners who have direct links with the business. Even raised expectations from this quarter, typically in connection with a change of generations or ownership, are widely regarded as symptoms of decline. These companies can live with profit margins which would make them 'corporate value destroyers' par excellence according to the criteria of value-based management. The prerequisite for their survival in this form is a reliable credit base that functions in accordance with other criteria. Thus, we typically find strong small- and medium-sized business structures or comparable economic structures where there is a significant public or cooperative bank sector with strong local or regional involvement. To the extent that this sector is effectively committed to observing global standards of risk assessment under the new version of the rules of the Bank for International Settlement, known as Basel II, the economic principle of the *Mittelstand* comes fundamentally under pressure, since all models for producing equity capital that fulfil one of these standards amount ultimately to financial-market financing instruments and, thus, to grounds for claims to corresponding profits and dividends.

Before the rules concerned come into effect, it is not possible to make anything but more or less well-founded presumptions about these developments. There are strong indications in this direction, though independent of Basel II. For years, complaints among SMEs concerning the extreme difficulties and embarrassments in obtaining credit have been notorious; there have been calls of alarm from the German engineering industry over a matter of years warning of a credit squeeze that could endanger the future of their industry; at least a few responsible figures in the *Landeszentralbanken* (state central banks), which back the *Sparkassen* (savings banks), stated back in the late 1990s that they no longer perceived their future role as an institution of public infrastructure policy but rather as players in the global business of commercial banking. Basel II and the endeavours of the EU to reduce elements of the German *Sparkassen* system alien to the markets would, thus, be the expression and regulative promotion of economic reorientation tendencies that, in practice, have long been in effect within the credit sector – that is, the re-embedding of economy in economics in the sense set out in the initial analysis.

Here, too, it must be said that the developments, as briefly described, are not the sole determinants for the enterprises. They constitute new options and, under certain circumstances, serious restrictions, but they take away the possibility and necessity of strategic choice only from such enterprises that can definitively no longer deal with these conditions. With regard to the others, the thoughts that we have set out can, with their combination of structural analysis and random experience, constitute useful heuristics. In order to allow further progress, systematic empirical research is needed, especially in the area of the *Mittelstand*.

2.5 Financialization and innovation

Finally, we would like to make a short remark on the connection between financialization and innovation. Notwithstanding a certain scepticism towards concepts that claim to see the way to *the* or *a* 'knowledge society' as the central feature of the global economy, we assume that the ability to innovate and the (further) development of specific competencies are the central prerequisites for companies in early industrialized countries to hold their own and develop, where worldwide cost-competition is not an option. The re-embedding of economy in financial-market-oriented economics raises questions. This is because, in our view, companies as organizations in general are 'systems of collective action' (Friedberg 1993). 'Their consistency and capacity to act as organizations consist in a complex of relatively stable balances of powers and influence and in a stock of conventions that makes it possible to decide questions of adequacy and legitimacy in a generally accepted manner' (Kädtler 2001: 223). That applies particularly to enterprises that set store by innovation, which is typically based on recombining different competencies and knowledge in an original way.

The common denominator of all finance-market-related management principles and evaluation systems is their reference to processes that at the same time are highly transparent, can be planned in detail and can be 'broken down' into steps. The business process appears to be the logical implementation of an unambiguous and fully defined 'right' strategy – that is, as a company-based planned economy in which risks and levels of productivity may be calculated at any time and surprises excluded as far as possible (for a detailed account of this, see Nicolai and Thomas 2004). The complex, and in many points open and tentative, circumstances of organizational learning and the processes of innovation, which *per definitionem* cannot be fully planned in advance, have no place in this model. However useful risk capital may be when considered under other aspects, transferring this problem into the risk-capital financial-segment merely relocates it, as risk capital financing requires a sufficiently advanced innovative idea and with this the social background from which such early innovations emerge, as well. There can be no spin-offs without publicly financed research and no complex economy on the basis of this innovation model alone.

The French sociologist Frédéric Lordon (2000) has summed up this dilemma as a halved interpretation of Schumpeter, in which the creative part of creative destruction has been lost, since only the question of how to make the most out of given resources is addressed but not that of how the resources are to be generated. In the same sense Michael Faust et al. point out the obvious contrast between analysts' passion for innovations, on the one hand, and their lack of interests for the initial conditions of innovation, on the other (Faust, Fisecker and Bahnmüller 2007). The implementation of company evaluation and governance taking the financial markets as its frame of reference could prove to hinder innovation in many companies, not only the small ones. Worldwide, pharmaceutical companies today, for instance, are caught in a dilemma between the demand for innovative products, on the one hand, and business models and corporate structures that conform to the financial markets, on the other.

2.6   Summary – Companies' perspectives in a financializing economy

A fundamental shift in how corporate decisions are made lies at the heart of financialization. Increasingly, corporate strategies are not decided upon primarily on the basis of internal development opportunities but in response to external conditions and models. These models are based on the ability of the financial-market public sphere to generate models, concepts of reality and criteria of success (not only) for economic action and to stage it effectively. Once an idea has reached the status of being a generally accepted and recognized view, it is guaranteed a sufficient following for the foreseeable future, because it is definitely much less risky to lose when one is in keeping with the tide of opinion than to seek success against it. This was already true under the conditions of earlier models and management fashions that were less influenced by financial-market players.

This power, like power in general, has its limits. The ability or the extent of the ability to control other players' room for manoeuvre depends on what these other players themselves are aiming to achieve. Regarding the relationship between financial investors and the real economy, the power of the financial markets extends as far as there are real economic strategies that may be realized under its influence. That is not true of individual cases, but certainly is a necessary principle of the reality in general and in the long run. Otherwise, the erosion of the economic substance of the companies concerned would be likely in the long term – a consequence that authors such as François Chesnais (1997), Mary O'Sullivan (2000) and Frédéric Lordon (2000) certainly see as a possibility. Their key argument is that substantiating investor claims before the event lacks a corrective mechanism to prevent them spreading to the social level. In this point critical economists and sociologists concur with Claude Bébéar – former CEO of AXA and current chairman of the supervisory board, who is often referred to as the 'godfather of French financial capitalism'. He published a polemic paper in 2003 accusing external financial players, such as consultants, investment bankers, rating experts and the like, of 'killing capitalism' (Bébéar and Manière 2003). We would add that the role perception of strategic management, as the representative of internal real economy and/or of financial markets, is one of the most critical issues from this perspective, and that the answers to it vary significantly in different cases. The structure of ownership matters, but we also find central aspects of management oriented towards financial-market principles in companies that are dominated by strategic shareholders or companies that are not listed at all. Amongst the large companies, we find hardly any to which these principles do not apply, at least in significant aspects.

However, in any case financialization affects different categories of companies very differently. Managers of large, cash-rich companies have a great deal of scope for action, while players in small, cash-strapped companies have minimal scope for action. Large companies find attractive credit conditions on the global capital market and are able to pass on the costs of their own strategies of financialization to subcontractors. On the other side, especially SMEs find themselves in a quandary, with cost and margin pressure, on the one hand, and deteriorating credit conditions, on the other. Therefore, with respect to the systemic effects of financialization, SMEs may, in a way, become 'payers of last resort'. This would cause deep-rooted change in economies, such as in Germany, where SMEs and the *Mittelstand* are an important sector not only in quantitative terms but also with respect to crucial qualitative dimensions, such as the qualification of the social workforce and innovation.

It is not possible to make any positive statement on the consequences that these trends, once established, will bring in their wake, or how far the financialization of the economy at social and corporate levels can and will go. This is because there are no clear solutions in the social field of the financial markets, but only temporary compromises between conflicting trends, orientations and interests.

There is an irresolvable tension between financial-market models and the conditions of the production of goods and services in the real economy, particularly where strategic objectives cannot be calculated in principle, which holds true for investments in innovation, for example. Orientation for real economic strategies that is stable in the long term cannot be gained in this way. Rather, continual change from one provisional state of balance to the next is likely, with restructuring being a permanent feature at the corporate level. This includes the assumption that considerations and negotiation processes concerning corporate strategies will continue to be more important in future than current theories of the hermetic subsumption of all economic activity under the power of the financial markets sometimes suggest. That applies to the level of the company itself and to the financial-market public sphere. However, it appears questionable whether the financial-market public sphere and its collective learning potential alone could effectively counteract the immanent tendency towards exaggerated demands to the detriment of the real economy's potential for development. In particular, this concerns the area of small- and medium-sized enterprises – the *Mittelstand* in Germany. To them, it is not the changing moods and sentiments in financial markets that are problematic but rather increasing debt services going along with a growing dependency on financing via financial markets. The debate here ought to be, once again, rather about the general political and social public opinion on the deregulation and reregulation of financial markets, the role of a public banking system, and also such issues as pensions systems.

Notes

1. By analogy to the English term 'real investment', we understand the term 'real economy' to mean the development, production and sales of goods and services in contrast to the financial markets as markets of promises (to pay) (Giraud 2001). It is obvious that the latter are also real.
2. Thus, we refrain from explicitly discussing macroeconomic aspects, such as the perspectives of a new 'finance-led growth regime' (Boyer 2000) or *'capitalisme patrimonial'* (Aglietta 1998, 2000). It will become clear from our observations on financial market-oriented corporate strategies, however, that we are extremely sceptical towards the relevant prognoses about new-style accumulation or growth regimes, and why this is. Another argument against the positions concerned is that they make unrealistic assumptions about the social distribution of financial assets (cf. Froud, Sukhdev, Haslam and Williams 2001).
3. We consider it more appropriate to speak of 'organized investors' but go along with the generally established terminology below.
4. For a detailed analysis see Lavigne (2002: 158–79).
5. Lordon uses the term *'idée simple'* to cover simple yet diversely interpretable models, which may function in a certain era or society as a standardized and generally accepted reference-point for substantiating and legitimizing economic practice, just as 'growth' and 'competitiveness' once did.
6. For the significance of the rating agencies as 'governance without government', that is, as institutions of corporate regulation founded on a private basis, and on procedures and criteria of the rating process, see Sinclair (1994).
7. In German statistics there are two definitions of *Mittelstand*: a quantitative one, as SMEs (<500 employees and <€ 50 mil. turnover); and a qualitative one (family-owned/owner-managed). In 2004, SMEs represented 70.8 per cent of

employees, 39.8 per cent of turnover, 46.7 per cent of gross value added and 82.9 per cent of apprentices; family-owned companies represented 41.5 per cent of gross value added and 57.3 per cent of employees in Germany. (Hauser and Wolter 2007).

References

Aglietta, M. (1998) 'Le capitalisme de demain', Notes de la Fondation Saint Simon, Paris.

Aglietta, M. (2000) 'La globalisation financière', in CEPII (ed.), *L'économie mondiale 2000* (Paris: La Découverte), 52–67.

Bébéar, C. and P. Manière (2003) *Ils vont tuer le capitalisme* (Paris: Plon).

Becker, S. and T. Sablowski (1998) 'Konzentration und industrielle Organisation: Das Beispiel der Chemie- und Pharmaindustrie', *Prokla*, 113, 619–42.

Berle, A. and G. Means (1950) *The Modern Corporation and Private Property* (17th ed.) (New York: Macmillan).

Bourdieu, P. (2001) *Das politische Feld. Zur Kritik der politischen Vernunft* (Konstanz: UVK).

Boyer, R. (1999) 'Le politique à l'ère de la mondialisation et de la finance: Le point sur quelques recherches régulationnistes', *L'année de la régulation*, 3, 13–75.

Boyer, R. (2000) 'Is a Finance-Led Growth Regime a Viable Alternative to Fordism? A Preliminary Analysis', *Economy and Society*, 29, 111–45.

Callon, M. (1998) 'Introduction: The Embeddedness of Economic Markets in Economics', in M. Callon (ed.), *The Laws of the Market* (Oxford: Blackwell Publishers), 1–57.

Child, J. (1972) 'Organizational Structure, Environment and Performance: The Role of Strategic Choice', *Sociology. The Journal of the British Sociological Association*, 6, 1–23.

Crozier, M. and Friedberg (1977) *L'acteur et le système* (Paris: Editions du Seuil).

Cutler, T. (2001) 'Social Insecurity and the Retreat from Social Democracy: Occupational Welfare in the Long Boom and Financialization', *Review of International Political Economy*, 8, 96–118.

Chesnais, F. (1997) *La mondialisation du capital* (Paris: Syros).

Davis, G. F. and T. A. Thompson (1994) 'A Social Movement Perspective on Corporate Control', *Administrative Science Quarterly*, 39, 141–73.

Ehrbar, A. (1998) *EVA: The Real Key to Creating Wealth* (New York: John Wiley & Sons, Inc.).

Faust, M. (2002) 'Consultancies as Actors in Knowledge Arenas: Evidence from Germany', in M. Kipping and L. Engwall (eds), *Management Consulting: Emergence and Dynamics of a Knowledge Industry* (Oxford, New York: Oxford University Press), 146–63.

Faust, M. (2006) 'Consultants', in J. Beckert and M. Zafirovski (eds), *International Encyclopedia of Economic Sociology* (London New York: Routledge), 96–9.

Faust, M., C. Fisecker and R. Bahnmüller (2007) 'Was interessiert Analysten? Versuch über erklärungsträchtiges Desinteresse an Personalpolitik', *Berliner Debatte Initial*, 4(18), 1–11.

Friedberg, E. (1993) *Le pouvoir et la règle* (Paris: Èditions du Seuil).

Froud, J., C. Haslam, S. Johal and K. Williams (1999) 'Car Companies and the Challenge of Financialisation', paper prepared for the GERPISA colloquium, 18–20 June 1999.

Froud, J., C. Haslam, S. Johal and K. Williams (2000) 'Shareholder Value and Financialization: Consultancy Promises, Management Moves', *Economy and Society*, 29, 80–110.

Froud, J., J. Sukhdev, C. Haslam, and K. Williams (2001) 'Accumulation under Conditions of Inequality', *Review of International Political Economy*, 8, 66–95.

Froud, J., J. Sukhdev, A. Leaver and K. Williams (2006) *Financialisation and Strategy: Narrative and Numbers* (London, New York: Routledge).

Giraud, P. N. (2001) *Le commerce des promesses. Petit traité sur la finance moderne* (Paris: Seuil).

Hauser, H.-E. and H.-J. Wolter (2007) *Die volkswirtschaftliche Bedeutung der Familienunternehmen*, IfM-Materials, no. 172, Bonn.

Henwood, D. (1997) *Wall Street* (London, New York: Verso).

Huffschmid, J. (2002) *Politische Ökonomie der Finanzmärkte* (Hamburg: VSA).

Ittner, C. D. and D. F. Larcker (2001) 'Assessing Empirical Research in Managerial Accounting: A Value-Based Management Perspective', *Journal of Accounting & Economics*, 36, 349–410.

Jensen, M. C. (1998) *Foundations of Organizational Strategy* (Cambridge/Mass., London: Harvard University Press).

Jensen, M. C. and W. H. Meckling (1976) 'Theory of the Firm: Managerial Behavior, Agency Costs, and Ownership Structure', *Journal of Financial Economics*, 3, 305–60.

Kädtler, J. (2001) 'Social Movements and Interest Groups as Triggers for Organizational Learning', in M. Dierkes, A. Berthoin Antal, J. Child and I. Nonaka (eds), *Handbook of Organizational Learning and Knowledge* (Oxford, New York: Oxford University Press), 221–41.

Kädtler, J. (2006) *Sozialpartnerschaft im Umbruch. Industrielle Beziehungen unter den Bedingungen von Globalisierung und Finanzmarktkapitalismus* (Hamburg: VSA).

Kädtler, J. and H. J. Sperling (2001) *'Financialization - A New Software for Car Manufacturing'*, paper presented at the Reconfiguring the Auto Industry: Merger & Acquisition, Alliances, and Exit (9th GERPISA Colloquium), Paris, 7–9 June 2001.

Kädtler, J. and H. J. Sperling (2002) 'After Globalisation and Financialisation: Logics of Bargaining in the German Automotive Industry', *Competition and Change*, 8, 149–68.

Knight, F. H. (1921) *Risk, Uncertainty and Profit* (New York: A.H. Kelly).

Lavigne, S. (2002) *Investisseurs financiers et convention d'évaluation des firmes* (Toulouse: Université des Sciences Sociales de Toulouse 1).

Lordon, F. (2000) 'La "création de valeur" comme rhétorique et comme pratique. Généalogie et sociologie de la "valeur actionnariale"', *L'année de la régulation*, 4, 117–68.

MacKenzie, D. (2004) 'The Big, Bad Wolf and the Rational Market: Portfolio Insurance, the 1987 Crash and the Performativity of Economics', *Economy and Society*, 33, 303–34.

MacKenzie, D. (2005) 'Opening the Black Boxes of Global Finance', *Review of International Political Economy*, 12, 555–76.

MacKenzie, D. (2006) *An Engine, Not a Camera. How Financial Models Shape Markets* (Cambridge/Mass., London: MIT-Press).

Malmi, T. and S. Ikaheimo (2003) 'Value Based Management Practices – Some Evidence from the Field', *Management Accounting Research*, 14, 235–54.

Montagne, S. (2000) 'Retraite complémentaire et marchés financiers aux Etats-Unis', *L'année de la régulation*, 4, 13–45.

Nicolai, A. T. and T. W. Thomas (2004) 'Kapitalmarktkonforme Unternehmensführung: Eine Analyse im Lichte der jüngeren Strategieprozesslehre, *Zeitschrift für betriebswirtschaftliche Forschung*, 56, 452–69.

O'Sullivan, M. (2000) *Contests for Corporate Control - Corporate Governance and Economic Performance in the Unites States and Germany* (Oxford, New York: Oxford University Press).

Orléan, A. (1999) *Le pouvoir de la finance* (Paris: Éditions Odile Jacob).

Ortmann, G. (ed.) (1995) *Formen der Produktion. Organisation und Rekursivität* (Opladen: Westdeutscher Verlag).

Sinclair, T. J. (1994) 'Passing Judgement: Credit Rating Processes as Regulatory Mechanisms of Governance in the Emerging World Order', *Review of International Political Economy*, 1, 133–59.

Sinclair, T. J. (2000) 'Reinventing Authority: Embedded Knowledge Networks and the New Global Finance', *Environment and Planning C: Government and Policy*, 2000, 487–502.

Stewart, B. (1999) *What is EVA?*, retrieved 02-09-2001, http://www.sternstewart.com/evaabout/whatis.shtml.

Streeck, W. and M. Höpner (2003) 'Einleitung: Alle Macht dem Markt?', in W. Streeck and M. Höpner (eds), *Alle Macht dem Markt? Fallstudien zur Abwicklung der Deutschland AG* (Frankfurt/Main, New York: Campus), 11–59.

Windolf, P. (2005a) 'Die neuen Eigentümer', in P. Windolf (ed.), *Finanzmarkt-Kapitalismus. Analysen zum Wandel von Produktionsregimen* (Wiesbaden: Verlag für Sozialwissenschaften), 8–19.

Windolf, P. (2005b) 'Was ist Finanzmarkt-Kapitalismus¿, in P. Windolf (ed.), *Finanzmarkt-Kapitalismus. Analysen zum Wandel von Produktionsregimen* (Wiesbaden: VS), 20–57.

Zugehör, R. (2000) 'Unternehmensinvestitionen zwischen Kapitalmarkt und Mitbestimmung: Eine empirische Analyse', paper for the workshop 'Institutioneller Wandel in den industriellen Beziehungen', held at MPIfG, Cologne, 8–9 December 2000.

3
Change within Traditional Channels: German SMEs, the Restructuring of the Banking Sector, and the Growing Shareholder-Value Orientation

Katharina Bluhm and Bernd Martens[1]

3.1 Introduction

Small- and medium-sized enterprises (SMEs), especially in the manufacturing sector, have been an essential part of the German coordinated market economy in the second half of the 20th century. Hence, to understand the departure of the German economy from this model since the mid-1990s, it is valuable to scrutinize changes within SMEs. To the 'varieties of capitalism' approach (VoC), the positive mutual reinforcement between the institutional systems and firm strategies has been decisive for the explanation of institutional stability and path dependency (cf. Hall and Soskice 2001). In many dimensions, manufacturing SMEs have a stake in the process: they are a major player in the reproduction of the occupational system; have accepted co-determination in labour relations – at least when they are medium-sized; prefer high-quality niche strategies accommodated to the institutional opportunities and constraints; and have moved into a symbiotic relationship with the bank-based financing system.

Two institutions of the specific German three-pillar banking system – public savings banks and cooperative, or mutually-owned banks – are specialized in providing SMEs with capital on friendly terms and represent a major mediator in state finance-support programmes.[2] Neither capitalization on stock markets, nor a high rate of capital and reserves has been necessary to finance niche strategies and increase internationalization. Thus, there has been little need to share control in corporate governance. The equity ratio[3] of German SMEs dropped in the second half of the 20th century from more than 50 per cent in the 1950s to less than 20 per cent in 1998, thus becoming the lowest rate in the EU-15, especially among small-sized enterprises (cf. Berghoff 2003; KfW 2006; Observatory Network of European SME 2003: 20); in the manufacturing sector, however, the equity ratio is higher. The 'debt capital culture' of German SMEs supported an *insider corporate-governance system* typical for the coordinated market economy (CME). In this system, decisions over firms' credibility are based on long-term, trustful relationships between enterprises and banks. The personal reputation of the entrepreneur and a good reputation in an informal network that monitors the firms' performance are crucial (Hall and Soskice 2001; Deeg 2006). Those 'reputation networks' consist of memberships in business associations and chambers, and on supervisory boards of other firms, often with strong regional bonds.

During the New Economy Bubble, and in consequence of reforms in stock corporation law facilitating SMEs' access to the capital markets at the end of the 1990s, a shift towards new equity-oriented ways of financing had been expected. This was supposed to accompany a cultural change towards a new, shareholder-oriented type of entrepreneur emerging first in high-tech industries, but also being triggered by the generational change within the SME sector as post-war entrepreneurs were replaced by successors with different attitudes and concepts. The historian Hartmut Berghoff portrays the new entrepreneurs as a 'transition group' perceiving leadership in one enterprise as no longer a lifetime or family project (2004; 2006; cf. Kühl 2003). In other words, the capital-market-driven dissolution of the German insider system among large firms, and the cultural change in top management echelons (cf. Jackson, Höpner, and Kurdelbusch 2005), appears to have found its counterpart in the SME sector.

In this chapter, we argue that the change in SMEs does in fact contribute to the departure from the traditional German CME. Yet, this change is less spectacular and radical. Neither new capital-market investors nor a young generation of managing directors are the predominant driving forces. Rather, it should be understood as *change within traditional channels* of doing business; and the increasing profit sensitivity appears to be more the outcome of the *professionalization of corporate governance* via improved accounting practices and financial planning, than an aggressive embracing of the shareholder-value ideology.

This chapter is organized into five parts. Section 3.2 briefly describes the samples and research methods on which the findings are based. Section 3.3 indicates that the influence of new financial actors on SME corporate governance is still weak. Section 3.4 outlines the institutional change in the SME-related bank sector and explores how SMEs in the manufacturing sector deal with the new demands. Section 3.5 highlights aspects of the social change occurring in the upper ranks of SMEs, the relevance of the new concept of entrepreneurship for our sample, and differences between predecessors and successors in company managements. The paper concludes with a brief summary of the findings.

3.2 Sample and methods

Our sample comprized two surveys with nearly 800 respondents each and 50 guided in-depth interviews with leading personal in SMEs. Survey data were collected in two waves: in 2002 and 2005. Of the enterprises 538 responded twice. We approached managing directors first and were successful in 716 cases (2005 survey). If it was possible, designated successors of managing directors were additionally interviewed. We selected some enterprises in manufacturing, such as textiles and plastics, but the bulk of the businesses were in the metal, electrical, and mechanical engineering sectors. Enterprise size ranged from 50 to 1,000; roughly half of the enterprises had more than 100 employees.

The in-depth interviews were carried out between 2002 and 2007. They explored topics from a quantitative questionnaire, such as succession, leadership concepts, and how the firms were meeting the new institutional and economic challenges of globalization. In addition, we conducted interviews with banks (cf. Schmidt 2005).

3.3 Limited influence of new financial investors

German newspapers repeatedly tell stories of family firms partly or completely taken over by new financial investors alongside dramatic changes in their management culture towards strict shareholder-value orientation. These enterprises are usually relatively large and, therefore, important for the German insider system, where big family firms could afford to stay away from the financial market. At the same time, they do not represent the SME sector, not even the manufacturing branches. Representative surveys confirm that new external actors and ways of equity financing still play a minor role (KfW 2006: 174). The same holds true for our sample. Although the percentage of managing directors without any shares in the company is relatively high at 45 per cent, the majority are employed in owner-led or family firms. Other corporations and organizations (such as foundations) hold shares in 22 per cent of the enterprises. Amongst other corporations, only 2.1 per cent are equity companies of any sort. As in the KfW survey (2006) our sample includes few stock corporations: in absolute numbers, just 34 enterprises. Only one-third of them are listed on stock markets. All the others spread their shares among families and friends allowing management to raise equity without having professional financial actors involved in corporate governance.

While SMEs prefer to finance their business and growth from their own cash-flow (with all the limitations involved), bank loans remain the most important external source for German SMEs. According to the 2005 survey, 96 per cent of the SMEs use bank loans, with 60.4 per cent on longer terms.[4] One of the owner-managers interviewed pointed to reasons that make SMEs hesitant in adopting new ways of equity-based finance, stating:

> Mezzanine and other such types of financing are absolutely [unsuitable] for small-sized operations. (...) Well, if you've got a good company and can manage a 15 or 20 per cent return, then it's maybe an alternative to classical financing over 5 to 10 years. But I don't even know whether we'll be here tomorrow, let alone say whether in 10 years we'll be making 20 per cent returns. And if we don't, then I've got some big insurance company, or worse, on my back. With banks (...) one can perhaps still talk things over, but with an insurance corporation – certainly not. (Owner-manager, SME 56 2006.)[5]

The traditional approach to financing often goes together with strict refusals of shareholder value ideology. Two statements from our in-depth interviews may illustrate this:

> For us there is no such thing as the shareholder-value idea or quarterly results. (...) We reckon in decades, generations. (Senior owner-manager, SME 6 2002.)

> It's not middle-class firms that are ruining the country. Well, OK, there may be a few black sheep in there too. It's the high-paid managers who are ruining the country. (...) I won't name Ackermann, that's just getting too old. Ackermann[6] bought his way out. (...) That Herr Sommer, Telekom, the 11 millions etc., Karstadt 8 millions, and that Esser![7] That Esser! Now don't get angry, if I just ask: where did this guy come from anyway? What did he accomplish? I'll tell you. He was just at the right time in the right place. (...). Sells an excellent company for a song, and gets 30 million. Just let this sink in a bit! (Owner-manager, SME 56 2006.)

The only SME in our sample which was actually taken over by a private equity company confirms a radical change in management culture. The deal saved the old family firm from insolvency, which was then consolidated for a high price, as the investor planned to shift the complete production abroad for cost reasons. The personnel director described the cultural change as follows:

> Earlier, a businessman was something more of the classical entrepreneur, meaning he also had social responsibility. Not every rationalization measure was carried out 100 per cent right away. Some decisions could be deferred, the effects counterbalanced or such. But not anymore. Now the only rule is: maximize profits! (SME 34 2004.)

3.4   Bank restructuring and proactive strategies of SMEs

3.4.1   What is new?

Although the 'debt capital culture' of German SMEs appears to be untouched, it would be misleading to assume that no serious changes have occurred. On the contrary, the banking sector has been one of the forces driving change in corporate governance of German SMEs in recent years.

The German three-pillar system is under huge pressure from three sides. First, the globalized financial markets have also raised bank shareholders' expectations of returns on investment in continental Europe. While other European banks have reacted to the new global benchmarks with large-scale mergers and acquisitions (also in east-central Europe) (Belaisch et al. 2001), German private banks can hardly take over state-owned savings and cooperative banks – both of which have a non-profit mission.[8] Private institutes hold, in particular, the savings bank system responsible for low profits in the German banking sector, since savings banks can afford to be less focused on profitability, offer loans to customers on better terms, and, therefore, distort competition.[9]

Commercial banks are also a driving force behind the efforts of the European Commission to abolish the three-pillar system. Since July 2005 public guarantees for savings banks, which allowed savings banks to give loans to lower costs, have been abolished.[10] This decision represents a systemic shift in the institutional trajectory of the German market economy (cf. Lane and Quack 2002). With the abolition of the public guarantees, the EU stipulated a longer *transition period* until 2015, as all liabilities taken on before July 2005 are still covered by the old law. According to Mullineux and Terberger (2006: 6), the EU decision met the savings-bank sector not unprepared, that is, they had covered their refinancing needs in advance.[11] Savings banks succeeded, however, in keeping their public status, regional structure and trade marks, which were under scrutiny. Hence, in spite of the dramatic institutional change, *path dependency* in the German SME-oriented financing sector appears to be more likely than a quick switchover to the Anglo-Saxon banking system.

Second, long before the Second Capital Accord (Basel II) came into effect in 2007, German banks began to introduce the new requirements. Basel II aims at a more far-reaching integration of the European financial system by introducing joint minimum equity standards and unified criteria for measuring lending risks. This implied a 'little revolution' for the German insider system which long-term consequences are still to be explored (KfW 2006: 148; cf. Kädtler and Faust in this volume). Right away, two things changed: a) all banks began to make SME[12] lending tied to detailed information and credit rating procedures, which became a general standard, and b) the equity ratio of an enterprise gained a 'signal' function as indicator of lending risk (as proposed in economic theories), unusual heretofore in the German system.

Credit rating itself is nothing completely new to German banks. Commercial banks like the Dresdner Bank have already been rating their firms since the mid-1990s, while the savings banks began later. Basel II, however, provides banks with new power to actually *get* the information they demand. This change allows them to not only require *retrospective information* about the business, but also *specific financial updates* and *strategic information* necessary for profit *planning*. In the past, SMEs often declined to hand over sufficient information, especially concerning medium and long-term liquidity planning out of fear of harming their creditworthiness (director of a private bank affiliate, interview 2006). And the lack of information flow is not just a German phenomenon.[13] With Basel II, banks acquire the institutional right to request this kind of information; the rating procedure as a general standard barely leaves applicants any choice. In short, the institutional changes alter the power relationship between banks and SMEs in spite of the persisting bank diversity in Germany. SMEs are forced to become more 'transparent' in order to prove creditworthiness (cf. KfW 2006; Observatory Network of European SME 2003: 24; Schmidt 2005).

Today a formalized credit rating is common in the interaction between SMEs and banks. Only 3 per cent of German savings banks have not elaborated their own rating system by 2006; in addition, 41 per cent of their firm customers also utilized external ratings (mostly provided by other banks) (DSGV 2007b: 83–85). From the SMEs we surveyed in 2005, 65.4 per cent already had experiences with rating systems. In 2002 only 47.8 per cent had had such experience. Most of the interviewees reported this experience as positive (61.1 per cent, survey 2005).

Formalized credit rating as generalized standard has not dissolved or even weakened the close German bank-customer relationship so far. However, it has altered the character of the relationship by changing information-gathering from the trust- and network-based way towards a formalized information system combined with intense monitoring by a loans officer in case of financial difficulties. With the pronouncedly number-based communication, bank relationships have become more sensitive to firms' actual profitability and future prospects. Banks act more like a *'principal'* who is concerned about whether the *'agent'* (the bank customer) pursues strategies with highly profitable efficiency and who puts pressure on rising equity capital. While in the past banks were more concerned about securities that companies or owners can provide, they now take a much more *active* role in the corporate governance of German SMEs.[14]

In addition, commercial banks have started to sell debts to financial investors in order to clear their portfolios. This, too, brings a new kind of risk into the relationship (director of a private bank branch, interview 2006). Savings banks are trying to combine better risk-management and long-lasting, trustful relationships with customers by selling debts only *within* the savings bank group ('loan pool') (Haasis 2007). Yet, they also began to sell uncollectible loans to external investors (DSGV 2007c).

The new profit sensitivity of banks has been an issue in our in-depth interviews. As the personnel director already quoted states: it's now a fact that, as a rule of thumb, if you have a profit margin of less than 3 per cent and a cash-flow yield of less than 8 per cent, then banks are not really interested. And then you've got a problem (SME 34 2004).

3.4.2 How do SMEs react?

We observed three major reactions to the changing role of banks: a) a *professionalization in the accounting instruments and methods of corporate control* occurs; b) SMEs take up a proactive *transparency* strategy; c) they raise their *equity capital* not only to meet the new requirements, but also to become more independent of bank loans.

Professionalization of corporate control

Our data for 2005 indicate a significant correlation between equity ratio, experience in rating, and the range of reorganization measures, especially in accounting. While 75 per cent of SMEs with constantly low equity capital (in our sample, less than 25 per cent) have experience with rating, 'only' 48 per cent of the enterprises with a stable, high equity rate (more than the average of 38 per cent) have experienced rating. For the second panel in 2005, logistic regressions show that negative or undecided responses with regard to rating often correlate with more reorganization measures, especially with changing or improving accounting standards and evaluating individual units according to ratios for earnings and productivity. Other influential features are the company's size, the region, and the respondent's age. Thus, more precisely, firms without rating experience, smaller firms, and firms run by East Germans or by older managing directors are significantly reorganized to a smaller extent. This was not the case in the first panel wave. For the 2002 data, only a negative operating result of the company showed significant effects on the probability of undertaking restructuring measures (Table 3.1). In recent years organizational restructuring has been conducted more selectively and banks have acquired an indirect influence on the internal structure of firms via rating outcomes.[15]

Our in-depth interviews reveal that the introduction of, or improvements in, accounting methods often occurs due to economic and, above all, liquidity crises. This consequence of a crisis may be interpreted as the catching-up of laggards. Yet, the interviews prove that banks are frequently a driving factor in the implementation of elaborated accounting standards. In case of financial crisis, SMEs must report to their creditors quarterly or even monthly, just like subsidiaries to a parent company or an institutional investor.

Yet, there are also other, more indirect but influential factors involved. Innovative management methods often move down from large firms to SMEs. When the historian Harm G. Schröter (2004) identified a third 'wave of Americanization' of European corporations – after for example the implementation of marketing and market research – he was referring to the trickle-down effect from large firms to small ones. The new 'wave' he terms a 'triumph of finance' (Schröter 2005: 190). A profound empirical proof of the trickle-down effect in the implementation of accounting systems developed during the last decades is provided by Martens and Schmidt (2003): In a sample of 328 enterprises – members of the German branch of the International Controller Association (ICV) – firms with more than 1,000 employees introduced accounting systems up to the

Table 3.1 Result of two logistic regressions with the German 2002 and 2005 data sets (the dependent variable is the probability that organizational restructuring occurred up to three years before the survey)

Independent variables*	2002		2005	
	Odds ratio	Discrete change	Odds ratio	Discrete change
The loan situation is problematic	1.224	1.2%	1.147	3.3%
West-German firms directed by West Germans	1.062	1.2%	0.865	−3.5%
East-German firms directed by East Germans	0.915	−1.8%	0.627*	−11.3%
Reference: East-German firms directed by West Germans				
fewer than 50 employees	0.524	−14.5%	0.579	−13.5%
50–99 employees	0.743	−6.2%	0.504*	−16.5%
100–300 employees	1.261	4.7%	0.692	−8.9%
Reference: Company has more than 300 employees				
Rating negative or undecided	1.204	3.7%	1.885**	14.6%
Rating positive	1.084	1.6%	1.491*	9.5%
Reference: no rating				
Balance negative	2.093*	16.5%	1.054	1.3%
Age of respondent	0.982°	−0.4%	0.974**	−0.6%
Nagelkerke's Pseudo R^2	0.053		0.070	
Number of cases	722		674	

Notes: $°p < 0.10$, $*p < 0.05$, $** p < 0.01$

end of the 1980s; firms between 500 and 1,000 employees did so about five years later, while even smaller members of the association adopted the approach at the end of the 1990s.[16]

The introduction of new standards and more detailed parameters allow managers and owners a more detailed and on-time corporate control, enabling them to react more quickly to emerging financial problems. We suggest that as *learning processes* occur in business, a more commercial approach emerges with a stricter profit orientation – even though SMEs may still reject the shareholder value ideology. The learning process can be more easily detected in the in-depth interviews, and managing directors themselves chose the term 'professionalization' to describe the change. One accounting manager pointed out:

Before, we approached some things quite differently, saw their value differently. [The change] begins already with keeping strictly to agreements – if it says in the contract that a quarterly business assessment is due, we give them a profit-and-loss statement. We've kept precisely to this. Earlier we wouldn't have seen things from this point of view. They called us up once and said, 'give us another business assessment.' No problem. But then they must have looked exactly at the contract and said, 'hey, they really have kept to their deadlines after all!' So now you can see an automatic, completely new way of thinking in yourself (SME 40, 2005).

Transparency policy of SMEs

The substantial change in bank-firm relationships also alters how enterprises acquire reputation. Although personal trust in the capabilities and skills of a potential creditor has not vanished completely from the relationships, the *foundation* that trust is built on has experienced a significant shift from informal reputation gained in a (business) community towards formal standards and balance-sheets. This shift has been adopted as a new strategy by many managers we interviewed who started to feed banks proactively with detailed figures and strategic information on a regular basis, and even exceeding requirements. Once again, in-depth interviews provide examples of new strategies for improving weak reputations:

> One of the East German companies, we observed for a longer time, fought back its bad credit image by setting up a monthly 'management information system' with the most important company statistics and to which banks were 'connected'. After the first data transfer, the officers of one credit institution called up the firm's managing director and said: 'Your performance is really incredible, we didn't know anything about this, your company is outstanding, we've got to start doing business' etc. That the strategy was a success shows the changed behaviour of creditors, who now only check up deviations from the business plan and already start to become edgy if the firm 'threatens' to deliver new data. (Managing director, SME 1 2005.)

We term this shift in communication *'transparency policy'* in order to stress the partial break in the communication culture of German SMEs, which in general used to behave very anxiously in releasing any figures about the firms' economic performance following the traditional concept of unilateral corporate control by the owner or family (the 'master of the house' attitude). Transparency policy is a firm strategy that copes with the new bank requirements *without* leading necessarily to more distance in their relationships with the banks.

Growth from firm cash

For a few years, surveys have been indicating a rise in the equity ratios of German SMEs (cf. KfW 2006; DSGV 2007b). Their authors interpret this as a sign of the success of institutional changes, that is, of the new requirements and incentives. In our sample, too, there is a slight rise in the equity ratio from the already high average of 37 per cent, to 38 per cent. We also note a remarkable growth in the utilization of alternative financial methods from 48 per cent in 2002 to 59 per cent in 2005, which mainly occurs in younger firms and firms owned by other corporations and organizations. Increasing equity and leasing have a high priority. Forty-four per cent of the firms in the hands of private owners or families and 30.2 per cent of companies owned by other corporations and organizations use *equity* as an alternative source to bank loans. *Leasing* constitutes 74.3 per cent of the privately or family-owned firms and 68.6 per cent of the others a major alternative.

In light of our in-depth interviews, we interpret the data as success of the established 'signal function' of high-equity capital. It also suggests an intentional strategy of becoming more independent from banks. Yet in contrast to large German firms (cf. Deeg 2006), it would be too much to say that German SMEs are turning away from credit financing (cf. section 3.3; BDI 2003: 22). What's more, the satisfaction with banks was persistently very high (roughly 80 per cent), indicating no deterioration in relationship, as had been predicted in the debate about the institutional changes – a finding that contributes to our main argument that the change occurred does modify and not break yet with the traditional channel of financing of the German *Mittelstand*.

3.5   Changes through succession

Social change in management is more of a long-term process than the institutional change we have discussed in the previous section. The connection between the two processes is only weak. Yet, we should note that the new professionalized standards of corporate control do contribute to cultural change in the *traditional management culture* of large German firms as well as SMEs (cf. Lane 1989; Eberwein and Tholen 1990). In spite of the expectation of the emergence of a new, shorter-term and project-oriented type of entrepreneur, as was observed in the New Economy (cf. Berghoff 2004; 2006; Kühl 2003), the 'traditional' German owner-managers in manufacturing have not altered their concept of the family business. Once again, changes occur more gradually

Table 3.2   Distribution of succession planned or carried out in per cent

	2002 (n = 233)	2005 (n = 204)
Relatives	39.1	44.1
Employees	18.5	21.6
Managing directors	5.2	7.8
Fellow owners	3.9	8.3
External managers	6.0	6.4
Successor is being sought	22.7	13.7
Pass on to other firm	1.3	1.5

and within traditional channels (cf. Martens and Michailow 2006). Succession does play a role here but is less crucial for the new generation of entrepreneurs than predicted (cf. Berghoff 2004; 2006). In the following sections, we provide evidence for the unbroken relevance of the traditional concept of succession (3.5.1) and highlight some indicators of the ongoing cultural change in German SMEs (3.5.2).

3.5.1   Preference for insider solutions

An early solution to the problem of succession in SMEs became a high priority in the new banking regime.[17] In our survey of 2005, 31 per cent of managers had to deal with the succession question at the time of the interview (in 2002 this figure was 36 per cent). Of the interviewees 44 per cent declared that the 'who' is, or will be, a *relative*; in 22 per cent of the cases this is an *employee*; in about 8 per cent this person is already a *managing director* or a *fellow owner*. Additionally, it seems that the situation has become more 'definite', because the percentage of successors sought has decreased significantly during the period 2002/05 (Table 3.2). A similar tendency is shown by the study of Günther and Gonschorek (2006: 17): 63 per cent of their interviewees plan to pass the firm on to family members.

In sum, succession *within* families is still the dominant pattern. But owners also compensate a lack of suitable relatives by considering a *wider circle of insiders*. There is no East-West difference in this respect. The East German founders, too, wish to establish family firms within the next generation. Of the managers 84 per cent we questioned perceived the search for a successor as unproblematic.

We also asked for the reasons for passing on a firm. In 87.7 per cent of the cases (survey 2005) the reason for the change was retirement. In just

2.5 per cent the owner accepted another assignment or job offer, and only in one case was there simply an 'irresistibly good offer'. In sum, the new type of entrepreneur who perceives running a firm as just a 'transition stage' is far from the reality of the manufacturing SME-sector.

3.5.2 Features of the succession process and career modes

In order to explore social change among the managers in question according to socio-structural features and attitudes, we tested age differences (cohorts), variations between forerunners and designated successors, and differences between heirs (recently in charge), other owners (such as founders), and the employed managing directors. These three independent features emphasize different aspects: *phases of life* of the respondents, *life cycles* of the organization, and *effects of ownership* in relation to the age of the company.

Concerning *strategic company goals,* differences between the older and the different groups of younger managers are not statistically significant. Company founders, who are usually older in our sample, and especially founders in East Germany, are most interested in liquidity (about 65 per cent of the East-German did emphasize this target, compared to 57.1 per cent of the whole sample). The figures indicate the still weaker financial base of East German SMEs. An increase in equity is ranked in privately owned firms notably higher (24.3 per cent) than in other firms (12.8 per cent). Older age cohorts in general emphasize turnover and liquidity in comparison to younger managing directors, but the correlations are not significant.[18] Designated successors rank profitability, as one of the most important parameters for corporate governance, higher than predecessors: 81 per cent of West German successors and 67 per cent of the East Germans reported this parameter to be crucial (the corresponding figures for the forerunners are: 64 per cent of the West Germans and 56 per cent of the East Germans). Although succession has not recently played a decisive role in pushing the professionalization of corporate control ahead, we conclude that it could act as a promoter of the process.

With respect to *qualifications,* successors (in West Germany) tend to prefer management to engineering degrees (63 per cent and 41 per cent), whereas the corresponding East Germans confirm the traditional technical dominance with 27 per cent of the degrees in management and 80 per cent in engineering.[19] With regard to the whole West German sample, astonishingly no correlation between qualifications and age exists: management degrees are *always* more frequent than technical ones (59.4 per cent and 47.6 per cent). This is a new trend in the 2005 data set, since a negative correlation between age and management degrees still existed in the 2002 sample. It seems that a trend towards management degrees also affects older age cohorts of managing directors of SMEs – at least the ones directed by West Germans – indicating that it is also becoming more and more decisive for running manufacturing SMEs. There is also no correlation between the qualification of the managing director questioned and the reorganization measures the firms gave priority to in the recent years. That is, directors with management degrees do not stress market and accounting issues more than engineers (both East- and West-German managers). The link between the qualifications of top management and firms' strategy that was supposed to cause the German 'over-engineering' in the 1980s and early 1990s appears much weaker nowadays.

As with their counterparts in large German firms, younger managers of SMEs tend to bypass vocational training on their career paths, something once considered decisive for the German engineer culture in management (in comparison to French or British management for example), which combines theoretical with practical competences (cf. Lane 1989). For West-German as well as East-German managing directors, the percentages of persons who enter vocational training is decreasing continuously. In the age cohort < 1940 (78 per cent of the East Germans and 77 per cent of the West Germans) and in the age cohort born between 1940 and 49, about 84 per cent of the East Germans, and 62.4 per cent of the West Germans had vocational training, while in age cohort ≥1960, only 56 per cent of the East Germans and 43 per cent of the West Germans did. For the same age cohort, the frequencies of academic degrees amount to 81.3 per cent (West Germans) and 94.4 per cent (East Germans).

The German management culture has been famous for its *in-house careers* or *chimney careers* contributing to a strong commitment to the firm. This finding is also believed to be true for SMEs, although it mainly rests on biographic data about managers of larger firms. In our SME survey, the in-house career is only typical for the heirs to a family business. Of the heirs 56 per cent (survey 2005) made their careers within their own firm only. Only one third of all heirs[20] gathered experience in other firms, while 41 per cent of the founders did so. By contrast, the majority of the employed managing directors had previously been in one or two firms.[21] One-third of them even reached the position without any previous employment in the enterprise – a type of career we term a *skydiver career*. Taking the flatter hierarchies of SMEs into account, we assume that also in the past employed managers were often recruited externally, which suggests a stronger differentiation in career patterns in large firms and SMEs. Hence, the growing relevance of skydiver careers may be the result of the growing number of employed managers on the managing boards of SMEs, rather than of a shift in career patterns. Yet, employed managers, too, are far from being a 'transition group' with high fluctuation. Their average tenures in the 2005 sample vary between 10.0 and 13.8 years, the corresponding means for the heirs and founders are 20.6 and 15.4 years.

In contrast to our expectations, the variables *ownership* and *qualification background* revealed small correlations with attitudes. Firm founders, successors or employed managers vary in their concept of leadership, but do not differ significantly in their attitudes about, for example, the social responsibility of the firm or state regulation (Martens and Michailow 2006). The East-West differences are much more significant and stable here. One explanation could be socialization processes within the SME sector, since even the skydivers among managing directors rarely come from large firms. The finding might also prove the general distance towards the shareholder value orientation as a new manager ideology, which we have found in the in-depth interviews. Yet, those interviews also suggest that managing directors underestimate the challenges posed to traditional social relationships in SMEs caused by the professionalization of corporate governance and the intensification of financial efficiency and cost control (Becker, Bluhm and Martens 2008).

3.6 Conclusion

In this chapter we have explored the change in management of German SMEs from two perspectives: the impact of the institutional change on corporate governance of medium-sized manufacturing firms due to further European integration and globalization, and the role of succession in this process. We argue that major changes have occurred in the traditional channels of business and are contributing to the gradual dissolution of the nationally embedded, coordinated German market economy. In recent years the banks have played a major role. The new surge in the professionalization of corporate control improves not only the information flow to investors (transparency of external actors) but also increases the transparency of profits and losses *within* firms. It can be proved that the results of ratings have an influence on restructuring processes in companies. This impact of financial ratios is new in the context of German SMEs. Although many owners and managers of manufacturing SMEs still reject the idea of strict shareholder value – as they frequently stressed in the qualitative interviews – the new 'rating perspective' will also provide opportunities and incentives to turn much more attention towards profit and efficiency even in firms of this size.

This change does not correspond to the spread of a new type of entrepreneur who perceives managing a firm as a temporary project. Yet it contributes to the ongoing decline of the traditional engineering culture in German management. Successors in the manufacturing sector have social ties to the firm they take over either as relatives or former employees, and do not consider leading that particular firm as a transition stage in their personal life. Although they do not undertake an open ideological shift toward shareholder value, they appear to more readily embrace the new requests and incentives of a financially-oriented and professionalized concept of corporate governance.

Notes

1. This paper presents results of the DFG project 'Generational change in SMEs. Persistence or change of management strategies in East and West Germany'.
2. According to the savings bank, three-quarters of German SMEs are customers of savings banks. Firms also more often use savings and cooperative banks in order to obtain state financial aid.
3. Equity ratio = equity as a percentage of total capital.
4. The German state has traditionally supported 'debt capital culture' with tax concessions. (cf. more KFW 2006: 144; Plattner et al. 2005: 34f.).
5. Mezzanine capital is a form of equity that gives the investor few rights in corporate control. Nevertheless, the expected return on investment is often so high that the new form has attracted only few customers among SMEs so far (cf. KfW 2006). The abbreviation refers to the enterprise where the interview took place (in this case SME 56), additionally the year of the interview mentioned.
6. Josef Ackermann, as CEO of the Deutsche Bank, agreed as a member of the supervisory board of Mannesmann to the Vodafone deal after a fierce takeover battle that led to the dissolution of Mannesmann and job losses in Germany. The deal included a large bonus for Klaus Esser (and others), the head of the managing board at that time. While Ackermann set the bonuses by 'international standards,' they were exorbitant in the German context.
7. Ron Sommer is former CEO of Deutsche Telekom. For Esser, see footnote 6.
8. Concentration processes have occurred within the three pillars, not between them (cf. Belaisch et al. 2001). Germany, along with Finland, is still the country with the highest share of state-owned banks in Europe. The public mission does not exempt savings banks from commercial aims (Mullineux and Terberger 2006: 6). In 2006, for example, the savings banks dedicated 415 million Euros to public welfare (DSGV 2007a). They are the largest non-governmental cultural sponsor in Germany.
9. In the same direction argue Belaisch et al. from the IMF. According to this study, Germany has the largest number of credit institutions – over 3,000.

France has fewer than half as many (2001: 13f.). Other authors dispute this view (cf. Millineux and Terberger 2006).

10. Yet, Kädtler and Faust also observe a changing relationship between the state central banks and the savings banks as former perceive their future role in global business of commercial banks (see ch. 2 in this volume).

11. Until 2005, German savings banks had two guarantees: first, the state was unrestrictedly liable for all debts of the bank in the event of bank insolvency *(Gewährsträgerhaftung)*; second, state entities have an institutional liability *(Anstaltslast)* that obliges them to keep a German public-sector institution, including the savings banks, functioning and solvent at all times. In addition, the German tax system still provides incentives for bank loans, as paying interest can be claimed for tax relief (in contrast to equity capital).

12. This is not true for small and micro-firms, as Germany and Austria prevailed in introducing exemptions for them.

13. According to the *Observatory Network of European SMEs*, inadequate information about enterprises in the assessment of applications is a general problem in Europe (2003: 23f.).

14. In more detail see: Schmidt 2005; Martens and Bluhm 2007; Becker, Bluhm, and Martens 2008.

15. The 'discrete changes' in Table 3.1 show the impact of the independent variable on the probability of adopting restructuring during the three years before the surveys took place. The change in the probabilities is computed under the assumption that all independent variables (with exception of the one in question) take the values of the average (Long 1997: 77).

16. Regarding measurements strongly linked to shareholder value or value-based approach, some scholars observe an increase, but SMEs (and even large firms) are still far from taking on the complete set of measurements as the literature proposes (cf. Günther and Gonschorek 2006; Horváth and Minning 2001).

17. See also Kramer 2005, who discusses succession as a criterion in rating processes.

18. Turnover is perceived as crucial parameter for corporate governance in the age cohort = 1939 by 60 per cent of the interviewees; in the cohort born between 1940 and 49, 53 per cent of the interviewees stressed the same, while in the whole sample 48.7 per cent did so. With regard to the parameter 'liquidity', a similar pattern emerges: 71.4 per cent of the cohort = 1939 reported the parameter to be one of the most crucial, in the whole sample 58.2 per cent did so.

19. The percentages do not sum up to 100 per cent because of the possibility of multiple responses. East Germans have a much higher percentage of engineers among managing directors, which remains high but is declining among successors. In the categorie 'engineer' we also included degrees in natural science, which is not widespread though. For more see Geppert and Martens in this volume.

20. Seventeen per cent of the interviewees who inherited the firm are women, while in the total sample only 5 per cent of the founders and 7 per cent of the employed managers are female (2005).

21. The figures are similar for managing directors of family- or privately-owned firms (68.7 per cent), and of SMEs belonging to a larger group of firms (62.6 per cent of this category).

References

BDI and Ernst and A. G. Young (2003) *Der industrielle Mittelstand – ein Erfolgsmodell* (Berlin: Industrielle Förderung).

Becker, K., K. Bluhm and B. Martens (2008) 'Unternehmensführung in den Zeiten des "Shareholder Value": Zum Wandel des industriellen Mittelstands', in R. Benthin and U. Brinkmann (eds) *Unternehmenskultur und Mitbestimmung* (Frankfurt/Main, New York: Campus), 215–244.

Belaisch, A., L. E. Kodres, J. Levy and A. J. Ubide (2001) 'Euro-Area Banking at the Cross-roads', IMF Working Paper, no. 01/28.

Berghoff, H. (2003) 'Abschied vom klassischen Mittelstand', in V. Berghahn, S. Unger and D. Ziegler (eds) *Die deutsche Wirtschaftselite im 20. Jahrhundert* (Bochum: Klartext-Verlag), 93–113.

Berghoff, H. (2004) *Moderne Unternehmensgeschichte* (Paderborn: Schöningh).

Berghoff, H. (2006) 'The End of Family Business? The Mittelstand and German Capitalism in Transition 1949–2000', *Business History Review*, 80, 263–96.

Deeg, R. (2006) 'Institutional Change and the Uses and Limits of Path Dependency: The Case of German Finance', *Discussion Paper*, 1. (Cologne: Max Planck Gesellschaft für Gesellschaftsforschung).

Deutsche Sparkassen- und Giroverband (DSGV) (2007a) 'Sparkassen-Finanzgruppe steigert gemeinwohlorientiertes Engagement auf 415 Mio. Euro', Pressemitteilung 28/2007, <https://www.dsgv.org/dsgv/Presseex.nsf/4e94713f94c26b5ec125688e005179a0/1f4df7ec66f43ee1c12572d500413a16/$FILE/PI%2028-07%201.0.pdf>.

DSGV (2007b) 'Diagnose Mittelstand 2007. Deutsche Unternehmen auf der Überholspureine starke Partnerschaft von Mittelstand und Hausbank' (Finanzgruppe Deutscher Sparkassen- und Giroverban: Berlin).

DSGV (2007c) 'DSGV-Stellungnahme zu Spiegel-Artikel: Vertragstreue Kunden werden nicht an Finanzinvestoren weitergeleitet', Pressemitteilung 41/2007, <https://www.dsgv.org/dsgv/Presseex.nsf/4e94713f94c26b5ec125688e005179a0/d52a1793c781f620c12572ec0042b8b5/$FILE/PI%2041-07% 201.0.pdf>.

Eberwein, W. and J. Tholen (1990) *Managermentalität. Industrielle Unternehmensleitung als Beruf und Politik* (Frankfurt/Main: FAZ).

Günther, T. and T. Gonschorek (2006) 'Wert(e)orientierte Unternehmensführung – Erste Ergebnisse einer Empirischen Untersuchung', *Dresdner Beiträge zur Betriebswirtschaftslehre*, 114/06.

Haasis, H. (2007) 'Sparkassen in Deutschland. Starke Partner für den Mittelstand', speech at the 7th Sparkassen-Forum 'Deutscher Mittelstand', Berlin, 27 February 2007, <http://presse.dsgv.de/owx_medien/media15/1551.pdf>.

Hall, P. A. and D. Soskice (2001) 'An Introduction to Varieties of Capitalism', in P. A. Hall and D. Soskice (eds), *Varieties of Capitalism. The Institutional Foundations of Comparative Advantage* (Oxford: Oxford University Press), 1–70.

Horváth, P. and F. Minning (2001) 'Wertorientiertes Management in Deutschland, Großbritannien, Italien und Frankreich. Eine empirische Analyse', *Controlling*, 13, 273–82.

Jackson, G., M. Höpner and A. Kurdelbusch (2005) 'Corporate Governance and Employees in Germany: Changing Linkages, Complementarities, and Tensions', in H. Gospel and A. Pendelton (eds), *Corporate Governance and Labour*

Management. An International Comparison (Oxford: Oxford University Press), 84–121.

KfW Bankengruppe et al. (eds) (2006) *Mittelstandsmonitor 2006* (Frankfurt/Main: unpublished).

Kramer, J. (2005) 'Unternehmensnachfolge als Ratingkriterium', *Wismarer Diskussionspapiere*, 15.

Kühl, S. (2003) *Exit: Wie Risikokapital die Regeln der Wirtschaft verändert* (Frankfurt/Main, New York: Campus).

Lane, C. (1989) *Management and Labour in Europe. The Industrial Enterprise in Germany, Britain and France* (Aldershot: Edward Elgar).

Lane, C. and S. Quack (2002) 'How Banks Construct and Manage Risks. A Sociological Study of Small Firm Lending in Britain and Germany', *WZB Discussion Paper*, FS 02–101 (Berlin: Social Science Research Center Berlin).

Long, J. S. (1997) *Regression Models for Categorical and Limited Dependent Variables* (Thousand Oaks: Sage).

Martens, B. and Michailow, M. (2006) 'Wandel und Kontinuität mittelständischer Unternehmen – Eine Untersuchung zu Differenzen zwischen und Gemeinsamkeiten von Unternehmensleitern', *Zeitschrift für KMU & Entrepreneurship*, 54, 221–42.

Martens, B. and R. Schmidt (2003) 'Aufgaben zwischen betriebswirtschaftlichem Service und strategischer Unternehmensteuerung', Ergebnisse einer Mitgliederbefragung des Internationalen Controller Vereins, Jena.

Martens, B. and K. Bluhm (2007) ' "Shareholder Value" ohne Aktionäre? Diffusion und Mögliche Folgen wertorientierter Unternehmenssteuerung im Industriellen Mittelstand', *Working Papers: Economic Sociology Jena*, Lehrstuhl Arbeits-, Industrie- und Wirtschaftssoziologie, no. 3.

Mullineux, A. and E. Terberger (2006) *The British Bank Sector a Good Role Model for Germany?* (London: Anglo-German Foundation of the Study of Industrial Society).

Observatory Network of European SME (2003) 'SME and Access to Finance', no. 2, European Commission, <http://www.insme.org/documenti/smes_observatory_2003_ report2_en.pdf>.

Plattner, D., D. Skambracks und M. Tchouvakhina (2005) 'Mittelstandsfinanzierung im Umbruch', in D. Engel (ed.), *Mittelstandsfinanzierung, Basel II und die Wirkung öffentlicher sowie privater Kapitalhilfen*, Veröffentlichungen des Round Table Mittelstand, 5, 13–38.

Schmidt, R. (ed.) (2005) 'Reorganisation unter Marktzwang. Finanzierung von kleinen und mittleren Unternehmen nach Basel II', *Jenaer Beiträge zur Soziologie*, 15.

Schröter, H. G. (2004) 'Zur Geschichte der Marktforschung in Europa im 20. Jahrhundert', in R. Walter (ed.), *Geschichte des Konsums* (Stuttgart: Steiner), 319–41.

Schröter, H. G. (2005) *Americanization of the European Economy. A Compact Survey of American Economic Influence in Europe since the 1880s* (Dordrecht: Springer).

4

Corporate Financing, Management and Organization in SMEs: An Anglo-German Comparison

Mike Geppert and Bernd Martens

4.1 Introduction

In this chapter we will analyse corporate financing, management and organization of small- and medium-sized manufacturing enterprises (SMEs) from a comparative angle. Our comparison of German companies with their British counterparts proves to be quite important, as this method helps one to better understand the direction and depth of the current changes in Germany and, what is more, to put these into a broader international perspective.

There is an ongoing debate in recent international management research about whether national institutions are retaining their importance in understanding what is going on inside business firms, or whether this is declining, especially due to the increasing impact of the internationalization of capital markets and corporate financing. Besides economic and technological pressures, the rise of global institutions is seen as leading to convergence at the level of the nation-state. Related to the idea of global isomorphism is the assumption that organizations and organizational structures in different countries are becoming increasingly similar. In the centre of the debate is the future of coordinated market economies, such as Germany's, where a transformation of core features, such as company financing by banks, is predicted. Thus, some scholars – for example, Höpner (2003), Beyer and Höpner (2004) and Lane (2006) – see the influence of 'shareholder value' as crucial to understanding the current institutional change in coordinated market economies such as Germany. Especially changes in the German financial sector, it is argued, have irreversible effects on the German business system as a whole. It is assumed, in other words, that Germany is moving closer to 'shareholder value' capitalism, and that this is already having knock-on effects on other features of the societal system, such as the industrial relations system, especially on the role of *Mitbestimmung* (co-determination) in firms, the educational system and, accordingly, on the organization of German firms.

It is striking that most arguments about internationalization and increasing 'shareholder value pressures' on the German production model are often not representative enough to be generalized over different industrial sectors and company sizes. Many arguments about changes in the 'German model' of capitalism are based on recent strategic decisions of large firms. For example, Höpner's convergence thesis of the *'Durchkapitalisierung'* (marketization) of formerly non-market-organized processes in Germany (2003: 229) refers to the analysis of changes in career patterns, bank monitoring, management pay, and industrial-relations issues in the 40 largest stock-market-listed companies in Germany. There have rarely been any systematic studies, however, about how small- and medium-sized enterprises (SMEs) react to recent capital-market pressures, especially in Germany. What is more, knowledge about the corporate financing of SMEs in the UK is also rather limited. One important issue addressed in this chapter is whether German SMEs are becoming more similar to their British counterparts due to institutional change in the financing sector. By taking a comparative angle, we go beyond the debate mainly concerned with institutional isomorphism and the diffusion of shareholder-value practices. Thus, we respond to Arndt Sorge's concern that it is 'extraordinary (...) that rigorous international comparison has gone into decline just as 'globalization' has become conceptually more and more prominent' (2005: 226).

The focus of debate over institutional change is clearly on recent developments in the so-called coordinated market economies, such as Germany. However, there is also an ongoing discussion about the effects of financialization and deregulation on British capitalism. This research highlights the strengthening of 'short-termist culture' as a major effect that causes 'skill shortages' (Hughes 1992), 'recruitment difficulties' (Johnson 1991) and 'borrowing/financing difficulties' (Mullineux 1994), especially in SMEs.

In contrast to the majority of studies undertaken to date, our cross-national comparison a) uses both quantitative survey data and qualitative interview materials; and b) compares Germany with England, putting German institutional changes in a much-needed broader context. Accordingly, we will discuss how far and deep the shift in German SMEs towards Anglo-Saxon mechanisms of corporate financing has gone and compare it to recent developments in a matched sample from the UK.

Using these comparisons we will argue that, despite (isomorphic) financialization pressures, corporate financing and management patterns in SMEs in both countries remain significantly different.

4.2 The data

We conducted a telephone survey among English[1] small- and medium-sized companies in the summer of 2005. The aim was to survey the first hierarchical level, principally managing directors of firms with 50 to 1,000 employees in the manufacturing industry. The companies were randomly chosen on the basis of the KOMPASS database. Key topics in the questionnaire were:

- corporate governance – financing and the role of management concepts;
- company design – human resources, organization and control, market strategies;
- characteristics of staff – qualifications;
- managerial orientations – management styles, employee participation in decision-making, socio-political attitudes.

The structure of the English questionnaire was comparable to that used in Germany. The English survey was made as similar as possible to two surveys conducted in Germany in 2002 (Martens, Michailow and Schmidt 2003) and 2005. In England, the response rate was about 10 per cent, while it was higher in Germany (20–25 per cent). The response rate in England, however, is comparable to similar surveys made by the Centre for Business Research in Cambridge (Cosh and Hughes 2003) and the Federation of Small Businesses (Carter et al. 2006), which both had a response rate of about 13 per cent. The number of companies participating in the English survey was 131. The sample size of the 2005 survey in Germany was 762 cases, matching the features of the English ones.

The surveys in England and in Germany were accompanied by expert interviews. In England this included 12 with managing directors and two with financial experts. In Germany a total of approximately 50 qualitative interviews were conducted during the period 2002–7.

An initial comparison of the data sets from both countries shows that the *size of the companies* is only slightly different: small firms (10–99 employees) made up 50.4 per cent (GB), 51.1 per cent (G); medium firms (100–499) 45.5 per cent (GB), 43.6 per cent (G); and firms with 500 or more employees 4.1 per cent (GB), 5.3 per cent (G). The size of the

Table 4.1   Distributions of the three above-mentioned surveys

Industrial sector	Cambridge survey 2002	Surrey survey 2005	Jena survey 2005
Chemicals, man-made fibres, rubber and plastics	13.1	15.3	13.7
Metal manufacture and metal goods	16.2	16.1	26.6
Electrical and electronic engineering	17.8	28.8	13.2
Food and beverages	5.1	0	6.0
Textiles, leather, footwear and clothing	7.4	5.1	4.7
Timber, furniture, paper and printing	21.1	5.9	8.9
Mechanical engineering	12.6	28.8	19.4
Other manufacturing	6.9	0	7.5

industrial sectors in each sample does not always match. Strong industrial sectors include chemical, metal manufacture, electrical, electronic, and mechanical engineering (Table 4.1). However, the distributions of the *founding decades* of the company reveal some interesting features. In particular, the West-German companies are rather old: almost 29 per cent of them are older than 65 years, and more than 60 per cent were founded prior to 1970. The comparable number of English firms was only 35.2 per cent. It seems that the companies in the English sample are to some extent influenced by the deregulation policies of the Thatcher government, which, on the one hand, led to the dismantling of large manufacturing firms, job losses and unemployment, but also encouraged some self-employment and entrepreneurial activity. This might explain the higher business founding rates, especially in the 1980s (cf. Johnson 1991). The strong presence of West-German firms in former decades, however, clearly illustrates the long tradition of these companies in the manufacturing sector. The East-German sample, with its peak founding years in the early 1990s, reflects deregulation after the collapse of the GDR economy, which, interestingly enough, matches developments in the 1980s in England after the Thatcher government took power.

4.3   The findings

In this section we present the empirical findings of our comparative project, along the dimensions of a) corporate financing and b) management and organization in SMEs.

4.3.1 Comparison of recent developments in corporate SME financing

There are, at first sight, some similarities between English and German SMEs. In both countries banks are the main source of external funding. There are hardly any signs in either country that outside equity or venture capital as sources of finance have gained large influence. Thus, the stock market has less direct influence on the corporate governance and management of the firms analysed than it does on that of large companies.

However, compared to German SMEs, British SMEs are more dependent on a single bank (72.6 per cent), whereas German firms usually have relationships with several banks (57.3 per cent), and only 39.2 per cent are customers of a single bank (survey 2005). These findings reflect ongoing structural differences in the banking sector. While the German banking sector is still decentralized, with cooperative and savings banks playing a much larger role especially in the case of SMEs, (cf. Bluhm and Martens in this volume) – the British banking system is highly concentrated and dominated by a few large commercial high-street banks. In Britain the four large high-street banks control 80 per cent of the SME financing market (Lane and Quack 2002: 8–9). If one also takes into account that about one-third of English firms are dependent on one customer while in the West of Germany this is the case for only 10 per cent (15 per cent in the East), we see that English SMEs face a *double handicap* when economic performance and the market situation decline. This means, in other words, that in terms of resource-dependency theory (Pfeffer and Salancik 1978) British SMEs are more 'vulnerable' and less autonomous than their German counterparts.

From a dialectical perspective, it can also be argued that the reluctance of British managers to deal with more than one bank cannot just be understood in reference to external resources and institutions. These findings also indicate local managers' strong, institutionally supported mistrust of banks as reliable partners. Another significant difference between German and UK SMEs is indeed the managers' relationship with their banks. Our research confirms earlier findings of Vitols (1995) that, with regard to 'insider' influence of banks on local company management, Germany and Great Britain seem to be opposites. Thus, even when the survey findings on the role of short- and long-term credits in SMEs shows only slightly more short-term financing in the British cases, we found in the qualitative interviews with British managers a strong reluctance to talk about their bank relationship. Especially the qualitative interviews revealed the difficulties British firms have getting closely involved with banks or indeed having any relationship with banks at all.

Therefore, in line with previous studies (Johnson 1991; Mullineux 1994; Vitols 1995; Sorge 2005) we come to the conclusion that for manufacturing SMEs in England 'relationship banking' remains largely unknown. It is also important to notice that the English firms we studied, compared to the German ones, are more dependent on overdraft credits from their banks (cf. Cosh and Hughes 2003; Hughes 1997), and that some contractual elements of the relationship can be more short-term or more long-term.[2] Thus, our qualitative interviews give evidence that the strong reliance on overdraft financing not only makes businesses more vulnerable, but also means that managers as company owners are at high personal risk of going bankrupt if their business fails.

The relations of bank managers with their clients are much more impersonal and at arm's length in the English context. Thus, one company manager complained about the 'high turnover' of bank managers dealing with his company. He stressed that bank managers are replaced so quickly that it is difficult 'to keep track of who is responsible' for his firm. This confirms the findings of Mullineux, for example, who found that British SMEs seem to 'want "transaction banking" in booms and "relationship banking" in recession' (1994: 25). This raises the question, however, whether long-term finance is regarded by UK SMEs as too expensive (in comparison to overdraft-based financing) or 'whether it reflects a lack of education/training on part of potential borrowers' (ibid: 26) – an issue we will come back to in the next section. However, it seems that banks are also not interested in getting too closely involved in SME business affairs; if they do get involved it is limited to 'transaction banking' and only as long as the firms perform well. UK banks are less willing to provide long-term credits to companies (Lane and Quack 2002: 8–9) and see industrial companies to a great extent as an 'incalculable risk' (Sorge 2005: 207) and are, therefore, generally reluctant to invest in manufacturing businesses. One manager describes his situation by stating: 'They give you an umbrella when the sun's shining and take it away when it's raining' (MD, Advance CS).

It is stressed in various other studies (Binks 1991; Hughes 1997; Mullineux 1994) that the British financial system is not supportive, especially of capital-intensive manufacturing firms, and that this is even worse when the firms are small. In an interview, a British bank manager stressed: 'The problem of SMEs is that they are often too big for smaller banks and too small for large or medium-sized banks' (Relationship Manager, A-Bank).

The lack of bank interest in SMEs is also reflected in an interview with a company manager who stated: 'When we used to borrow money...we had a good relationship, friendly, they used to take me out to cricket matches... I'm caught in my business 'cause they're not making money out of us these days' (MD, Wood A.).

In Germany we find a much more differentiated banking system where large commercial and investment banks deal with larger firms, while a relatively high density of cooperative and savings banks are specialized in offering various services, forms of credits, and financial advice to medium-sized and smaller firms, especially in the manufacturing sector – which is traditionally strong and much larger than Britain's (see also Bluhm and Martens in this volume for a more detailed discussion of the structure of the German banking system and current modifications).

Another striking societal difference is the role of *company ratings*. As already illustrated above, at first sight we seem to have found similar patterns in the two countries, for both surveys indicate that firms there possess experience with some form of ratings (69.8 per cent in England, 65.9 per cent in Germany). However, after taking a closer look and attempting to interpret the data, we found that the term 'company ratings' has different connotations in England and Germany – a common problem in cross-national research (see Maurice 2000 and Sorge 2005 for a more detailed discussion). In Germany ratings were clearly connected with new mechanisms banks are using to assess company performance. In England, however, bank ratings *seem not to be common* for SMEs. When asked, the interviewees connected this issue with active or passive 'ratings' of such measures as performance or quality by clients or customers.

Rating of SMEs by banks, however, has become a common procedure in Germany. In comparison to the past where mutual trust, personal relationships and networking helped to reduce risks by 'getting closer' (Deeg 2006: 40), the increasing importance of bank ratings shows that German banks are more interested in assessing risks on the basis of impersonal economic figures and performance (cf. Bluhm and Martens in this volume). The percentage of companies that have had experiences with such credit ratings rose in the time period 2002–5 from 47.8 per cent to 65.9 per cent. Additionally, a statistical correlation between a 'bad' development of the equity ratio and ratings exists: Our panel data (only those firms that responded twice in the period 2002–5) show that 75 per cent of the companies with constantly low capital resources (an equity ratio of less than 25 per cent during the time frame in question) were also rated by banks more frequently, whereas only 48 per cent of the firms with a constantly high equity ratio (greater than average) reported similar experiences.

In contrast to common quality-management measures, which are often used in relation to customers or suppliers (such as marketing instruments), it seems that bank ratings do not have the same function in Germany. They are confined to their primary purpose – current measures of solvency and creditworthiness. Our German data also show some *effects of ratings* that, up to now, have been rather unusual for the German Mittelstand. It can be shown that negative and undecided results of ratings correlated with more efforts to control firms by quantitative indicators. Where the rating was positive, 40.7 per cent of the companies reported improvement of accounting standards taking place in the three years before the survey (data set 2005). The percentage of restructuring activities for negative and undecided rating results, however, is 58.2 per cent (Chi^2, $p < 0.00$).

The findings of increasing accounting activities in 'badly' performing German firms do match with experiences of managers in our British sample. In the qualitative interviews, managers in both countries who experienced performance problems in the past described situations of banks' increasing pressure and influence on the businesses by asking for detailed monthly reports. In Germany, one company with a bad reputation in the past developed a monthly management information system to which the bank had access. According to its managing director, the new transparency of the firm's operating figures changed its image fundamentally (interview 1). Similarly, one of the interviewed British managers stated:

> (. . .) we had a bank manager who used to insist with our management about reports, that we gave some commentary on how the business was performing, the strengths. I mean the habit I've kept up. I mean, it is useful when you know what's going on in the business, and um, but um, they said to us they were increasing the interest rate, um, because we weren't performing well, (. . .) (MD, Outsource E.).

Thus we see that external monitoring by banks produces some learning effects for 'bad performers'. It leads to the implementation of accounting measures which were not in place before.

By contrast, in Germany, despite banks' increasing monitoring activities of some companies, we see no general patterns of emerging difficulties for SMEs in gaining solid corporate financing. In the qualitative interviews we find some hints that managers combine the 'new rules of the game', imposed by banks, with established behavioural patterns. Here are selected story lines illustrating these learning processes:

- A managing director is talking about the monitoring system of the firm, which is capable of computing many different indices. In the new era of bank ratings, the company's reports 'have gone down totally well at the banks (...) it is a factor which guarantees a relatively good rating' (interview 38).
- Another manager interviewed says that he exercises 'complete transparency with the bank, they (the bankers) get once a year a forecast of 120 pages'. As the interviewer remarks that this is not necessary, the managing director replies, 'but I want money from them' (interview 31).
- A managing director, who is a member of the board of a savings bank, relates a change in communication with banks. 'It is essential to know how banks are thinking. That is very important. I have learned a lot in connection with this board story.' He is not using his membership on the board to build up confidence in the relationship with the bank, but rather to learn about the needs of creditors (interview 40).
- Another entrepreneur relates a similar experience. He is also a member of a savings bank board. Colleagues of his frequently ask him whether he could lobby for them in regard to loans that the bank has rejected. In the interview sequence, the manager adopts the perspective of the creditor and says that if the bank refused the request, the entrepreneur in question ought to be very happy, because the bank has saved the company from a great misfortune. He gives this advice: 'They do not approve the loan. (...) Then go and hug the banker, because he has saved you' (interview 35). The interviewee is both stressing the necessity of corporate transparency and characterizing the creditor's perspective as rational and useful.

To sum up, our discussion has shown that SMEs and banks in England continue to maintain a 'distant' relationship. We found that the German – in comparison to the English – traditionally close and mutually trust-based system of relationship banking is becoming more formal, relying more on quantitative performance indicators and less on good reputation. A consultant well known to German SMEs confirms our findings by writing:

> The relationship between customer and bank will increasingly move from an emotional towards a rational level. That credits will in the

future not be based on a handshake with a deep look in the eyes, but only on the presentation of a convincing business plan and corresponding operating figures, is a sign of increasing professionalization (Hennerkes 2004: 367).

4.3.2 Comparison of recent developments in SME management and organization

English SMEs, in comparison to German ones, seem to be less interested in restructuring in general and, especially, in the restructuring of their *accounting system*. The percentages of companies restructuring their organization, accounting system, and production are as follows: 74.0 per cent, 6.1 per cent, 12.2 per cent, respectively (England); 65.9 per cent, 48.1 per cent, 61.3 per cent, respectively (Germany). German firms exhibit in particular activities intended to improve *accounting*, which are not present in English SMEs. The corresponding percentages are 6.1 per cent (England) and 58.0 per cent (Germany). As we discussed earlier, the German case additionally provides evidence that *rating* (by banks) and the *implementation of accounting systems* correlate significantly; such activities are not at all connected in England. Our findings indicate a relative institutional stability of corporate financing of English SMEs as compared to SMEs in Germany, where we see a more institutional and organizational dynamics.

Restructuring of accounting and corporate finance practices in Germany can be presumably interpreted as being related in part to emerging 'regulative' isomorphic pressures (Scott 2001: 51) triggered by significant modifications in parts of the European Union and German legal systems, which have led banks to introduce closer monitoring measures of their assets and led companies to provide more 'transparent' financial information to their banks.[3] Similar institutional changes with regard to regulating corporate finance of SMEs have not been relevant in the UK because banks there have been historically less engaged in the corporate financing of manufacturing firms and in the creation of close social links with management, as discussed earlier.

Besides important differences in the focus of restructuring activities in England and Germany, we found further evidence of remaining societal differences. As illustrated above, compared to their German counterparts, British SMEs have focused primarily on organizational structure changes and significantly less on production and accounting systems.

These findings can be related to other differences in management and organization structures of firms in each country:

1. The percentage of managers compared to the number of employees is higher in England than in Germany. In England 9.6 per cent of the whole workforce are called 'managers'; in Germany this percentage amounts to 6.3 per cent;
2. The hierarchies in Germany are slightly steeper; the average number of hierarchical levels there is 1.9, in contrast to 1.3 in England.

A result similar to that of the previous discussion about national differences in SME corporate financing shows that the higher proportion of managers in English firms seems to indicate different institutional logics of firm management and organization. Thus, the higher percentage of managerial roles in English SMEs might reflect a more radical shift towards neo-liberal economic principles, which is discussed by British social scientists under the label of escalating 'new managerialism' – an ideology closely linked to the politics of the Thatcher government but continued under New Labour, especially in the public sector (cf. Beckmann and Cooper 2004). For example, Mueller and Carter (2007) show that financialization of a former electricity utility firm led not just to a narrowing of the firm's strategy but also to a significant increase in managers. Many of the previous engineers and other employees are 'all called managers now' (ibid). Organizational change has mainly been driven by newly brought-in financial experts and accountants. In comparison with much bigger, formerly public-owned firms and the SMEs in our German sample, the English SMEs have not become more professional.[4] In short, SMEs in England employ more managers in a less hierarchical way, but this seems not to go hand-in-hand with a greater *professionalization* of managers, an issue we will discuss next.

The members of staff in managerial positions in English SMEs seem to have classical expertise in general management, if they have a professional background at all, as indicated in earlier studies (cf. Child et al. 1983; Sorge and Warner 1986). In our English sample, in only 15.1 per cent of cases did all managers have such an education; in 36.8 per cent the proportion of professionally educated managers exceeded 50 per cent; in 42.5 per cent less than half of the managerial staff was professionally educated; and in 5.7 per cent of English companies no manager fulfilled this criterion. In the case of the German surveys, we lack figures concerning the formal qualifications of management. However, comparative studies suggest that figures from our English survey are representative and that in German management a professional education is still typical (Windolf 2003: 317; Walgenbach and Kieser 1995).

These findings can be related to former cross-national comparisons stressing that English manufacturing firms and engineering expertise have a lower status in the society, in contrast, for example, to Germany (Child et al. 1983; Sorge and Warner 1986). This might explain the lack of expertise, even in finance and accounting, in smaller English manufacturing firms. Compared to larger British firms, however, SMEs also have a poorer reputation and pay lower salaries and, thus, seem not to attract the increasing numbers of young business-school graduates. For some of them, larger manufacturing companies might be more attractive. For significantly higher-paid accountants, in particular, these definitely are.[5]

In addition to societal differences with regard to the overall number of managers in SMEs, we also found that managers in England continue to have less technical or engineering expertise. However, since the 1980s in the Federal Republic of Germany, the proportion of engineers relative to managers with other qualifications has also been continuously declining. Managers with an economic education have become more important (Eberwein and Tholen 1990), which is confirmed in our study, as well.

Interestingly, the percentage of West-German companies with a high proportion of engineers (49.8 per cent) is now approaching that in England (41.6 per cent), having declined to a remarkable extent during the last years. According to our survey in 2002, 57.8 per cent of managerial staff in the West still have engineering degrees. This trend is also seen in East Germany, where the proportion of engineers to the number of all managers in the company declined from 77.7 per cent in 2002 to 67.3 per cent in 2005. The following percentages further clarify these findings: in Great Britain less than 30 per cent of the firms interviewed had more than 50 per cent engineers, whereas the East-German portion was 66.7 per cent. The West-German share is situated between these (44.9 per cent).[6]

Another indicator of the institutional distinctiveness of British companies is the relatively marginal role of training and education provided at the firm level, again a confirmation of investigations conducted more than 20 years ago (cf. Sorge and Warner 1986) and new studies concerned with the performance of British SMEs (cf. Cosh and Hughes 2003). Only 19.8 per cent of the English sample had provided training or continuing-education measures in the last three years, compared to 53 per cent in Western, and 50.3 per cent in Eastern Germany. This emphasises the problem of 'governmentally regulated deregulation', which further undermines the already weak basis of vocational training systems in the UK (Almond and Rubery 2000).

The increased liberalization of values and norms in Britain is also reflected in the level of performance-related payment. At first sight, it was surprising that performance-related payment of managers is more common in German firms than in English ones. In 55.4 per cent of the East-German SMEs headed by East Germans and 68.2 per cent of the West German firms directed by West Germans such incentive schemes were chosen for managers. But only 26.7 per cent of the English firms pay their managers according to their performance. Where this is the case, salaries depend more on individual performance than on the revenue of the whole company. The latter is more common in German companies, especially in East Germany, owing to the more difficult economic situation of many firms there.

Not surprisingly, another striking difference between the two countries is their industrial relations systems, especially as to the role and influence of trade unions and formal workers' representation. Formalized forms of co-determination (*Mitbestimmung*) are traditional parts of the German management model, which cannot be found in England and which are, according to our surveys, more or less accepted by German management (see Schmidt for more details, in this volume). In 68.4 per cent of the West-German firms there is a works council *(Betriebsrat)*; the corresponding figure for the East German cases is 51.5 per cent. A large majority of managing directors (87 per cent) characterize their relationship to the works council as 'unproblematic' or as 'trustful'. The English situation is quite different. There are no formal works councils in England, though we found unexpected evidence of employee representative bodies. In 40.5 per cent of the companies there are stewards' committees, but only 17.1 per cent of the respondents see any influence of trade unions on the industrial sector. If they concede any union power at all, this is primarily confined – according to the opinions of our interviewees – to wages, customers' issues, and health topics. However, while we do not know much about the role, influence, and composition of the employee committees, it is clear that they have a different function and influence than German works councils. They are often created by the local management as a vehicle to communicate decisions to staff.[7] They can also be easily dissolved if managers face problems. Thus, one manager reports that he decided to do dissolve the works council in his firm, because another local employer was poaching some of his company's employees, and he was concerned about communicating strategic decisions (MD, Advance CS).

Finally, the analysis of managerial opinions shows that German SMEs are more positive about the issue of *globalization*, in contrast to the more negative attitude of English managers. Combining 'coordinated' with 'liberal market' approaches seems to provide a competitive advantage for most of the firms in our sample. According to our qualitative interviews, in the German entrepreneurial discourse globalization and competition are seen more as an opportunity than they are in Britain. German managers believe that they have a variety of corporate strategies and options at their disposal (for example outsourcing, 'going east', or more internal competition within the firm) that can be used to the benefit of their enterprise. They only seldom describe global competition as a potential danger for the existence of their company, seeing it rather as a challenge and an opportunity for partial organizational restructuring.

Characteristics of discourses reflect differences in industrial structures and societal institutions. The German Mittelstand, both in manufacturing and SMEs in general, is still seen as an important feature of the German economy (cf. Köhler 2006). In the UK, however, the media are full of praise for 'the City' and the strength of the financial services industry, which are seen as much more important than manufacturing. The decline of manufacturing businesses in the country and the increasingly internationally diverse ownership of the economy are interpreted as signs of successful economic development (cf. *The Economist* 2007). Thus, it is no wonder that many English manufacturing managers referred to banks and the 'the City' in terms of 'us' and 'them' in interviews, indicating not just the lack of corporate financing for SMEs, but also the strong hegemony of the financial service industry in the British economy. The latter is interpreted as a main cause for the further weakening of manufacturing in the UK and the explanation for why managers – compared to their German colleagues – are more pessimistic about global competition and the prospects for their firms.

4.4 Conclusions

Our Anglo-German comparison has shown that current developments in German banking and corporate financing are not leading to a radical change of the production system of German SMEs. In Germany we did not find any signs of a trend 'towards the low-pay and low-quality axis', which is seen as a problem especially for British manufacturing firms and is directly related to the deregulation of the economy that started nearly 30 years ago (Almond and Rubery 2000).

Our empirical findings indicate that British and German SMEs are still significantly different in terms of corporate finance, management, and organization. British banks, in comparison to German ones, remain distant with their clients, while SME managers prefer to avoid dealing with banks whenever possible. This mutual distrust is also reflected by the preference of British firms for bank overdrafts, which does not require much commitment on either side. However, in Germany the increasing importance of bank ratings can be interpreted as a sign of financialization, leading to more 'transparency' in companies and thus, more influence for banks. Nevertheless, we have seen that societal institutional change is not just a straightforward isomorphic process, but is moderated and shaped by local actors. The 'new rules of the game' have been locally adapted, negotiated and modified in a way that retains the influence of local managers. Thus, relationship banking in Germany is not disappearing or moving in the same direction as banking in England, where SMEs managers prefer to keep banks at a distance and avoid close banking relationships.

Moreover, our comparison confirms earlier findings (cf. Child et al. 1983) that managerial decisions in English manufacturing firms are based more on individualistic values and are more short-term oriented, than they are in Germany. In Britain we can see evidence of related, deeper changes on the culture-cognitive level (Scott 2001). That is, a growing impact of managerialist ideology on firm behaviour, an issue that is largely unknown in most of the German SMEs so far. We also see relevant changes in German firms, including an increased importance of financial control measures and a growing importance of non-engineering expertise. However, we found little evidence in German SMEs similar to our UK findings of disparaging effects of new managerialism, short-term and individualistic management and leadership styles.

In contrast to their German counterparts, most of the English SME managers, however, seem to follow more 'traditional' leadership styles and are more concerned with keeping their market position and share, while being rather reluctant to actively develop strategies for dealing with increasing international competition, in particular from firms pursuing low-cost strategies. Our interviews with English SME managers seem to confirm that the ongoing 'market liberalization' of the British economy has had damaging effects on manufacturing SMEs, which contrasts with the neo-liberal discourse widely reflected in the British media. Compared to their German colleagues, English SME managers are more pessimistic about the future. In line with other studies, we have some doubts whether the 'governmentally regulated deregulation' – started by the Conservatives and continued under New Labour (Almond and Rubery 2000) – has helped to improve entrepreneurship, innovation, and performance in manufacturing SMEs. Instead, British manufacturing firms seem to be more conservative and, compared to their German counterparts, are managing by 'muddling through', remaining at best at arm's length in relations with their banks and customers. In contrast to the British context, however, the future of the Mittelstand in Germany – a social phenomenon that has never developed in the UK due to well-described institutional constraints (cf. Lane 1995; Sorge 2005; Vitols 1995) – might be much brighter than often assumed.

From a theoretical angle, our comparative research has shed additional light on the dialectical nature of institutional change and on how it is intertwined with changes in strategies and cultures at the national societal and managerial levels. From this point of view, references to global isomorphism do not seem to explain the whole story of institutional change. For example, the focus on global isomorphism and the diffusion of certain practices is only one aspect of institutional change. Further, our comparison of Germany with England has shown that the reconstruction of the bank–company relationship, along with managerial and organizational change in SMEs, cannot be understood only in reference to isomorphism and diffusion. As we have demonstrated, the diffusion of the 'financial conception of the firm' (Fligstein 1990) is not the straightforward process often assumed. From an interpretative perspective, 'external isomorphic pressure "is not simply what it is" but what it turns out to be when filtered through the domestic understanding of local actors' (Sorge 2005: 45). Our comparison also reveals how and why local British SME managers remain reluctant to cooperate with local banks and do not develop the same professional approach to corporate finance as their counterparts in German SMEs.

Notes

1. Our British survey did not cover Northern Ireland, Scotland or Wales, but in this paper, for brevity, 'UK' is also used to identify the survey area.
2. We refer to Vitols' research findings emphasizing that 'banks prefer to give SMEs short term credits in the form of overdrafts (authorizations to overdraw checking accounts up to a certain limit), which are renegotiated periodically (. . .) While overdrafts are often "rolled over" to finance long-term investments in equipment, the fluctuation of overdraft interest rates according to market conditions renders the costs of financing uncertain over the medium- and long-term' (1995: 13).

3. For example, see Lane (2006) and Deeg (2006) who give an overview of these issues.
4. Thus, Mueller and Carter (2007: 191) stress that the company studied, 'Coast-Electric', employed some 1000 professional engineers at the time of privatization. The paper shows impressively how all these engineers either transformed themselves into managers or just became victims of 'managerialist' changes and lost out.
5. Thus, in a study of British subsidiary management in the heavy engineering sector, it is reported that a sales manager, educated as an engineer, decided to complete another degree in accounting because of pay constraints and better career chances with his US-owned employer after finishing his studies (cf. Geppert 2003: 322).
6. An explanation for why the figures for East German management are still rather different is the history of the GDR and its economic transformation in the 90s (cf. Salheiser 2006; Pohlmann and Gergs 1997).
7. This reflects findings of a recent study exploring employee involvement that found that European legislation actually led to the implementation of information and consultation measures in many British SMEs. Nonetheless, the study also concludes that managers ' "buy into" a notion of information-sharing and involvement policies that reinforce togetherness, they seem much more reluctant to embrace processes based on consultation as these threaten their prerogative' (Wilkinson et al. 2007: 1294).

References

Almond, P. and J. Rubery (2000) 'Deregulation and societal systems', in M. Maurice and A. Sorge (eds), *Embedding Organizations* (Amsterdam: John Benjamins), 277–93.

Beckmann, A. and C. Cooper (2004) '"Globalisation", the New Managerialism and Education: Rethinking the Purpose of Education in Britain', *Journal for Critical Education Policy Studies*, 12(2), <http://www.jceps.com/?pageID=article&article ID=31>.

Beyer, J. and M. Höpner (2004) 'The Disintegration of Organised Capitalism: German Corporate Governance in the 1990s', in H. Kitschelt and W. Streeck (eds), *Germany. Beyond the Stable State* (London: Frank Cass), 179–98.

Binks, M. (1991) 'Small Businesses and Their Banks in the Year 2000', in J. Curran and R. A. Blackburn (eds), *Paths of Enterprise: the Future of Small Business* (London: Routledge), 149–62.

Carter, S., C. Mason and S. Tagg (2006) 'Lifting the Barriers to Growth in UK Small Businesses', *The FSB Biennial Membership Survey 2006* (London: Federation of Small Businesses).

Child, J., M. Fores, I. Glover and P. Lawrence (1983) 'A Price to Pay?: Professionalism and Work Organization in Britain and West Germany', *Sociology*, 17(1), 63–78.

Cosh, A. and A. Hughes (2003) 'Enterprise Challenged: Policy and Performance in the British SME Sector 1999–2003', *CBR Small Business Survey Research Report* (Cambridge: Centre for Business Research).

Deeg, R. (2006) 'Path Dependency, Institutional Complementarity, Contradiction and Change in National Business Systems', in G. Morgan, R. Whitley and E. Moen (eds), *Changing capitalisms?: Internationalization, Institutional Change, and Systems of Economic Organization* (Oxford: Oxford University Press), 21–52.

The Economist (2007) *British Manufacturing – In Praise of Shopkeepers and Sellers: In the Contrasting Stories of Tesco and ICI, Britain Offers a Lesson to the World*, print edition, 21 June 2007.

Eberwein, W. and J. Tholen (1990) *Managermentalität: Industrielle Unternehmensleitung als Beruf und Politik* (Frankfurt/Main: FAZ).

Fligstein, N. (1990) *The Transformation of Corporate Control* (Cambridge, MA: Harvard University Press).

Geppert, M. (2003) 'Sensemaking and Politics in MNCs: A Comparative Analysis of Vocabularies within the Global Manufacturing Discourse in One Industrial Sector', *Journal of Management Inquiry*, 12(4), 312–29.

Hennerkes, B.-H. (2004) *Die Familie und ihr Unternehmen. Strategie. Liquidität. Kontrolle* (Frankfurt/Main, New York: Campus).

Höpner, M. (2003) *Wer beherrscht die Unternehmen?: Shareholder Value, Managerherrschaft und Mitbestimmung in Deutschland* (Frankfurt/Main, New York: Campus Verlag).

Hughes, A. (1992) *The State of British Enterprise: Growth, Innovation and Competitive Advantages in Small and Medium-Sized Firms. Report of the Small Business Research Centre* (Cambridge, UK: University of Cambridge).

Hughes, A. (1997) 'Finance for SMEs: A UK Perspective', *Small Business Economics*, 9, 151–66.

Johnson, S. (1991) 'Small Firms and the UK Labour Market: Prospects for the 1990s', in J. Curran and R. A. Blackburn (eds), *Paths of Enterprise: the Future of Small Business* (London: Routledge), 88–113.

Lane, C. (1995) *Industry and Society in Europe: Stability and Change in Britain, Germany and France* (Aldershot: Edward Elgar).

Lane, C. (2006) 'Institutional Transformation and System Change: Changes in Corporate Governance of German Corporations', in G. Morgan, R. Whitley and E. Moen (eds), *Changing Capitalisms?: Internationalization, Institutional Change, and Systems of Economic Organization* (Oxford: Oxford University Press), 78–109.

Lane, C. and S. Quack (2002) 'How Banks Construct and Manage Risk: A Sociological Study of Small Firm Lending in Britain and Germany, *WZB Discussion Paper*, FS I 02–101 (Berlin: Social Science Research Center Berlin).

Köhler, P. (2006) 'Eigentümergeführte Firmen im Mittelstand als Antriebsmotor für wirtschaftliche Dynamik', *Handelsblatt*, 25 May 2006.

Martens, B., M. Michailow and R. Schmidt (eds) (2003) *Managementkulturen im Umbruch*, SFB 580 Mitteilungen, 10 (Jena: SFB).

Maurice, M. (2000) 'The Paradoxes of Societal Analysis: A Review of the Past and Prospects for the Future', in M. Maurice and A. Sorge (eds), *Embedding Organizations* (Amsterdam: John Benjamins), 13–36.

Mueller, F. and C. Carter (2007) "'We Are All Managers Now'": Managerialism and Professional Engineering in UK Electricity Utilities', *Accounting, Organizations and Society*, 32, 181–95.

Mullineux, A. (1994) 'Small and Medium Sized Enterprise (SME) Financing in the UK: Lessons from Germany', *Discussion Paper* (London: Anglo-German Foundation for the Study of Industrial Society).

Pfeffer J. and G. Salancik (1978) *The External Control of Organizations: A Resource Dependence Perspective* (New York: Harper & Row).

Pohlmann, M. and H.-J. Gergs (1997) 'Manager in Ostdeutschland – Reproduktion oder Zirkulation einer Elite?', *Kölner Zeitschrift für Soziologie und Sozialpsychologie,* 49, 540–62.

Salheiser, A. (2006) 'Professionalisierung und Angepasstheit. Eine empirische Untersuchung zum Leitungspersonal der DDR-Industrie vor dem Hintergrund differenzierungstheoretischer Fragestellungen', *SFB 580 Mitteilungen,* 18 (Jena: SFB) 77–98.

Scott, R. W. (2001) *Institutions and Organizations* (Thousand Oaks: Sage).

Sorge, A. (2005) *The Global and the Local: Understanding the Dialectics of Business Systems* (Oxford: Oxford University Press).

Sorge, A. and M. Warner (1986) *Comparative Factory Organization: An Anglo-German Comparison of Management and Manpower in Manufacturing* (Aldershot: Gower).

Vitols, S. (1995) 'Financial Systems and Industrial Policy in Germany and Great Britain: the Limits of Convergence', *WZB Discussion Paper,* FS I 95–311 (Berlin: Social Science Research Center Berlin).

Walgenbach, P. and A. Kieser (1995) 'Mittlere Manager in Deutschland und Großbritannien', in G. Schreyögg and J. Sydow (eds), *Managementforschung 5* (Berlin: de Gruyter), 259–309.

Wilkinson, A., T. Dundon and I. Grugulis (2007) 'Information But Not Consultation: Exploring Employee Involvement in SMEs', *International Journal of Human Resource Management,* 18(7), 1279–97.

Windolf, P. (2003) 'Sind Manager Unternehmer? Deutsche und britische Manager im Vergleich', in S. Hradil and P. Imbusch (eds), *Oberschichten – Eliten – Herrschende Klassen* (Opladen: Leske + Budrich), 299–335.

5
Stakeholder or Shareholder Orientation? Entrepreneurial Careers and Value Preferences of Entrepreneurs in East Germany

Rainhart Lang

5.1 Introduction

Entrepreneurs and managers play a decisive role not only in firm restructuring but also in building trust and commitment of co-workers, which are essential pre-conditions for economic survival and success (Puffer et al. 2000; Kandil and Walter 2002; Waldner 2003; Lang 2007). This is especially true in transforming societies, where entrepreneurship and private management have been newly institutionalized, thus making it necessary to re-invent corporate values and leadership styles. (Marinov and Marinova 1996; Clark, Lang and Balaton 2001; Edwards and Lawrence 2000; Ardichvili 2001; Lang and Steger 2002; Steger and Winkler 2003; Lang et al. 2005). As a result of 'recombination' (Stark 1996) or 'bricolage' (Clark et al. 2001) new practices emerge that contribute to the specific features of a new Central and East European capitalism that differs from western models.[1]

The specific situation in transformational settings of instability and insecurity have provided a similar environment for all responsible actors in the new as well as in the established private or privatized firms – a lack of institutionalized norms, rules and standards – which gives them more room to act according to their personal values and dispositions (cf. Waldmann et al. 2001). The latter is shaped by the professional careers as well as the respective experiences of owners and managers (see contributions in Kirby and Watson 2003).

For East Germany, a number of studies have highlighted social background (cf. Koch, Thomas and Woderich 1993) or selected motives, attitudes and strategies of the new entrepreneurs, owners and managers (cf. Pistrui et al. 2003; Martens 2007; Hess 2006) but do not link the attitudes and activities of the new owners and managers to other members of the firm, their values or attitudes. The studies also fail to include leadership issues.

Taking into account the above shortcomings, this chapter investigates value preferences, their links to leadership styles and to the professional careers of entrepreneur-/owner-managers and employed managers in East Germany, and their respective consequences for the development of corporate social values in the privatized or new firms. The exploratory in-depth study is based on data from the GLOBE-CEO study of 52 firms in East Germany and includes questionnaire and interview information from owner-managers and employed managing directors as well as questionnaire information from immediate subordinates of these managers. The quantitative and qualitative analysis of these data is combined to describe the differences in value orientations towards shareholder or different stakeholder interests between the two groups of managers and the subsequent impact on the attitudes of their respective subordinates in the firms. Moreover, the data allow for the identification of different patterns of values and dispositions and illustrate their relations to experiences during the managerial careers and the privatization and restructuring of the firms. The results point to the development of a number of specific patterns of shareholder and stakeholder orientation under conditions of radical environmental changes.

5.2   State of research, theoretical background and preliminary assumptions of the study

The scientific theoretical discussion in the field of values, attitudes and the behaviour of entrepreneurs, owners and managers, and their careers in transforming societies are characterized by a number of serious shortcomings. Especially the early contributions in the field are influenced by an inbuilt normative argument of the 'good entrepreneurs', who are seen as being the decisive group of actors in a transformation towards a western type of market capitalism. Some contributions (cf. Johnson and Loveman 1995) have often contrasted the entrepreneurial spirit of this group with the conservative attitudes of the old managerial elite of state-owned enterprises, who are held responsible for a slowdown in the speed and success of company transformation. The theoretical underpinnings of such claims include: modernization theory based on a universal assumption of the capitalist modernity in a western sense; and economic institutionalism, in particular property-rights theory, with a focus on private ownership influence on actors' behaviour (cf. Nee and Matthews 1996; Ullmann and Lewis 1997; and Pfirrmann and Walter 2002). The influence of culture, especially dominant cultural values such as group collectivism and power distance, on social value preferences of the actors is still underestimated (see Brouthers et al. 2007; exception from Waldmann et al. 2007; and partly some contributions in Habisch et al. 2005). At the level of individual actors, the values and attitudes of managers or employees have been mainly used to explain the above-mentioned shortcomings and problems within the process of organizational transformation, privatization and restructuring (see Johnson and Loveman 1995; Edwards and Lawrence 2000; Wade, 2003). The group of 'new' entrepreneurs and their respective values and attitudes, however, have often been portrayed as the reason for their positive impact (ibid; McGrath and MacMillan 2000; Pistrui et al. 2003; Hess 2006). Interestingly, the studies have not yet adequately explored similar situational contexts or the role of transformational careers of entrepreneurs, owners and managers.

The studies on East-German management and managers have underlined the importance of social background (cf. Koch, Thomas and Woderich 1993), or selected motives, attitudes, and strategies of the new entrepreneurs, owners and managers (cf. Lang and Müller 2001; Pistrui et al. 2003; Martens and Michailow 2006; Martens 2007; Hess 2006). Especially the results of Pistrui et al. (2003: 120–29) that compare motives and orientations of entrepreneurs in East and West Germany are of further interest. On the basis of questionnaire data from 102 East-German and 58 West-German entrepreneurial owners, of which 79 per cent and 38 per cent were start-ups, respectively, the authors conclude that East-German entrepreneurs are characterized by a greater commitment, willingness to make greater and more sacrifices, need for independence and freedom instead of achievement and recognition, and a social-achievement motivation stressing the importance of co-workers and the community (Pistrui et al. 2003: 128). In more detail, the authors point to the fact that East-German entrepreneurs showed a greater social motivation associated with community influence and social respect. Newer entrepreneurs also expressed a strong preference to working with people they choose. The authors describe this as '... a more traditional cultural orientation' (2003: 125).

Contrary to these results, Martens (2007) reveals that a pattern of orientation close to a 'competitive capitalism' instead of 'social market economy' is widespread among the entrepreneurs and managers in East Germany, especially in smaller enterprises and start-ups. A number of other contributions (see Lang 1994; Pohlmann and Gergs 1996; Alt and Lang 1998; Schreiber et al. 2001; and Kulke 2005) have highlighted the importance of careers, referring to the different professional backgrounds of managers and entrepreneurs from East and West Germany, but do not go into detail concerning entrepreneurial firms managed by the founders and owners themselves (with the exception of Martens 2007). Finally, a lack of qualitative studies on the link between professional careers and patterns of values and behaviours must be noted (with the exception of Lang 2000; Breu 2001; and, in part, Schreiber et al. 2001; Steger and Lang 2003).

The theoretical background of the following analysis is fourfold. With respect to the contextual orientation, the *stakeholder theory* (Freeman 1984 and 1995; Donaldson and Preston 1995; McWilliams and Siegel 2001) assumes that firms consist of a variety of different constituencies such as employees, suppliers, customers, shareholders, and the broader community. Different ownership structures and a differentiation in the importance of the various groups of stakeholders may, therefore, lead to contextual differences between entrepreneurial, or owner-led private firms, and private firms run by employed managers, or state- and community-owned firms (cf. Green 1992), with some influence on strategy, management style, organizational structure, and performance (Brouthers et al. 2007). A stronger focus on shareholder values and interests could be expected for private and owner-led firms. Value preferences of owners who run their firms are to a large extent directed towards economic and performance targets based on a stronger individual achievement motivation (McClelland and Boyatzis 1982), whereas employed managers must consider various other aspects such as interests of stakeholders, regional welfare and so on. 'Senior management often faces problems, such as enhancing the viability of the firm while simultaneously balancing the needs of various stakeholders' (Waldmann et al. 2007: 824). While stakeholder orientation is focused more on the physical environment, which has a direct influence on the viability and survival of a firm, the community orientation represents a larger societal entity beyond particular groups and is more amorphous in nature (ibid: 825).

The contextual orientations can be seen as linked to managerial values and leadership behaviour. Here, the literature on the relation between *national and organizational values and leadership attributes* suggest an influence of values on decision-making. Values and leadership behaviour may be seen as culturally embedded stable patterns of leader-follower interaction (cf. House et al. 2004). The values and behaviour of entrepreneurial owners seem to differ from those of employed managers, as the literature on entrepreneurial mindsets (McGrath and MacMillan 2000), basic entrepreneurial motivation (McClelland and Boyatzis 1982), and leadership behaviour of entrepreneurs suggests ('entrepreneurial leadership', cf. Gupta et al. 2004; Ardichvili 2001). The above-mentioned authors point to a universally valid difference in values, motives and styles (see also Malach-Pines et al. 2002). Entrepreneurial owners are characterized as more visionary, inspiring, charismatic, performance-oriented, individualistic and less bureaucratic, while managers may be more team-, humanist- and participation-oriented (Lang et al. 2005 and 2007).

Transformation theory and literature describe organizational change in radically changing environments as a 'follow-up modernization' (Grancelli 1995) towards new structures of ownership and enterprise restructuring; whereby the local cultures and historical heritage must be taken into account, especially in the case of the transformation of big state-owned companies (Clark, Lang and Balaton 2001; Langer et al. 2005; Lang 2007). Moreover, cultural factors and the enduring transformation have led to a revival of the state with its respective influence on the organizational field (Grabher and Stark 1997; Stark 1996). The transformation process is also accompanied by a reproduction of the old elites (Schreiber et al. 2001; Steger and Lang 2003; Waldner 2003). Finally, the transformational context has led to a similar situation for entrepreneurial owners and managers that could be characterized as psychologically weak. Instead of strong norms and incentives for specific types of behaviour, and clear expectations concerning by what rules behaviours are rewarded, as in well-established organizations, weak situations are less formalized, more flexible, and allow the actors a stronger behavioural expression of personal values and dispositions (cf. Waldmann et al. 2001). In the face of this situation it may be hypothesized that owner-managers and employed managers display similar value patterns, while the often-stressed differences in the values and dispositions of entrepreneurs in contrast to employed managers may be less striking. This might be even more so the case if we take the great stability within the social structure of the economic elite into account. In addition, it also might be assumed that subordinates share the views of their CEOs and by this stabilize the values and dispositions of managing owners and employed managing directors.

CEO values may also be influenced by other factors, such as the professional background, personal experience and career of the entrepreneur, owner or manager as suggested by theoretical concepts like theories of professionalization or identity. Professional values may be seen as influencing the individual decision-maker, while experiences during such critical events as transformation crises may have led to a massive process of individual learning and identity formation within the 'new' environment (cf. Breu 2001; Clark et al. 2001). With respect to the professional background, the empirical literature describes entrepreneurs with an engineering background as more individualistic, logical and less administration-oriented or bureaucratic. Entrepreneur-manager with long-term experience in state-owned firms may be more procedural and administration-oriented, but also more humanistic and focused on regional and state welfare, while also possessing a broader stakeholder orientation.

5.3 Methodology and methods of the study

This study is an exploratory in-depth research examining patterns in value preferences, styles and careers under conditions of fundamental societal and organizational changes. The data were drawn from case studies in 52 East-German small- and medium-sized enterprises, 27 firms led by the founder/owner, and 25 firms led by employed managers. The sample covers firms from several industrial branches, trade and service companies, with the number of employees ranging from 20 to 500 in the majority of cases.

The material consists of a 1–2-hour interview with Chief Executive Officers (CEOs), owners as well as employed managers, about the development of the firm, their own professional careers, and a special CEO questionnaire on firm development, changes, strategies and their value preferences in critical decisions. Furthermore, 205 questionnaires from immediate subordinates as co-workers of the CEOs, other managers or leading experts, with an average of 4–5 questionnaires per firm, were included. The data were collected in 2000–3, applying instruments from the CEO study within the GLOBE project[2].

The value preferences of the CEOs and their subordinates in critical management decisions were drawn from the respective questionnaires using a 7-point Likert-scale from 'highest importance' (7) to 'no importance' (1) with respect to 17 different factors including: customer satisfaction, long-term competitiveness of the firm, ethical considerations, professional growth and development of employees, and contributions to the region or state.

Following the literature and empirical studies on stakeholder theoretical reasoning (cf. Waldmann et al. 2007), I also summarized the appropriate items from the study to describe shareholder-value orientation, stakeholder-value orientation, or community welfare orientation. For example:

- *Shareholder orientation (3 items)*: 'effect on firm profitability', 'effect on sales volume', 'effect on cost control'.
- *Stakeholder orientation (5 items)*: 'employee relations issues (well-being, safety, working conditions)', 'effect on the environment', 'effect on customer satisfaction', 'effect on the relations to other important organizations and groups'.
- *Community/state welfare (2 items)*: 'contribution to the economic welfare of the local community', 'contribution to the welfare of the state'.

The descriptions of leadership behaviour of entrepreneurial owners and managers are based on single items in the subordinates questionnaires with a 7-point scale, ranging from 'strongly agree' (7) to 'strongly disagree' (1), for example: 'Has a clear understanding of where we are going' (visionary), 'Sets high standards of performance' (performance-oriented) or 'Has empathy for others, is inclined to be helpful or show mercy' (humanistic). According to the GLOBE methodology, the data on the leadership items were summarized to leadership sub-scales (leadership attributes) and main factors (leadership style patterns or dimensions), like value-based or transformational, participatory, team-oriented, humanistic, or autonomous leadership.

The basic motives as well as contextual data were drawn from CEO interviews. Therefore, the data of interview transcriptions were subjected to motive coding (Winter 1991a; 1991b; 1992). The motives were counted according to McClelland's motive types: power, achievement and affiliation, and responsibility (for typical example items see Lang et al. 2007). Moreover, I included statistical data from interviews or questionnaires regarding firm size, professional background of the entrepreneurial owners and managers, the decision structure in the firm (single owner or CEO, number of deciders), entrepreneur age, and the branch of activity.

The data were subjected to quantitative analysis of value preferences and leadership styles with comparisons of owner-managers and employed managers, CEOs with engineering and other professional backgrounds, and with respect to the former management experience and institutional settings, for example, firm size. An exploratory cluster analysis was applied to identify typical patterns of CSR values within their respective personal and institutional settings. Related factors of influence, such as motive structure and leadership behaviour, were found using correlation analyses, as well as a possible impact on value-orientations of co-workers. The interview analysis of representative CEOs was used to find typical contextual factors, career steps and experiences as possible explanations for value types.

5.4 Main results

5.4.1 Characteristics of the firms and CEOs

The firms involved are, with one exception, private firms. Two firms continued their business after 1989. Of the firms 45 per cent were newly founded after 1989, and 50 per cent were privatized – approximately 90 per cent between 1989 and 1993. The firms mainly belong to branches such as manufacturing; approximately 70 per cent are in the metal, machinery, and computer industries. Yet, firms from the construction industries, textiles, trade, publishing and media, health care and education are also included in the sample. Of the firms 51 per cent have between 100 and 500 employees, and 38 per cent have fewer than 100 employees. Most of the firms are led by the entrepreneur or owner (55 per cent), while 45 per cent are run by an employed manager.

The CEOs of the firms are mainly male (more than 90 per cent) and between the age of 40 and 60 years old (73 per cent). Of the firms 58 per cent are of East-German origin, while 42 per cent have a West-German background. More than one-third of the participants in the study (36 per cent) have worked more than 10 years in the very same firm and 44 per cent of the CEOs fewer than 10 years. The CEOs share long experience in management positions: 74 per cent have more than 15 years' experience.

As for professional experience, the sample consists of 62 per cent of CEOs with a professional background in engineering and only 21 per cent with an economics background. All CEOs, with one exception, have a university degree (98 per cent with diploma or master's degree).

5.4.2 Value preferences in critical decisions

The value preferences of the owner-managers and employed managers are very similar throughout the sample. The ranking is dominated by a focus on customer satisfaction followed by product quality, competitiveness of the firm, cost control, profits, and turnover. All in all, short- and long-term economic factors seem to build the core of the preferences of entrepreneurial owners and managers. The stakeholder focus is mainly

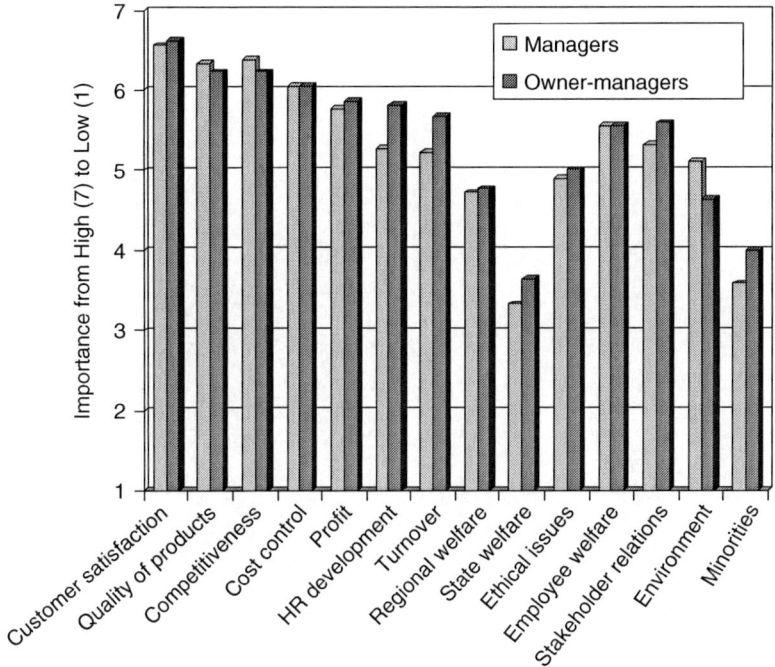

Figure 5.1 Value preferences of owner-managers and employed managers in critical management decisions

on the customers. Contributions to the welfare of the region and state, the natural environment, ethical issues, and, especially, the inclusion of minority issues in decisions are seen as less important. In this respect, no striking differences between entrepreneurial owners and managers could be found. However, the data show quite interesting differences between the two groups with respect to the importance of turnover, short-term profit, professional staff development and minority issues, which receive more emphasis from owner-managers, while their employed counterparts pay more attention to environmental issues. Long-term economic issues seem to get similar attention, with a slightly higher focus on customers by the owner-managers and on product quality and long-term competitiveness by managers. In addition, CEOs who own the firms are slightly more concerned with other organizational groups of stakeholders like suppliers, members of strategic alliances or public organizations. The variety of stakeholder interests is, however, slightly more focused on core groups (see Figure 5.1).

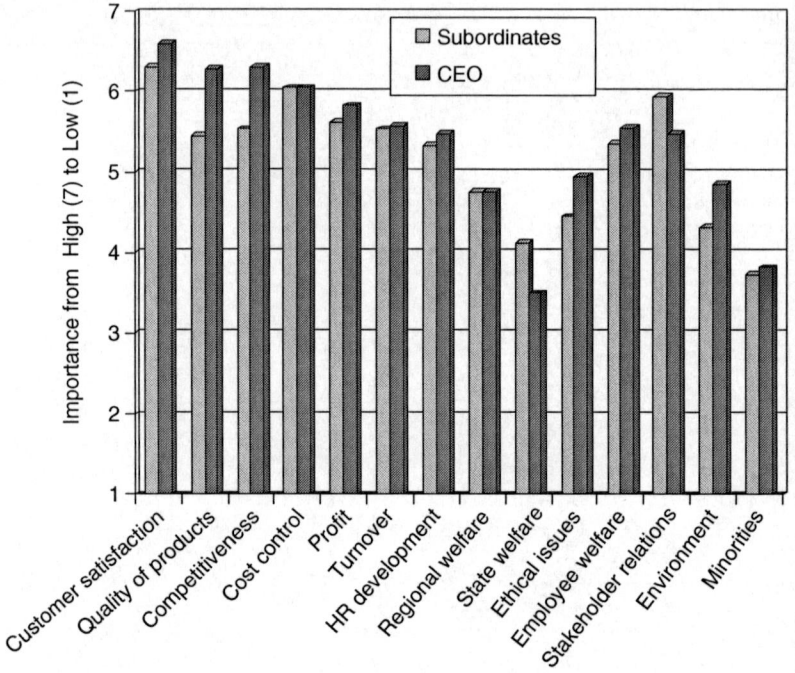

Figure 5.2   Value preferences of all CEOs and immediate subordinates in critical management decisions

The ranking of the immediate subordinate managers or employees is quite similar to those of their CEOs, indicating an adaptation of their own world-view to those of their 'bosses'. But again, a number of interesting differences must be noted. Product quality and long-term competitiveness are considered more important by the CEOs, while contribution to the state's welfare and a broader stakeholder orientation is more important to the co-workers. A bit surprising is the owners' and managers' increased awareness of ethical and environmental issues compared with the assessment of these factors by their employees (see Figure 5.2). Despite a potentially higher demand for socially desirable behaviour in managers, the result also points to a long-term orientation of CEOs' perceptions and world-views.

5.4.3   CSR value preferences in critical decisions

A summary of corporate social responsibility (CSR) values from the material shows again a similarity between CEOs and their immediate

Table 5.1   CSR value preferences in critical decisions

	Shareholder values	Stakeholder values	Community/ State welfare values
All managers (CEOs)	5.80	5.58	4.12
Owner-managers	*5.90*	5.61	4.20
Employed managers	5.70	5.55	4.03
Immediate subordinates	5.54	5.45	*4.44*

subordinates (see Table 5.1). Only community values and the contribution to state and regional welfare are seen as more important by the employees. A clear difference can be seen for owner-managers with respect to the higher importance of shareholder values, than (short-term) profits, turnover or cost reduction.

Within the whole group of CEOs, five clusters were identified using the three factors 1) shareholder orientation, 2) stakeholder orientation and 3) community orientation as suggested by Waldmann et al. (2007) as selection criteria.

The first cluster with a *stakeholder focus* (26 per cent of the whole group) consists of approximately two-thirds CEOs from mainly privatized medium-sized firms, 40–60 years old, with a non-engineering background and mixed East- and West-German origin.

The second cluster can be described as *overall value focus* (26 per cent), consisting of 80 per cent managing owners from smaller, often outsourced and privatized firms, with an engineering background, from all age groups and two-thirds with an East-German origin. All scores are clearly above the average.

A smaller third cluster is characterized by a *dominant stakeholder focus*. The three managers (8 per cent) are from larger, new or privatized firms, on average between 40 and 50 years old, with two of West-German origin and mixed professional backgrounds.

The fourth cluster, with 35 per cent the largest group, is one with a *shareholder focus*. The group consists of East-German engineers between 40 and 60 years old, from small, more recently founded and owner-led firms.

Finally, cluster five consists of only two older West-German entrepreneurs and managers with non-engineering backgrounds, heading larger privatized firms and characterized by a strong *community focus*. Table 5.2 shows the score patterns for the CSR value clusters. The figures

Table 5.2   CSR value preferences in critical decision clusters

	Cluster 'Stakeholder focus' (10)	Cluster 'Overall value focus' (10)	Cluster 'Strong stakeholder focus' (3)	Cluster 'Shareholder focus' (14)	Cluster 'Community focus' (2)
Shareholder values	5.65	*6.30*	3.83	*5.89*	4.50
Stakeholder values	*5.92*	*5.68*	*5.80*	5.27	5.30
Community/ State welfare values	*4.65*	*5.30*	3.50	2.89	*5.50*

in italics indicate results significantly above average and describe the typical patterns of the various clusters.

The cluster analysis allows one to identify CEOs in each cluster and to describe the value orientations as well as the biographical and contextual settings. The following section describes representatives of each of the three larger clusters. According to the focus of the article on managing owners, I selected four CEOs from this group. With the italic letters in the quotations, I would like to indicate typical references to both career aspects and value- orientation aspects. Moreover, the case descriptions permit a more differentiated picture of the managerial orientations.

Example 1: A new owner-manager with an (internal) stakeholder focus (Cluster 1)

The entrepreneur (age 45) was *one of three* founders of a trade and distribution firm for computer systems with 143 employees. He studied electrical engineering and worked in a large computer enterprise and a smaller firm before 1990. He characterized his special qualifications in the field of engineering as follows:

> During my studies in *engineering* I learned mainly how to *solve problems* ... that helped me a lot ... in my further work at 'Robotron', where I had to design, develop and test electronic steering systems and components ... for different machines, *every machine was unique.* (Author's italic emphasis.)

The collective founding process was described as a fundamental entre-preneurial experience:

> Like other computer firms, we founded ours in 1990, in a garage ... it was really a child of the German 'Wende'.

The experiences of the early years after founding have led to a special pattern of orientation towards problem-solving, with a strong focus on internal stakeholders, especially the professional competence of the employees.

> We learned that *cooperation* with other firms is *difficult*, especially if you need a high degree of flexibility ... that is impossible with another firm if they do not work after 5 or 6 p.m. That is why *we are doing a lot by ourselves*, because we are simply more flexible ... we try to *solve all problems with our own know-how* ... also *marketing*. (Author's italic emphasis.)

Example 2: A value-based and committed owner (Cluster 2)

This entrepreneur is about 60 years old. He is one of three owners and the CEO of a firm that was *privatized* in the early 1990s and now has 115 employees. The mechanical engineering firm produces spare parts and was originally founded in 1905. From 1963 to 1990 it was state owned. The CEO studied *engineering*, a field in which he worked within and outside the firm before he received a *management position in the state conglomerate* ('*Kombinat*') which the firm belonged to.

> In a large enterprise a lot of people live anonymously, the top management doesn't know the employees, but with around 120 employees *you know everybody personally* ... and if you have to tell someone 'it's the end for you' with a consequence not only for the job but for the whole family, it's really difficult ... I think we did it [*refers to the early 1990s*] in the proper way if that's at all possible, but *we try to respect their feelings* ... but *you have to withstand* that as *CEO and owner*, you have no other choice, otherwise you endanger *the whole enterprise.*' (Author's italic emphasis.)

Example 3: An owner with an explicit shareholder orientation (Cluster 4)

This CEO is founder and one of the owners of an engineering firm with around 130 employees. He is 43 years old, studied *physics and material science* in the late 1980s and earned his PhD in the same field. He worked as a technologist and in an R&D department in a foundry and for a few years also as a technology consultant.

After the *Wende* (German political transformation) in 1989, he had the idea to set up his own business that would have a long-term perspective. As he left his former company, a privatized state enterprise, the firm was on the way to bankruptcy:

> When I left the firm in 1994, they were not investing any longer. There was no product development. There were no perspectives. ... but as I said, it was a middle-term *aim to become independent*. (Author's italic emphasis.)

In 1995 he started his own business together with financial investors and co-owners:

> My idea was to develop a new innovative product and/or service for the industry that would be *nationally and internationally competitive and profitable*. (Author's italic emphasis.)

But in order to get credit, he had to present a well-balanced business plan, *'to convince investors to participate'* in the businesses. Because of increasing competition in their field, permanent development of the product/service had to be ensured. This resulted in a *large investment* in new machines in 2000 and 2001 as the basis for *further firm development and growth*. Again, the development of the firm had to be financed with the help of investors and public funding, creating a dependence on the group of co-owners and shareholders.

Example 4: An owner with a shareholder orientation, but also a long-term economic view (Cluster 4)

This entrepreneur re-founded an existing firm in the printing business with 80 employees. He is 50 years old and studied *electrical engineering*. After his studies, he worked at a university as academic assistant. His family background was an entrepreneurial one: his father had been a private owner. So he took over the substance of the old enterprise, but he completely changed its products and structures, which finally led to the re-foundation of a new firm:

> What I'm interested in is the *new idea, the product* ... Yes, *market share* is very important, growth, *but with profit*.

Despite a clear shareholder orientation, he is also aware of problems coming from a short-term shareholder focus, and he consequently stresses aspects of long-term economic competitiveness.

simple profit-making brings problems if you would cut down research and development . . . certainly for a good profit, but fails to set seeds for the *future growth* and development of the firm.

The four examples show some *typical characteristics of East-German entrepreneurs* or owner-managers:

- a background in science or engineering and, as a consequence;
- a focus on technology and products;
- prior management experience in state-owned enterprises and, at least partly;
- long-term experience in their own firms, often including the process of privatization and restructuring.

The differences in value preferences may, therefore, be influenced by other factors. The interviews indicate that the unique experiences during the transformation process had a strong impact on value orientations, as expressed in cases 1 ('internal stakeholder focus') and 2 ('value-based committed owner'). Example 3 ('explicit shareholder orientation') points to the influence of financial sources and ownership structures as possibly driving a stronger shareholder focus, while example 4 ('shareholder and long-term orientation') shows the limitations of a quantitative analysis. It turned out to be difficult to find simple and short-term shareholder views. Beyond showing the intentions of the interviewed managers, the qualitative data point to a necessary differentiation within the shareholder cluster.

But the statistical data, in spite of their limitations, also show the influence of the process of restructuring and privatization. In privatized firms, contrary to newly-founded firms, a higher importance of costs, environmental and ethical issues, and long-term competitiveness are combined with a stakeholder focus. Moreover, personal factors such as the basic motivation of the owners and managers, and their leadership styles, can be regarded as important.

5.4.4 Influence of basic motivations, leadership behaviour and value preferences of employees

The data point to the fact that stakeholder orientation is greater when CEOs have above-average motives based on their social affiliations to

Table 5.3 Differences in leadership dimensions between owner-managers and employed managers

	Employed managers Mean	Std. dev.	Owner-managers Mean	Std. dev.	T-Test
Value-based leadership	5.53	0.52	*5.73*	0.55	*0.05*
Participatory leadership	*5.47*	0.98	5.15	1.20	n.s.
Team-oriented leadership	4.95	0.49	4.97	0.66	n.s.
Humane leadership	*4.87*	0.73	4.70	0.71	n.s.
Autonomous leadership	3.78	1.10	*4.35*	1.17	*0.05*
Self- protective leadership	*3.04*	0.51	2.79	0.51	*0.05*

others. Greater shareholder orientations are connected with motivation for achievement of the owners and managers, and, in part, lower-level social affiliation motives. The responsibility motives are essential for a balanced inclusion of community and stakeholder values; if CEOs' basic motivations have a high share of the responsibility motive within the overall motivation, it is more likely that CEOs will include not only shareholder issues but also stakeholder and community welfare aspects in their decision-making processes. Moreover, stakeholder and community orientations seem to be linked to each other, while a greater importance of ethical considerations for the CEO influences stakeholder as well as community orientations in a positive way.

CEO leadership behaviour seems to have a moderating effect on the value preferences of CEOs and subordinates, especially if it is perceived as transformational, integrative and fair.

Entrepreneurial managers are described as more transformational but also more individualistic and, of lesser importance, less participatory and self-protective (see Table 5.3). Moreover, significant single-item differences can be found with respect to a more self-conscious, less calm and less bureaucratic behaviour of the entrepreneurial CEOs compared with that of CEO-managers. At the same time, CEO management behaviour is seen as fairer, more integrative, informative, and power-sharing.

Consequently, participatory, power-sharing and communicative styles have the strongest influence on the importance of staff development, minority issues and long-term competitiveness, but do not foster a focus of subordinates on shareholder issues. This points to a clear disadvantage for entrepreneurial CEOs in comparison with CEO managers. The more bureaucratic and procedural styles of the latter group also foster the higher priority in subordinates of issues regarding state and regional welfare.

This may be regarded as an explanation for the fact that in manager-led firms the welfare of the state and the region, ethical considerations as well as the development of the employees are seen as more important in critical decisions of subordinates.

5.5 Discussion and conclusions

The results seem to prove that transformational settings may equalize the difference between entrepreneur-owners and employed managers in the sense that a situation of similar psychological weakness leads to a convergence of the value orientations of managers and entrepreneurs. Similar results have been reported for other transforming societies such as Estonia and Romania (Lang et al. 2005).

Similar value orientations in CEOs and their subordinates can be seen as a result of the transformational *Notgemeinschaft* of former years – a sort of implicit contract that emerged out of the ongoing transformational crisis which meant that the firms avoided substantial change in employment levels in order to keep loyalty in spite of low pay (see also Schmidt in this volume). This may be relevant for employed managers and owner-managers as well, in light of the large share of new enterprises emerging out of old ones through re-privatization, privatization or management buy-out as shown by Hess (2006). At the same time this implicit contract can be seen as an obstacle to creating an 'entrepreneurial organization' in a western sense (Jelinek and Litterer 1995).

The differences in perception of leadership behaviour suggest a higher commitment and dependency of employed managers on various stakeholder interests. Only the managers in smaller firms with a professional background in engineering and a stronger shareholder orientation seem to depart from this dependence. Like small-firm owners they are highly selective having only a few internal stakeholders in mind, such as experienced and highly skilled employees. But at the same time these owner-managers become partly dependent on financial services or other co-owners, which may explain the stronger shareholder focus and short-term economic orientations, as also found by Brouthers et al. (2007) in a Romanian sample and Martens (2007) in East Germany. The differences within the shareholder cluster as found in the qualitative interviews may support the assumption that short-term shareholder views can rarely be found in East German SMEs. The transformational actors seem to be rooted in a more selective but still influential cultural setting.

Thus, the results also refer to the influence of basic motives in the personalities of owner-managers and employed managers on decision preferences, although the influence of different motive structures seems to be moderated by the respective leadership style. The results point here at least to a more differentiated motive structure than expressed in the study of Pistrui et al. (2003) and also challenge the generalizing results classifying East-German owners and managers as 'competitive capitalists' (Martens 2007: 127).

The value orientation and the differences found in the analysis are obviously connected with experiences of the CEOs and followers in the process of privatization and restructuring, especially in the support received from different groups of stakeholders during the transformation crisis, which could be seen in the interview text examples. Here the results are challenging the traditional CSR analysis with its very rough categorizations and summarizing approaches to stakeholders, but also to shareholder orientations. A more differentiated analysis can help to overcome this problem. Moreover, the focus on qualitative and process data, taking into account the life cycle of organizations and its impact on managerial motivation, can help to explore the influence of early experiences and learning processes in the owners and managers of newly set-up firms (see the basic work of Smith and Miner 1983).

Finally, the empirical material challenges the short-handed economic analysis focusing only on ownership structure as the decisive factor and following a more general trend back to actor-centred approaches in transformation studies (cf. Lang 2007). Instead, factors like personal motives, professional background and the experienced importance of stakeholders and communities may be seen as more influential in shaping corporate social values in the new and transformed East-German firms.

Notes

1. This phenomenon is partly misinterpreted as a limited understanding of the concept of ownership in CEE countries (see Heering and Pfirmann 2002: 62).
2. For a description of the instruments, see House et al. (2004) or Lang et al. (2005). Similar data from Romania, Estonia and Austria are available for further generalization.

References

Alt, R. and R. Lang (1998) 'Wertorientierungen und Führungsverständnis von Managern in sächsischen Klein- und Mittelbetrieben' in R. Lang (ed.), *Führungskräfte im osteuropäischen Transformationsprozess* (Munich, Mering: Hampp), 247–69.

Ardichvili, A. (2001) 'Leadership Styles of Russian Entrepreneurs and Managers', *Journal of Developmental Entrepreneurship*, 6, 169–87.

Breu, K. (2001) 'The Role and Relevance of Management Cultures in the Organizational Transformation Process', *International Studies of Management & Organization*, 31(2), 28–47.

Brouthers, K. D., M. Gelderman and P. Arens (2007) 'The Influence of Ownership on Performance: Stakeholder and Strategic Contingency Perspectives', *Schmalenbach Business Review (sbf)*, 59, 225–42.

Clark, E., R. Lang and K. Balaton (2001) 'Making the Transition: Managers and Management in Transforming and Reforming Societies', *International Studies of Management & Organization*, 31(2), 3–8.

Donaldson, T. and T. Preston (1995) 'The Stakeholder Theory of the Corporation: Concepts, Evidence and Implications', *Academy of Management Review*, 20(1), 65–91.

Edwards, V. and P. Lawrence (2000) *Management in Eastern Europe* (Basingstoke, UK: Palgrave Macmillan).

Freeman, R. E. (1984) *Strategic Management: A Stakeholder Approach* (Boston: Pitnam).

Freeman, R. E. (1995) 'The Politics of Stakeholder Theory: Some Future Directions', *Business Ethics Quarterly*, 4(4), 409–21.

Grabher, G. and D. Stark (eds) (1997) *Restructuring Networks in Post-Socialism: Legacies, Linkages and Localities* (Oxford: Oxford University Press).

Grancelli, B. (ed.) (1995) *Social Change and Modernization: Lessons from Eastern Europe* (Berlin: de Gruyter).

Green, S. (1992) 'The Impact of Ownership and Capital Structure on Managerial Motivation and Strategy in Management-Buy-Outs: A Cultural Analysis', *Journal of Management Studies*, 29(4), 513–35.

Gupta, V., I. C. MacMillan and G. Suric (2004) 'Entrepreneurial Leadership: Developing and Measuring a Cross-Cultural Construct', *Journal of Business Venturing* 19, 241–60.

Habisch, A., J. Jonker, M. Wegner and R. Schmidpeter (eds) (2005) *Corporate Social Responsibility Across Europe* (Berlin: Springer Verlag).

Heering, W. and O. Pfirmann (2002) 'Private Ownership in Markets: Limits to Privatisation in the Transition Process', in O. Pfirrmann and G. H. Walter (eds), *Small Firms and Entrepreneurship in Central and Eastern Europe: A Socio-Economic Perspective* (Heidelberg, New York: Physika), 47–72.

Hess, U. (2006) *Unternehmer in Sachsen* (Leipzig: Militzke).

House, R. J., P. J. Hanges, M. Javidan, P. Dorfman and V. Gupta (2004) *Culture, Leadership, and Organizations: The GLOBE Study of 62 Societies* (Thousand Oaks, CA: Sage).

Jelinek, M. and J. A. Litterer (1995) 'Toward Entrepreneurial Organizations: Meeting Ambiguity with Engagement', *Entrepreneurship Theory and Practice*, spring, 137–68.

Johnson, S. and G. W. Loveman (1995) *Starting over in Eastern Europe: Entrepreneurship and Economic Renewal* (Boston: HBR Press).

Kandil, F. and G. H. Walter (2002) 'Industrial Modernisation in Post-Socialist Economies: Primary Endogenous and Elites Oriented Modernisation as a Socio-Economically Oriented Strategic Concept', in O. Pfirrmann and G. H. Walter (eds), *Small Firms and Entrepreneurship in Central and Eastern Europe: A Socio-Economic Perspective* (Heidelberg, New York: Physika), 73–95.

Kirby, D. A. and A. Watson (2003) *Small Firm Development in Developed and Transition Economies: A Reader* (Aldershot, Burlington: Ashgate).

Koch, T., M. Thomas and R. Woderich (1993) 'Akteursgenese und Handlungslogiken – das Beispiel der neuen Selbständigen in Ostdeutschland', *Berliner Journal für Soziologie* 3(3), 275–92.

Kulke, D. (2005) *Politisches Kapital, soziales Kapital und Humankapital in Ostdeutschland* (Munich, Mering: Hampp).

Lang, R. (1994) 'Führungskräfte in Ostdeutschland', Working Paper 3, Chemnitz, University of Technology.

Lang, R. (2000) 'Economic, Social and Cultural Resources of Russian and East German Managers', *Journal of Cross-Cultural Competence and Management*, 2, 167–210.

Lang, R. (2007) 'Transition Economies', in G. Ritzer (ed.), *The Blackwell Encyclopaedia of Sociology*, vol. 10 (Malden, Oxford, Carlton: Blackwell), 5050–54.

Lang, R. and S. Müller (2001) 'Privatisation, Perception of Success and Attitudes of Managers in the East German Transformation Process', in K. Liuhto (ed.), *Ten Years of Economic Transformation, Volume III: Societies and Institutions in Transition. Studies in Industrial Engineering and Management*, no. 16, Lappeenranta University of Technology, 391–407.

Lang, R. and T. Steger (2002) 'The Odyssey of Management Knowledge to Transforming Societies: A Critical Review of a Theoretical Alternative', *Human Resource Development International*, 5(3), 279–94.

Lang, R., R. Alas, R. Alt, D. Catana and R. Hartz (2005) 'Leadership in Transformation – Between Local Embeddedness and Global Challenges', *Journal of Cross-Cultural Competence and Management*, 4, 215–46.

Lang, R., A. Catana, D. Catana and J. Steyrer (2007) 'Impacts of Motives and Leadership Attributes of Entrepreneurs and Managers on Followers Commitment in Transforming Countries – A Comparison of Romania, East Germany and Austria', in P. Jurczek and M. Niedobitek (eds), *Europäische Forschungsperspektiven – Elemente einer Europawissenschaft* (2008).

Malach-Pines, A., A. Sadeh, D. Dvir and O. Yafe-Yanai (2002) 'Entrepreneurs and Managers: Similar Yet Different', *The International Journal of Organizational Analysis*, 10, 172–90.

Marinov, M. and S. Marinova (1996) 'Characteristics and Conditions of Entrepreneurship in Eastern Europe', *Journal for East European Management Studies*, 1(4), 7–24.

Martens, B. (2007) 'Orthodoxie der Proselyten – Einstellungsmuster ökonomischer Funktionseliten im Ost/West-Vergleich', *Zeitschrift für Soziologie*, 36(2), 118–30.

Martens, B. and M. Michailow (2006) 'Wandel und Kontinuität mittelständischer Unternehmen – Eine Untersuchung zu Differenzen zwischen und

Gemeinsamkeiten von Unternehmensleitern', *Zeitschrift für KMU und Entrepreneurchip*, 54(3), 221–42.

McClelland, D. C. and R. E. Boyatzis (1982) 'Leadership Motive Pattern and Long Term Success in Management', *Journal of Applied Psychology*, 67, 737–43.

McGrath, R. G. and I. C. MacMillan (2000) *The Entrepreneurial Mindset* (Boston: Harvard Business School Press).

McWilliams, A. and D. Siegel (2001) 'Corporate Social Responsibility: A Theory of the Firm Perspective', *Academy of Management Review*, 26(1), 117–227.

Nee, V. and R. Matthews (1996) 'Market Transition and Societal Transformation in Reforming State Socialism', *Annual Review of Sociology*, 22, 401–35.

Pfirrmann, O. and Walter, G. H. (eds) (2002) *Small Firms and Entrepreneurship in Central and Eastern Europe: A Socio-Economic Perspective* (Heidelberg/New York: Physika, 2002).

Pistrui, D., H. P. Welsch, H. J. Pohl, O. Wintermantel and J. Liao (2003) 'Entrepreneurship in the New Germany', in D. A. Kirby and A. Watson (eds), *Small Firm Development in Developed and Transition Economies: A Reader* (Aldershopt, Burlington: Ashgate), 115–30.

Pohlmann, M and H.-J. Gergs (1996) 'Manageriale Eliten im Transformationsprozess', in M. Pohlmann and R. Schmidt (eds), *Management in der ostdeutschen Industrie* (Opladen: Westdeutscher Verlag), 63–98.

Pohlmann, M. and R. Schmidt (eds) (1996) *Management in der ostdeutschen Industrie* (Opladen: Westdeutscher Verlag).

Puffer, S., D. J. McCarthy and A. I. Naumov (2000) *The Russian Capitalist Experiment: From State-Owned Organizations to Entrepreneurship* (Cheltenham: Edgar Elgar).

Schreiber, E., M. Meyer, T. Steger and R. Lang (2001) *Eliten in Wechseljahren – Verbands- und Kombinatsführungskräfte im ostdeutschen Transformationsprozess* (Munich, Mering: Hampp).

Smith, N. R. and J. B. Miner (1983) 'Type of Entrepreneur, Type of Firm, and Managerial Motivation: Implications for Organizational Life Cycle Theory', *Strategic Management Journal*, 4, 325–40.

Stark, D. (1996) 'Recombinant Property in Eastern European Capitalism', *American Journal of Sociology*, 101(4), 993–1027.

Steger, T. and R. Lang (2003) 'Career Paths of Elite of Former GDR Combinates During Post-Socialist Transformation Process', *Journal of World Business*, 38, 168–81.

Steger, T. and I. Winkler (eds) (2003) 'Leaders and Leadership in Central and Eastern Europe', *Journal for East European Management Studies (JEEMS)*, 8/4, Special issue.

Ullmann, A. A. and A. Lewis (eds) (1997) *Privatization and Entrepreneurship. The Managerial Challenge in Central and Eastern Europe* (New York, London: International Business Press, Haworth Press Inc.).

Wade, M. D. (2003) 'Differences in Values, Practices, and Systems Among Hungarian Managers and Western Expatriates', *Journal of World Business*, 38(3), 224–44.

Waldmann, D. A., G. G. Ramírez, R. J. House and P. Puranam (2001) 'Does Leadership Matter? CEO Leadership Attributes and Profitability under Conditions of Perceived Environmental Uncertainty', *Academy of Management Journal*, 44, 134–43.

Waldmann, D. A., M. S. de Luque, N. Washburn and R. J. House (2007) 'Cultural and Leadership Predictors of Corporate Social Responsibility Values of Top Management: A GLOBE Study of 15 Countries', *Journal of International Business Studies*, 37, 823–37.

Waldner. A. G. (2003) 'Elite Opportunity in Transitional Economies', *American Sociological Review*, 68, 899–916.

Winter, D. G. (1991a) 'Measuring Personality at a Distance: Development of an Integrated System for Scoring Motives in Running Text', in J. M. Stewart, J. M. Healy Jr. and D. J. Ozer (eds), *Perspectives in Personality: Approaches to Understanding Lives* (London: Jessica Kingsley Publishers), 61–91.

Winter, D. G. (1991b) 'Manual for Scoring Motive Imagery in Running Text', Department of Psychology, University of Michigan, 8–30.

Winter, D. G. (1992) 'Content Analysis of Archival Materials, Personal Documents, and Everyday Verbal Productions', in C. P. Smith (ed.), *Motivation and Personality: Handbook of Thematic Content Analysis* (New York: Cambridge University Press), 110–25.

6

SMEs in France: New Perspectives and New Generation of Small-Business Owners

Alain Fayolle and Salma Fattoum

6.1 Introduction

When starting up a business, three different approaches are possible: reproduction, imitation, and innovation (Bruyat 1993). From the reproduction perspective, individuals wish to continue doing what they did in their previous employment but work for themselves. Individuals who start up businesses based on imitation follow a well-established pattern but do not always have the required skills or resources. Finally, innovative start-ups rely on the introduction of new products, services, technologies or practices that break away from existing ones. Innovation usually entails a great deal of uncertainty due to the inherent novelty.

Our question is whether innovation and growth are within the reach of all entrepreneurs and SME owner-managers. Building on Laufer's contribution (1975), typological studies carried out in France show that the typical innovative manager generally graduated from a prestigious school and occupied important positions in large firms. However, until now in France, this type of actor was not socially destined for the kind of professional orientation that led to starting up a business or managing SMEs, as numerous authors have shown (Bauer and Bertin-Mourot 1987; Bourdieu 1989; Fauconnier 1996; Lojkine 1992; Maurice et al. 1982; Ribeill 1984; Robin 1994). Recent institutional changes linked to globalization, the changes of the job market and the educational system lead us to believe that from now on more and more graduates will choose the world of SMEs and new-venture creation for their careers (Aghion and Cohen 2004; d'Iribarne 2006).

This change in orientation and behaviours in people that used to see their careers in terms of nobler career paths and jobs in large companies and administrations is happening in a context where the need for innovation, growth and development has never been higher. Several short-term transformations are expected in the world of SMEs. Demographic changes will lead to the retirement of numerous SME owner-managers. European Commission sources[1] and the Directorate-General for Enterprise and Industry forecast an average of 610,000 SME transmissions each year in Europe, among which are 300,000 SMEs that employ staff, implying a total of 2.1 million jobs. In France alone, 450,000 companies will have changed owners by 2013.[2] Moreover, several studies underline France's structural deficit in high-growth firms (which American economist David Birch terms 'gazelles') and medium-sized companies (between 250 and 500 employees), which both constitute indispensable elements of economic and job-creation dynamics.[3]

The stance we take in this chapter is in line with the above mentioned institutional transformations and changes. Indeed, we assume that in the next few years more and more graduates will choose venture creation and SME ownership and management, notably by seizing opportunities offered by the generation of owners who are to retire. This new generation of entrepreneurs should bring numerous changes into the strategy and management of these firms. Yet, there is no clear link between generational change and an increase in research and development in French SMEs, as the reality of innovation in SMEs cannot be approached from the simplistic viewpoint that consists of thinking that a person with good education and qualifications is naturally attracted to innovation and the growth of the firm they manage. The laws that rule the world of innovators and innovation appear far more complex and depend, also, on contextual factors.

In this chapter, we will first present the situation of SMEs in France in both qualitative and quantitative terms. We will look into their contribution and specificities and we will outline a few perspectives of change. Secondly, we will focus on the new generation of French entrepreneurs and SME owner-managers in order to show that their emergence is linked to a certain extent to ongoing institutional changes. Even though these new entrepreneurs seem to be innovative managers, we will show, through the example of engineers, that SMEs and their managers generally combine both innovation and reproduction attributes.

6.2   Small- and medium-sized enterprises in France

In this section, we will first attempt to give a precise representation of the distribution of SMEs in terms of sectors and jobs (6.2.1). Then we will underline the main contributions of these SMEs, especially as regards employment and innovation (6.2.2). Thirdly, we will look at the specificities of SMEs in relation to their managers' profiles (6.2.3). Finally, we will conclude by discussing several key issues and perspectives of change (6.2.4).

6.2.1 First insights based on quantitative data

Official figures reveal that on 1 January 2005[4], there were about 2,613,000 SMEs with less than 250 employees in the sectors of industry, trade and services in France.[5] Five years earlier (1 January 2000), there were 2,284,000. Therefore, a 14 per cent increase occurred over this time period (OSEO 2006).[6] This sharp increase can be explained by the rising number of business start-ups over the last few years[7], and by the stability of the failure rate, which has remained around 2 per cent of the total number of companies in the last five years.

Table 6.1 presents the distribution of companies by sector and number of employees and shows the evolution of venture creation in the last five years. It also highlights three sectors that have experienced significant

Table 6.1 Distribution of French companies (1 January 2005) by number of employees and activity sector

Activity sector	0	1–9	10–49	50–99	100–249	250+	Total
Food industry	20,520	36,980	6130	660	480	320	65,090
Industry (except food industry)	82,770	65,620	26,790	3970	2750	1710	183,600
Construction	178,710	149,460	23,460	1400	640	260	353,930
Wholesale/ retail	347,610	252,760	37,730	3670	1810	830	644,400
Transport	52,740	24,920	8980	1200	730	370	88,940
Real estate	58,260	22,500	2310	90	40	20	83,220
Professional services	295,250	121,970	23,370	2430	1390	1040	445,440
Services (to individuals)	226,730	165,150	17,250	1030	370	230	410,760
Education, health, social activities	267,520	68,810	5010	620	390	140	342,500
Total	1,530,110	908,180	151,010	15,050	8600	4910	2,617,870

Source: INSEE (French National Institute for Economic Statistics – www.insee.fr)

growth over the same period: real-estate, construction, and professional services; whereas the transport sector has diminished. These national data hide regional disparities that can be quite significant in terms of SME density and business start-up rates. Geographic and economic dividing lines separate northern from southern, rural from urban, and touristic from non-touristic areas (OSEO 2006).

Around 30 per cent of the total number of companies proposes services to individuals; one in six is a wholesaler or retailer. In terms of jobs, independent firms that employ fewer than 250 employees account for 55 per cent of the working population (employees and self-employed), whereas 10 per cent work in subsidiaries of large companies and 35 per cent in large companies (OSEO 2006). SMEs with fewer than 20 employees account for 37 per cent of the employed population. 35 per cent of firms employ fewer than ten people, while 58 per cent have no staff. Consequently, more than one in two wholesale or retail businesses (54 per cent) and one in three firms specialized in professional services rely solely on the activity of the manager (OSEO 2006). In 2005, 86.5 per cent of all business start-ups in France generated only one job – that of the entrepreneur.

6.2.2 Role and importance of SMEs in the French economic system

Although many approaches can be taken towards the analysis of these data, we will focus on the role and importance of French SMEs by looking closely into their contribution to employment and innovation.

SMEs and job-creation

Although the 2005–6 period has been identified as particularly favourable to employment by the *INSEE* (French National Institute for Economic Statistics), SMEs have been particularly dynamic in this regard despite the fact that it can be difficult to evaluate their contribution precisely. In 2005 in France, companies of over 250 employees represented around 2 per cent of the total number of firms and employed 9 per cent of the working population, whereas independent firms from of up to 250 employees (55 per cent of companies) represented 9 million employees and self-employed people while producing 40 per cent of the added value of the French economy.

Moreover, if one examines the evolution of employment over a longer period of time, one will notice a significant increase in employment in small-sized structures. Over a period of 13 years (1990–2003), companies with more than 500 employees witnessed an increase of 5 per cent in their staff, that is, fewer than 200,000 new employees. Over the same period of time, companies with fewer than 500 employees increased their staff by 40 per cent – approximately 3 million new employees (OSEO 2006).

However, not all SMEs contribute to job creation to the same extent. A July 2006 study of the *Conseil D'analyse Économique* (French Council of Economic Analysis) shows that some companies, the 'gazelles' (around 20,000 in France), created 582,000 jobs between 1993–2003. Compared with the 1,115,000 jobs created by the total number of SMEs over the same period, this comprises 52 per cent of the total number of jobs created (Betbèze and Saint Étienne 2006).

SMEs and innovation

According to the fourth Community Innovation Survey (CIS4) focusing on the innovative activities of non-agricultural trading companies of ten or more employees between 2002 and 2004, almost one in two French companies made innovations during this period.[8] Innovations in this survey comprised products, processes, or organization and distribution methods.

The results of this fourth survey confirm the results from the previous studies: company size and tendency to innovate are linked; 43 per cent of small-sized companies (between ten and 49 employees), 59 per cent of medium-sized companies (between 50 and 249 employees) and 76 per cent of large companies (250 and more) made innovations.

SMEs tend to innovate more in the industrial, banking and insurance sectors. Their innovations concern mainly organizational methods and some of the more traditional products and fabrication processes.

Innovative SMEs commit 1–1.3 per cent of their turnover to research and development programmes and to the acquisition of new machines and knowledge. They are also significantly more open to international markets and contribute largely to the total turnover of French SMEs of similar size.

6.3   SME owner-managers – types and profiles

The specificities of SMEs can be studied from various angles. Torrès (2003), for instance, adopted an original approach by studying the size of firms and the inverse proportional importance of proximity effects[9] within them. As for our approach, we have chosen here to focus on SME managers in a typological perspective in relation to innovativeness. We distinguish between two main types of SME owner-managers: 'innovators' and 'reproducers'.

6.3.1   First insights

Numerous typologies are available that characterize SME managers. Weber (1988) identifies two categories in a study that clearly opposes two different profiles: a) 'innovators' and b) 'reproducers'.

1. Entrepreneurs are owner-managers characterized by a capitalist spirit and entrepreneurial culture and who are also strongly innovative.
2. Family-business owners are characterized by their family culture and, in some cases, consider the family business simply as a source of regular income. Often routine-oriented, conservative and authoritarian, the majority of SME owner-managers fall into this category.

Other studies distinguish three different paths to becoming an industrial SME manager (Bunel and Saglio 1979). These various paths determine as many types of managers: *founders*, who have little or no qualification and own the capital; *heirs and heiresses*, who have little qualification in the first generation but increasingly high qualifications as the generational distance to the founder increases and who share ownership with other members of the family; and *engineers*, who graduate from prestigious schools but do not have a share in the ownership of the company. At the beginning of the 1980s, a fourth type of manager emerged: *raiders*. Most raiders worked as executives in SMEs. When the opportunity arose (as in bankruptcy) to take over the company in which they were employed (or another), they seized it, thus becoming owner-managers (Saglio 1984). The two former types of managers behave in more traditional and conservative ways and are more like reproducers than the later two types, who are most interested in innovative behaviours. Both studies from Weber (1988) and Bunel and Saglio (1979) lead us to focus on two categories of SME owner-managers: the reproducers and the innovators.

6.3.2   Two categories of SME owner-managers

In this section, we will look closely at two categories of SME owner-managers: reproducers and innovators.

The reproducer

In his vision of economy and industry, Jean-Baptiste Say (1972) distinguishes three main actors: the scientist who studies nature; the entrepreneur who benefits from and uses the scientist's knowledge to create useful products for society; and the worker who works under the supervision of both. To a certain extent, the reproducer is Say's worker who applies the scientist's discoveries and inventions into successful innovations by the entrepreneur.

The *Centre de Recherche Euro PME* (Euro SME Research Centre, part of the ESC Rennes School of Business) carried out a study of 601 French SME owners, which focused on an essential element of the manager's behaviour: his or her capacity to anticipate or follow[10] the changes of the environment (Duchéneaut 1997). This study showed that the average age of 'reproducers' is 46 and that they work mainly in the industrial and trade sectors. They do not really export, and their vision of competition is mainly regional. They are also not particularly oriented towards the growth or development of their company.

The innovator

For Joseph Schumpeter (1935) individuals who are capable of innovating deserve to be called entrepreneurs. These individuals are creative and show initiative and strong will. The 'innovator', according to Jean-Baptiste Say (1972), is a dynamic economic agent with a strong rationality and the capability of safeguarding the general balance.

For this type of manager, building, creating and imagining as well as informing, communicating and listening are essential abilities strongly linked to development and innovation (Duchéneaut 1997). These skills are also highly representative of a management style that relies more on training than experience.

According to the same study by the Euro SME Research Centre, innovative SME owner-managers have a more or less precise medium-term vision; and the vast majority are willing to make profound changes in their company in the near future. Most of them are members of professional organizations or are actively involved in associations.

In comparison with the reproducers – as presented previously – we note that innovative managers are noticeably younger. The origin of ownership is very specific, too: few innovators inherit their business, even fewer take them over, and thus most of them are founders.

Another essential and significant difference between innovators and reproducers is their will to develop their companies (60 per cent for innovators in comparison to 26 per cent for reproducers).

6.3.3 Key issues and new perspectives

A 2003 study by the Ifop institute (*French Market Research Institute*)[11] of SME managers showed that out of the 843 people interviewed, 76 per cent plan to sell and 24 per cent plan to pass on their companies within the next five years. According to European Commission sources (2003) and the *Direction Générale des Entreprises* (Directorate General for Enterprise), 450,000 businesses in France will have changed hands by 2013.

A business transmission is a delicate operation, not only as regards legal or fiscal matters, but also the risk of serious social and economic problems for company's development. For many years questions of transmission and succession have been the subject of serious concern for SME owners and those who advise and support them. The influence of SME managers on management culture and practices is a well-established fact. Owner-manager qualifications and profiles play an important role in their ability to open up to new management concepts and strategic orientations for their firms.

The above figures give us an idea of the scale of this business transmission phenomenon and how crucial the issue is. We would like to note here that the issue of transmission and takeover in France is often approached from the angle of the age pyramid as well as from the social and societal acknowledgement of the effects of an aging population (Gilles Lévy 2007).[12] This author does not question the number of business owners who will reach the age of retirement in the next few years. However, he questions the number of companies that can effectively be transmitted.

This leads us to another question regarding the structure of SMEs in France and its consequence for the economic situation of the country. Even though SMEs play a great role in creating jobs and developing innovation in a broader sense in France (as discussed in section 6.2.2), according to Betbèze and Saint-Étienne (2006), the French economy seems badly affected by three shortages: a lack of job creation; a lack of exports; and a lack of research and development in firms, especially in private firms and even more so in SMEs. They argue that these shortfalls originate in the insufficient number of medium-sized businesses (between 50 and 500 employees[13]), which in turn produces an insufficient number of small French groups (between 500 and 3,000 employees). France lacks 'gazelles', those high-growth SMEs that generally employ 20 to 250 staff members (or 20 to 500 staff members in a broader definition). Indeed, we believe that conditions necessary for the creation of this type of firm should be improved and reinforced in order to ensure their growth and development. Among these conditions, the emergence of new entrepreneurs in French SMEs could play a significant role.

6.4   Emergence of new entrepreneurs in French SMEs

The emergence of a new generation of owner-managers is not only a demographic issue but is also linked to institutional changes in the educational system and on the graduate job market (6.4.1). We will look at the new generation of owner-managers who possess higher qualifications and are more prone to adopting behaviours oriented towards innovation and growth (6.4.2). We will conclude this section by showing that, even though higher education is correlated with innovation, the factors behind the emergence of this type of behaviour appear to be far more complex (6.4.3).

6.4.1 Institutional changes in the educational system and the job market

In France since the beginning of the 1990s, society has expressed much apprehension as regards its difficulties in facing a reality far removed from the reality of the Glorious Thirties (Le Goff 2006). The globalization of the economy and its impact in terms of necessary adaptations and unwanted consequences, such as the precariousness of employment, has fuelled mistrust and suspicion in social relations; this mistrust is focused on the elites, the state and its institutions.

For certain categories of employees, executives in particular, other factors have reinforced this negative feeling towards the opening of the market.[14] Executives benefit from better protection than the rest of employees when it comes to redundancy, thanks mainly to their qualifications and degrees. Although the unemployment rate for this group is three times lower than the national average, figures show that the risk of losing their jobs has increased steadily since the beginning of the 1990s approaching the same rate as that of other employees and workers (Maurin 2002). Moreover, today they represent 15 per cent of the working population, versus 4.7 per cent in 1962 and 10.7 per cent in 1990 (Dupuy 2005). Executives are more and more numerous and their status increasingly resembles that of simple employees. Finally, the law on the 35-hour work week has hit them very hard by compelling them to work faster, not better. This is how, 'contrary to forecasts (...) we have not witnessed a general extension of leisure time, but a displacement of the work load towards better-qualified categories of workers' (Chenu and Herpin 2002).

The categories of employees with the highest degrees and qualifications, who had benefited the most from the Glorious Thirties when the priority of firms was to work for the good of their employees, are now becoming the first victims of the new situation (Dupuy 2005). One of the effects of globalization has been to reverse the relation of power between suppliers and their customers. This translates into the domination of customers followed closely by that of shareholders.

In short, the educational system produces increasingly more graduates who feed the legions of executives who are hardly or not at all protected by their organizations and are more and more exposed to the fluctuations of the market. Graduation from the 'Grandes Ecoles' does not guarantee top-positions in large firms anymore. The disintegration of labour spares no one, apart from those who can leave employment and, thanks to their qualifications and knowledge, determine their own destiny and working conditions (Dupuy 2005). These fundamental changes, which began more than 30 years ago, lead these categories of employees to consider more seriously the possibility of starting up their own businesses or taking over existing firms and drive them away from more traditional career orientations.

6.4.2   A new generation of French entrepreneurs

Numerous studies of SME manager qualifications and training profiles in France seem to indicate the emergence of a new type of entrepreneur. This new entrepreneur benefits from a higher level of education, notably owing to higher degrees from business and engineering schools and universities (Duchéneaut 1997).

A study led by Silvestre and Goujet (1995) in Rhône-Alpes illustrates this trend. This study identifies three types of SME managers. First, self-taught managers without qualifications and who, at best, have their *Baccalaureat* (French secondary-school diploma). This category of manager is fundamentally a founder who created his or her company a long time ago. The second category includes multiple-experienced managers. They usually completed engineering studies and reached the position of owner-manager by taking over the company or following their designation by shareholders. They acquired their experience in middle-management positions or by managing businesses. The last category is a sort of stable administrator. These managers typically graduated from a business school or a business university. They became business managers through family transmission or internal promotion, and they acquired their previous professional experience in another position in the company that they now own and manage. In this sample, the proportion of graduate managers is significant and represents 83 per cent of the total.

The training of business owners, their previous experience and how they came to own and manage a business all play an important role in their adopting innovative or reproductive behaviours. A study led by Duchéneaut (1997) provides first insights into the distribution of these behaviours in relation to the level of education. One can note that the higher the degree, the more innovative the SME manager. Among the graduates, one finds a large proportion of business and engineering-school graduates. Finally, one can note that engineering graduates are present in equal numbers among reproducers and innovators, whereas the number of business-school students is twice as high among the innovators as reproducers.

Another study shows that factors related to strategic management and the level of education of managers are important determinants of technological innovation in manufacturing SMEs (Bechelkh et al. 2006). In a slightly different approach, Aghion and Cohen (2004) attempted to demonstrate causal links between education and growth at the national level.

In conclusion, a recent study that we completed in France in 2006[15] confirms that the new generation of owner-managers is better qualified and, consequently, perhaps more prone to innovation than reproduction. Nine out of 13 owner-managers we met were graduates (two engineers, five business-school graduates, and two university graduates).

6.4.3   Towards more innovation or reproduction?

The results of a study we carried out at the end of the 1990s on the careers of French engineering graduates may help us better understand the logic of the career path and its consequences on innovative and reproductive behaviours (Fayolle 2001; 2006). In what follows, engineer-entrepreneurs can be likened to SME owner-managers. We have tried to better understand the way engineers reached the position of business owner-managers. We also noticed that the paths taken were not without an effect on their innovative or reproductive behaviours.

The sample we used can be divided into four sub-groups:[16]

- 157 engineers who had never been entrepreneurs and had never wanted to become entrepreneurs (type A);
- 135 engineers who had never been entrepreneurs and who no longer wanted to become entrepreneurs (type B);
- 186 engineers who had never been entrepreneurs but who wanted to become entrepreneurs (type C);
- 182 engineer-entrepreneurs who had created or taken over at least one business (type D). In this last group, 143 were still entrepreneurs at the time of the study.

To better understand the various career paths taken by engineers who become entrepreneurs, we studied more closely the group of 182 engineer-entrepreneurs (type D), which enabled us to identify three main types or profiles of engineer-entrepreneurs with specific career paths and entrepreneurial behaviours:

- 71 type X engineer-entrepreneurs;
- 87 type Y engineer-entrepreneurs;
- 24 type Z engineer-entrepreneurs.

Career paths of the engineers in our sample

Figure 6.1 shows career paths of the engineers in our sample. Two main paths can be distinguished as regards the entrepreneurial dimension. The first path (path 1) represents the young engineering graduate who develops a career without any entrepreneurial intention. The second path corresponds to the young engineering graduate who, after a few years of professional experience, sees entrepreneurship as a possible career option (path 2). After taking a closer look at these itineraries, we will present in more detail what profiles of engineer-entrepreneurs they correspond to.

First possible itinerary

The first path (path 1) corresponds to the situation of engineers who belong to type A. Type A engineers are aged 45 on average with around 20 years' professional experience. They have a small family, often come from a family in which the father was an engineer himself and

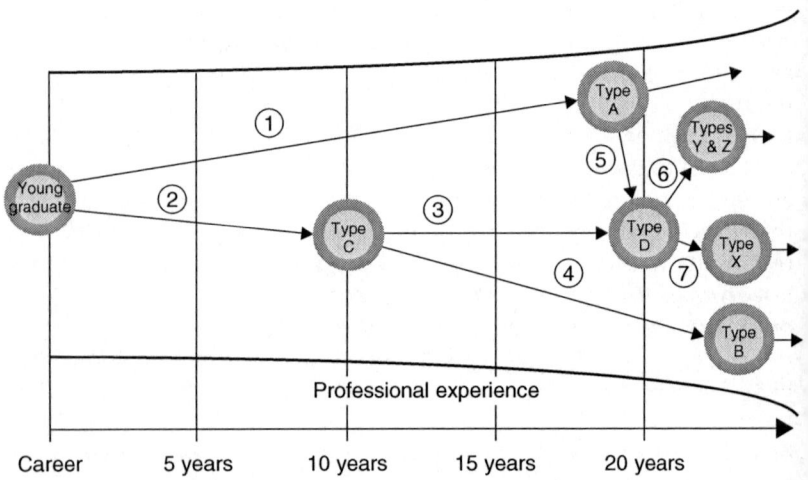

Figure 6.1   Possible paths

have a solid scientific and technical background. Type A engineers have little geographical and professional mobility and their preferences as well as their career orientation are closely related to the technical dimension. Their professional identity is based on technical and scientific expertise, values and references. Type A engineers do not wish to become entrepreneurs, and they do not consider the possibility of an entrepreneurial career. However, accidents or events in their professional life may lead them to reconsider their position and follow this path despite having had no particular vocation hitherto. These accidents and events may be linked to situations of redundancy, professional dissatisfaction or the desire to complete a technical project they could not complete within the company in which they were employed. Type A engineers commit to entrepreneurship, trough discontinuity and displacement. Their motivation can be described as being 'negative' (Shapero and Sokol 1982). When type A engineers actually become entrepreneurs, they capitalize on their scientific and technical knowledge and skills.

Second possible itinerary

The second path represents engineers who early on had the intention of becoming entrepreneurs (path 2). These type C engineers are potential entrepreneurs, aged 35 on average, and have about ten years' professional experience. Type C engineers have followed complementary training, principally in the fields of business administration and management, which has given them a good vision of the company environment and its relative complexity. They are professionally and geographically mobile and have occupied various positions, including some in non-technical fields. Their professional identity is built on supervision and hierarchy. Managerial values are predominant for them. Type C engineers attach a lot of importance to professional orientations in relation to business administration and management. Their future may, therefore, lead them to realize their intention of becoming entrepreneurs, or confirm them in their career choice of employment in management positions in SMEs or large firms. In this case, the professional orientation they favour is that of hierarchy and management. These possible itineraries are represented in Figure 6.1 by paths 3 and 4, which respectively show type C engineers becoming either engineer-entrepreneurs (type D), or engineers who no longer desire to become entrepreneurs (type B). This last situation is that of satisfied engineers who once wanted to become entrepreneurs and changed their mind for various reasons that may be linked to their family, personal or professional environment.

Type B engineers represent the oldest age group (48 years on average) in our sample and have around 23 years' professional experience on average. They carry a large amount of family responsibilities and have acquired important management skills and qualifications. They have favoured hierarchy and management in the various positions they have occupied, most of the time in large companies. Type B engineers are professionally and geographically mobile. They look for security and stability in their career choices and attach great importance to the prestige of the position and the visibility of their status and achievements. Their professional attachment is strongly marked, and they display a high level of professional satisfaction.

Itineraries of engineer-entrepreneurs

Engineer-entrepreneurs (type D) are on average a little over 47 years old and have around 22 years' professional experience. They benefit from wide-ranging complementary training and professional experience acquired in various positions and situations, and are professionally mobile.

When engineers become entrepreneurs they can be positioned on an axis that separates the technical and managerial poles. This position is linked to the engineers' career development process, as described by Robin (1994), Bouffartigue (1994), Riverin-Simard (1984) and Lojkine (1992). When they move into entrepreneurship, engineers may be at a technical stage in their career or out of the technical field and at least partially involved in managerial and administrative roles. We have identified three different profiles of engineer-entrepreneurs (X, Y, and Z) in our sample. Their positions are illustrated in Figure 6.2.

The engineer-entrepreneur can have a marked technical positioning. We will call this type of engineer-entrepreneur 'technical engineer-entrepreneur' (this status concerns types Y and Z[17]). If the engineer has a marked managerial positioning, we will designate this profile as 'managerial engineer-entrepreneur' (this status concerns type X). In our opinion, the 'managerial engineer-entrepreneur' is principally the product of paths 2 and 3 in Figure 6.1, whereas the 'technical engineer-entrepreneur' results from path 1. 'Managerial engineer-entrepreneurs' are innovative entrepreneurs to the extent that they develop innovations in the broad sense of the term. These engineer-entrepreneurs rely less on their technical capital than the 'technical engineer-entrepreneurs' and their technical specialization does not necessarily determine the activity sector of the business they start up or take over. Their professional identity is focused on management and hierarchy whereas that of

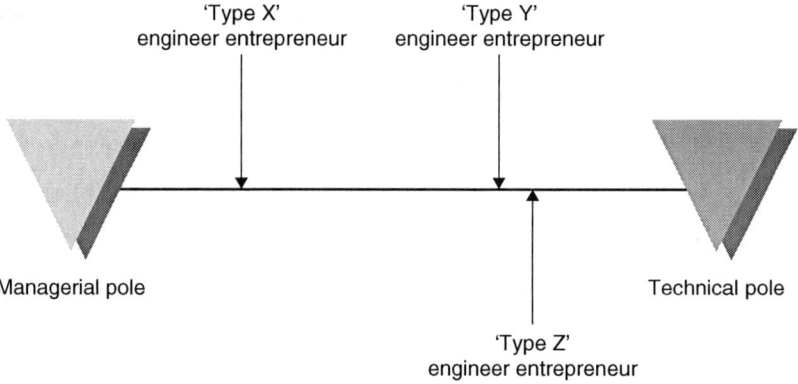

Figure 6.2   Positioning of the various types of entrepreneurs

'technical engineer-entrepreneurs' is more focused on expertise and technique. 'Technical engineer entrepreneurs' display reproducer behaviours and use their technical capital in windows of opportunity that are more closely linked to their previous professional experience and their engineering specialization. These engineer-entrepreneurs behave in a marked technical and professional continuity.

The positioning of the various profiles of engineers in relation to the managerial and technical poles has an influence on the type of activity they choose and the behaviours they adopt. The further engineers are from the technical pole, the more prone they are to creating firms in tertiary activity sectors that are unrelated to their previous professional experience. They display less reproductive behaviours and the innovations they develop are more closely linked to services and products than technology.[18] 'Managerial engineer-entrepreneurs' rely more on relational resources and less on technical capital. The opposite is true for 'technical engineer-entrepreneurs'.

6.5   Conclusion

Demographic changes (the arrival of a new generation of entrepreneurs to compensate for the mass retirement of the 'baby-boom' generation of entrepreneurs), structural and technological changes (the boom in tertiary activities, role of new information and communication technologies) and, finally, cultural transformations (the re-evaluation of entrepreneurship) are affecting the world of SMEs. Simultaneously, the educational system and the job market are experiencing similar upheavals with the lengthening of education, the increasing number of graduates and the high rate of unemployment among young people – including graduates. All these changes are converging towards the emergence of a new category of company founders and managers with higher qualifications and better training. They seem to be bearers of a new vision of the business world.

Among these new entrepreneurs, graduates with higher education are not like any other SME owner-managers. Up to now, their training as well as their intellectual and social capital has oriented them towards careers and jobs that were largely outside the scope of SMEs and new venture creation. The training they received shaped their behaviours and over-developed their rational capacities. Those who reached the position of SME owner-managers did so as a result of strong motivation, influence of their family environment, as an escape from dead-end situations, or as a result of career 'accidents'.

Generally, graduates have not been specifically prepared to innovate or become entrepreneurs. The diversity of their career paths constitutes pools of opportunities and innovations on which they can draw. However, it seems more crucial than ever that French society should think about the best ways to direct and use the scientific, technological and managerial knowledge, know-how and skills of these new would-be SME owner-managers.

In this chapter, we have looked at some of the institutional changes that are appearing in France as well as their demographic, strategic and managerial consequences for SMEs. We believe it is necessary to go further and research the interactions between these changes at various levels and how they translate into career orientations and careers of graduates. Finally, the next step should be a closer study of the SME management strategies and methods of these new entrepreneurs.

Notes

1. In OEC (2003) Créer, Développer, Pérenniser, Transmettre, 58ème Congrès de l'Ordre des Experts Comptables (OEC), français, 25–27 September.
2. Ibid.
3. There is no unique definition of what a 'small- and medium-sized' enterprise is. For a long time in France we have considered SMEs to be firms with a size between 10 and 500 employees. In 1996, the European Union proposed the following classification: from 0 to 9 employees are micro-enterprises; from 10 to 49, small enterprises; from 50 to 249, medium-sized enterprises; more than 250, large enterprises. Depending on the literature we have used in this

work, SMEs can be presented differently. In any case, we will mention the definition or classification on which the research or the study we are quoting is based.

4. The figures rise to 3.2 million if we include the agricultural sector.
5. Even if international comparisons are not always easy, we notice some differences between European countries when examining data from the data base *Eurostat Newcronos*. For example, in the South of Europe countries such as France, Italy and Spain highlight a higher percentage of micro-enterprises (0–9 employees) than countries located in the North such as Germany or UK. The 2001 figures for France, Italy and Spain are 91.6 per cent, 94.9 per cent and 94.4 per cent, respectively, while they constitute 82.3 per cent in Germany and 85.7 per cent in the UK. Inversely, in the later countries the percentages of small- and medium-sized companies (10–249 employees) are higher than those from the South of Europe. For instance, the percentage of medium-sized enterprises (50–249 employees) in 2001 was 1.2 per cent in France, 1.9 per cent in the UK and 2.4 per cent in Germany.
6. OSEO is an organization specialized in financing and supporting entrepreneurial projects and SMEs in particular.
7. New business start-ups have increased by 26 per cent compared to the figures in 2002.
8. The data for France is available on the SESSI website (*Service des Études et Statistiques Industrielles* – Industrial Studies and Statistics Office): http://www.industrie.gouv.fr; for the 25 European countries, see the Eurostat website: http://epp.eurostat.cec.eu.int.
9. The proximity effect is a concept proposed by Olivier Torres that means a very close and affective relationship between the owner-manager and his/her firm.
10. We prefer the terms 'innovator' and 'reproducer' to the terms 'anticipator' and 'follower' used by Bertrand Duchéneaut.
11. Study ordered by the *Conseil Supérieur de l'Ordre des Experts-Comptables* (French institute of chartered accountants), the *Agence pour la Création d'Entreprise* (APCE – French business start-up agency) and the *Assemblée des Chambres Françaises de Commerce et d'Industrie* (Assembly of French Chambers of Commerce and Industry).
12. http://www.agoravox.fr/article.php3?id_article=21965
13. This classification comes from Betbèze and Saint-Etienne. It is not ours or that from the EU.
14. Here the word 'executive' refers to the French notion of '*cadre*', which corresponds to an official status in French law. '*Cadres*' refers to graduate employees who generally occupy middle-management positions in companies and administrations.
15. Our sample consists of 13 French firms. The data were collected in face to face interviews. The firms in the sample were founded between 1840 and 1981; their activities are located in different industrial sectors such as metallurgy or mechanics. Among them, five have less than 50 employees, five have about 100 employees and, finally, three have between 250 and 500 employees. The average age of the managers we interviewed is 39.
16. The four sub-groups that are presented here were determined at the time of the survey based on the respondent answer to a specific question. It does

not mean, however, that these positions could not change over time. For example, engineers belonging to the types A and B who had never been entrepreneurs at the interviewed could change their mind and adopt an entrepreneurial position later on.

17. Engineers belonging to the type Z are older and more anchored in the technical dimension than those belonging to the type Y. Their entrepreneurial behaviours are based on resource control orientation and technological reproduction. They innovate much more in process technologies and manage businesses in industry and high-technology. For more details, see Fayolle (2006).

18. Conversely, a closer positioning to the technical pole will tend to entail radical technological innovations.

References

Aghion, P. and E. Cohen (2004) *Education et croissance* (Paris: La Documentation Française).

Bauer, M. and B. Bertin-Mourot (1987) *Les 200. Comment devient-on un grand patron?* (Paris: Editions du seuil).

Betbèze, J. P. and C. Saint-Étienne (2006) *Une stratégie pour la France: favoriser l'essor des gazelles, entreprises moyennes en forte croissance*, http://www.cae.gouv.fr.

Bechelkh, N. R. Landry and N. Amara (2006) 'Les facteurs stratégiques affectant l'innovation technologique dans les PME manufacturières', *Canadian Journal of Administrative Sciences*, 23(4), 275–300.

Bouffartigue, P. (1994) 'Ingénieurs débutants à l'épreuve du modèle de carrière', *Revue Française de Sociologie*, 35(1), 69–100.

Bourdieu, P. (1989) *La noblesse d'Etat. Grandes Ecoles et esprit de corps* (Paris: Les éditions de minuit).

Bruyat, C. (1993), 'Création d'entreprise: contributions épistémologiques et modélisation', PhD thesis in Mangement Science, Université Pierre Mendès France, Grenoble II.

Bunel, J. and J. Saglio (1979) *L'action patronale, du CNPF au petit patron* (Paris: PUF).

Chenu, A. and N. Herpin (2002) 'Une pause dans la civilisation des loisirs', *Economie et Statistique*, 352–53, 15–37.

Duchéneaut, B. (1997) 'Les dirigeants de PME "anticipateurs/innovateurs" et "suiveurs"': une typologie comparative', research paper, Rennes School of Business.

Dupuy, F. (2005) *La fatigue des élites. Le capitalisme et ses cadres* (Paris: La République des Idées/Le Seuil).

Fauconnier, P. (1996) *Le talent qui dort* (Paris: Editions du Seuil).

Favier, J. (1987) *De l'or et des épices* (Paris: Fayard).

Fayolle, A. (2001) 'D'une approche typologique de l'entrepreneuriat chez les ingénieurs à la reconstruction d'itinéraires d'ingénieurs entrepreneurs', *Revue de l'entrepreneuriat*, 1(1), 77–98.

Fayolle, A. (2006) 'Engineers as High-Tech Entrepreneurs: French Engineers' Paths to Entrepreneurship', in M. Bernasconi, S. Harris, M. Moensted (eds), *High-Tech Entrepreneurship*, (London: Routledge), 50–68.

Gilles, L. (2007) Idées reçues sur la reprise d'entreprise, AGORA Le media citoyen, arrie,<http://www.agoravox.fr/article.ph3?id_article=21965, downloaded 2 May 2008.

Iribarne, d', P. (2006) *L'étrangeté Française* (Paris: Editions du Seuil).

Laufer, J. (1975) 'Comment on devient entrepreneur', *Revue Française de gestion*, 2, 11–26.

Le Goff, J. P. (2006) 'Les lendemains de la révolte', *Le Nouvel Observateur*, 20–26 April, 98–9.

Lojkine, J. (1992) *Les jeunes diplômés: un groupe social en quête d'identité* (Paris: PUF)

Maurice, M., F. Sellier and J. J. Silvestre (1982) *Politique d'éducation et organisation industrielle en France et en Allemagne* (Paris: PUF).

Maurin, E. (2002) *L'Egalité des possibles* (Paris: La République des Idées/Le Seuil).

OEC (2003) 'Créer, Développer, Pérenniser, Transmettre', 58ème Congrès de l'Ordre des Experts Comptables, 25–27 September.

OSEO (2006) *PME 2006* (Paris: La Documentation Française).

Ribeill, G. (1984) 'Entreprendre hier et aujourd'hui: la contribution des ingénieurs', *Culture Technique*, 12, 77–92.

Riverin-Simard, D. (1984) *Etapes de vie au travail* (Montréal: Editions Saint Martin).

Robin, J.-Y. (1994) *Radioscopie de cadres: itinéraire professionnel et biographie éducative* (Paris: l'Harmattan).

Saglio, J. (1984) 'Les ingénieurs sont-ils des patrons comme les autres?', *Culture Technique*, 12, 93–101.

Say, J.-B. (1972) *Traité d'économie politique* (Paris: Calman-Lévy).

Schumpeter, J. (1935) *Théorie de l'évolution économique* éditions Dalloz.

Shapero, A. and L. Sokol (1982) 'The Social Dimensions of Entrepreneurship', in *Encyclopaedia of Entrepreneurship* (Engelwood Cliffs: Prentice Hall, Inc.), 82–113.

Silvestre, H. and R. Goujet (1995) 'Approche typologique du tissu industriel des PMI indépendantes et filiales de groupe de la région Rhône-alpes, à partir de facteurs constituant la démarche stratégique de leurs dirigeants', IRE research papers (ESC Lyon), September.

Torrès, O. (2003) 'Petitesse des entreprises et grossissement des effets de proximité', *Revue Française de Gestion*, 29(144), 119–38.

Weber, H. (1988) 'Cultures patronales et types d'entreprises: esquisse d'une typologie du patronat', *Sociologie du travail*, 4, 558–66.

7
Family Business and Family Change: The End of Patriarchalism

Hermann Kotthoff

7.1 Introduction

The EQUA-Foundation, or 'Family-Owner Qualification Academy' (*Eigentümer-Qualifizierungs-Akademie*), offers training for family business owners, especially those of the younger generation. To quote the EQUA website: Family Business! Business Family! These terms mean stability, tradition, responsibility. Family businesses are more successful in the long run. Their main success factor is the owner family. But the owner family is as well the main risk factor for the family business. Quarrels, misunderstandings regarding succession, disputes about dividends and family fights threaten the stability of the business, which depends not only on economic conditions but also on the solidarity within the owner family. What are the configurations that lead to conflict between family-shareholders? And what are the means to securing peace in the family and, thereby, the stability of the firm? (author's translation).

The problem described on this website is in my view the core problem of family businesses but often neglected in the research on SMEs. Peace and harmony in the family are the preconditions to a successful family business, because they guarantee stability and continuity. The appearance of EQUA underlines the importance of peace and harmony in the business family: more and more family businesses fail because of internal family quarrels that often end up – to put it in economic terms – in the unnecessary destruction of capital and jobs. That is one reason to call for alternatives, for instance, non-family shareholders, as in private equity firms. Is the better outlook for strengthening the economic power of family firms offered by 'family therapy', or by opening the door to 'greedy vultures'?

The purpose of this chapter is to show the significance of linking family business to the families behind them and to explore the ways to approach the issue.

7.2 Generational change of families in family business

In the media one finds nearly nothing concerning small family businesses. However, one finds quite a lot in the case of large family businesses, as in the 25 August 2006 *Frankfurter Allgemeine Zeitung (FAZ)*, which wrote that the large German pharmaceutical family enterprise Schwarz was likely to be up for sale. The 85-year-old founder Rolf Schwarz was quoted as saying: 'Once an owner, always an owner – you are obliged'. His 50-year-old son Patrick, and the ten other family shareholders, are of another spirit. The article describes them as cool calculators keen to make a lot of cash. Loyalty to the family business and its employees seems just not so important any more.

On the same day, the same newspaper reported that the Quandt family, one of Germany's largest family empires, had sold its pharmaceutical enterprise Altana. The article portrays the psychology of the Quandt-family daughters – who are now the main family shareholders in the fourth generation – as being very different from that of the Schwarzes, stating that 'the descendants are devoted to the dynastic philosophy', and that 'the Quandts like discretion'. There seems to be peace and solidarity in this family. The article concluded that the daughters had inherited the entrepreneurial spirit of their famous grandfather Herbert Quandt.

The same week the *FAZ* reported as well on the end of the clothing family enterprise Steilmann, which was some years ago Europe's largest ladies' garment firm. Once more there were remarkable insinuations about the family's psychological situation. The founder Klaus Steilmann is supposed to have had an early inclination to the 'Buddenbrook syndrome', that is, a penchant for the fine arts, culture and sports. For this he earned a doctorate *honoris causa*. Of the two successor daughters a newspaper has written:

> Since the 'patriarch' left the company, there has been a lack of continuity due to constant conceptual changes and replacements in top level management. Of all the top managers, daughter Britta was the most charismatic. When she entered the company for the second time in 2001, she was celebrated as a 'business savvy, cost-cutting manager with sex appeal'. She created a line of environmentally friendly

clothing, restructured the corporation and still found time to be ever-present in the German media. As Britta handed control over to her sister Ute in 2003, she argued that the restructuring was completed and new managers were firmly in place. However, three years later, the family is faced with the ruins of what was once a big enterprise (FAZ, 22 August 2006).

The message is quite clear – here the Steilmann daughters, there the Quandt daughters – two opposite types of female family-owners. The former failed because of extravagance and gossip, the latter succeeded through reliability and loyalty to the dynastic spirit.

Why examine such newspaper stories? We hear almost nothing from science about the family life of family-business owners. The business family is a black box. There is the sociology of the family, the psychology of the family and those of business – but they are not talking to each other. There are the classic German centres for SME research (*Mittelstandsforschung*), but these take 'the family in the family business' for granted and do not invest in the topic. As the Australian social scientist Michael Gilding points out: 'It is curious that researchers have almost completely overlooked the relationship between family business and family' (2000: 241). The accountancy house PricewaterhouseCoopers (2005: 15) writes in a report on owner succession: 'It is a well-confirmed assumption that succession processes are mainly an emotional problem. But there are no researchers who pay attention to this aspect.'

While sociological and economic research has neglected the subject until now, in other fields the topic has already become important. Leading business schools, business consultants and family therapists consider relationships in the family the key to understanding family businesses. The small amount of available literature comes mainly from these fields. It is estimated that in the US nearly 100 universities, management schools and colleges offer further education and training in family business ownership.

As for German-speaking countries, the following institutes, all established within the last few years, are devoted to family-business ownership:

- Deutsche Bank Institut für Familienunternehmen, University of Witten-Herdecke;
- Center of Family Business, Hochschule St. Gallen, Switzerland. Training topics there include: 'Conflict and emotions in family business'; 'Socialization impact of family business on youth personality

and career motives'; 'Leadership satisfaction in family business as a motivator of organizations'.

- Center of Family Business of the Otto Beisheim School of Management, Vallendar;
- European Family Business Center of the European Business School, Schloss Reichartshausen;
- the above-mentioned EQUA-Foundation, Herrsching a. Ammersee;

Particularly the consultant houses Ernst&Young and Pricewaterhouse-Coopers have reported regularly on succession issues. In 2000 a group of German family therapists organized the first congress on 'The family of the family business' in Heidelberg. These institutes and activities seem to indicate that the modern family business has a problem that did not exist some 40 years ago.

From a theoretical and conceptual point of view, there are two ways of structuring the study of the business family, namely according to either:

1. the *psychodynamics* of the business family, which is seen as a special type of family that develops particular priorities or in a particular direction. The core questions are the continuity and the *life cycle of the family*. Characteristic for this type of family is an increased demand for collective behaviour and solidarity and a particular attitude towards individualism and personal autonomy; or
2. the presently occurring changes in family structure in the western world and their impact on the *social dynamics of business families*. The important issues here are value change, increasing individualism, democracy and partnership in the family, the new role of women and, above all, the rapid increase in divorce rates, numbers of couples without children, and single parents.

7.2.1 The life-cycle approach

A good description and deep analysis of the first approach can be found in the work of some economic historians. While some, of course, might question what we can learn from history for our time, for me this is the most profitable way to investigate the black box.

Hartmut Berghoff (1997) excellently analysed the Hohner business family and identified typical configurations and conflict patterns and the means to securing peace in business families. Matthias Hohner founded the business in 1857 in Trossingen, Baden-Wuerttemberg. He manufactured mouth harps (harmonicas) and accordions. In the first 20 years, the family was a small, home-industry production community. The most important labour was provided by Anna Hohner, the wife of the founder. She seemed to be the driving force behind the business. Only 20 years later, Hohner had 300 employees and was a millionaire. Anna might have retreated from this hard work to play the role of a bourgeois lady, but that was not for her: she lacked the education for upper-class habits; her hands weren't fit for piano playing. The couple walked the long road to the bourgeois life at quite a different tempo.

Life in the enterprise was mirrored, as well, in the education of the children – five sons and eight daughters. The three elder sons attended only elementary school and were integrated very early into production. The two younger sons were allowed to attend *Gymnasium* (secondary school) in Stuttgart, but they were unable to finish school because of their father's fear that they could become interested in the fine arts (like Thomas Mann's Hanno Buddenbrooks) and resulting alienation from the family business. The other daughters were sent to 'housekeeping school' to learn the bourgeois lifestyle.

For Hohner it was self-evident that all his five sons would inherit his business and become his successors in joint management. In accordance with the traditional pattern, the daughters were simply paid off as renouncing heirs. The father imposed a rigid inheritance contract on the sons, forbidding sales of their shares as well as majority decisions. That was a very narrow family concept: nobody could leave. It was more a family prison than family business. However, it functioned into the second generation, even when the conflicts became so serious that the sons communicated only in writing. The main source of conflict was the relative status of the elder and younger sons. They tried to step out of the shadow of their father and, at the same time, fulfil his will. Things that did not fit into the picture of an intact family were taboo. The divorce of the youngest son Hans, the black sheep of the family, was not even mentioned in his obituary and was left out of the family tree.

In the 1920s the succession to the third generation was arranged according to primogeniture: only the eldest son of each brother inherited the shares and succeeded as head manager. However, two of the five brothers had no sons. Therefore, three cousins, all graduates of technical universities, ran the enterprise for the next 50 years. For the first three decades they were very successful. In the 1950s, however, the succession to the fourth generation caused many problems, because two of the three cousins in the third generation had no sons. Therefore, the sons-in-law should have become successors. They had already worked in the business and were well disposed to succeed, but it was nearly impossible for them to get recognition in the family. Ernst Hohner, the eldest of the third generation, refused to make room for them until he was 80 years old. During this never-ending waiting period, the would-be successors themselves became old, but as 'only' sons-in-law they couldn't, or wouldn't, dare to force Ernst out. This succession conflict came as sales dramatically decreased in the wake of Rock and Pop music's popularity in the 1960s. In his obstinacy, Ernst remarked: 'As long as there are boys in the world, mouth harps will be played'. He hated electric guitars and refused to produce them. The agony of the enterprise lasted into the 1990s, when its remains were bought out by a Korean group.

The Hohner story contains many of the components of the inner life of a family business – above all the very different configurations of follow-up generations. In the first generation, business is about subsistence economy. It embodies the dream of its creator, who tries to fulfil its promise. This is simply a matter of economic survival: hard physical work and very long working hours. There is a nearly complete identification of the family with the business. The family is the business. Then, with the transition to the second generation, growth becomes more and more important. Above all, the desire to build a dynasty emerges. The conscious steering of the children into their role as heirs and successors is now crucial. In the third generation, we are dealing with an established enterprise with a differentiated hierarchy. In the case of Hohner, the third generation is a kind of prolongation of the second one and did not drift off track as often happens in many other cases.

The psychologists and family therapists Fischer and Retzer (2001) published a detailed interview with a German mechanical-engineering family-business owner focusing on family psychology. The business was then in its second generation and shortly before transmission to the third. Despite the historical difference of some 80 years, the similarities with the Hohner family are striking. The core statements are: 'From the very beginning our family business was the central family event', and 'The business must not become the family gameball'. Similarities exist in the following aspects: the role of the wife; the socialization and professional education of the sons; the typical 'double bind' father-sons conflict; the strong desire of the founder and his son as second-generation owner that a natural son be their successor and build a dynasty; the status conflicts of the joint-successor sons; and the heritage rules (that is, primogeniture). There is only one difference: in this case, the heritage rules caused serious conflicts among the children, especially the daughters.

The generational cycle, as in the Hohner family and the case reported by Fischer and Retzer, is the structuring pattern to which all other important aspects are oriented. Those aspects are:

- The role of the wife. Particularly in the first generation the importance of her staying power and role in the business cannot be over-stressed.
- The socialization and professional education of the children, especially those who have been designated successors. Depending on the generation, this can vary greatly. In each generation there are different personalities and types of people and families, who all have to find their place under the roof of the family business. Already by the second generation, 'family' means more and more a branched-out clan, where it is increasingly difficult to maintain cohesion and trust. To arouse the desire for succession in the children and to educate them to own and manage an enterprise are the biggest challenges for the business family.
- The tendency towards a patriarchal, narrow concept of family, including the tabooizing of conflicts. The result is the subordination of individual wishes for self-actualization to the business. Securing a dynasty in combination with a looser, more tolerant and 'democratic' concept of family is the great challenge – but also precondition – to the viability of the business family in modern times.
- An ambivalent relationship between fathers and sons that causes many conflicts – called a 'double bind'. The father persists in the belief that his son must follow in his footsteps, but at the same time has little confidence in the son's competence and belittles him. The son would like to imitate the father but feels himself handicapped. Some authors see in this pattern the cause of later physical and mental diseases of business successors.
- Social advancement and prestige (or 'cultural capital') of an entrepreneurial family is one very important aspect that is often entirely lacking in the papers of economists concerning family businesses. The strong motivation to acquire and defend this cultural capital is one of the main reasons for continuity.
- The desire for autonomy and independence.
- An order of values in which long-term goals and prospects are more important than short-term gains.

All of these aspects involve special emotional dynamics and, therefore, pose dangers to cooperation and peace in the owner family. The most typical occasions and situations in which they give rise to conflicts are:

- the distribution of the family estate inheritance – are the norms, rules or standards applied equal and fair, especially regarding the gender question, or is male priority (primogeniture) applied?
- the succession by the owners' children or other relatives to positions in the top management of the family business (active/ entrepreneurial family shareholders). Important are early planning, good timing, careful preparation, and wise advice;
- succession by owner-trusted non-relatives, as in 'management buy-outs' (MBO) or 'management buy-ins' (MBI);
- the need for profit discipline of non-active family shareholders, that is, their consent to reinvesting most of the profit in the business instead of paying out dividends;
- the need for consent of non-active family shareholders in essential business decisions (like restructuring) to be made by the entrepreneurial shareholders or a non-family manager;
- the desire of non-active family shareholders to sell their shares and leave the family business;
- the relationship between employed non-family top managers and the family shareholders – often a very complex and tentative relationship. Therefore, the first criterion in the recruitment of external mangers is that they are well suited to the family.

7.2.2 Social dynamics of business families

One of the first authors who explored the current change in families in the western world and its impact on the owner family is Michael Gilding (2000). He specifies the general phenomena of family change: a rapid increase in divorce rates, childless couples, single-households, and so on. This decline of paternalistic family patterns has been caused by an increase in individualism and democratic norms in family life. The core statement is that 'people have moved toward the belief that investments in oneself are likely to be more profitable than investments in the family' (Gilding 2000: 241); and quoting Anthony Giddens (1998): 'There is only one story to tell about family today and that is democracy'.

Gilding interviewed 50 Australian owners of family enterprises who were chosen out of a list of the wealthiest Australians, so these enterprises were all larger ones. The result, in short: succession within the family – the building of a dynasty – is still very important for most owners. But not – and this is new – at any price. In contrast to traditional patriarchal

patterns, the tolerance of autonomy of the children and their opportunities for choosing is much greater than in the past. The interest in
equal and fair distribution of inheritance among the children – including
daughters – has priority over that of dynasty. Male privilege and primogeniture seem definitely out of fashion. Above all, parents want to avoid
conflict among the children. The most remarkable changes, at least in
declaration and intention, seem to regard gender – the rights and roles
of wives and daughters – and the birth order of sisters and brothers.
Whether this is becoming evident in real life will be revealed in further
research.

One of the above-mentioned real-life conflicts in family business is
the conflict between active and non-active family-shareholders. This is
found most often in multi-generation family enterprises (third, fourth
and later generations) in which family shareholders are often distant relatives who hardly know each other and, perhaps, would not meet at all if
not for the business. Michael Gilding (2000) gives the following example:
a female shareholder of an Australian family enterprise was insulted that
her brother received the succession to the enterprise alone, 'whereas [she]
was expected to get married and have babies'. As she had the opportunity
to sell her shares to a family trust and so leave the family business, she
wanted to clarify the value of the enterprise, but received no response
from her brother – 'There was a systematic marginalization of me and my
interests for a very specific purpose. How dare I ask questions?' Gilding
(2000: 246) adds: 'This woman recalled huge, overwhelming, almost life-
threatening pain that she felt as rejection, betrayal and invalidation of
her whole life. Her fight for her fair share led to the complete breakdown
of the family relationship.'

The solution to succession-, inheritance-, and profit-discipline conflicts stands at the centre of current debates on family businesses
(Anderson et al. 2002; Kotthoff 1993). Basically, two solutions are proposed. One is to 'open the family prison', – that is, facilitate family
members' leaving the business and avoiding the conflicts – by creating
suitable financial tools such as a market for family shares (Mezzanine, Private Equity, and so on). The other proposal is for a new 'stay in' strategy –
revitalization of the family spirit through the conscious re-organization
of the business family, meaning 'professional family management' –
assisted, of course, by external consultants. What was once the 'natural' source of vitality and solidarity in the family business now must be
reactivated artificially. Proposed tools for doing so are family assemblies,
family codes of conduct, cultivation of traditions and, above all, the early
owner-education of the young family shareholders, as in training courses

on family management in modern business schools. Does the existence of 'family management' training only presage a last struggle to keep the tradition of the family business alive, or is it the harbinger of the modern form of it? In the past, family business and the patriarchal type of family were very well suited to each other. The question now is: is the end of patriarchalism the end of family business, or is family business compatible with less closed, more individualistic or even self-centred forms of family?

7.3 Erosion of patriarchalism

The characteristics of the traditional, patriarchal model of family business are: the dominance of the father-owner in all important business and family decisions; a high degree of fusion of the person and the business on side of the father-owner and his hesitation even in advanced age to give up control; the expectation of the father-owner that family members sacrifice personal happiness for the welfare of the business and the attendant negation of individualism and liberality; a strong inclination to dynasty-building and, as a consequence, the early determination of the son as successor including his socialization and the renunciation of autonomous life-planning. The father-son relationship that follows typically, but not inevitably, out of these contexts is often described as emotionally very tense, even antagonistic and traumatic, and following the pattern of a strong father and a weak son. Characteristic of these relationships are a high degree of compliance – or of rebellion – in the sons and a lack of equality, balance, and democracy in the family relationship. Yet this pattern was the guarantee for the priority of the business in the family-business relation and a high degree of continuity in the business.

A recent representative Swiss study (Frey et al. 2004) shows that 88.14 per cent of all Swiss enterprises are family enterprises (the comparative figures quoted in this study are 68 per cent in Germany and 71 per cent in Spain), of which 13 per cent were founded after 2000, 28 per cent between 1970 and 1999, 23 per cent between 1946 and 1969, 19 per cent between 1914 and 1945 and 17 per cent before 1914. The average lifetime of the business is almost half a century (45.5 years); the average business holds for nearly two family generations (the mean owner generation sequence is 1.8). These data indicate a very great continuity.

However, the near future may bring some changes. While 90 per cent of current owners wish to transmit the enterprise to a family member of the next generation, and 60 per cent already have concrete plans for doing so, out of these 'prepared-for-transmission' owners, only 57 per cent already have a specific family member as successor in mind. Of the other 43 per cent, 16 per cent have no children and 16 per cent say their children are still too young or not qualified enough for succession. However, in 52 per cent of the cases, the owners say the children have no interest in becoming successors. Even if in some cases the desired successor might have a change of mind, this is a crucial fact in probable change. Instead of transmission to a family-member, the next-preferred option for owners is transmission to a qualified employee inside the enterprise (MBO) as a quasi-family owner.

Such findings are exemplary for the erosion of the dynastic and patriarchal pattern and are also supported by a representative study from the Institut für Mittelstandsforschung (IfM 2004) on German family businesses – for 71,000 of which the matter of succession was acute in 2005. Although the majority of owners desired a family-internal succession, this desire could be realized in only 44 per cent of cases. In 17 per cent of the firms, an external manager (MBI) was the successor, in 10 per cent an internal manager (MBO), 21 per cent of the firms were sold (mostly to large companies), and 8 per cent closed down. This means that in more than half of the transfer cases the dynastic line came to an end. The MBOs and MBIs may become once more family businesses, but probably not traditional, patriarchal ones. Of the transfer cases (sales, closures) 29 per cent disappeared from the category of family business and, thus, abandoned the patriarchal pattern completely.

The erosion of the traditional patriarchal pattern is occurring generally in the western world, including other European countries besides Germany and Switzerland, America and Australia (Gilding 2000) and even in migrant-owned family businesses.

Janjuha-Jivraj (2006) examined in a very subtle study the process of succession in Indian family businesses in three different migrant situations: in Kenya, Britain, and the US. She constructs very sensitive types of the succession situation, according to the psychological determination or self-determination at work in the decision about succession, reflecting the degree of patriarchalism or liberality in the family relationships. The son might be compelled into succession by the family, or it could be his free decision. The work relationship between father-owner and son-successor exhibits variety. The key concept is the extent of 'filial obligation'. Janjuha-Jivraj posits two types of filial obligation: the *anticipated entry* and the *unanticipated entry*.

In the case of the anticipated entry, the son is pushed into becoming the successor from early childhood and has little chance of autonomous life-planning; this belongs to the patriarchal pattern.

In the case of *unanticipated entry*, dynasty-building is not planned by the father-owner; the family business is only a means of supporting the family household. Although the sons grow up with the business and the family expects sporadic help from them, they still realize their own life plans (pursuing a higher education, maintaining an external professional career, and so on). An unanticipated event (such as parent illness or unanticipated growth of the business) creates the situation in which the son revises his previous decision and re-enters the business. Different from the first scenario, he now comes as an autonomous and mature person into the business. The working relation between father-owner and son-successor is not patriarchal but rather smooth, balanced and democratic. The father feels gratitude and respect for his son.

In Kenya where Indian family businesses are isolated in a hostile environment, the patriarchal pattern is still very strong. It is quite another situation in Britain, where 'the younger generation of South Asians find they have a wider number of opportunities available to them when considering career prospects.... [that] enables them to consciously decide if they wish to join the family business' (Janjuha-Jivraj 2006: 116). While it is true that parents desire the succession of their son, and many sons follow this path, 'entry is not a straightforward emotional attachment to creating a family dynasty. Both generations consider the options available to the younger generation' (ibid). Here the patriarchal pattern is weakened by parents' respect for the autonomy and individuality of the children. They prefer family succession but do not try to achieve it by force.

Yet another migration situation is that of Indian family businesses in the US, which are welcome in their environment. The parents do not expect family succession, but 'instead ... expected to enable the younger generation to continue their education. They have flexibility in their future choice of careers' (ibid: 117). Nevertheless, these children tend to join the businesses, but in a specifically different way. Together with other young family members they start up their own 'spin offs' – separate from the main family business. 'They build up their own credibility as entrepreneurs, which helps to establish authority amongst family' (ibid: 115) In the American situation, the patriarchal pattern of a working relationship between the father-owner and the son-successor is coming to an end. The relationship is 'much more smooth and less extreme in the volatility of emotions' (ibid: 118).

In all three migration situations, Janjuha-Jivraj found some cases where a daughter is the successor. This leads to a surprising change in the patriarchal work and family relationships. '[Daughters] bring a different dynamic to the much-cited antagonistic father-son relationship' (ibid: 117). The author predicts that daughter-successions will increase, not only in western family business in western countries, but also in Asian migrant firms in western countries. 'Daughters provide a new source of successor, they have the educational skills, often external work experience ... their impact on future family businesses cannot be underestimated' (ibid: 117).

Gilding (2000) reports that daughters' succession in Australia is a general phenomenon. Daughter-succession is increasingly becoming a topic in journals in family business research. According to Kirkwood (2007) male and female owners are differently influenced by their parents: 'Many women entrepreneurs looked to their parents for advice, support and encouragement, while some men desired independence from their parents (primarily fathers) or were trying to compete with them.' The relationship between a father-owner and daughter-successor was smoother and more harmonic than that of a father and his son-successor.

Vera and Dean interviewed daughter-successors in the USA and found: 'Although participants reported few problems with their fathers upon succession, many experienced difficulties succeeding their mothers' (2005: 332). Habermann and Danes (2007) compared son versus daughter succession while examining the relationship between female family members who are passive shareholders and those family members who are active managers of the business. 'The women in the father-son business experienced feelings of exclusion, incidents of higher conflict among family members and lower levels of integration among family members. On the other hand, women in father-daughter businesses experienced feelings of inclusion, resulting in lower conflict and high levels of collaboration' (Habermann and Danes 2007: 167).

These findings illustrate that daughter-succession is increasingly becoming a reality in different western countries and support the assertion of Janjuha-Jivraj concerning the future role of female succession: it is one of the most important developments undermining the patriarchal pattern of relationships in family business.

In conclusion, we can distinguish between several levels in the erosion of the patriarchal pattern:

1. Succession of the son is anticipated, but he is allowed to gain his own external experience at an institution of higher education and in professional jobs elsewhere.
2. Succession is planned long-term – the father-owner prepares for his replacement.

3. Unanticipated entry – filial succession is not planned, but a sudden event motivates the son to revise his career decision. This is welcomed by the father-owner with gratitude and respect.
4. The splitting of ownership may require the recruiting of an external senior manager for the day-to-day management of the firm.
5. Professional 'family management' may be necessary for the constitution and formalization of the family business relationship (family assembles, codes of conduct, and so on) when the family is large and widespread among the third and later generations.
6. In the case of daughter succession, the daughter's unique psychological dynamic transforms the classic patriarchal pattern.
7. With the transfer of the family business to an MBO or MBI, the old family abandons the business and a new family takes over ownership. Since new owners have not experienced the act of foundation or the psychological drama of prioritizing the family business over the business family, it is free of these issues.

The relationship between business and family in the family business is becoming increasingly open and flexible. New relations between individual happiness, on the one hand, and dedication to the business, on the other, will be tested. The two expectations are no longer 'naturally' antagonistic. A plurality of options for combining the two worlds is developing – the private sphere and family emotions with the demands of business rationality and viability. The family business is reacting increasingly positively to the changing forms of family life.

References

Anderson, T., J. Carlsen and D. Getz (2002) 'Family Business Goals in the Tourism and Hospitality Sector: Case Studies and Cross-Case Analysis from Australia, Canada, and Sweden', *Family Business Review*, 15(2), 89–106.

Berghoff, H. (1997) *Zwischen Kleinstadt und Weltmarkt. Hohner und die Harmonika 1857–1961* (Paderborn: Schöningh).

Ernst&Young (2005) *Rendite und Spielregeln in Familienunternehmen* (St. Gallen: University of St. Gallen).

EQUA-Stiftung: Familienunternehmen! Unternehmerfamilie! <www.equastiftung.orgis>.

Fischer, H. R. and A. Retzer (2001) 'Das Geschäft war von Anfang an das zentrale Familienereignis. Die Familie und das Familienunternehmen', *Familiendynamik*, 4, 379–97.

Frey, U., F. Halter and T. Zellweger (2004) 'Bedeutung und Struktur von Familienunternehmen in der Schweiz', Center of Family Business, University of St. Gallen.

Gilding, M. (2000) 'Family Business and Family Change: Individual Autonomy, Democratization, and the New Family Business Institutions', *Family Business Review*, 13(3), 239–348.

Giddens, A. (1998), The Third Way: The Renewal of Social Democracy (Cambridge: Polity).

Habermann, H. and S. M. Danes (2007) 'Father-Daughter and Father-Son Business Management Transfer Comparison: Family FIRO Model Application', *Family Business Review*, 20(2), 163–84.

Institut für Mittelstandsforschung (IfM) (2004) 'Unternehmensnachfolge', *Jahrbuch Mittelstandsforschung* (Bonn: IFM).

Janjuha-Jivraj, S. (2006) *Succession in Asian Family Firms* (London: Palgrave).

Kirkwood, J. (2007) 'Igniting the Entrepreneurial Spirit: Is the Role the Parents Play Gendered?', *International Journal of Entrepreneurial Behavior & Research*, 13(1), 39–59.

Kotthoff, H. (1993) ' "Unternehmer sein, das lernt man nicht auf der Schule... ". Ökonomie, Organisation und Führung in mittelständischen Unternehmen', in H.-D. Ganter and G. Schienstock (eds), *Management aus soziologischer Sicht* (Wien: Gabler), 234–262.

PricewaterhouseCoopers (2005) *Nachfolger gesucht. Empirische Erkenntnisse und Handlungsempfehlungen für die Schweiz* (PricewaterhouseCoopers).

Simon, F. B. (2001) 'Die Familie des Familienunternehmens', *Familiendynamik*, 4, 359–77.

Sund, L. and K. X. Smyrnios (2005) 'Striving for Happiness and its Impact on Family Stability', *Family Business Review*, 18(2), 155–70.

Vera, C. F. and M.A. Dean (2005) 'An Examination of the Challenges Daughters Face in Family Business Succession', *Family Business Review*, 18(4), 321–45.

Part II
SMEs in Globalized Production Networks

8
SMEs in the Global Economy: A Comparison of the Global Production Networks of German and British Clothing Firms*

Christel Lane and Jocelyn Probert

8.1   Introduction

Trans-nationally active firms are conventionally held to be large and well-resourced, but in the German and British clothing industries most firms are small- and medium-sized enterprises (SMEs). These firms are global in that they independently construct sourcing networks stretching over several continents. However, their sales operations have remained mainly nationally oriented. In terms of ownership structure, turnover and number of employees, too, they resemble domestic rather than global firms.

This comparison of German and British clothing enterprises aims to show that firms' national institutional context, including the divergent nature of SME sectors, shapes both the competences that firms develop and the product strategies they adopt. As a result of their embeddedness in divergent national structures, these firms pursue different sourcing strategies, as well as locational choices. The construction of global production networks (GPNs) and control over supplier firms is mediated by clothing firms' degree of dependence on national retailers.

However, firms' strategies are influenced not only by national institutions, but also by global and regional trade rules and by the opportunities to escape national institutional constraints inherent in GPNs. Both exposure to global rules and the opportunities for 'regime shopping' mediate the impact of the national institutional environment.

Our analysis seeks to integrate three sets of theoretical literature. The 'strategic management' literature on the development of capabilities within firms is linked with global value chains/networks analysis (Gereffi 1994; Henderson et al. 2002) and the Varieties of Capitalism (VoC) thesis of Hall and Soskice (2001).

This chapter has the following structure. Section 8.2 outlines the theoretical framework. Section 8.3 analyses German and UK clothing firms in their national contexts. In section 8.4, GPNs and supplier relationships are examined. The Conclusion highlights the theoretical insights developed, focusing on the interaction between globalization and national varieties of capitalism.

The data draw on the analysis of 50 in-depth interviews conducted in 2003–4 with high-level managers/owners of British and German firms and associations in the textiles, clothing and retail industries. To preserve confidentiality names have been disguised. Official statistics and secondary sources from both countries supplement findings.

8.2   Theoretical considerations

8.2.1   The competence-based approach in strategic management

To gain competitive advantage, managers develop organizational competencies/capabilities that facilitate innovative responses to market pressures (Grant 1996; Stalk et al. 1992; Teece et al. 1997). They define capabilities as the development and combination of various types of knowledge which, when embodied in products or processes, are difficult to imitate by competitors. In the clothing industry, such idiosyncratic, value-generating competencies take the form of 'services', such as styling features, product images (Quinn et al. 1991: 302) or special sourcing capabilities (Teece et al. 1997: 515). The knowledge sedimented in competencies depends on the provision of relevant educational qualifications and skills (Quinn et al. 1991: 301; Teece et al. 1997).

Managers' competitive strategies must distinguish between capabilities unique to the firm and fundamental to its competitive advantage, and those which may be externalized, either through market links or in strategic networks (Grant 1996; Jarillo 1995).

8.2.2   Power and control in global commodity chains/production networks

Gereffi's work (1994) on global commodity chains (GCCs) in the clothing industry centres on the analysis of power surrounding a dichotomy of 'drivers'. However, his focus mainly on buyer-driven chains and large retailers gives insufficient attention to the fact that branded marketers, particularly if they are significant exporters, may develop a countervailing power to retailers. The concept of GPNs as sets of firms linked in complex, variable and multi-level (in spatial terms) relationships, developed by Henderson et al. (2002), makes it possible to focus on the social embeddedness of networks.

Following Gereffi (1994), we focus on shifts in control over the organization of the value chain and over the gains and losses from it accruing to the three main parties involved – the coordinating firm, its supplier(s) and retailers. But unlike Gereffi (1994) we contend that large retailers are not invariably the dominant network actor. Based on managerial and employee capabilities, together with financial resources, coordinating firms can develop their own power resources. Two sets of capabilities are particularly important: first, the development of a high-quality, high-fashion, branded product, which makes it possible to cultivate a wide retailer base; and second, skilful management of the GPN, in order to retain a high degree of control over the final product.

8.2.3   Explaining cross-national differences

The VoC approach (Hall and Soskice 2001) suggests that the comparative advantage of firms in differing industries originates in the institutional foundations of their home nations. Hall and Soskice (2001) conceive of firms as developing competencies in interaction with other actors, compelling them to solve a number of coordination problems. Of the five areas of such interaction they outline, vocational training and education is of particular importance for this paper. But reference will also be made to regulatory regimes regarding entrepreneurship, as well as to aspects of financing the firm.

Hall and Soskice (2001) further suggest that different national political economies resolve these coordination problems in contrasting ways. They develop two basic types of political economy: in liberal market economies, markets and hierarchies are the most prevalent coordinating mechanisms, whereas in coordinated market economies, firms depend more heavily on non-market mechanisms, entailing extensive relational contracting. Although these theorists have not been concerned with SMEs, their differential institutional shaping may be explained by reference to the VoC thesis.

8.3   National firms in their domestic contexts

8.3.1   National industry structure and capabilities of firms

In recent decades, the UK and German clothing industries have experienced a precipitous decline in the face of developing country competition. In Britain, both employment and production value declined by around 40 per cent in the period 1995–2000 (BATC 2003, estimates from ONS data). In Germany, by 2000, both employment and the number of firms remaining had fallen to around one-third of their 1990 level (Groemling and Matthes 2003).

Table 8.1 shows the different size composition of the British and German industries and the higher productivity of German firms. In the German industry, 85 per cent of turnover is generated by firms employing 100–999 people (Euratex 2002). Only a handful of firms are very large, yet some 20–30 brands are globally traded (BBI 2002: 11). The UK industry, since the break-up of three large to giant companies during the late 1990s, comprises a small number of large- and medium-sized firms and a very large number of small firms (CAPITB Trust 2001: 8). Nearly three-quarters of British clothing manufacturers are reported to turn over less than £250,000 per annum (Warren 2003: 233). Ethnic minority owners are prominent in this latter group (CAPITB Trust 2001: 5), and their firms constitute a sizeable informal sector. No equivalent low-wage informal sector exists in Germany, due to greater regulation of both entrepreneurship and the labour market (Donath 2004; Rath 2002: 16).

Our interview data reveal how divergent firm size, capital bases and ownership profiles affect firms' ability to invest in capability building. Due to the differing modes of raising capital in the two economies (Hall and Soskice 2001), we found family ownership to be widespread in Germany, even among large '*Mittelstand*' firms, while in the UK such firms are not common. In the UK since the late 1990s, de-listings of firms, acquisitions by private equity funds and management buyouts have occurred, following the break-up of large firms. Whereas several German firm owners emphasized that, after paying their own salaries, all profits are reinvested, in the UK priority goes to investors/creditors.

Table 8.1   Structure of the German and UK clothing industries, 2001–02

	No. of firms	Turnover (€ billion)	No. of employees
German industry (firms with >20 employees)*	560	9.65	53,901
German industry (all firms)**	6,159	14.4	–
UK industry (all firms)*	5,820	8.92	127,000

* Data for 2002; ** data for 2001
Sources: VR2003; IHK Bielefeld data, 2002; ONS Annual Business Inquiry 2001 and BATC estimates

The impact on training and skills acquisition of these different financial models, together with national institutionalized practices of vocational training, is significant. In the British industry, levels of education and training, particularly of the technical kind, are very low at all levels of the hierarchy, from managers, through designers and supervisors, to shop floor workers (PSS 2000; EMDA 2001: 29; TCSG 2000: 12; CAPITB 2001: 16). The opposite applies in the German industry, where skill levels are uniformly high (Interview Notes 2003; BBI 2002). Following the decline in domestic manufacturing, skilled production work no longer holds great importance in either country. However, for German firms, technical-level operatives have become the backbone of production organization and quality monitoring in foreign production sites (Interview Notes 2003; Faust 2005). These differences between the UK and German clothing firms indicate that UK managers face much greater constraints in capability building and are unable to combine creative and technical competencies to develop brands.

8.3.2 Product and market strategy

An understanding of product/market strategy necessitates a representation of the value chain and the different types of clothing firm resulting from the combination of functions/capabilities required to execute the various steps in the value chain.

We identify three main types of clothing enterprise, each with its own way of organizing the clothing value chain (for a more elaborate typology, see Lane and Probert 2006).

The first type, Branded Marketers, puts a high emphasis on all the steps in the value chain and only leaves out manufacturing, although retailing is only sometimes included, as in the New Verticals. Type 2, Producers of Retailers' Own Labels, also dispense with marketing and have only a weakly developed design function. This type never integrates forward into retailing, lacking a distinctive product. Finally type 3, the Cut-Make-and-Trim Firm, engages only in manufacturing to order.

These three types of clothing enterprise evidently differ in the capabilities and capital invested, and in the types of product they develop.

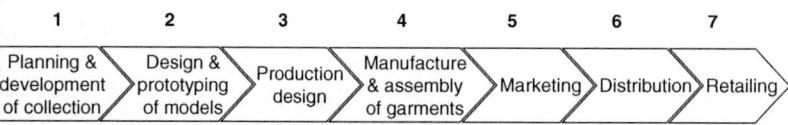

Figure 8.1 Steps in the clothing value chain

As will be shown in section 8.4, they also possess varying degrees of autonomy and network power.

German firms cater mainly to the middle and upper-middle market, with an emphasis on quality, fit and, often, brand – a strategy dependent on high skill levels (BBI 2002). Most UK firms have abandoned brand-building in favour of manufacturing under retailers' labels for the middle to low market segment.

These contrasting patterns affect the export performance of the two industries. German firms have a relatively high export ratio of 32 per cent (Volksbanken Raiffeisenbanken 2003), and its 6 per cent growth rate since 1995 exceeds that of the UK, the US and even Italy (Groemling and Matthes 2003: 77). British exports, by contrast, were only half the German level in 2000 (Trends Business Research, cited by EMDA 2001: 21), and trade with both EU and non-EU countries is below the EU average (Euratex 2002: 105–6).

Although both Germany and the UK have powerful retailers, the index of market concentration in the UK, at 75 per cent, is the highest in Europe (Retail Intelligence 2000: 4, quoted by Baden and Velia 2002: 62). The expansion of large clothing multiples has virtually eliminated independent retailers. In Germany, small independents, although in decline, still represent around 38 per cent of clothing outlets (Baden and Velia 2002: 58; BBI 2002: 3). Supermarkets have rapidly increased their share of both the German and UK clothing markets during the last 20 years (Faust 2005; Oxborrow 2005). Further, supermarkets and department stores are creating their own labels and increasing the share of garments sourced directly from foreign suppliers (Interview Notes 2003; Oxborrow 2005; Volksbanken Raiffeisenbanken 2003). Finally, in both countries the capture of considerable market share by foreign 'New Verticals' poses an additional challenge to coordinating firms.

Retailers in both countries have sought cost reductions from suppliers to compensate for lower margins during the last decade or so (Retail Intelligence 2000, cited by Baden and Velia 2002). However, the negative impact on British clothing firms' margins is much greater because of the high level of buyer and low level of seller concentration (Warren 2003: 233). Thus British firms, which have tied themselves to only one or a few large multiples, have lost control over their market.

To sum up, the two national clothing industries contain very different populations of firms, with divergent capabilities, strategies and market ambitions. In the German '*Mittelstand*'–dominated industry, branded marketers predominate, and 'New Verticals' are emerging. In the UK, most firms are suppliers to retailers and, in the informal sector, we find mainly CMT firms. Whereas the production paradigm of German firms is that of 'diversified quality' production, that of British firms is closer to 'diversified mass' production. Although retailer-buyers are also increasing their market power in Germany, the countervailing power of branded and exporting clothing producers prevents the overwhelming dominance that Gereffi (1994) identifies in the US (for more detailed information on all the firms interviewed, see Lane and Probert 2006).

8.4 Development of global production networks

The clothing industry is a highly labour-intensive industry in which wages for relatively low skilled workers account for a significant share of the production costs. With intensification of international competitive pressures, the manufacturing function has been relocated to countries in Asia-Pacific, the Mediterranean Rim and Central and Eastern Europe (CEE). In addition to labour cost considerations, quota availability (until January 2005), tariffs, shipping times and the location of fabric producers have shaped the geographical focus and control of GPNs. Additionally, considerations around quality and lead time reduction determine sourcing strategies. Finally, the home country's institutional environment exerts significant influence over sourcing strategy and the resulting GPNs. Notwithstanding the fact that off-shoring partly serves to escape domestic institutional effects, the latter remain notable.

Whereas reference to secondary survey data help to sketch the larger picture, our interview data afford unprecedented insights into the reasoning behind strategy and the quality of relations with suppliers.

The competencies externalized by coordinating firms may be described as fairly standard and facilitate easy substitution of one supplier firm by another. But suppliers nevertheless have complementary capabilities. Supplier relations, therefore, are subject to contradictory pressures and are informed by an incongruous mixture of attitudes and expectations. On the one hand is the need for close coordination to develop acceptable product and process standards and cultivation of longer-term and cooperative relations; on the other hand, coordinating firms constantly endeavour to hold or preferably reduce product cost – compelled by the relentless pressure for price reduction from retailers. Therefore a purely transactional mode of contracting is often practised, with little acceptance of mutual obligation. While this paradoxical make-up was identified *within* many relationships, we also found differences in weight given to each element *between* firms from different VoCs.

8.4.1   Types of strategies and modes of sourcing

To explain sourcing strategies, we outline two basic elements: varying combinations of in-house and third party manufacturing; and modes of third-party contracting.

Coordinating firms utilize three basic variants of the make-or-buy decision, either in pure form or, more commonly, in some combination:

1. retain production in the home country;
2. retain manufacturing in-house through FDI/joint ventures in lower-wage countries;
3. manufacturing to order by third-party contractors in low-wage countries.

Concerning the mode of third party sourcing, there are at least three important distinctions:

1. Cut-Make-and–Trim (CMT) – the buying of fabric/trim remains in the hands of the coordinating firm. It is often described as Outward Processing Trade (OPT) in the context of overseas sourcing, in reference to its (now defunct) implications for customs duty. This mode requires substantial pre-manufacturing investment in fabric buying and lengthens total lead time. However, more positively, it affords the coordinating firm greater control over the quality of the final product.
2. Full Package (FP) – the coordinating company no longer buys/pays for the fabric and trim but may retain some influence over purchasing. The fabric goes directly to the supplier, thus reducing lead time. FP implies some transfer of control over the final product from the coordinating firm to suppliers.
3. Direct Buying – buying of the finished product without prior input by the western firm is currently used sparingly, either for very basic garments or for accessories to products developed in-house.

Although there exists a good deal of commonality in the way German and UK firms utilize and combine these two elements of strategy – make-or-buy and mode of sourcing – we highlight the more interesting contrasts. These are primarily differences between providers of own-brand garments, on the one hand, and suppliers of retailers' more standardized own label garments, on the other, which result from, and may be mapped onto, two different varieties of capitalism with divergent SME sectors.

8.4.2   Sourcing strategies of German coordinating firms

German firms, due to high domestic wage costs and more stringent employment regulation, began to abandon manufacturing in Germany from the 1970s onwards (Froebel et al. 1980). Nevertheless, most firms in our sample withdrew from Germany very gradually, and some were relinquishing their last fully owned domestic operations only at the time of our interviews. Four firms, due to strongly held sentiments of social obligation to their locality, continued either a fully-owned, exclusively domestic production facility or still produced a small part of output in that way. Data from a larger interview sample (Adler 2003: 74, Table 1) put the proportion of turnover from in-house, domestically produced garments in 2002 at 17 per cent.

Only a small minority of our German interviewees set up fully owned or (more rarely) joint venture manufacturing facilities in lower-wage countries. No firm adhered solely to this strategy – a result that corresponds with Adler's finding (ibid). In these cases, CEE was the main FDI destination. This strategy was variously motivated by reluctance to relinquish control; the wish to utilize the machine park from closed-down German facilities; or to create a competence centre for working out cost-efficient 'best practice'. On the debit side, this strategy was seen to seriously restrict flexibility of geographical movement and of response to new fashion trends, while also entailing maintenance and employment costs during quiet periods in the fashion cycle.

Use of third-party suppliers is the dominant strategy among German firms (Interview Notes 2003; Adler 2003) for the following reasons. It offers a high degree of flexibility of movement between suppliers; sufficient, even if not complete, control; and low tie-up of capital. Because German firms have, on average, much higher turnover than their UK counterparts and retain less in-house foreign production, they have significantly larger supplier networks, encompassing up to 100 very large suppliers in the case of one of the largest firms. Such large and far-flung global production networks require well honed supply chain management capabilities.

Concerning the mode of third party contracting, CMT, and specifically OPT, is by far the dominant choice (Adler 2003: 74, Table 1). In 1998, Germany had easily the largest share – in terms of value – of outward processed clothing among major European countries (Dunford and Greco 2004). In a distant second place come both the FP and 'direct buying' strategies (Adler 2003: 74, Table 1). Our data indicate that FP was significantly more important than 'direct buying', but was rarely the only mode. We additionally found that German firms are less likely than UK firms to use agents to source either fabric or garments. This overview of the sourcing strategies of German firms still shows the imprint of the German VoC, including the higher capabilities of '*Mittelstand*' firms. However, the surrender of ownership control and the preparedness, in some cases, to move between locations in search of lower wages are more consistent with a liberal-market approach.

8.4.3　Sourcing strategies of British coordinating firms

In the UK, outsourcing of manufacturing to low-wage countries started comparatively late, from the mid-1990s onwards (BATC 2003). Nevertheless, at the time of our interviews in 2003, the last vestiges of domestic in-house production were being surrendered. Hence, retention of manufacturing domestically in either fully-owned or third-party facilities was even less common than in our sample of German firms.

However, this picture of the end of domestic production is a partial one. Industry sources reminded us that domestic manufacturing still exists in the UK, particularly among the smaller, often ethnic minority-owned firms in the informal sector, to whom we gained no access. The prevalence of this sector, together with the late surrender of the 'buy British' policy by Marks & Spencer (M&S), explains why this strategy continued so much longer in the UK. It also explains the large and continually shifting population of micro firms (KFAT et al. 2000; Ram et al. 2002; Warren 2003). Such firms thus have little in common with German '*Mittelstand*' firms.

FDI in lower-wage countries was more prevalent than among German firms. It was the dominant strategy among the firms exclusively supplying M&S, and its rationale is best expressed in the words of one CEO: 'If we didn't own the factories, I'd be sitting here, and I'd be worried ... Otherwise, what value do I add if I am going to a third party? I am only a middleman, so why doesn't the customer [M&S] go direct?'(UK-C-10). The positive aspects of ownership were deemed to be greater control over production for changing orders and avoidance of supplier preferential treatment of customers with bigger orders. When asked about the restriction of geographical movement entailed by ownership, two respondents declared their preparedness to move again – 'Closing things down is a core skill, unfortunately' (UK-C-4).

Outsourcing to third-party suppliers in lower-wage countries was favoured by most UK firms as either the dominant or supplementary strategy. In contrast to the German situation, the number of each firm's third-party contractors was relatively small, ranging from only one supplier to at most ten. The reasons for choosing outsourcing differed subtly from those given in Germany. Some firms simply did not want the financial and organizational burden of in-house manufacturing. Others welcomed the flexibility this mode implied, such as being able to accommodate a sudden increase in capacity (UK-C-4). In sum, the two dominant strategies of UK firms were also shaped by domestic institutional influences and market demands. Suppliers to M&S felt compelled to invest in their own production facilities to retain the level of control their exclusive buyer requires. Most other firms retained comparatively low indirect control over the final product – consistent with diversified mass production for low-to-middle market customers.

Firms that used mainly third-party contractors utilized a mixture of CMT and FP, with higher recourse to FP than among German firms. Lower use of OPT is indicated by more general statistics: outward processing of clothing in 1998, to the value of 444 million Euros, was small compared with Germany's 3,196 million Euros (Dunford and Greco 2004).

8.4.4   Geographical Locations of German and UK Firms' GPNs

According to the study by Groemling and Matthes (2003) of German firms' locational choices, four fifths of outwardly processed clothes came from central and east European states (CEE), plus Turkey. Among Asian countries, China is the most popular, supplying about 4.1 per cent of clothing imports during the decade 1990–2000 (Groemling and Matthes 2003: 49, Figure 13b). Our own data broadly support this distribution of supplier locations, chosen mainly for reasons of proximity to German design centres and west European markets. While the underdevelopment of a domestic textiles industry in CEE is now seen by some firms as a locational disadvantage, Turkey scores highly for its well developed fabric industry, together with good manufacturing and proximity to Europe. But for some of our respondents China has, since 2002, become one of the most important locations, having most of Turkey's advantages but much lower costs. Because of longer lead times and sometimes for 'image' reasons, no firm relied exclusively on Asia.

UK firms' locational choices show a strong focus on Asia Pacific countries, together with some Mediterranean Rim countries. Their selection of more distant suppliers is consonant with the greater use of FP rather than CMT. However, CEE locations were not negligible. A few smaller firms (in terms of turnover) used only CEE locations for either third party contracting or overseas in-house manufacturing, whereas for other firms CEE countries supplemented far-flung locations. Turkey and China are popular locations, for the same reasons as in Germany. Some sourcing countries, such as Sri Lanka, Bangladesh, Mauritius and Cambodia, had no evident locational advantages beyond low costs and were rarely mentioned by German respondents.

8.5   The nature of supplier relations

A notable paradox in building supplier networks is the widely expressed wish to build longer-term relationships, while simultaneously wanting to retain freedom of movement, to escape feared wage increases. The actual length of relationships – which was much longer for German firms, because of the earlier start in foreign sourcing – showed that foot-loose behaviour is rampant in neither German nor UK firms. But it was nevertheless a strategy that firms in both countries had practised. 'Every season, we have to work on their quality and on their price level, other-wise we are not married' (GER-C-7), or 'I'd just move again ... we only ever plan for seven years in any country, anyway' (UK-C-10). More UK firms seemed intent on chasing price reductions, due to the greater pres-sure experienced from large retailers, but also financial pressures arising from management buy-outs (UK-C-6).

At the same time, there were firms in both countries making credible commitments to longer-term partnerships. 'It's a long, very good rela-tionship, we definitely do not move about' (GER-C-7) or 'We would not give up a supplier lightly' (UK-C-3).

Many firms in both countries talked of partnership, give-and-take, trust and gentlemen's agreements. Indeed, many small services were pro-vided by the western firms, and time is granted 'to improve and adapt' (GER-C-11). But, at the same time, most suppliers received no contract guaranteeing a seasonal volume of business, only promises regarding capacity utilization. Coordinating firms themselves receive no guaran-tees from their retail customers and simply pass on the insecurity they are exposed to.

Owing to the oversupply of suppliers, coordinating firms generally hold the power in the sourcing relationship. The degree of leverage enjoyed over suppliers was widely connected to order volume. Hence firms in both countries took measures to ensure sufficiently high vol-ume buying – among German firms sometimes 100 per cent of any one supplier's capacity – to secure supplier commitment. As German firms on average have a significantly larger turnover than UK firms, their ability to achieve control over the supplier through volume buying is superior.

However, several larger firms made it clear that they would not exploit their power advantage. 'We do have the leverage, but we tend not to use it to pursue transactional issues' (GER-C-3). In contrast, one UK manager of a medium-sized firm vividly illustrated the degree of power his firm enjoyed. 'When I tell them to jump, they only ask "how high"?' (UK-C-9).

Another aspect of network management, the criteria for supplier selection, well illustrates the different objectives of German and UK firms. When asked for the selection criteria, the fairly uniform answer in both countries was 'price, quality and reliability of delivery'. However, UK managers more often mentioned price first and subsequently re-emphasized the absolute priority of getting a low price. In contrast, several German firms, but only one high-end UK firm, either did not mention price or emphasized that quality was more important. 'We do not put cost uppermost, usually we go to countries other suppliers have left, where there is accumulated experience. I do not want them to build experience with our high-end products' (GER-C-6).

A final important issue is to what degree vertically disintegrated firms manage to exert control over their nominally independent third-party suppliers, particularly over the quality of the garments they make. At first sight, it seemed that there was no discernible difference between German and UK firms in this respect. Both expressed themselves highly concerned to safeguard the quality of their supplies. QC was particularly stringent among the several suppliers to M&S. But closer analysis revealed several important differences, indicating more sustained and direct monitoring by German firms. Particularly noteworthy was that many German firms had permanent technical employees stationed with their suppliers, whereas UK firms more frequently used either roving inspectors or appointed agents to execute QC. German firms also invest considerable effort in training and therefore in upgrading their suppliers (Faust 2005), a practice rarely found among UK firms. Thus, the remark by Wrona (1999: 161), that production of outsourced garments remains firmly under the influence of the German coordinating firm, ensuring virtual vertical integration, is largely confirmed by our research. 'With our quality control system with production, I think we influence our suppliers heavily, so sometimes they are treated as our own factories' (GER-C-1). For the UK firms, such virtual vertical integration was assured only for those with wholly owned subsidiaries.

This overview of the nature of relationships between coordinating and supplier firms illustrates the different imprint of the two VoC and of the production paradigm connected with each. Although firms from both countries demonstrated some market-type behaviour, supplier integration and control was found to be significantly more pronounced in German than in UK firms, whereas a search for low costs is more prominent among the latter. These divergent approaches enable German firms to maintain product standards consistent with branded marketing strategies, whereas UK firms looked more for conditions enabling them to compete on costs. (For more detailed information on firms' GPNs, see Lane and Probert 2006).

8.6 Conclusions

We have shown that, to understand the role of firms in global production networks, they need to be studied also in their domestic institutional context, focusing on the way it shapes different sets of capabilities and competitive strategies. We have demonstrated that market strategies, in turn, influence the ways in which firms create and govern GPNs. Even though networks are constructed to escape domestic institutional constraints, the latter still structure locational choices and network governance style.

Our contextualization of firm strategy lends support to the VoC framework, confirming the claim that differing institutional environments shape firm size and ownership, as well as investment and training behaviour. British firms have been shown to be more atomistic in their development of resources and capabilities. The German institutional environment, in contrast, has facilitated the development of larger '*Mittelstand*' firms, with better capital bases and providing more support for skill development among higher-level domestic and suppliers' employees. Although the VoC thesis was developed by reference to large firms, many of its claims may be adapted for the analysis of SMEs.

This chapter has additionally offered an in-depth examination of the nature of network governance, drawing attention to its contradictory mix of relational and 'market-type' contracting. Although the latter is more developed in the networks of UK firms, German firms do not adhere consistently to relational contracting. In both cases, the achievement of lower (than at home) wage costs motivated the creation of GPNs. Despite a variety of other managerial objectives it remains a strong, even if not always dominant, concern for German firms. However, the considerable investment in training suppliers (Faust 2005) is also consistent with a more relational type of contracting.

Hence we suggest that the VoC approach is not sufficient for the analysis of cross-border networks. National influences, although important, are not the only explanatory factors. First, global production networks have been established specifically to escape national institutional constraints, such as industrial relations systems and employment regulation.

Second, these networks and their constant spatial reconfiguration are influenced by the rules of both global and European trade agreements. Last, these networks are shaped by capabilities in supplier countries.

Finally, we have shown that SMEs in the clothing industry maintain a balancing act between enduring domestic embeddedness and being independent global actors. On the one hand, they are independent firms with some trans-national operations. On the other, they are dependent on large, powerful and mainly domestic retail customers who strongly influence their global strategies and networks. The stronger German '*Mittelstand*' firms have been better able to develop some countervailing powers than the smaller and worse-resourced British firms.

Notes

*This paper is an output of the project, The Globalising Behaviour of UK Firms in Comparative Context, which was funded by the Cambridge-MIT Institute (CMI).

References

Adler, U. (2003)*Suche nach Kernkompetenzen als Daueraufgabe – gibt es Grenzen der Produktionsverlagerung? Bekleidungsindustrie mit Zukunft,* Report on Conference organised by Textil- und Kleidungsverband Nordwest and IG Metall in Halle/Westfalia, 26 November 2003 (Frankfurt/Main: IG Metall) 65–78.

Baden, S. and M. Velia (2002) *Trade Policy, Retail Markets and Value Chain Restructuring in the EU Clothing Sector* (Brighton: University of Sussex, Poverty Research Unit).

BATC (2003) *Trend Data 2002* (London: British Apparel and Textile Confederation).

BBI (2002) *Jahresbericht 2001/2002* (Cologne: Bundesverband Bekleidungsindustrie).

CAPITB Trust (2001) *Sector Workforce Development Plan for the UK Clothing Industry 2001–2005* (Leeds: CAPITB Trust).

Donath, P. (2004) Personal communication to C. Lane IG Metall: 7 January 2004.

Dunford, M. and L. Greco (2004) *Textiles and Clothing: Industrial Districts, Magic Circles and Delocalisation,* unpublished manuscript (Brighton: University of Sussex).

EMDA (2001) *Developing the Clothing and Textile Cluster in the East Midlands* (Nottingham: East Midlands Development Agency).

Euratex (2002) 'Evolution of the Textile and Clothing Industry in the European Union between 1996 and 2000', *Euratex Bulletin,* 5, 18–159.

Faust, M. (2005) 'Reorganization and Relocation in the German Fashion Industry', paper presented at the conference on 'Organisational Configurations and

Locational Choices of Firms: Responses to Globalisation in Different Industry and Institutional Environments', Cambridge, 14–15 April 2005.

Froebel, F. J. Heinrichs, and O. Kreye, (1980) *The New International Division of Labour,* (Cambridge: Cambridge University Press).

Gereffi, G. (1994) 'The Organization of Buyer-Driven Global Commodity Chains: How US Retailers Shape Overseas Production Networks', in G. Gereffi and M. Korzeniewicz (eds), *Commodity Chains and Global Capitalism* (Westport: Greenwood Press), 95–122.

Grant, R. (1996) 'Prospering in Dynamically-Competitive Environments: Organizational Capability as Knowledge Integration', *Organization Science,* 7, 375–87.

Groemling, M. and J. Matthes (2003) *Globalisierung und Strukturwandel der Deutschen Textil- und Bekleidungsindustrie* (Cologne: Deutscher Institutsverlag).

Hall, P. and D. Soskice (2001) *Varieties of Capitalism: The Institutional Foundations of Comparative Advantage* (Oxford: Oxford University Press).

Henderson, J. P. Dicken, M. Hess, N. Coe and W.-C. Yeung (2002) 'Global Production Networks and the Analysis of Economic Development', *Review of International Political Economy,* 9, 436–64.

IHK Bielefeld (undated) *Manufacturing in Germany,* Photostat (Bielefeld: Industrie und Handelskammer).

Jarillo, J. (1995) *Strategic Networks: Creating the Borderless Organization* (Oxford: Butterworth-Heinemann).

KFAT (Knitwear, Footwear and Apparel Trades), National Group on Homeworking, Women Working Worldwide and Labour Behind the Label Network (2000) *UK Garment Workers Report* (Leicester: KFAT (Knitwear, Footwear and Apparel Trades), National Group on Homeworking, Women Working Worldwide, and Labour Behind the Label Network).

Lane, C. and J. Probert (2006) 'Domestic Capabilities and Global Production Networks in the Clothing Industry: A Comparison of German and UK Firms' Strategies', *Socio-Economic Review,* 4, 69–91.

Oxborrow, L. (2005) 'Global or Global? Restructuring in the UK Apparel Industry', paper presented at the conference on 'Organisational Configurations and Locational Choices of Firms: Responses to Globalisation in Different Industry and Institutional Environments', Cambridge, 14–15 April 2005.

PSS (2000) *People Skills Scoreboard: Clothing, Textiles and Footwear* (London: DTI).

Quinn, J. T. Doorley, and P. Paquette (1991) 'Beyond Products: Service-Based Strategy', in C. Montgomery and M. Porter (eds), *Strategy. Seeking and Securing Competitive Advantage* (Cambridge MA: Harvard Business Review), 301–14.

Ram, M. B. Jerrard, and J. Husband (2002) 'West Midlands: Still Managing to Survive', in J. Rath (ed.), *Unravelling the Rag Trade: Immigrant Entrepreneurship in Seven World Cities* (Oxford: Berg), 73–87.

Rath, J. (2002) 'Needle Games: A Discussion of Mixed Embeddedness', in J. Rath (ed.), *Unravelling the Rag Trade: Immigrant Entrepreneurship in Seven World Cities* (Oxford: Berg), 1–27.

Stalk, G. P. Evans and L. Shulman (1992) 'Competing on Capabilities: The New Rules of Corporate Strategy', *Harvard Business Review,* March–April, 57–69.

TCSG (2000) *A National Strategy for the UK Textile and Clothing Industry* (London: British Apparel and Textile Confederation, Textile and Clothing Strategy Group).

Teece, D., G. Pisano and A. Shuen (1997) 'Dynamic Capabilities and Strategic Management', *Strategic Management Journal*, 18, 509–33.

Volksbanken Raiffeisenbanken (2003) *Branchen Special*, 32 (July).

Warren, C. (2003) 'Implications of Garment Industry Subcontracting for UK Workers', in *Garment Industry Subcontracting and Workers Rights: Report of Women Working Worldwide Action Research in Asia and Europe* (Manchester: Women Working Worldwide), pp. 231–254.

Wrona, T. (1999) *Globalisierung und Strategien der Vertikalen Integration* (Wiesbaden: Gabler Verlag).

9
Flexibility and Formalization: Rethinking Space and Governance in Corporations and Manufacturing Regions

Gary Herrigel

9.1 Introduction

This chapter rethinks assumptions about space and governance that have structured debate concerning flexible production within old-line manufacturing industries over the last 20 years in the United States and Europe. Two assumptions, in particular, are reexamined. The first is that industrial communities are located in specific and discreetly bounded territories in which social[1] and territorial proximity perfectly overlap.[2] The second assumption (often embedded in discourses about trust and informality) is that flexibility and cooperation are possible where formal organizational rules fail to apply, or where they are so general that one must rely on informal cooperation and tacit knowledge in order to get anything done. In much of the literature on cooperation and flexible production systems, producers are simply generalizations of the old sociological notion of a craft producer who turns the limitations of formal rule into a virtue in contexts where production volume is low, the demand for customization high and/or where demand is volatile and frequently changing (Stinchcombe 1959; Sabel 1981; Piore and Sabel 1984).

This chapter suggests that the restructuring of supply chains in old-economy manufacturing industries (for example, motor vehicles, mechanical and electrical engineering industries) in North America and Europe calls these basic assumptions into question.[3] In what follows, I will make two arguments. First, I claim that the peculiar contradictory pressures felt by all producers within industrial supply chains (customers and suppliers alike), in the context of a general trend toward vertical disintegration, have given rise to new, more porous and recombinatory organizational forms that have, among other things, dislodged industrial communities from their traditional territorial moorings. The new, vertically disintegrated organizations are characterized by pervasive collaboration among specialized units. Yet because all producers are driven by the need to both innovate and reduce costs, all collaborative ties are highly unstable and subject to more or less continuous recombination and redefinition. In this context, industrial communities are constituted on multiple scales and the spatial character of community, much like the division of roles in production, has become extremely fluid and subject to constant change.

Second, I argue that the same contemporary pressures that have led to the diffusion of new organizational forms and new spatial coordinates have also generated new style governance practices. Most prominently, these alternative governance practices make constantly recurring and unstable collaborative ties subject to formal procedures of joint goal setting and mutual evaluation. These procedures, which Charles Sabel (2006) has recently called the 'new pragmatic disciplines', systematically make tacit knowledge explicit in order to achieve continuous improvement in efficiency, cost reduction and innovation. Taken for granted in the earlier discussion on flexible industrial organization, flexibility today seems to be driven far more by formalization than by a reliance on informality and tacit forms of knowledge in organization.

After making these arguments, this chapter concludes by pointing out that newly emerging spatial and governance dynamics reveal inadequacies in many of the existing traditional regional architectures of public governance in the industrial economy. Many experimental efforts to cope with this new spatial governance problem borrow and adapt the principles of deliberative goal setting and accountability through systematic mutual comparison, which have diffused in manufacturing supply chains at the project, operating unit and intra-corporate levels of practice. Understanding the character of these experiments, determining the conditions for their success and identifying obstacles to their diffusion is an extremely significant area for future research.

9.2   Vertical disintegration, ambiguity and new relations of proximity and distance in the old economy

Production in old-line metal manufacturing industries such as automobiles, construction machinery, agricultural equipment and other forms of industrial machinery is dramatically different today than it was 20 years ago. A broad trend toward vertical disintegration has profoundly changed the character of relations between suppliers and customers (OEMs) in these industries. In order to understand the distinctiveness of the new 'disintegrated' relations and practices it is useful to contrast them to those that existed in the more vertically integrated past.

Vertical integration was a widely undertaken, yet incompletely realized, project for large producers during the middle decades of the twentieth century. Prior to the wave of vertical integration, production in industries such as automobiles, machinery and electrical equipment, in both Europe and North America, was more disintegrated, in many cases with strong and capable suppliers collaborating with strong and capable customers in a specific regional context (Schwartz 2000; Herrigel 1996). The move toward integration came in different ways, and for different reasons, in different places, but on the whole it sought to internalize as much know-how (manufacturing and design) about a firm's end product as possible. These vertical relationships were organized into bureaucratic hierarchies and governed by principle-agent logics of incentive alignment. Both hierarchy and principle-agent governance relied on the separation of conception and execution not only into different phases but also into different roles in the design and production of a product.

Hierarchy created a series of specialized and non-overlapping roles. Information travelled from the top, and most conceptual, down to the bottom, and most practical, part of the organization. Principle-agent governance was a system to enforce orderly coordination among the specialties and prevent hold-up and recalcitrance on the part of the specialists. Principles – top managers – coordinated roles among agent – specialists – and devised sanctions to ensure that the specialists had an incentive to comply with the goals of the organization. In many cases, these new organizational forms were achieved through the incorporation of capable external suppliers (for example, Fischer Body into General Motors). But they were also achieved through internal expansion and development, replacing the services rendered by suppliers with those provided internally. Many strong suppliers survived this wave of integration, such as Robert Bosch and the Zahnradfabrik Friedrichshafen in Germany, or Timken and Borg Warner in the automobile industry. However, in many other cases, the process of integration fundamentally altered the terms and conditions under which supplier firms related to OEMs.

The historical regime of vertical integration minimized collaboration with suppliers. Indeed, apart form the prominent cases where strong suppliers had successfully defended their position in proprietary technologies, OEMs did not cooperate with their suppliers at all. Instead, when they turned to suppliers, they did so when their in-house capacity was under-supplying the market, or when they required large volumes of normed and standard components (such as nuts and bolts, or spark plugs). In the former case, suppliers placed bids on very specific, already designed parts and the contract went to the bidder with the lowest price. In the standard product cases, suppliers did not produce with specific customers in mind; while firms purchased the parts from catalogues and warehouses. In both cases, the role of the supplier and the role of the customer were very well defined: OEM's designed and developed parts and suppliers produced them. In cases where the OEM also produced, the supplier's role was clearly a secondary one. That is, there was never competition between OEM production and supplier production. Customers showed no loyalty to suppliers. Longstanding relations produced familiarity and routine but never commitment.

Such arms-length contracting had two paradoxical consequences for the community of producers in a particular industry. First, it resulted in huge numbers of OEM-supplier relations, all dominated by the leverage of the OEM. OEMs cultivated multiple suppliers for each individual part in order to avoid bilateral monopolies. This produced large, and often quite vibrant, agglomerations of suppliers around the OEM. Daimler Benz, for example, had relations with nearly 10,000 suppliers in the mid 1960s. Numbers for other European and American producers were of similar magnitudes (Daimler Benz AG 1962). Relations of power in such agglomerations were, of course, massively unbalanced. Individual suppliers were often dependent on the OEM, but the OEM was never dependent on any one individual supplier.

The second consequence of arms-length contracting was that suppliers were located in close territorial proximity to OEMs. Transportation costs affected the price of parts, and price was a crucial determinate of the supplier-OEM relation. Moreover, geographic closeness to the OEM, and to other firms with relations to the OEM, enabled suppliers to gain information about potential jobs to bid on. This classic locational logic produced agglomerations of suppliers in the vicinity of OEM production facilities – a bit like clouds around mountain peaks. Regions with dense supplier populations were also regions with strong OEMs: Baden Württemberg and North Rhine Westfalia in Germany, Piedmont in Italy, the Great Lakes States in the United States. Suppliers produced for *their* local OEM (or OEMs). They had very little contact with OEMs, or even other suppliers, in other regions.

The trend toward vertical disintegration on the part of OEMs has both disrupted the internal mechanisms of governance within the firm and shifted supplier relations from arms-length contracting among large numbers of suppliers to closer collaborative ties with fewer suppliers.[4] This shift has thrown the kinds of local communities of (unequal) producers that existed under the old contracting regime into crisis. Industrial communities are currently recomposing themselves with new sets of relations that involve significantly different conceptions of proximity and distance and, indeed, new conceptions of the boundaries and structure of community.

The shift toward vertical disintegration and collaboration has occurred because contemporary OEMs experience contradictory pressures in their competitive environment. They must divert increasing amounts of resources to new areas of technological development and the discovery of new market possibilities, *while at the same time* continuously improving design, production quality, customer service and lowering costs on existing product lines. This has led a) to the break up of hierarchies, the abandonment of principle-agent mechanisms for control and the introduction of new forms of collaborative and re-combinable forms of internal organization inside the corporation; and b) to the increasing reliance on the expertise and production capability of outside suppliers by OEMs.

The old hierarchical and principle-agent governance structures have been cast aside, because they are too cumbersome, slow moving and wasteful. In today's volatile environment it is rarely possible to formulate clear and precise goals in advance for a complex new product, so it is difficult to identify, *ex ante*, all the required roles and specialties that will be needed for the design, development and production of the product. Moreover, efforts to control from the top, and circumscribe the role of specialist units, place barriers on the flow of information through an organization and discourage the creativity of specialists. Such practices inhibit, rather than enhance, the capacity of the firm to innovate and keep up with new developments in technology and markets.

Hence, firms are breaking up hierarchies and constructing general organizational roles that are re-definable, both from product cycle to product cycle, and, crucially, within a given product development cycle itself. At the same time, boundaries of the firm are becoming porous: new local specialists, seeking innovation and cost reduction, turn to specialized outsiders to help them achieve their goals. The deconstruction of hierarchy and the growth of collaboration with suppliers, in other words, are linked. Firms are creating organizational conditions under which information can flow both upwards and downwards (as well as sideways), by creating groups with general competences, rather than narrow specialties, and by fostering collaboration and encouraging openness among them (both within and across firm boundaries).

In the new organizations, product ideas, designs and the means to produce them emerge together through iterated processes of collaborative problem solving. General designs are set provisionally at the higher levels and are revised in light of proposals by lower level groups responsible for executing key sub-systems. Roles among in house team actors and outside suppliers are made more precise, iteration by iteration, as a design moves toward production, and as specialists are drawn in and defined out. With each iteration in the process, everyone involved knows that the roles they have jointly defined are provisional and subject to change either after greater definition is achieved, or in the next round of iterations with a new product. Collaborators are rewarded for achieving broad goals according to standards defined through the process by which the goals themselves are set. But everyone also has an incentive to enhance their knowledge and capacity to creatively contribute to the iterated development process.

As we will see in the next section, this broad diffusion of collaborative and recombinatory relations has produced a distinctive, and quite new, set of governance arrangements both within and across firm boundaries. Before turning to that aspect of the problem, however, it is important to note the consequences that this 'collaborative turn' has had for the development of supplier-customer relations as a social space.

First of all, the move toward collaboration has drastically reduced the number of suppliers an OEM uses. Daimler Benz's suppliers, to follow the previous example, now number in the high hundreds, rather than the multiple thousands (Kwon 2003; Enrietti and Bianchi 1999). The role of suppliers has shifted from providing a service or part to the OEM that the latter has designed and developed to providing something known to both parties only through the process of collaboration itself. Unlike the arms-length supplier's work, the collaborative supplier's product can only with great difficulty and expense be replaced by that of another. Supplier concentration is an artefact of the growing dependence of OEMs on the increasingly sophisticated development and production input of suppliers.

This concentration process is pronounced, but it is not unfettered. There are counter pressures as well. OEMs rely on suppliers for knowhow, but the intensity of competition in manufacturing is such that they must continually search the global terrain in their industry for innovative technologies and organizational forms. This is done very frequently by cultivating collaborative ties with an array of specialist suppliers, and in particular ones from different locations with experience with different markets and other OEMs. Terrain searching and collaboration go hand in hand, but they produce conflicting pressures for exclusivity and openness on relationships among suppliers and OEMs.

Naturally, this shift in practice on the part of OEMs has created great turbulence and opportunity in the community of suppliers. They must develop strategies and competences to match the changing needs of OEMs. This means investing in new equipment, improving their production quality, enhancing their own internal development and design capacities *and* developing expertise in the areas of continuous improvement and cost reduction. Under such circumstances, suppliers increasingly specialize on a narrow range of competences in order to maximize the quality of value added they can offer their customers. At the same time, however, they also avoid longstanding bilateral ties, even when they are lucrative, in order to collaborate with other OEMs and a broad array of knowledgeable sub-suppliers in the interest of technological and organizational learning. Such serial collaboration is a search practice and a mechanism for learning. It facilitates innovation and improves cost reduction capability.

All of this competence redefinition and continuous terrain searching among both OEMs and suppliers, however, makes the division of competences among producers ambiguous. Who in the inter-firm division of labour has competence, and how their role in its provision will be defined, is continuously changing for both OEM and supplier. *Ex ante*, neither party knows the role it will play. Roles are defined and allocated through negotiation. Sometimes a supplier is integrated strongly and intimately in a fully cooperative project. Other times the OEM may ask that same supplier for only a small slice of its competence (for example, production only) because it chooses to use its own, or another supplier's, competences instead. On still other product development rounds the same supplier may be shut out completely. The supplier indulges the OEM in this relational variety for two reasons. First, a variety of more and less intimate ties – the ability to play multiple roles – creates flexibility for the producer to cultivate (a variety of) ties elsewhere. Second, taking unchallenging contracts from an OEM, with whom one has long standing and often much more intimate and collaborative ties, shows good will. Though the developmental attentions of both the OEM and the supplier may, at the moment, be turned elsewhere, the tie is not broken and the availability of the supplier for future business is demonstrated.

Over time this process of negotiated role (re)definition produces heterogeneous relations between an OEM and its suppliers as a collective, as well as an ever changing bilateral relation between OEMs and individual suppliers. Collaborative and arms-length, intimate and distant relations can be found in the supply chain at any given point in time and can characterize relations between the same OEM and supplier over time. Elsewhere, we have called this emerging bundle of practices: 'sustained contingent collaboration' (Herrigel and Wittke 2005).

This transformation in the way in which roles are constituted in production has radically changed the quality and spatial scope of community among producers in three ways. First, the contradictory pressures for collaboration and search (exclusivity and openness; intimacy and distance) on both OEMs and suppliers has led each to enlarge and redefine the scope of their community. OEMs have expanded their operations into foreign national markets (many of which contain the home regions of rival OEMs) in an effort both to secure market access and to survey the innovative capabilities within those (previously) foreign communities. As a consequence, the space of reasonable collaborators has been enlarged and redefined as OEM ties to suppliers located in the community agglomerations of other OEMs across the globe have begun to expand significantly. German automobile companies, for example, collaborate with French, Italian and US suppliers, not only in operations located in those regions, but also in their home regions. The industry's community has become global and in many cases 'close' and 'intimate' supplier partners can be located quite far away. Similar trends exist in construction machinery, agricultural equipment and electrical engineering.

For their part, suppliers have been following similar trajectories of community enlargement (and spatial compression). For a time, many larger 'local' suppliers were encouraged by 'their' OEMs to follow their example and move operations to foreign markets. The constantly changing quality of the relation with 'their' OEM, however, driven by both parties' desire to expand access to new technological and organizational competences, inexorably led the follower supplier firms to cultivate ties with other OEMs (and suppliers) in the new regions. Suppliers serviced those customers not only with local resources, but with the resources and competences of their organizations in their home markets. Further, constantly self-recomposing, disintegrated production chains created the possibility for ties between smaller specialist suppliers with operations in only one region and large OEMs and supplier collaborators located in other regions.

All of these changes recast old notions of proximity, distance and community. In the old world of OEM-supplier relations, intimacy, proximity and community were all rooted in specific territorial spaces. The new industrial dynamic severs the link between community and territory by creating the possibility for intimate and self-reproducing ties across significant distances.

Second, role ambiguity produces a specific kind of power levelling across the community of producers. In the old subcontracting world, power was structurally stable: suppliers were a community of proximate producers dependent on one or a few local OEMs for work. The OEM, in turn, could view itself as a kind of privileged prince capable of producing prosperity for its underling suppliers, but ever conscious of its need to do so with a firm and strict hand. In the new world, power continues to be a central dimension of OEM-supplier relations – especially in cases where role definition is relatively clear *ex ante* and/or arms-length ties are in play. But even in the latter cases, there is the crucial difference that neither the OEM nor the supplier views their power advantage as privileged, nor even secure: power relations are contextually defined and constantly shifting in both local and foreign contexts.

In cases where roles are ambiguous and ties are collaborative, power in the sense of asymmetric advantage is elusive: Ambiguity, mutual dependence and joint competence definition not only continually shifts the leverage that players are able to hold, but it also causes interest in the identification of possibilities for opportunism and the realization of asymmetric advantage to give way to the imperatives of joint problem solving. So, in an important sense, the new paradoxical mixture of exclusivity and openness in the supply chain has produced a levelling in the community (though, significantly, without eliminating power imbalances!).[5]

Third, the same pressures that have disconnected industrial community from specific territory and destabilized power relations have also produced a new and more fluid conception of the meaning and boundaries of the 'local' among members of the new industrial communities. The old notion of 'local' was identified with territorial proximity, communities with stable roles and hierarchies and a sense of self-containment. Baden Württemberg machinery producers, for example (Herrigel 1993), were thought to have a comparative advantage on world markets because of the special institutional and cultural features of their districts. They took their knowledge (which they themselves often believed to be completely tacit) to the world. Today, those producers (and the regional institutions that support them) do not have the same kind of confidence. They need to cultivate, very systematically, an openness to the know-how that is being generated in the rest of the world in order to be able to remain competitive even in their own region; part of the current transformation in the 'local', in other words, is that it has become (or needs to become) global (Sabel 2003; Zeitlin 2006).

But there is more than that. The new 'local' is also a highly fractured one that contains multiple scales. With the expansion of intimate ties across wider territories, conventions for understanding even territorial proximity have been changing. Southern German automobile producers integrate Italian, French and Northern German suppliers (not to mention Czech, Polish and Hungarian ones) into the flow of their production in ways that are indistinguishable[6] from their ties to specialists on the Schwaebisches Alb or in the Allgaeu – all are in a sense 'local'. Similarly, in the US, 'Detroit' can refer to a city, producers in the Great Lakes region or, indeed, to the entire US automobile complex. The same pressures that have given rise to pervasive role ambiguity in production, in other words, have also produced significant scale ambiguity for both producers and regions.

9.3 The governance of fluidity, contradiction and ambiguity

The recurrent juxtaposition of pressures for exclusivity and openness, mutual dependence and contingency, within firms and in the supply chain has led to the widespread diffusion of new style governance arrangements that ensure transparency and mutual accountability in collaboration. This is taking place on three discrete levels: a) the inter-firm division of labour in production; b) intra-firm relations between and among the centre and operating units; and c) at the level of the region in which firms are (were) embedded.

9.3.1 Inter-firm division of labour in production

Here the new style governance relations have been referred to as the 'new pragmatic disciplines', for example: benchmarking, simultaneous engineering, procedural quality standards, 'root cause' error detection and correction analysis and so on. (Sabel 2006; Helper et al. 2000). Initially developed in Japan, the new forms of governance deploy formal practices to make tacit organizational knowledge explicit to actors, uproot routines, and force participants to search for superior alternative possibilities in design, organization, strategy, technology and policy. These mechanisms have been called 'pragmatist' because they oblige those engaged in collaboration to routinely identify and question the suitability of their own taken for granted practices. They must continuously readjust their ends and means to one another in light of the results of such questioning.

In the case of benchmarking, for example, the participants in a design team (representatives of OEMs and suppliers) by formal agreement engage in systematic surveying of the terrain of technologies relevant for the composition of the product (or sub-system) they are charged with making – for example, a front end system on an automobile. The team identifies the range of functional features that exist on competing products throughout the industry as well as the various engineering and technological ways in which those functions have been elaborated. The results are then compared to one another and to the team's own capacities, giving rise to the revision and re-specification of original design ideas for the sub-system. This process of iterative self-examination through external comparison produces learning and innovation, because it reveals to the participants strengths and weaknesses in their own capacities that they were not initially aware of (for an extensive discussion of these 'new disciplines' see Sabel 2006; see also MacDuffie 1997).

From the point of view of traditional organizational and economic analysis, the success of the new pragmatic forms of governance is counter-intuitive: They combine flexibility with formal procedures, learning with monitoring, local experimentation and creativity with central discipline and optimization. The core innovation of these new pragmatic disciplines is that formal procedures for deliberative goal setting and for the evaluation of performance are devised. The procedures are explicitly open and it is expected that they will be redefined in light of experiences. Such procedures seek to make tacit forms of knowledge in organization and technical designs explicit to actors. This facilitates constant improvement and innovation in design and production across functional and geographic boundaries. As such, these modes of governance enforce a regime of continuous collaborative self-revision and improvement (learning by monitoring) at virtually all levels of product design, development and production.[7]

9.3.2   Intra-firm relations between and among the centre and operating units

The problem at the intra-corporate level is posed in the following way: How is it possible, as central corporate management, to monitor the performance of lower level units in a way that allows for local experimentation and innovation, while at the same time disciplining those units and holding them to best practice standards consistent with an overarching set of goals and strategies for the corporation as a whole? How to allow for broad experimentation without making everything allowable? Too much autonomy can be counterproductive for the centre, while too little can be counterproductive for the local units. Both scenarios lead to corporate underperformance. It is crucial to be able to strike a balance and come up with an agreed upon method for establishing effective and legitimate enterprise-wide priorities.

Evidence from the AMP project (and elsewhere) suggests that the core pragmatic governance principles of benchmarking, iterated co-design and self correction are increasingly being applied to this broad set of problems inside multi-unit enterprises. Take, for example, the choice of strategy or goals for the corporation and its units. The centre, in conjunction with sub-units, can benchmark its overall objectives by scanning the corporate landscape, looking for goals 'like' its own, but better on some dimension. In the same way, each of the corporation's business units can do the same regarding its own responsibilities. The results of this process then can be compared to the initial general goals and the latter can be revised accordingly. By involving both the centre and the local units in the construction and re-evaluation of central goals, corporate wide pragmatic searches can be made consistent with those being undertaken locally.[8] Collaborative and iterated pooling of benchmark goals makes it possible for the centre and the sub-units to establish organization-wide priorities that make it further possible to rank the kinds of projects and searches that the sub-units undertake.

I will present two examples of how these general principles are being realized in particular settings.[9] The first is the Illinois Tool Works (ITW), a second tier, broadly diversified manufacturer of plastic and metal components for end users in a broad array of old-line manufacturing sectors. The firm is organized as a federation of approximately 600 units. The units look to the central headquarters for financing as well as access to corporate research and development facilities. But within these limits the units are largely independent. Each is responsible for setting its own goals, and is held accountable for outcomes.

The key governance rule for goal setting in ITW is a seemingly innocuous formal mechanism derived from Pareto's general principle that only a small fraction – about 20 per cent – of all the causes of an outcome account for some 80 per cent of the total effect. In accordance with the rule the units are regularly obligated to re-determine *which* 20 per cent of their activities account for (roughly) 80 per cent of their profits. They are then expected to strengthen those activities that are successful and spin off or simply abandon the rest. Naturally, this is a very complicated process that forces units to explore the counter-intuitive: each unit bundles its capacities to different customers in different ways, so the way in which a core 20 per cent bundle is established unavoidably involves a process of deep strategic self examination by the unit. It must decide what to be through a process of benchmarking its current goals against a variety of hypothetical versions of itself. The process forces the unit to dis-entrench its own taken for granted routines.

Because the centre recognizes that this process of self re-invention is speculative, ITW has a subsidiary governance rule that provides that managers should not be penalized for (some small number) of wrong decisions. Unit managers do, however, face immediate sanctions if they are caught pursuing strategies that have not been disclosed and justified to headquarters. Thus, paradoxically, managers, throughout the broadly federated enterprise engaged in formally imposed processes of self-re-creation are encouraged by the transparency of the process to take risks, and be innovative. In large part due to this kind of intra-enterprise system of corporate governance, ITW has been able to continuously grow in a sector that has been plagued by anaemic growth and bankruptcy.

A second example is the system of governance in place at Cisco Systems, a manufacturer of network routers, switches and interface devices. Cisco is a research intensive firm, but the most distinctive element of its corporate strategy is its systematic practice of acquiring technology and products developed by small firms and then working with the management of the acquired unit to develop them further. The success of this strategy hinges on two governance rules.

The first is a dis-entrenching rule, which obligates business units to conduct a 'make or buy' review when preparing their annual business plan. This requires each unit to compare the strengths and weaknesses of its current product or service, and closely related variants of these, to those alternatives under development or already produced by competitors. As in the ITW case, business units are enjoined to re-conceive themselves, though in this case by surveying the landscape of their competition for alternative possible versions of themselves. With an acquisition, a second governance rule provides that the inside managers are rewarded for retaining the managers of the target firm, and integrating them into Cisco. Together the two rules not only encourage (as at ITW) regular re-assessment and occasional brusque change of strategy at the business-unit level, but also, by making outsiders into insiders, increase the cognitive diversity of management generally. The governance of the process itself facilitates the next round of assessment and change.

9.3.3 Governance at the regional level

The new pragmatic principles of governance are also being mimicked by non-firm actors within the regions in which old-line manufacturing industries have traditionally been located. In most regions with traditions of old economy manufacturing, the architecture of institutions serving the regional economy was constructed to deliver services to producers with clear roles who were positioned within a stable hierarchy. Moreover, the boundaries of those architectures (more or less) reflected the prevailing identity of community and territory. Under the more volatile conditions of vertical disintegration in which role ambiguity, exclusivity and openness, power levelling and spatial fracturing have come to the fore, the traditional extra-firm architectures have become less effective. Consequently, they are less attractive to producers. Because markets, technologies, organizational boundaries, actor's roles and the character of 'local' ties are constantly changing, the content of useful public services and public goods must continuously change as well. New channels of communication among all actors in the region must be created that can respond to the fluidity of identities, roles, and goods.

Given the nature of these challenges, it is not surprising that some of the most interesting contemporary experiments in industrial regional governance either involve entirely new (and improbable) sets of public actors or the engagement of traditional actors in very new ways. Nor is it surprising, given the character of fluidity of industrial needs, that the new experiments involve many of the sorts of deliberative, mutual accountability enforcing, self-revising procedures that one finds in the supply chain and within large corporate groups.

I will present two examples that illustrate the character of contemporary adjustment in regional industrial governance. Both cases show actors seeking to develop self-revising regimes of mutual accountability at the level of multiple firms and multiple projects.[10] Both cases have important limitations, however, and the limits point to the importance of incorporating more attention to the spatial dimensions of regional policy adjustments in future research.

The first example is the Wisconsin Manufacturers' Development Consortium (WMDC), a public-private consortium of large OEM firms, public agencies and regional technical colleges in the Midwestern United States (for a full description, see Whitford and Zeitlin 2004, and Whitford 2005). The WMDC was created in response to the observed need in the region for the improvement of component supplier competence. OEMs were vertically disintegrating and were relying increasingly on suppliers for significant design and manufacturing input. This turn to suppliers created an upgrading challenge for suppliers. Many were not able to improve quickly and effectively enough to meet OEM needs. The existing infrastructure of industrial policy was not in a position to address this rapidly emerging public good problem, so the OEMs allied with one another and with sympathetic public actors to provide for supplier training. Participants in the consortium collaborate in the construction of the curriculum for suppliers and continuously revise it in response to regular evaluation of the results, as presented by both training participants and other evaluators from within and outside of the consortium. Component supplier firms serving the members of the consortium have their participation subsidized by public money and they gain significant access to OEM know-how through participation in consortia-sponsored courses.

The second example is of the efforts by the IG Metall Metalworker's union in the German city of Wuppertal to coordinate the regional upgrading of supplier firms (Herrigel and Wittke 2005). Wuppertal is located in the Bergisches Land, the densest agglomeration of, especially small- and medium-sized, automobile suppliers in Germany. The IG Metall began pushing firms to upgrade and embrace newer forms of work and production organization, as well as new production services and logistics, when it became clear that the changing demands on local producers made by OEMs were proving to be overwhelming and none of the other local industrial policy institutions proved either willing or able to take action. IG Metall both directly consults with firms (offering firms advice on how to restructure their product palette, their labour and production arrangements, and their finances in order to be able to achieve the quality and cost targets demanded by large automobile industry OEMs) and acts as an intermediary between the firm and consultants who audit the company and provide advice and consulting on how to restructure the firm to be competitive. In addition, the Union has constructed networks of works councils, employers and other relevant local players in the region who meet regularly to discuss ways in which knowledge about how to continuously improve firm competences and performance can be transferred to local producers. The trade union has also begun to construct a formal procedure for the evaluation of its own role and the role of consultants in this process.

In both cases, new collaborative and mutually accountable mechanisms of governance have emerged because local actors have recognized a new form of public good problem that the existing industrial policy infrastructure was not capable of addressing. Also, in both cases, the new arrangements seek to enhance capacity of the participants to revise their role (as well as the joint assessment of the public good) based on systematic and open evaluation of the effects of their own actions. The results in both cases are not only effective; they are innovative (even contextually novel) institutional experiments in governance.

Neither example is without limitations, however. And, as a way to conclude this essay on space and governance in the new old-economy, I will highlight the ways in which space constitutes a significant limitation on the effectiveness of both experiments in public governance. In both cases, the collaborative projects confine themselves to territories that are much smaller than the actual community of producers that could benefit from the services rendered. In the Wisconsin case, the seven participating OEMs actually engage with significant numbers of suppliers that are outside the state of Wisconsin – especially in Iowa, Minnesota, Illinois, Indiana and Michigan. Those producers are part of the industrial community that the WMDC serves, but they cannot benefit from the services the WMDC provides, because public subsidies (provided by the state of Wisconsin) may only be given to producers within the state's boundaries. Hence, the innovative effort is actually prevented by law from providing the public good to the entire community of producers.

Similarly, in the Wuppertal case, the IG Metall in Wuppertal has jurisdiction only over firms located within the boundaries of the Union's administrative unit. Firms in the neighbouring city of Remscheid, for example, which are equally in need of the services provided by the public network, are legally prevented from participating. The IG Metall in Remscheid has begun to develop a similar programme, but its traditions are different and the 'local' players in that city have different interests in the process of adjustment. At best, a public good common to a community of producers is served in a number of different and incommensurable ways; at worst, as in Wisconsin, parts of the community are left unserved.

The fractured character of the 'local' in the contemporary industrial environment is both a result of and a stimulant for the continuous flow of knowledge and innovation among firms. Yet it also poses problems for the effective delivery of public goods and infrastructural services. The limitations apparent here in the two cases discussed show how the fracturing of space actually can undercut the ability of regional institutions to provide public goods to the community of producers. An analogue to the mechanisms in production that allow producers to overcome role ambiguity through joint goal setting and mutual evaluation is needed in this realm of scale ambiguity.

It is not impossible to think of ways in which these limitations could be overcome: The creation of supra-regional deliberative bodies of affected actors (public and private) charged with monitoring the performance of lower-level experiments, evaluating the results and transferring best practices would seem to be one logical move to make. At the moment, however, we know too little about the political and social processes that shape (enable and deter) the construction of such higher-order govern-ance arrangements. Regional experiments and the character of spatial fracturing are very heterogeneous, as is the specific content of local pub-lic goods. More spatially informed research on the specific character of these processes of adaptation and experimentation is needed in order to properly understand the changing character of extra-firm governance in the spatially fractured contemporary manufacturing environment.

Notes

1. On the idea of social proximity, see Simmel 1950a and b; Allen 2000.
2. There were many voices in this discussion: see Piore and Sabel 1984; Saxenian 1992; Storper 1998; Streeck 1989; Grabher 1991; Pyke and Sengenberger 1992; Hirst and Zeitlin 1997 for overviews.
3. My position stems from my own research in these industries. My research has been in conjunction with the Advanced Manufacturing Project (AMP) and its affiliates. AMP was a research consortium of scholars from the University of Wisconsin (Jonathan Zeitlin, Joshua Whitford and Joel Rogers), the Uni-versity of Chicago (Gary Herrigel), Case Western Reserve University (Susan Helper) and the Michigan Manufacturing Technology Center (Dan Luria). There are also affiliated scholars from Germany (Volker Wittke of the SOFI Institute in Goettingen), Italy (Aldo Enrietti, Massimo Follis of the Univer-sity of Turin), and Denmark (Peer Hull Christiansen, Copenhagen Business School). The project has been funded by the Alfred P. Sloan Foundation. A link to AMP's website, where research papers, policy reports and conference proceedings are available, URL: http://www.cows.org/supplychain/. My own contributions are (Herrigel 2000; 2002; 2004 and Herrigel and Wittke 2005). In slightly altered and re-composed form, the consortium is now turning to look at the way in which the same cluster of industrial players is coping with the rise of offshore outsourcing and transnational production networks.
4. Though as we will see, new ties are neither exclusively collaborative, nor entirely exclusive.
5. There are also governance problems that emerge within the new serially collaborative relations. For a discussion see Whitford and Zeitlin 2004.
6. Indistinguishable in terms of the character of intimacy in cooperation, Eastern European collaborators, as a group, may be distinguished from south German producers by their level of wages.
7. As I suggested, these new forms of governance are quite widespread in old-economy manufacturing today (though the coverage is far from complete and their implementation is not always free of contradiction and self-blockage) (Whitford and Zeitlin 2004; Herrigel 2004; Whitford 2005).

8. For an excellent description of this kind of systematic corporation-wide benchmarking process, see the description of Emerson Electric by its former CEO C. F. Knight (2005).
9. The ITW example comes from my own interviewing in conjunction with the AMP project. Wittke and I interviewed people in multiple operating units of ITW as well as in the central administration. The Cisco example comes from an article by Mayer and Kenney (2002). Sabel (2006) also provides a gloss on the ITW case. This section is culled from an unpublished memo on which Sabel and I collaborated.
10. There are many other examples, see Schmidts (2004) for further interesting examples.

References

Allen, J. (2000) 'On Georg Simmel: Proximity, Distance and Movement', in M. Crang and N. Thrift (eds), *Thinking Space* (London: Routledge), 54–70.

Daimler-Benz, AG (1962) *Das Großunternehmen und der Industrielle Mittelstand: Eine Untersuchung über die Klein- und Mittelbetrieblichen Zulieferer der Daimler-Benz AG* (Stuttgart-Untertuerkheim: Daimler-Benz AG).

Enrietti, A. and R. Bianchi (1999) 'The Dynamics of Innovation in the Automotive Technology District of Piedmont', Manuscript, (Paris, Dipartimento di Economia, Turin: CREI).

Grabher, G. (ed.) (1991) *The Embedded Firm* (London: Routledge).

Helper, S., P. J. MacDuffie, and C. Sabel (2000) 'Pragmatic Collaborations Advancing Knowledge While Controlling Opportunism', *Industrial and Corporate Change*, 9(3), 443–88.

Herrigel, G. (1993) 'Large Firms, Small Firms and the Governance of Flexible Specialization: Baden Wuerttemberg and the Socialization of Risk', in B. Kogut (ed.), *Country Competitiveness: Technology and the Organizing of Work* (New York: Oxford University Press).

Herrigel, G. (1996) *Industrial Constructions. The Sources of German Industrial Power* (New York: Cambridge University Press).

Herrigel, G. (2000) 'Large Firms and Industrial Districts in Europe: De-regionalization, Re-Regionalization and the Transformation of Manufacturing Flexibility', in J. Dunning (ed.), *Regions, Globalization and the Knowledge Based Economy* (Oxford: Oxford University Press).

Herrigel, G. (2002) 'Grossunternehmen und Regionen: Neue Formen des Engagements', in U. Mueckenberger and M. Menzel (eds), *Der Global Player und das Territorium* (Opladen: Leske & Buderich), 226–39.

Herrigel, G. (2004) 'Emerging Strategies and Forms of Governance in the Components Industry in High Wage Regions', *Industry and Innovation*, 11(1–2), 45–79.

Herrigel, G. and V. Wittke (2005) 'Varieties of Vertical Disintegration: The Global Trend Toward Heterogeneous Supply Relations and the Reproduction of Difference in US and German Manufacturing', in G. Morgan, E. Moen and R. Whitley (eds), *Changing Capitalisms?* (Oxford: Oxford University Press).

Hirst, P. and J. Zeitlin (1997) 'Flexible Specialization: Theory and Evidence in the Analysis of Industrial Change', in J. R. Hollingsworth and R. Boyer (eds), *Contemporary Capitalism: The Embeddedness of Institutions* (New York: Cambridge University Press), 220–39.

Knight, C. F. (2005) *Performance without Compromise. How Emerson Consistently Achieves Winning Results* (Cambridge MA: Harvard Business School Press).

Kwon, H.-K. (2003) 'Fairness and Division of Labour in Market Society: A Comparison of US and German Automotive Parts Markets', PhD dissertation, Department of Political Science, University of Chicago.

MacDuffie, J. P. (1997) 'The Road to Root Cause: Shop-Floor Problem Solving at Three Automobile Assembly Plants', *Management Science*, 43, 479–502.

Mayer, D. and M. Kenney (2002) 'Economic Action Does Not Take Place in a Vacuum: Understanding Cisco's Acquisition and Development Strategy' (Berkley: Berkeley Rountable on International Economics Working) Paper 148.

Piore, M. and C. Sabel (1984) *The Second Industrial Divide* (New York: Basic Books).

Pyke, F. and W. Sengenberger (eds) (1992) *Industrial Districts and Local Economic Regeneration* (Geneva: International Institute for Labour Studies).

Sabel, C. (1981) *Work and Politics* (New York: Cambridge University Press).

Sabel, C. (2003) 'The World in a Bottle, or, Window on the World? Open Questions about Industrial Districts in the Spirit of Sebastiano Brusco', Paper presented to the Conference on Clusters, Industrial Districts and Firms: the Challenge of Globalization, Modena, Italy, September 2003.

Sabel, C. (2006) 'A Real Time Revolution in Routines', in C. Heckscher and P. Adler (eds), *The Firm as a Collaborative Community* (New York: Oxford University Press), 106–156.

Saxenian, A. (1992) *Regional Advantage* (Cambridge MA: Harvard University Press).

Schwartz, M. (2000) 'Markets, Networks and the Rise of Chrysler in Old Detroit, 1920–1940', *Enterprise and Society*, 1, 63–99.

Simmel, G. (1950a) 'The Metropolis in Mental Life', in K. H. Wolff (ed.), *The Sociology of Georg Simmel* (New York: Free Press).

Simmel, G. (1950b) 'The Stranger', in K. H. Wolff (ed.), *The Sociology of Georg Simmel* (New York: Free Press).

Stinchcombe, A. (1959) 'Bureaucratic and Craft Administration of Production: A Comparative Study', *Administrative Studies Quarterly*, 4(2), 168–87.

Storper, M. (1998) *The Regional World: Territorial Development in a Global Economy* (New York: The Guilford Press).

Streeck, W. (1992) *Social Institutions and Economic Performance: Studies of Industrial Relations in Advanced Capitalist Economies* (London: Sage).

Whitford, J. (2005) *The New Old Economy: Networks, Institutions and the Organizational Transformation of American Manufacturing* (Oxford: Oxford University Press).

Whitford, J. and J. Zeitlin (2004) 'Governing Decentralized Production: Institutions, Public Policy, and the Prospects for Inter-Firm Cooperation in the United States', *Industry and Innovation*, 11(1–2), 11–44.

Zeitlin, J. and D. M. Trubek (eds) (2003) *Governing Work and Welfare in a New Economy: European and American Experiments* (Oxford: Oxford University Press).

10
Innovation Strategies of Non-Research-Intensive SMEs

Hartmut Hirsch-Kreinsen

10.1 Introduction

In the public and scientific debate, the prevalent opinion is that mainly high-tech industries are the key to future growth and employment. The statistical basis for this view is the common indicator measuring the ratio of R&D expenditure to turnover of a company or a business sector.[1] The OECD classifies industrial sectors as follows: sectors with an R&D intensity of more than 5 per cent are categorized as 'high-tech'; sectors with an R&D intensity of between 3 and 5 per cent are 'medium-high-tech'; 'medium-low-tech' sectors have an R&D intensity of between 3 and 0.9 per cent; and 'low-tech' sectors show an R&D intensity of below 0.9 per cent. The latter two are in the following subsumed under 'low- and medium-technology' (LMT) or 'non-research-intensive'. Pharmaceuticals, the electronics industry, motor vehicles, the aerospace industry as well as mechanical engineering are categorized as high-tech or medium high-tech. More mature industries, such as household appliances, foods, paper, print and publishing, wood, metal and plastic products manufacturing, are regarded as low- and medium-technology.

Of course science, research and high technology play a crucial role in the future development of advanced countries. But this outlook is accompanied by an inadmissible narrowing of perspective, which possibly misjudges the industrial and technological development potentials of industries not based on high-tech. An indication of this is the available data showing the surprisingly large number of these industries in OECD countries: between 1980 and 2002, 55–60 per cent of manufacturing value added was in these sectors; on average over 60 per cent of employment in manufacturing firms was in low- and medium-low technology sectors.

Certainly there has been a clear decline in the share of low-tech industries in manufacturing, while the share of high-tech industries has increased. However, these changes do not appear to be dramatic, and the LMT sector shows a remarkable stability.[2] Further evidence for the importance of this sector is provided by a number of empirical findings that emphasize the innovative ability of the LMT sector precisely in high-tech countries (cf. Maskell 1998; Palmberg 2001; Tunzelmann and Acha 2005). Hence, my thesis – after Mendonça's – is: 'Innovation in low-tech industries should, therefore, not be seen as a contradiction in terms' (Mendonça 2004: 15).

In the following I attempt to map out an innovation mode typical for LMT companies. The particular focus is on mainly small- and medium-sized enterprises (SMEs), because they represent a huge share of LMT companies in Europe. According to aggregated data on company sizes and R&D intensity (CIS 2004: 40), the LMT sector in Europe comprises mainly SMEs.

I will also address the question which innovation potentials small- and medium-sized LMT companies really have, which conditions foster these potentials and which conclusions can be drawn from these findings concerning the prospects for such companies in advanced industrialized countries. The following line of argumentation is empirically based on the findings of case studies in 43 LMT industrial enterprises – mostly SMEs – in nine EU countries, which were conducted from mid-2003 to mid-2004 in the context of an international research project funded by the EU.[3] The focus of that investigation was on the strategies, organization and internal and external conditions of technological innovation. The term 'technological innovation' has been extensively interpreted (cf. OECD 1997: 10; Fagerberg 2005: 4): Fundamentally, innovation is perceived to include research and development activities, development and successful marketing of new products, introduction of new production technologies, and process reorganization.

10.2   Innovation strategies

To be better able to conceptualize the 'innovativeness' of LMT companies, different strategy types can be differentiated as regards the main objectives and the primary subject area of the innovation activities of enterprises. In the above-named concept three typical innovation strategies can be distinguished.

A first innovation strategy is the *continuous further development of given products*. Individual product components are improved and changed as to their material, function and quality, but the structure and techno-logical principles of the product remain unchanged. This innovation strategy can be called step-by-step product development. Typically these are products for relatively stable market segments, such as a manufac-turer of punched or sintered components for special applications in the automotive industry. The products are of low complexity, more or less technologically mature and made in large amounts. The process tech-nologies often remain unchanged for longer periods of time and are at best gradually adapted to changed product requirements.

A second innovation strategy is characterized by innovation measures that are directed at improving the sales of the enterprise. This is applied in the fashion-oriented design of products, the functional and technical upgrading of products, a rapid response to changing customer wishes, taking advantage of market niches, skilful branding strategies and the expansion of product-related services. Concrete examples are the textile and clothing industries and furniture and leather-goods manufacturers whose product development is geared to anticipating fashion cycles, and whose product lines demand a more or less continuous variation. A fur-ther example would be an office-furniture manufacturer who – accepting at very short notice a rush order from a big retailer for a large amount of office furniture of a completely new type – as a consequence diversifies its product line. One can also see a broadening of the spectrum of offers as companies add services and logistics tailored to specific customer needs. This innovation strategy can be referred to simply as the *customer-oriented strategy*.

A third type of innovation strategy is *process specialization*. An example from the furniture industry is a process of extensive automation on the basis of a significantly reduced variety of parts. Another is the continuous development in woodworking of an extremely high level of process performance and precision unheard of in other industrial sectors. Similar trends are also found in sheet-forming, plastic-parts and mechan-ical components firms. A third example is the paper manufacturing and food-processing industries, where intricate, technologically elab-orate processes are continually being optimalized and developed further. Under these technical and organizational conditions, the safeguarding and constant improvement of product quality is achieved almost as a by-product.

In terms of their priorities and objectives, the different innovation strategies cannot, at first, be fundamentally distinguished from those of industrial sectors with a markedly higher R&D.[4] However, if one com-pares the process of innovation in the two sector types, the special characteristics of LTM strategies can be demonstrated. Following categories taken from innovation research (Henderson and Clark 1990), one can see that LMT innovation strategies move within a spectrum that is, on the one hand, bounded by the 'incremental' type of innovation, and on the other, by 'architectural' innovation. Both types use a core of given technological concepts and knowledge and develop these further along the development paths they mark out. They thus differ fundamentally from 'radical' innovations that leave behind established technological concepts. Incremental innovations are characterized by the further improvement of individual components without essentially changing their overall design. An example is the standard manufacturer's strategy of step-by-step product development. The term 'architectural innovation', on the other hand, denotes the recombination of existing components to obtain a new product design or a new structure of the production process and, in doing so, not leaving the well-established technological development path. An example here is the customer-oriented strategy, which combines almost unchanged product components and units into a new product and, thus, not only meets special customer requirements but also opens up new market segments.

10.3 Companies and inter-company relations

10.3.1 Knowledge base

If one delves into the structural preconditions for the innovation strategies outlined, the knowledge base of a company emerges as one of the most important fundaments of innovation. For an analysis of the knowledge base of the LTM enterprises, one has to assume that these pursue virtually no R&D activities of their own. Therefore, formalized processes of knowledge generation and use play only an insignificant role, and instead innovation activities proceed in the form of 'practical and pragmatic ways of doing and using' (Tunzelmann and Acha 2005: 417). The knowledge that is relevant to these enterprises is *application-oriented, practical knowledge*. This term stands for a complex bundle of different knowledge elements that are both explicit, codified and formalized, such as design drawing and requirement specifications for new products, and, above all, implicit elements, such as experience and well-established, proven and tested routines for solving technical problems. The latter are closely connected with everyday experience and processes of 'learning by doing' and 'learning by using', which are a typically individual, but also collective, way of acquiring practical knowledge.

An example of this is the innovation strategy of *process specialization*. Here, the enterprises already have, on the one hand, engineering knowledge inherent to the production facilities, their operating specifications and instructions. On the other hand, ongoing operations require constant intervention and adaptation measures, whereby indispensable practical knowledge is gained in various forms, such as about shortcomings and problems of the applied production technologies. Under these preconditions can emerge a grasp of new potential for their effective technical, organizational and, of course, economic application. Process innovations, thus, generally take place during operations and are usually initiated by staff responsible for the ongoing production, such as engineers, technicians, master craftsmen and qualified workers.

The acquisition and generation of knowledge by no means takes place only within the company; relevant, too, for all innovation strategies is the knowledge of other firms, organizations and actors. This is true for practical knowledge but also especially for scientifically generated knowledge in various forms. Examples of external knowledge sources, in the case of the customer-oriented strategy, are the experience of long-time customers in new market and demand trends, the expertise of consultants, or information about foreseeable market trends gained during trade-fair visits. Further important external knowledge sources are machine manufacturers and suppliers, who provide theoretically and scientifically generated knowledge in the form of knowledge incorporated into production technologies and materials, which is often essential to innovation in process specialization. A similar procedure is the step-by-step strategy of product improvement, which is often triggered by the specifications of corporate clients, such as the automotive industry. On the whole, the knowledge base of non-research-intensive SMEs can be characterized as a 'distributed knowledge base' (Smith 2003), meaning different forms of knowledge of actors often working in different sectors and technology fields. Empirical findings suggest that this is the main source of knowledge generation for LMT SMEs.

10.3.2 Organization and management of knowledge

Of decisive importance for the innovation strategies of companies is, moreover, the manner in which they effectively organize and manage their internally available, as well as externally accessible, knowledge. The ability to use knowledge effectively is largely based on the routines and structures of the company organization, for instance, the division of labour, prevailing communication and cooperation forms and related qualification and personnel structures (cf. Henderson and Clark

1990: 15; Cohen and Levinthal 1990: 131). In relation to the different innovation strategies, however, only few distinct connections have been empirically observed. In some cases, management attempts to approach product and process innovations strategically by defining development projects with a certain priority and setting up target agreements together with a few engineers and master craftsmen on staff. In other cases, for instance in the case of fashion-oriented clothing manufacturers (with a customer-oriented strategy), one can find relatively well-established procedures that generate product ideas within the context of the ongoing production process itself and have been well-rehearsed over the course of several years. In other cases, innovation ideas result from random trial-and-error processes or can often also be ascribed to the ideas of individual managers, technicians or salespersons. Other aspects, such as sufficiently open channels of communication, room for independent manoeuvre, and specific slack times (at least for certain employees), are of importance. Also, the intuitions and interventions of management that aim to mobilize available knowledge are a very important organizational precondition for the effectiveness of these practices, as well as being generally a defining feature of SMEs.

Due to the great importance of external actors and their specialist knowledge, the ability to manage and effectively coordinate network relations among companies, and especially to other companies within the value chain, is a central precondition for successful innovation strategies. An essential requirement for the efficiency of such relations is a company organizational structure that provides adequate channels of communication, gateways and personnel for cooperative work. A further important aspect in this respect is the professionalism of management, who must be able to harmonize and control the specific competencies and related interests of many different cooperation partners in such a way that transfer of the required knowledge is assured. Finally, as network research findings (cf. Semlinger 2003) also show, the management's ability to communicate intensively regarding both everyday matters and strategic aspects of cooperation is of great importance in this connection. Such management qualities lay the foundation for a continual attendance to the state and development of cooperation relations, the ability to overcome barriers and the creation of a necessary degree of reliability. With regard to the relations of these companies to customers and purchasers, the constellations are likewise very diverse. On the one hand, enterprises, especially those using the customer-oriented strategy, pursue an active market strategy that focuses on direct access to end customers by means of well-established distribution channels and long-term relationships. To achieve this, detailed information about changing customer preferences and sales strategies of large retailers is, as already mentioned, vital to sales success, the companies' ability to detect new sales opportunities, market niches and so on, and their ability to take advantage of these by means of, for instance, product modifications. On the other hand, one can identify market activities in which enterprises are merely reacting to the requirements and demands of powerful corporate clients for certain product innovations. This is, for example, the case for enterprises with a step-by-step product development strategy that undergo product modifications according to the general specifications of end producers. Normally, these product specifications must be accepted and realised by the non-research-intensive enterprises without modifications or adaptations to their own product and production conditions. Here, power-asymmetrical partner relations determine to a great extent the innovation strategies of non-research-intensive SMEs. This, however, can also mean that supplier SMEs profit from the need for innovation of their stronger corporate partners and the accompanying transfer of knowledge, which thus helps them overcome their own constraints on innovation.

10.4 Societal and institutional conditions

The knowledge base, and the enterprises' ability to make strategic use of it, is also always embedded in socio-structural conditions. This pertains especially to those socio-institutional conditions that are evidently linked to technology development and innovations, such as: forms of regulation of the labour market; institutions of the educational and training system; institutional structure of the research and science system; the economic structure that has evolved over time; and the rules and standards of state innovation and technology policy (cf. Lundvall 1992: 13; Freeman 2002: 194). The available empirical material on LMT innovations, however, points to the varying relevance of these relations. They can be positioned on a broad spectrum of couplings of differing intensity between innovation strategies and societal institutions, which can be found, more or less, in all European countries investigated in the above-mentioned empirical research.

10.4.1 Loose coupling of LMT-company strategies with vocational education and innovation policy

Few companies regard the conditions of the labour market and the institutions of vocational education and training as relevant to their innovation ability. Those that do, cite particular difficulties, such as personnel bottlenecks and restrictions on recruiting employees with specific qualifications. Above all, these companies invoke the lack of persons with so-called hybrid qualifications, which unite traditional technical and professional skills with fluency in new technologies and organization forms. This aspect is particularly emphasized by companies pursuing the strategy of process specialization with modern production technologies, who are, therefore, in need of experienced and competent workers often for complex robotized lines. Furthermore, this strategy, in many cases, results in organizational change towards hierarchy reduction, the introduction of teamwork and the deployment of qualified labour. This calls for qualifications described by keywords such as 'communication skills' and the 'ability to work in teams' – qualities not always available on the labour market. This issue – qualification deficits – is raised by many companies, irrespective of whether they can fall back on trained skilled workers, as in Germany, or on academically qualified staff, as in Scandinavia or Ireland.

For the majority of companies examined in this study, however, the institutions of the labour market and the system of vocational education proved to be of little significance to a company's innovation ability. Many non-research-intensive companies bundle their internal knowledge in the hands of a few managers and experts, while the majority of employees are more or less semi-skilled workers. This hardly entails special recruiting or qualification problems. These companies are, therefore, virtually not dependent on processes of socially regulated qualification acquisition. At best, as in the step-by-step strategy, company representatives may express interest in unskilled, but quickly trainable and motivated labour, such as migrant workers – though frequent right-to-work restrictions on the latter make them less attractive.

Similar connections can be discerned in the legal regulation of innovation strategies of LMTs (cf. Jacobson and Heanue 2005). For one thing, companies in almost all West-European countries pointed out decidedly negative political factors, such as high costs – particularly labour costs and taxes – or an inflexible and restrictive state bureaucracy. It is surely true that these aspects can be very serious for many LMT companies in the face of competitive pressure. Although on various occasions companies have referred to existing public promotions of technological innovations, state-aided expansion or even factory start-ups as innovation-promoting conditions, these promotion measures – national or EU-based – have often been seen as sector-unspecific and directed towards support of research and high technology and not to the specific concerns of LMT companies – a circumstance often referred to as a 'lack of awareness' on the part of institutional innovation and economic-policy actors towards the needs of non-research-intensive industries.

10.4.2 Tight coupling of LMT-company strategies with the given economic and industrial structures

Given the importance mentioned regarding the distributed knowledge base for the innovation ability of LMT enterprises, it is not surprising that a company's embeddedness in the economic and industrial structures around it often proves important to its ability to innovate. This aspect deserves emphasis. First, in the face of the pronounced concentration of suppliers in many West-European countries, which allows manufacturers to change suppliers more easily than they can in less industrialized countries, companies have the ability to quickly and flexibly adapt their value chains to new requirements. This connection is also important in relation to the developers and manufacturers of production technologies. This is particularly true when technical equipment is custom-designed or at least certain components and functions are adapted to particular user needs. Naturally, this presupposes relatively close coordination, communication and learning processes between the partners concerned. Second, service providers with specialized knowledge occasionally play an important role in the innovation strategies of LMT companies. In this regard, one can mention design companies that assume responsibility for parts of product design, firms or institutes that have special competencies and facilities at their disposal for quality testing or special technical development questions, as well as market-research institutions. Such cooperation relations often occur in the market-oriented strategy. Occasionally, specialized research institutes are also assigned development tasks, such as material tests or material calculation for a step-by-step innovation strategy or, in the case of process specialization, the design of installations. Such institutes furnish the engineering knowledge necessary for low-tech innovations. Finally, companies occasionally call on consultants to solve problems in process development and optimization. Networking among companies and organizations in R&D-intensive sectors is also especially important for the innovativeness of LMT SMEs. This, in particular, applies to the above-mentioned exchange relations between supporting companies as well as with developers and manufacturers of complex process technologies, service providers and, also, scientifically-oriented institutions that may, to some degree, make new knowledge and technologies available in the context of close cooperative relations.

However, tight coupling also means that innovation impulses may flow in the reverse direction – from 'low-tech' to 'high-tech'. These impulses result from the simple, but often overlooked economic fact that profits from the sale of new technologies are a vital condition for the amortization and continuation of R&D investments of research-intensive enterprises. A determining factor here is the rapid diffusion of new technologies, which is, in turn, very strongly influenced by the innovative capabilities of non-research-intensive companies (Robertson and Parimal 2007). Furthermore, they result from the technical and economic specifications from such companies regarding the requirements for the application of new technologies. These decisively influence the development directions of new technologies if the requirements of individual users converge with those of many other users and thus, from the manufacturer's point of view, open up a broad application for new products. Examples are process technologies in woodworking and paper manufacture, whose continuous further development is initiated by individual users; at the same time, however, this development maintains and creates industry-wide and inter-sectoral marketing and application opportunities. *Grosso modo*, the LMT enterprises can be regarded both as important 'recipients' of new technologies and as their 'carriers' in the course of further development.

10.4.3   Erosion of regional ties

This tight coupling of LMT-company strategies with surrounding economic and industrial structures, nonetheless, does not mean that the regional embeddedness of the enterprises is always relevant to their ability to innovate. Therefore, the empirical findings at hand can only be generalized to a few development trends. It seems advisable to proceed from the 'paradoxes of territories' thesis of the socio-scientific regionalization and globalization debate (Crouch et al. 2001: 21): On the one hand, many LMT companies are under pressure to spatially extend their cooperation with suppliers, as well as expand their customer relations in order to secure and perhaps improve their positions. As a result, some markedly regional industrial agglomerations, such as the industrial districts of Emilia Romagna, are threatening to erode. The changing patterns of spatial proximity less and less frequently allow the tightly networked and insular relation-structures and coordination forms of a comparatively closed regional innovation and production system. New findings show that market-regulated, formalized exchange relations that are regionally far removed yet cost-competitive are gaining importance (cf. Garibaldo and Jacobson 2005).

On the other hand, 'going global' implies a growing importance of spatial, and related social and cultural, proximity for the success of enterprises' general strategies, as this brings specific operative advantages over competitors. First, for companies with a customer-oriented strategy, spatial proximity is regarded as important to supplier relations, since logistical problems are so avoided and the rapid availability of parts and components is assured. Second, in many cases it also plays an important role in customer relations when the ability to deliver overnight is guaranteed. Third, for many companies following the strategy of process specialization, proximity to manufacturers of production technologies is advantageous for establishing a mutual information and communication base. Also worthy of mention are regionally established occupational training and continuing education institutions, which are credited with an important supporting function particularly by process specialists with their unique qualification needs. Furthermore, for some companies, regionally established and specialized scientific organizations, technology liaison offices, political institutions, associations, chambers of commerce and industry or regionally focused support programmes also play a certain role in their capability to innovate.

10.5 Development perspectives of LMT

In spite of the doubtlessly difficult economic situation of LMT companies, and particularly of SMEs, prospects for these companies are not necessarily poor, even in high-tech countries because of the following reasons:

- The specific competences that LMT companies often possess cannot be easily copied by potential competitors, for they are deeply embedded in the social system of a company and its local environment, making the transfer of such competences difficult and fairly inaccessible to competitors (cf. Maskell 1998). This, paradoxically, also applies to standardized products that are usually considered to be easy to imitate. At the same time, such products are often design-intensive and have a great potential for upgrading through knowledge inputs.
- The geographical and social proximity to sales markets and specific customer groups, as well as the capability to use these advantages in a flexible manner, are a further reason for the relatively favourable development perspectives of such companies. For cheaper competitors from other countries it is often a time-consuming, difficult task to establish the necessary contacts and gain needed information.

- Many LMT companies are evidently in a position to employ high-tech process technologies systematically and efficiently. Their specific process competencies, and their well-established contacts to manufacturers of such technologies, are the basis of this ability. Obviously, the high-tech environment is a central requirement for the development perspectives of such low-tech enterprises.

These considerations lead to a new understanding of the restructuring of the economic landscape in Europe at the beginning of the 21st century. This change does not appear to be a wholesale structural replacement of 'old' sectors with 'new' sectors, or of 'old' technologies with 'new' technologies, but rather a restructuring of sectoral and technological systems more from within than without. This transformation is not dominated by industrial activities generating competitive advantage, capability formation and economic change by front-line technological knowledge, but rather by what are – often disparagingly – termed low-and medium-tech industries, which are represented largely by SMEs, and is characterized by specific and continuous re-combination of high- and low-tech capabilities.

Notes

1. This indicator covers in-house expenditures for R&D staff, further R&D costs and investments as well as out-of-house expenditures, such as R&D tasks assigned to other companies and organizations (OECD 2002: 108).
2. Eleven OECD countries including Austria, Denmark, Finland, France, Italy, Japan, Norway, Portugal, Spain, Sweden and USA (Kaloudis et al. 2005).
3. For further information on the project and its methodological basis see http://www.pilot-project.org and Hirsch-Kreinsen, and Jacobson and Robertson (2006).
4. For example, see the description of innovation processes in different sectors with a high R&D intensity by Jürgens and Sablowski (2005).

References

CIS (Community Innovation Survey) 2004 *Innovation in Europe. Results for the EU, Iceland and Norway*. Data 1998–2001. Luxembourg.

Cohen, W. M., D. A. Levinthal (1990) 'Absorptive Capacity: A New Perspective on Learning and Innovation', *Administrative Science Quarterly*, 35, 128–52.

Crouch, C., P. Le Galès, C. Trigilia and H. Voelzkow (2001) *Local Production Systems in Europe* (Oxford: Oxford University Press).

European Communities: Community Innovation Survey (CIS) (2004) *Innovation in Europe. Results for the EU, Iceland and Norway. Data 1998–2001* (Luxembourg: Office for Official Publications of the European Communities).

Fagerberg, J. (2005) 'Innovation: A Guide to the Literature', in J. Fagerberg, D. Mowery and R. R. Nelson (eds), *The Oxford Handbook of Innovation* (Oxford: Oxford University Press), 1–27.

Freeman, C. (2002) 'Continental, National and Sub-national Innovation Systems', *Research Policy*, 31(2), 191–211.

Garibaldo, F. and D. Jacobson (2005) 'The Role of Company and Social Networks in Low-tech Industries', in G. Bender, D. Jacobson and P. Robertson (eds), *Non-Research-Intensive Industries in the Knowledge Economy, Perspectives on Economic Political and Social Integration. Perspectives on Economic Political and Social Integration*, special edition XI, no. 1–2, 233–69.

Henderson, R. M. and K. B. Clark (1990) 'Architectural Innovation: The Reconfiguration of Existing Product Technologies and the Failure of Established Firms', *Administrative Science Quarterly*, 35, 9–30.

Hirsch-Kreinsen, H., D. Jacobson and P. L. Robertson (2006) '"Low-Tech" Industries: Innovativeness and Development Perspectives – A Summary of a European Research Project', *Prometheus*, March, 3–21.

Jacobson, D. and K. Heanue (2005) 'Policy Conclusions and Recommendations', in G. Bender, D. Jacobson and P. Robertson (eds.), *Non-Research-Intensive Industries in the Knowledge Economy, Perspectives on Economic Political and Social Integration*, Perspectives on Economic Political and Social Integration, Special Edition XI, no. 1–2 (Lublin/PL: Catholic University), 359–416.

Jürgens, U. and T. Sablowski (2005) 'Die Vielfalt sektoraler Innovationsprozesse – Pharmaindustrie, Telekommunikation, Autoindustrie', *WSI-Mitteilungen*, 58, 121–129.

Kaloudis, A., T. Sandven and K. Smith (2005) 'Structural Change, Growth and Innovation: The Roles of Medium and Low-Tech Industries 1980–2000', in G. Bender, D. Jacobson and P. L. Robertson (eds), *Non-Research-Intensive Industries in the Knowledge Economy*, Perspectives on Economic Political and Social Integration, Special Edition XI, no. 1–2 (Lublin/PL: Catholic University), 49–74.

Lundvall, B.-Å. (1992) 'Introduction', in B.-Å. Lundvall (ed.), *National Systems of Innovation. Towards a Theory of Innovation and Interacting Learning* (London: Pinter Publishers), 1–22.

Maskell, P. (1998) 'Learning in the Village Economy of Denmark: The Role of Institutions and Policy in Sustaining Competitiveness', in H.-J. Braczyk, P. Cooke and M. Heidenreich, *Regional Innovation Systems*, (London: UCL Press), 190–213.

Mendonça, S. (2004) 'Brave Old World: Accounting for "High-Tech" Knowledge in "Low-Tech" Industries', paper to be presented at the DRUID Conference 2004, Elsinore, DK.

OECD (Organisation for Economic Co-operation and Development) (1997) *OECD Oslo Manual*, proposed guidelines for collecting and interpreting technological innovation data, 2nd revision (Paris: OECD).

OECD (2002) *OECD Frascati Manual*, proposed standard for surveys on research and experimental development, 6th revision (Paris: OECD).

Palmberg, C. (2001)*Sectoral Patterns of Innovation and Competence Requirements – A Closer Look at Low-Tech Industries*, Sitra Report Series no. 8, Helsinki.

Robertson, P. L. and Parimal R. P. (2007) 'New Wine in Old Bottles – Technological Diffusion in Developed Economies', *Research Policy*, 36(5), June, 708–721.

Semlinger, K. (2003) 'Vertrauen als Kooperationshemmnis – Kooperationsprobleme von kleinen und mittleren Unternehmen und Auswege aus der Vertrauensfalle', in H. Hirsch-Kreinsen and M. Wannöffel (eds), *Netzwerke kleiner Unternehmen* (Berlin: Edition Sigma), 61–88.

Smith, K. (2003) 'What is the Knowledge Economy'? Knowledge-Intensive Industries and Distributed Knowledge Bases', paper presented at the PILOT Workshop on Concepts, Theory, Taxonomies and Data, Dept. of Industrial Economics and Management, Royal Institute of Technology, Stockholm, 26–27 September 2003.

Tunzelmann von, N. and V. Acha (2005) 'Innovation in "Low-Tech" Industries', in J. Fagerberg, D. Mowery and R. R. Nelson (eds), *The Oxford Handbook of Innovation* (Oxford: Oxford University Press), 407–32.

11

From the 'Wild West' Towards Europe: Change and Challenges in SMEs in Poland

Tadeusz Borkowski and Aleksander Marcinkowski

11.1 Introduction

This chapter deals with the problems of formation and dynamics of the small- and medium-sized enterprise (SME) sector in Poland encountered during, and after, the period of state and market transformation, characterized as the gradual evolution from a 'Wild West' stage in the 1990s to 'Europeanization' at the onset of the new century. The evolution of this sector, together with that of the whole national economy, represents, however, more than just an economic transformation. We argue that it signifies the emergence of the country from a state of 'civilizational backwardness' that had resulted from long communist rule. An indicator of this 'backwardness' are data on innovations and patents of Polish firms, which reveal the distinctly better position of the EU-15 economies in comparison to that of Poland (and the other new member countries). Creating and using innovative potential will play a significant role in further transformations in the SME sector (but not only in this area). We shall define this notion of 'innovative potential' and describe how it has changed in Poland over the last decade. Polish SMEs are still burdened with numerous barriers to development, as well as by corruption. The development of innovative potential must be linked to the elimination of existing barriers and pathologies.

This chapter is organized as follows. Section 11.2 traces the origins of the new SME sector in Poland. In section 11.3 we outline the three-stage development of SMEs since 1988. Section 11.4 explores the innovation gap that Polish SMEs must overcome in order to begin the process we call 'Europeanization'. Finally, we summarize major challenges and pathologies encountered during this process.

11.2   The origins of SMEs in Poland

Before World War II, Poland was a mostly agricultural country. Thereafter, in the Communist period, two main types of SMEs existed: a) enterprises owned by the state or a cooperative; and b) small private enterprises.

Private enterprises, as ownership-determined market opportunities, were persecuted for both ideological and pragmatic reasons – ideologically, because private capital, however small, constituted a departure from the communist doctrine and, therefore, a potential threat. Yet, ideology was just a cover for more pragmatic considerations. Since state enterprises provided most employment, people were practically dependent on the state and its whims. Without loyalty to the state, there was no employment; the lack of a legal job made residence registration in a city impossible, *that is*, an unemployed person had no place to live. In addition, he or she was also deprived of paid medical care, to which only the employed were entitled. Thus, the entirely state-owned and state-governed economy kept the society completely pacified. In this situation, the existence of private enterprises, services and private agriculture challenged the omnipotence of the state by constituting a small area of independence and civil liberty.

The attitude of the communist state towards private enterprise, which in the overwhelming majority consisted of family-owned SMEs, was unstable. It depended on the particular 'stage of class struggle' defined exclusively by the communist party. When the 'class struggle' intensified, the state used instruments like taxes (sometimes exceeding the income of a firm), tax surcharges, rationing of raw materials, or production limits to reduce the number of private enterprises. When the class struggle lost intensity, the persecution decreased. The situation of private enterprises was especially difficult in the Stalinist period of the communist economy.

The position of state and cooperative firms was much better. Actually, it is more proper to speak only of state enterprises, because the so-called cooperatives were fully controlled by the state. The position of state enterprises was, naturally, privileged in regards to access to rationed materials, state subsidies, and tax relief.

In spite of the obstacles, however, the Polish private sector grew during the communist period; especially craftsmen's workshops managed to survive and develop in the niches of the planned economy (from 93,884 firms in 1950 to 226,600 in 1980).[1]

After the introduction of market economy and privatization, the number of SMEs continued to increase rapidly. In 2005, there were already 2 million private SMEs in Poland, whose entrepreneurs can be classed historically into three subgroups: a) traditional entrepreneurs; b) entrepreneurs who had been 'apparatchiks of the failed political system' (afps); and c) the new entrepreneurs (cf. Marcinkowski, 1996: 97–111). Persons in these groups differed in terms of:

- membership in the entrepreneurship tradition (or lack thereof);
- level of education;
- professional experience;
- 'social capital'; and
- personality traits (for example, intelligence, resourcefulness, pioneering spirit and willingness to take risks).

The subgroup of *traditional entrepreneurs* consisted of persons who inherited from their ancestors firms still existing before World War II. In the early days of the communist economy in Poland, all major enterprises, and a vast majority of medium-sized ones, were seized by the state; peasants were forced to give up their land to newly-formed Soviet-style *sovkhozes* and *kolkhozes* (collective farms). Only a certain number of small, family-owned craftsmen's workshops remained. The process of farmland collectivization ceased after 1956, and the seized land was returned to former owners.

The permanent threat from the state, but also the state's incomplete dismantling of the infrastructure of private enterprise, evoked a strong solidarity and induced the development of a defensive strategy. This was possible because the communist economy had always lacked consumer goods, while independent craft aimed to supply these goods. This made the craftsman's activity extremely profitable. Once someone was given permission for business activity, he joined the financial elite. Taxi-drivers, hairdressers, tailors, shoemakers, producers of cosmetics and other small consumer goods, and also tradesmen frequently earned more than directors of large state enterprises. This financial power also made it possible to bribe civil servants to defend one's own position.

The less hostile state policy became in relation to private property, the more efficient strategies of coping with difficult conditions of conducting business became. Because in the communist period young people were not taught the principles of business activity, this knowledge was passed down within families. The son or daughter learnt from his or her parents; his or her success did not result from a high level of educational (these were often people with only vocational training), nor from extraordinary qualifications, skills, entrepreneurship, diligence or innovations (though individuals with these also succeeded). The major cause of the success of traditional entrepreneurs was the huge gap between the demand to buy products and the supply of consumer goods.

We term this type of entrepreneur the 'traditional entrepreneur', because, both in view of accessible knowledge and the conditions for conducting business, the representatives of this subgroup did not introduce any significant innovations, emulating, above all, the style of work of their parents or other relatives active in private crafts and trades.

The second type of entrepreneur, the afps ('apparatchiks of the failed political system'), vastly differs from the one discussed above. In spite of economic and political changes, these people found themselves in a very favourable situation. At least one year before 1988 – the final days of communism – changes were being prepared that resulted in profound reforms easing business registration laws, thus making start-ups possible for anyone. These reforms were implemented before political reforms, meaning that prominent authorities, who had been preparing for this since the moment it was obvious that the communist economic system would finally fail, could establish their own firms. They did so by taking over bankrupt state enterprises for a song or cynically seizing bankrupt state enterprises using loans obtained from banks controlled by the former *nomenklatura*, including intelligence, counter-intelligence and other secret service operatives. The loans were distributed among communist party activists to give them a good start in business activities. Friends from banks provided them with advice and facilitated access to cheap loans. Similarly, civil-servant-friends gave both legal advice and protection for their businesses.

Representatives of the afps group were well educated; their knowledge of business stemmed from experts, not family traditions. Understanding the principles of market economy, they performed enterprisingly, dynamically. Thanks to their political experience, they were also quite familiar with the ways state administrations work. They also knew their rights. As a result they grew rich on privatization, taking over not only many large firms, but also SMEs. The afps group was to a considerable extent responsible for the dramatic upsurge in the number of Polish SMEs. In addition, they fundamentally changed the structure of ownership and management of SMEs. They absorbed personnel from the former system (as making former employees jobless would have only turned them into enemies); this, in turn, facilitated the continuing political transformation.

Like the afps, the *new entrepreneurs* came into being as a result of the violent economic transformations in Poland. This group is the most diversified, comprising people who sought self-actualization in business activities, as well as of those who were forced to undertake any activity at all to survive in the time of high unemployment (Borkowski and Marcinkowski, 2001). The former established comparatively modern private enterprises, while the latter dealt in simple trade, services or production. To the group of new entrepreneurs belong people with both high and low educational levels, with some professional experience and comparatively little experience in business or in that given sector. What unites these people is a certain pioneering personality (as in the Wild West), readiness to take risks, dependence on their own skills, willingness to work and fend for themselves and, simultaneously, an aversion to the excessive protectiveness of the state.

The three subgroups of SME owners had a substantial impact on the dynamics of change in the sector which started to emerge in 1989. The Afps and the new entrepreneurs – and not the old family businesses – turned out to be the dynamic forces in the SME sector. However, the new entrepreneurs had the greatest impact – people, who in the past could not, in spite of their great talent and willingness, participate in economic life. They utilized resources different to those of the afps. Under communism, huge personal assets inherited, acquired on the black market or received from the millions of Poles abroad, were idle. This money was not in circulation or was simply spent on consumer goods in special shops selling goods for hard currency. With the new opportunities of a market economy, these funds were used as private equity and to start new businesses. An additional driving force for people to start-up in business was the huge new extent of unemployment, something unheard of in communist times. Many unemployed persons, without much state support, exhibited great energy and ingenuity, while those with jobs limited their demands on employers. Some of the new entrepreneurs possessed experience gained from various work situations in the West. A long stay and work abroad sometimes functioned as practical lessons in the principles of democracy and free market. The violent transformations discussed above completely changed the principles of SMEs in Poland. Similar processes occurred in other post-communist countries.

11.3   The development of the SME sector after 1989

The development of SMEs after 1989 encompasses at least three stages.[2] The first we call, figuratively, the *Wild West* stage, to indicate its 'pioneering', dynamic, but also rather chaotic character. The Polish market, long deprived of wide access to consumer goods, absorbed products of even poor quality brought from abroad by clever entrepreneurs. This was the effect of a stereotype well established in communist Poland by special shops which, in exchange for western currencies, sold 'luxury' western products ranging from Chanel cosmetics, Scotch whisky, French brandy, jeans, and refrigerators, to western cars or flats (in Poland). This stereotype of a presumed superiority of western products was exploited to even sell in normal shops Polish products, which were labelled as intended for export, but which were actually never sold abroad. In this way, Poles were made to believe that anything foreign or intended to be sold abroad was better than that offered to the socialist society. This hunger for consumer goods triggered the development of SMEs.

At this stage, comparatively little capital was sufficient to start a small business. At the outset, Poland did not appear to foreign investors to be an economically trustworthy or politically stable country, a fact that favoured the development of domestic Polish SMEs. The lack of competition from western companies facilitated not only the founding, but also the strengthening of new Polish firms. Just as in the Wild West, negative processes accompanied the positive ones: on the one hand, there were huge opportunities for earning and spending money, but on the other, there was a weak legal system and law enforcement that led to considerable corruption.

The second stage we term *civilising the Wild West*, which began when foreign capital started to discover Poland. The involvement of foreign firms in our country made conditions for SMEs more and more difficult. Western supermarkets offered an ample choice of goods of better quality; western banks took over Polish banks. According to the National Bank of Poland, the participation of foreign investment in the Polish banking system amounts to 67 per cent, while in Holland it is only 2 per cent, in Sweden 9 per cent and in Germany 11 per cent.[3] Yet western banks' lack of trust made it difficult for Polish entrepreneurs to obtain loans and sometimes even contributed to the failure of Polish firms, whose competition, as in the furniture industry, was inconvenient to their foreign counterparts.

Yet, this stage also led to an increasing number of medium-sized firms cooperating with western firms or joining their networks. The Polish state also started to develop support programmes for SMEs. Facing constant high unemployment, the state discovered that SMEs were an important source of employment and included them in its unemployment prevention programmes.

The third, most recent stage of SME development we call the *European stage*: the increasing obliteration of developmental differences between Polish SMEs and those in other European countries. A symbolic beginning of this stage was Poland's EU accession. A precondition to gaining membership was the harmonization with Community Law, the *acquis communautaire*, which had a positive effect on business conditions in Poland. These, in a sense enforced changes, starting a process of convergence that is gathering momentum. International competition on the Polish market and, as a consequence, a broader choice of goods, has lead to more and more demanding consumers. On the other hand, the fact that two million Poles have left for the west in the quest for employment has forced employers to introduce pay increases reaching, in the years 2006–7, 8 to 10 per cent on average. Another change is the increasing number of consumers who no longer take into account only the price of goods, but are also paying more and more attention to their quality. This forces producers to improve quality; with export rising by 16 per cent annually, it is also no longer possible to differentiate production into goods designated for the internal market (poorer quality) and external markets (better quality). Increased innovation also improves product quality. From year to year the number of Polish SMEs participating in international networks and intensely cooperating with large corporations has been growing.[4] Such cooperation, usually with economically, technologically and organizationally more advanced western firms, and the increased export especially to EU countries, which comprises more than 70 per cent of all Polish exports, favours effective innovation. In addition the numerous business contacts, an increasing number of regulations binding all EU countries and tourism all favour Europeanization. Common regulations and markets, ever-increasing international cooperation, and the rapidly increasing number of western firms on the Polish market, all lead to still greater resemblances in the functioning of EU economies in general, and of SMEs in particular. Although they will not become identical, once set in motion, the process cannot be stopped.

During the first *Wild West* stage, and also at the beginning the second stage, *civilizing the Wild West*, it was not clear in what direction the SME sector in Poland would develop. It seemed that on account of organizational, technological, capital, cultural, legal, *and so on* backwardness, a natural tendency would be the 'Asian way', characterized by cheap mass production of technologically simple goods. The success of this type of economic activity is based on a very inexpensive, but fairly well educated labour force, a not very restrictive environmental policy, easy-to-please customers and the global policy of abolishing tariff barriers. Significant political and economic events, above all the accession of Poland to the European Union, solved the dilemma of whether to follow the Asian or the European way of development. Common regulations, economic cooperation inside the EU, the opening of the Polish market to foreign goods, as mentioned, changed the demands of a considerable portion of Polish consumers. The comparatively large economic migration brought a sudden shortage of workers in many key sectors and, consequently, a considerable increase in earnings. The Polish worker became more and more expensive, thus increasing production costs. This, in turn, created the need for automatization and computerization of production. Opening borders between EU member-states caused a diffusion of lifestyles and consumption models. These processes abolished the dilemma of 'Asian' or 'European' paths of development in favour of the latter.

11.4   The innovation gap in Polish SMEs

In spite of the forces driving towards 'Europeanization' outlined above, differences between Polish and West-European SMEs, especially in the industrial sector, cannot be overlooked. Most Polish SMEs are still on a lower technological level and display a more traditional work organization.[5] In our view, the lack of innovativeness of Polish SMEs is the most important factor hampering their progress on the European path. This innovation gap between Poland and Western Europe continues to be especially wide and represents the greatest challenge. To exemplify the size of the innovation gap, we will use some data concerning Poland, other 'new' member countries and 'old' EU members. In 2001 there were approximately 7.6 patent applications per million inhabitants across the ten acceding countries, compared to an average of 161 applications within the EU (SMEs in Europe 2003: 59). The average level of innovative activity estimated on the basis of patent applications per million inhabitants was thus in the 'old fifteen' over twenty times as high as in new member countries. As to small- and medium-sized companies, 'the proportion of these enterprises with innovation activity is only available for limited set of five candidate countries: Latvia, Lithuania, Poland, Slovenia and Slovakia. Data cover the manufacturing sector, where there was a fairly wide range of innovation, from 13.7 per cent of all manufacturing enterprises in Latvia to 31.9 per cent in Slovenia' (ibid: 59).

The figures for 2002–2004 were more optimistic for Poland: among small firms 17 per cent implemented innovations, while 50 per cent of the medium-sized ones did so. In 'old' member countries, these amounts constituted 39 per cent and 60 per cent, respectively (Żołnierski 2006: 10).

This disproportion calls attention to the concept of 'innovative potential' (Borkowski 2007). This means a recognition of the possibilities for increasing innovative activity in a given country or sector. Innovative potential consists of different resources and dispositions, both objective and in the sphere of social consciousness, such as *education, qualifications, capital, pro-innovation attitudes, technical and organizational infrastructure* and the *spatial mobility* of a society. The dynamics of this potential reflects changes in the perception of the significance of innovation for the economy on the part of political elites and entrepreneurs, and reflects the attempts to diminish the disparity between Polish and European SMEs, apparent in the transformations taking place in Poland that affect the features of the SME sector. In this perspective, Europeanization of the SME sector in Poland means no less than the *formation of a new institutional environment,* as well as a further *change in attitudes and mentalities* of both owners and workers.

In the following, we briefly sketch changes within components of the innovative potential in Poland.

11.4.1 Education

Many people, especially in the west, believed in the myth of communist states being interested in education, whereas access to comprehensive secondary and higher education was restricted by the state. In 1988 only 5 per cent of the Polish population had a higher education, 25 per cent had a secondary education, and 24 per cent had attended vocational schools (GUS 1993). Thus, the educational level of approximately 46 per cent of the population was as low as primary school, or even lower than that. This was the situation following 43 years of communism! During the 15 years in which Poland has, again, been independent, the number of persons with a higher education has tripled; the number of people with a completed secondary education has increased from 54 to 75 per cent. The difference between the educational levels of the rural and urban populations has considerably diminished (Stańczak and Waligórska 2007).

11.4.2 Qualifications

Like the level of education, the level of qualifications has also improved, which is reflected, among other things, by the fact that the R&D centres of 30 well-known companies, such as ABB, Avio, Fujitsu, Glaxo Smith Kline, IBM, Intel, Lincoln Electric, Motorola, Oracle, Siemens, TRW

Automotive and Whirlpool, have moved parts of their operations to Poland, as have the Business Process Outsourcing (BPO) offshore centres (call centres, financial, accounting and other services). BPO centres in Poland belong to such firms as Accenture, Avon, Electrolux, Fiat, Lufthansa, IBM, Hewlett-Packard, General Electric, Volvo, and KPMG. Also, the share of foreign investment in high and medium-tech sectors is growing. Dell has recently built a factory in Poland[6], and the Google Company has opened its only R&D centre in this part of Europe. Training workers constitutes a certain problem. Statistical data reveal that employees in Poland are not as intensively trained as workers in some EU countries. At the same time, foreign firms in Poland spend more on training than Polish firms. There could be several reasons for this situation:

- Polish managers underestimate the significance of training;
- the qualifications of many workers are already higher than those now required;
- the level of technology and organizational solutions is low.

This aspect of innovative potential is plagued by the poor adjustment – as reported by regional job centres – of the labour force's qualifications to the needs of different labour-market segments.

11.4.3 Capital

One of the major factors inhibiting competitiveness and innovation in the Polish economy is the scarcity of capital. Tentative data from GUS show GDP in Poland to be at approximately 270 billion Euros in 2006, while budget expenditures planned for 2007 consist of about 70 billion Euros. These macroeconomic data indicate, to some degree, the limited financial capacity of government innovation support. Small capital resources necessitate measures aimed at their more effective utilization. In Poland such pro-innovation steps have been taken comparatively recently in the form of a relevant law[7]. The so-called technological loan was introduced, granted by the Technological Credit Fund, financed in greater part by the state budget, and intended to enable firms to explore new technologies (their own or somebody else's) and launch the production of new products or technologies. The moment an entrepreneur can prove the sale of goods or services based on loan-purchased new technologies, he or she can apply for the remission of up to 50 per cent of the loan.[8]

Another new pro-innovation incentive is the law on R&D centres. A condition for being granted R&D centre status is the obtaining of at least 50 per cent of a firm's income from the sale of their own research or development work. The idea of R&D centres is directed towards foreign investors among others, by encouraging them to locate their R&D centres in Poland and work with Polish private research institutions. The status of an R&D centre includes certain privileges, such as deducting the amounts of money designated to cover innovation costs from their taxation base. They are exempt from taxes on buildings, land and forest as long as these are connected with research. Another advantage is the possibility of counting research and development spending as company expenses regardless of their result and hastening the depreciation of completed development work from 36 to 12 months.

Another pro-innovation tax instrument enables micro-, small- and medium-sized firms to deduct from their taxation base up to 50 per cent of expenses for the purchase of technology from Polish or foreign R&D institutes and centres. Other companies may deduct 30 per cent. Also in this case depreciation time has been shortened from 36 to 12 months, and it is possible to count spending on development work as company expenses. A 22 per cent rate of VAT has been introduced on R&D services, which encourages cooperation between institutions selling R&D services and other firms.

In December 2003, the PolBAN organization was set up, part of which are the 'Business Angels in Poland' – experienced businessmen and women who, having sold their own companies, use their business contacts, capital and skills to support new enterprise start-ups. Young entrepreneurs receive all-round support from the Angels, while the latter earn money in this way. PolBAN, a private organization, matches different business projects with investors ('angel investing'). In 2006 PolBAN signed a 2-year contract with the European Committee for the implementation of the international project EASY, whose purpose is supporting young 'knowledge-based businesses' (KBBs).

Although the numerous examples of initiatives financially supporting innovations presented above could suggest that the problem of financing innovative activity is being solved, in this sphere there still remains much to be done. With EU-integration further changes in loan policy are underway. The Basel II Accord will be legally binding in Poland at the end of 2007; many observers expect a negative influence on the accessibility of loans to SMEs, because companies will be required to provide banks with more information in a more transparent form, which, in some cases, may entail higher prices for loans or even refusal. Basel II introduces procedures that are quite complicated for many Polish entrepreneurs and their assimilation will take some time.

11.4.4   Technical and institutional infrastructure

Technology and machinery, organization of labour and management, access to state-of-the-art technological and organizational solutions, systems of technology transfer – all these have been barriers to innovation and competitiveness. Because the present infrastructure does not seem satisfactory, investing in it is a promising way of increasing the innovative potential of SMEs. Statistics on the structure of expenditure on innovation in 2004 indicate that mainly the modernization of machines has been predominant in technological development. As much as 60 per cent of total investment in innovative activities consisted of expenditures for the purchase of machines and equipment. At the same time, R&D spending, one of the major sources of innovation, stood at only 7.5 per cent, far behind that of more developed countries. Moreover, only about 3 per cent of total expenditure on innovative activities in enterprises was earmarked for acquisition of ready technologies in the form of knowledge and rights. This structure of outlays indicates that innovative activities in Poland are mainly the acquisition of so-called hard technology, which is rational in the context of the need to reduce the technology gap.

There is only a very weak institutional link between science and SMEs, resulting in a poor transfer of knowledge and technology between them. This lack of cooperation contributes to the low amount of patent activity and meagre innovation in Polish SMEs. SMEs also complain about restrictive industrial laws, slow industrial courts and the high costs of trials in industrial court actions.

11.5   Challenges and pathologies in the Polish SME sector

This chapter has outlined a three-stage concept of the development of the Polish SME sector. We have argued that there are institutional, cultural, structural and political changes going on that support a 'European way' for SME-development instead of the low-cost 'Asian way'. These positive tendencies coexist, however, with negative phenomena and pathologies of varying influence that may severely challenge further progress.

First, in spite of progress there is still a *lack of cooperation* among SMEs, which rarely form alliances to pool resources or improve their financial situation (Żołnierski 2005: 2–34). This is sometimes linked to the individualistic Polish national character[9] in which there is a certain deficit of orientation towards cooperation. This finds expression in a considerable atomization (fragmentation) of the sector and its institutional weakness in the face of banks. Against this background, the cases of networking or cooperation with foreign SMEs – not numerous and restricted mostly to Polish SMEs owned by western investors – hardly form an exception, since such networking is usually demanded (or suggested) by these owners.

Second, associations of producers and firms rendering services *must begin to be perceived as potential contractors* for regional and national programmes and, thus, be taken into consideration in development planning. There is an urgent need for the development and implementation of principles of cooperation between financial, trade, regional and labour-market institutions, which have so far functioned separately. The European Union seems to be the most competent tutor in this complex task.

Third, SMEs in Poland are not as frequently equipped with *standardized systems of quality management* as their western competitors; this hinders them on entering networks or other cooperation relationships with partners from the west and, thus, also limits the internationalization of firms and the diffusion of knowledge and innovation. The introduction of ISO standards, for example, still exceeds the financial possibilities of many medium-sized companies.

Fourth, SMEs benefit only to a small degree from *cooperation with research and development centres*. Polish SME innovations are, in most cases, not research-based, but rather result from the trial-and-error method. It is unlikely that this spontaneous mechanism will function with equal efficiency in the long run.

Fifth, in the longer perspective *dangers connected with the labour supply* are apparent. Population decline and the considerable drainage of workers to other EU countries will produce growing difficulties in finding employees in Poland; this could interfere with SME development in some industries and regions.

Sixth, another essential problem in Polish economic life, and therefore also in SMEs, is *corruption*. It has grown tremendously since the early 1990s. Rough estimates (accurate data in this case do not appear to be attainable) suggest that corruption costs Poland several billion Euros annually. Fighting corruption is difficult, as many actors profit from it. Civil servants on all levels often become corrupt on account of their decision-making power. They grant all sorts of licences, quotas, limits, certificates, toll stickers, entitlements, *and so on* – 'goods' that have a positive or negative effect on a firm's performance. Also, entrepreneurs sometimes have a vested interest in corruption: it helps them win tenders, obtain contracts, profit by 'cutting corners' on the quality of labour and products, and is often a less expensive option for them than financing research and development. Corruption is a particularly destructive influence on SMEs because it cuts into already limited financial resources, weakens motivation to improve product and service quality, and in many cases ruins the competition of other dynamic and honest entrepreneurs.

Notes

1. *Mały Rocznik Statystyczny 1966* (Warszawa: GUS 1967) and *Mały Rocznik Statystyczny 1980* (Warszawa: GUS 1981).
2. In more detail cf. Koźmiński A., 1998; Błaszczyk C., 1996; Grudzewski, W. M., Hejduk, I. K. 1998.
3. See the speech of Sławomir S. Skrzypek, president of the National Bank of Poland on 'Aspekty instytucjonalne stabilności finansowej a wyzwania europejskie' at *Banking Forum* 'Zmiany regulacyjne w bankowości europejskiej – skutki dla banków i gospodarki w Polsce', 14.03.2007.
4. For example, such Polish firms as HMS, belonging to the STACO network and comprising SMEs from Holland, Germany, Belgium and France, or WIET-POL, cooperate with the Goodrich Company and other SMEs in the so-called Aviation Valley in South-Eastern Poland.
5. Schmierl and Kohler (2005) note: '(. . .) forms of strictly taylorist-hierarchical work organization are indeed prevailing within our sample [comparative and deeper case studies done in 44 small- and-medium-sized LMT firms in old and new EU member-countries]. Its main characteristics are a high division of labour, a heavily specialized work-force and sophisticated hierarchic levels. Furthermore there is a strict separation of conception, planning, steering and control, conducted in technical offices, on the one hand and the subsequent execution, taking place within the shop-floor on the other hand' (p. 16).
6. Data presented by the Polish Agency for Information and Foreign Investments <http://www.paiz.gov.pl/index/?id=0004d0b59e19461ff1126e3a08a814c33 #centrum->.
7. Some Forms of Support of Innovation Activity Act of 29 July 2005, Dz.U. (Law Gazette), nr 179, poz.1484; Regulations of Science Funding Act of 8 October 2004, Dz.U. (Law Gazette), nr 273, poz. 2703; Research Institutions Act of 25 July 1985; Freedom of Economic Activity Act of 2 July 2004, Dz.U. (Law Gazette), nr 173, poz.1807 with later amendments.
8. The participation of the borrower may not be lower than 25 per cent net worth of the investment aided by the technological loan. The interest on this loan is subject to market conditions. The loan is given by the National Economy Bank. The loan value may not exceed 2 million Euro. The total remission may not be higher than 1 million Euros. In 2006 the Technological Credit Fund had at its disposal approximately 170 million zlotys (44 million Euros).

9. As far as individualist orientation is concerned, Poland occupies the 22–24th position on the list of 74 countries studied. The individualism indicator (IDV) for Poland is 60. For comparative purposes: USA – 91 (highest level of individualism), Japan – 46, Russia – 39, Bulgaria and Romania – 30 (Hofstede, G. and G. J. Hofstede 2007: 91).

References

Błaszczyk C., *Małe i średnie przedsiębiorstwa w perspektywie członkostwa Polski w Unii Europejskiej* (1996) in: J. Lewandowski (ed.) III Międzynarodowa Konferencja Naukowa: Małe i średnie przedsiębiorstwa w procesie transformacji polskiej gospodarki. Politechnika Łódzka, Wydział Organizacji i Zarządzania. Łódź.

Borkowski, T. (2007) 'Innovative potential, competitiveness and diversification of Polish SMEs', contribution to the international workshop *Low technology: Innovativeness, Development and Perspectives in the Knowledge Economy*, Dortmund, 15–16 March 2007.

Borkowski, T. and A. Marcinkowski (eds) (2002) *Socjologia bezrobocia* (Warszawa: Scholar).

Jackson, J. and A. Marcinkowski (1999) 'Entrepreneurial Attitudes of Poles', in E. Hauser and J. Wasilewski (eds), *Lessons in Democracy* (Kraków, Rochester: Jagiellonian University Press, University of Rochester Press), 171–200.

Grudzewski W. M. and I. K. Hejduk (1998) Małe i średnie przedsiębiorstwa w gospodarce rynkowej w Polsce. Warszawa.

Hofstede, G. and G. J. Hofstede (2007) *Kultury i organizacje. Zaprogramowanie umysłu*, 2nd ed. (Warszawa: PWE).

Kołodziejczyk, D. and M. Pawłowska (2006) 'Konkurencyjność polskich przedsiębiorstw po wejściu do Unii Europejskiej. Wyniki badania ankietowego', *Materiały i Studia*, Zeszyt no. 206 (Warszawa: NBP), 1–54 .

Kornai, J. (1980) *Economics of Shortage*, vol. I and II (Amsterdam, New York: North-Holland Publishing Company).

Koźmiński, A. K. (1998) *Odrabianie zaległości. Zmiany organizacji i Zarządzania w byłym bloku socjalistycznym* (Warszawa: PWN). *Mały Rocznik Statystyczny 1966* (Conscise Statistical Yearbook). GUS (Main Statistical Bureau). Warszawa 1967.

Mały Rocznik Statystyczny 1980 (Conscise Statistical Yearbook). GUS (Main Statistical Bureau). Warszawa 1981.

Mały Rocznik Statystyczny Polski 2003 (Conscise Statistical Yearbook of Poland) GUS (Main Statistical Bureau) Warszawa 2004.

Marcinkowski, A. (1996) 'Drobny przedsiębiorca i horyzonty kultury organizacyjne', in A. Marcinkowski (ed.), *Kapitalizm po polsku. przedsiębiorca, organizacja, kultura* (Kraków: Księgarnia Akademicka), 91–150.

Rocznik statystyczny 1992 (A Statistical Yearbook). GUS (Main Statistical Bureau). Warszawa 1993.

Rocznik Statystyczny 2002 (A Statistical Yearbook) GUS (Main Statistical Bureau) Warszawa 2003.

Schmierl, K. and H. D. Kohler (2005) 'Organizational Learning. Knowledge Management and Training in Low-Tech and Medium Low-Tech Companies', contribution to the conference 'Low-Tech as Misnomer: The Role of Non-Research-Intensive Industries in the Knowledge Economy', Brussels, 29–30 June 2005.

SMEs in Europe. Candidate Countries (2003) (Luxembourg: Office for Official Publications of the European Communities), <http://www.eds-destatis.de/downloads/publ/en4_sme_europe.pdf>.

Sosnowska, A. and K. Poznańska (2003) *Systemy wspierania innowacji i transferu technologii w krajach Unii Europejskiej i w Polsce. Poradnik przedsiębiorcy* (Warszawa: PARP).

Stańczak, J. and M. Waligórska, supervised by L. Nowak (2007) *Podstawowe informacje o rozwoju demograficznym Polski do 2006 roku. Materiał na konferencję prasową w dniu 29 stycznia 2007* (Warszawa: GUS), <http://www.stat.gov.pl/cps/rde/xbcr/gus/PUBL_podst_inf_rozwoj_demograficzny_2006.pdf>.

Tokaj – Krzewska, A. and A. Żołnierski (2004) *Raport o stanie sektora Małych i średnich przedsiębiorstw w Polsce w latach 2002–2003* (Warszawa: PARP).

Von Schuttenbach, L. (2000) *Sektor Małych i średnich przedsiębiorstw w Republice Federalnej Niemiec* (Warszawa: Polska Fundacja Promocji i Rozwoju Małych i Średnich Przedsiębiorstw).

Żołnierski, A. (2005) Potencjał innowacyjny polskich Małych i średniej wielkości przedsiębiorstw (Warszawa: PARP).

Żołnierski, A. (ed.) (2006) Innowacyjność 2006. Stan innowacyjności metody wspierania, programy badawcze. Raport (Warszawa: PARP).

Part III
Labour Relations in Change

12

Structural Changes and New Forms of Social Regulation in the 'Third Italy' — the Case of the Emilia-Romagna Region

Volker Telljohann

12.1 Introduction

The Italian production system is dominated by small and micro-enterprises. In general, these companies have established close relationships with their respective local areas. In many cases the small and micro-enterprises are part of industrial districts or local production systems. In 2003 the companies operating in industrial districts covered almost 50 per cent of the overall employment in the manufacturing sector (Coletto 2006).

An 'industrial district' can be defined as a territorial production system made up of small- and medium-sized enterprises (SMEs) specializing in single phases of the production process and bound into a dense network of horizontal, vertical and diagonal relations. A 'local production system' on the other hand, different from an 'industrial district', is a set of companies concentrated in a circumscribed territory that directly or indirectly produces for the same end-market (Brusco 1989). Thus a 'local production system' is broader than an industrial district. (Brusco 1989; Becattini 1987).

The regions of central and north-eastern Italy, characterized by a strong concentration of industrial districts and local production systems, are known as the 'Third Italy'. Historically, the economic development in these regions can be distinguished from that of the regions of North-Western Italy, which is driven by large industrial companies, and the development typical of the Southern Italian regions, which based on the dominant role of agriculture. Emilia-Romagna is one example of the regions of 'Third Italy' characterized by the important role of small firms.

Since the end of the Second World War, this region's economy has been characterized by the dominance of SMEs clustered in homogeneous industrial sectors and often confined geographically to a province or municipality. The average company in this region has about four employees.

Traditionally, thirteen industrial districts have been considered significant for the Emilia-Romagna economy, with concentrations in the following industries: packaging machinery, motor industry, soft furnishings and upholstery, footwear manufacturing, wood-working machinery, textiles and clothing, biomedical, farm machinery, ceramics, machine tools, food-processing machinery and footwear. The regional production structure is thus highly diversified.

The regional production system, created through endogenous processes, has generated significant levels of innovation thanks to a socioeconomic structure showing a positive correlation between high rates of collaboration among companies (although at times entailing strong competition) and honourable links with local authorities and associations representing business and labour. The region's capacity to generate wealth and innovation cannot be understood without considering the value of this well-constructed, abundant and interwoven socio-economic fabric (Brusco 1989).

However, according to Bardi (2007) forces opening up markets today are now redefining both the geographic and relational spaces within which the regional firms operate. In the context of globalization processes new, extra-regional connections with diverse actors have reorganized the patterns of cooperation and competition that traditionally characterized the industrial districts. Thus, the traditional industrial districts are going through a process of radical change.

The transformation of the region's production structure has entailed the reconfiguration of organizations at the company (micro-) level and the physiognomy of the territory at the meso-level in which these companies operate (Bardi 2007). The emergence of connections and synergies between different sectors is bringing about a recombination of locally rooted production factors and skills and thus generating new innovation paths (Fondazione Istituto per il Lavoro 2004). However, although these new paths represent the end of the traditional industrial-district model, they do not necessarily lead to a lessening of the importance of the local context (Poma 2003). It seems, in fact, that the local territory, traditionally a central element for enterprise development, maintains its importance.

On the one hand, regional production networks also maintain their importance in the context of globalization processes. On the other hand, structural changes have led to profound changes in labour with regard to job security, quality of working life and labour relations (Garibaldo 2007). We argue that the structural changes in the local production systems have undermined the bargaining power and the capacity of representation of the trade unions. In its argumentation this contribution will mainly draw on the results of various surveys and research projects carried out by the Institute for Labour Foundation in the recent past.[1]

Following a short introduction, section 12.2 examines the impact of globalization on the automotive supply industry as one of the most important local production systems in Emilia-Romagna. While section 12.2.1 focuses on the changing relationship between manufacturers and suppliers, in following sections the impact on the labour market (12.2.2), work organization (12.2.3) and working conditions (12.2.4) is analysed.

In section 12.3 the impact of structural changes on labour relations in Emilia-Romagna is the focus; in particular we will address the changing relationship between direct and negotiated participation (12.3.1). Analyses of the diffusion of participative experiences in the context of organizational change (12.3.2), including a distinction between direct participation, negotiated participation and forms of economic participation are undertaken. Section 12.3.3 focuses on the impact of restructuring processes on participation, while section 12.3.4 examines the role of social partners in the context of change processes. In the concluding remarks the major shortcomings of and challenges to industrial relations *vis-à-vis* the structural changes taking place in the Emilia-Romagna Region will be discussed.

12.2   The case of the automotive supply industry

In the following sections the impact of globalization on one of the most important local production systems in Emilia-Romagna, the automotive supply industry, is examined in more depth. In this context the dynamics between co-operation and dependency in the relations between manufacturers and suppliers is examined. In particular, the role of processes of modularization as the driver of the reorganization of the supply chain is analysed. Furthermore, the role of the labour market as well as the impact of the reorganization processes on work organization and working conditions is examined.

The results presented in the following sections are the outcome of a research project carried out on the automotive supply industry in Emilia-Romagna and was based on 50 case studies (Bardi and Garibaldo 2005).

12.2.1 The relationship between manufacturers and suppliers

Because of globalization companies have to combine two trends: on the one hand they have to be regionally located; on the other hand, a global strategy is indispensable to being competitive at the market (Warschat, Wagner and Edelmann 2005).

The role of the territory, that is the social context and the competences rooted in it, remains central to developing the innovative and competitive capacities of the local production systems. According to Bardi and Garibaldo (2005) local actors, such as universities, local public bodies and business associations, represent important actors with regard to innovation processes.

The role of the territory becomes crucial, in particular where a diffuse entrepreneurship is strong and deeply-rooted, with a typically strong presence of SMEs. These territorial realities can be defined as productive filières, or clusters (Calabrese and Erbetta 2005; Bardi and Gaibaldo 2001; Bardi and Garibaldo 2005; Warschat, Wagner and Edelmann 2005).

Ferro-Camacho (2005: 183) defines clusters as 'a concentration of competing, collaborating and interdependent companies and institutions which are connected by a system of market and non-market links'. Stressing again the importance of the immaterial and non-tangible aspects of the territorial development, he states that there are other elements in this social process that do not directly involve economic or technological aspects. They do, however, play a fundamental role in its success. In particular, these aspects are honest communication among actors and the development of spaces of trust.

With regard to the processes of development and transformation of clusters, Bardi and Garibaldo (2005) stress the role of the territorial dynamics, that is, the intersectoral connections that characterize a local productive structure. Referring to the automotive cluster in Emilia-Romagna they point out that the region is characterized by the presence of a fully-fledged motor-vehicle filière. Within the regional boundaries there are close ties between the traditional industries, such as the motorcycle and farm-machine industry, as well as the producers of specific technologies satisfying the various types of demand, such as for machine tools. These industries are interwoven with the producers of intermediate or complementary goods (such as automotive components and modules) and with industries of productive or related diversification (sports cars sector, alternative power vehicles and the like). The inter-sectoral dimension also appears to be important because it contributes to forging a specific supply-chain architecture that is, to some extent, less hierarchically vertical.

The collapse of profitability and the need to be present in the new industrialized countries has led the automobile manufacturers to increase the outsourcing of activities, while at the same time reorganiz-ing the chain starting from the concept of modularization. Calabrese and Erbetta (2005: 214-5) state that 'the speedy decrease of profitability along with the growing financial requirements due to competition and production expansion in emerging countries has induced many carmak-ers to reinforce outsourcing'. These choices contribute to increasing the global presence of the suppliers as well as growth in terms of size and competencies possessed.

The integration between clients and suppliers becomes a strategic elem-ent to foster competitiveness and product innovation processes. Thus Bardi and Garibaldo (2005) observe an increasing dependency of car pro-ducers on suppliers in regard to the global development strategies. Such a dependency clashes with the manufacturers' increasing need to cut supply costs. Car producers use their bargaining power to impose cost containment strategies aimed at offloading the indirect costs onto the suppliers. Referring to the automotive cluster in Emilia-Romagna, Bardi and Garibaldo (2005) note that the need for cost reduction imposed by the market on the end-producers and offloaded by these onto the sup-pliers implies the risk of undermining the economic and financial stabil-ity of the companies operating in the supply chain in the medium term.[2]

These tendencies clearly show that the previous equilibrium of the filière is changing. The elements of the previous equilibrium that are today challenged are the nature and modalities of the relation-ship between companies as well as their organizational and managerial strategies. According to Bardi and Garibaldo (2005) the process of tran-sition is characterized by uncertainty and the difficulty of focusing clearly on the priorities and the direction to be pursued. This uncer-tainty is clearly expressed by the companies' demand for specific public policies. In view of the SMEs involved in the research project, public poli-cies should, above all, support the construction of integrated company networks. In particular, SMEs are asking for support in regard to:

- integration into networks with other companies;
- development of co-design; and
- raising the level of supply.

These demands suggest a growing sensitivity of supply companies to the role of company networks as a way to face the critical factors typical for SMEs. In Emilia-Romagna the Ministry for Productive Activities already started to introduce a series of specific measures supporting the development of company networks at the beginning of the decade.

The role of regional production networks is not only important for SMEs but also for global players, as their strategies of delocalization imply increasing information and transaction costs. For this reason reliable regional networks are of crucial importance, in particular in the case of high-quality production. As Hoffmann (2006) points out, the success of global players depends very much on how successfully they are embedded into regional production networks. For the Emilia-Romagna Region this is confirmed by Poma (2003) who describes the intense relations of subsidiaries of transnational enterprises with actors in the local context in which they have settled. That means that the subsidiaries are embedded there in various ways. Also, Garibaldo (2007: 520) confirms the role of the regional level, stating that 'the de-structuring and reinvention of organizational structures due to globalization does not imply the disappearance of regional spaces but rather their redefinition'.

12.2.2   The regional labour market

According to Bardi and Garibaldo (2005) the research carried out in the regional automotive cluster confirms that the knowledge accumulated and disseminated across the territory represents a central element in the overall competitiveness of the filière. In the SMEs there is still a strong dependency of the companies on the knowledge and competencies of the entrepreneurs themselves.

Due to the low rate of unemployment, the lesser propensity of young people to choose industrial jobs and the lack of workers in certain professions of strategic importance, there is strong competition between large and small companies in labour-force recruitment. As a consequence companies increasingly revert to the extra-regional labour force, first and foremost from southern Italy and from non-EU countries. The competition between companies is not limited to professions in production but also affects others such as quality managers, management staff and divisional supervisors (cf. Bardi and Garibaldo 2005).

Precarious forms of labour contracting are widespread and utilized in order to manage productive peaks as well as to select staff for a long-term contract. However, after a sharp increase in the use of temporary agency workers between 1997 and 2002, companies now tend to use temporary work agencies less often. The most important reason for this is the fact that the temporary agency workers are not sufficiently qualified for the work to be carried out in the highly specialized companies of the automotive filière. A growing number of companies, therefore, prefers directly selecting the workers and stipulating fixed-term contracts. In other cases companies prefer to manage the peaks by using overtime.

With regard to training, continuous training is practically absent. The practices of knowledge-management – that is, techniques of managing, stimulating and transferring knowledge inside companies – are still largely underdeveloped.

12.2.3 Changes in work organization

With regard to processes of organizational innovation, company strategies are characterized by a scarcely coherent approach. Processes of change are often the result of trial and error, and reactive actions, rather than of mediated strategies. According to Bardi and Garibaldo (2005) the main innovative trends, from both the technological and the organizational point of view, are represented by processes of modularization.

Modularization seeks to use assembly lines in the most flexible way. In modularization assembly lines are able to process a range of different parts according to a random order that depends on the market demand. Such flexibility is achieved through the integration of the suppliers, for example in so-called Module Assembly Units (Bardi and Garibaldo 2005). These processes of integration are characterized by a strong pressure on the employees' rhythm of work in the supply and sub-supply companies. That means that the client – the market – becomes the point of reference for internal company processes. The workers are directly faced with the demands of the market and the clients. As a consequence, the individual management of the growing dynamic of the market and customer demands becomes increasingly important.

Another trend in the reorganization processes in the automotive cluster in Emilia-Romagna is represented by the diffusion of forms of cooperative work between workers. As already described by Cooke, Meyer and Huxley (2006) these forms of cooperative work appear to be generally limited to task-based team structures and processes in which employees have become more flexible in the tasks and jobs they perform and are held more accountable for improving their own performance against management-designed and controlled work routines. That means that teams are directed from the outside and do not possess any substantial autonomy. In general, management does not concede anything with regard to performance control. Not surprisingly employees in work teams experience, on average, greater strain than employees not working in teams. In general that means that team-work provides little added empowerment and increases the intensity of work.

12.2.4 The impact on working conditions

Controlling the integrated production cycles focal firms (OEMs), in general, also control the value chain. This implies that focal firms indirectly determine working conditions and levels of remuneration in the other companies of the respective productive filières. Integrated production organization based on just-in-time principles leads to an increasing work intensity having a negative impact on work conditions and quality. Surveys on working conditions in Emilia-Romagna (Bonora and Garibaldo 2006; Bonora et al. 2006) report experiences in working at high speed and under strict deadlines. The pace of work is widely determined by the work done by colleagues, production targets and the speed of automated machinery (Garibaldo and Rebecchi 2006: 105). Therefore, the main negative factors in the changing work environment involve stress and the pressure of management demands. High-strain jobs are also concentrated among workers with non-standard labour contracts, in which working conditions are characterized by a highly flexible working time, heavy workloads and poorer health and safety conditions.

The most widespread forms of alienation are lacking opportunities to participate in work organizations, poor economic reward and difficulties in maintaining a good work-life balance. Other widespread reasons for discontent are rather limited career prospects and growing job insecurity.

The segmentation of internal labour markets leads to a gap between standard and non-standard workers. The former group with open-ended labour contracts more often enjoy functional flexibilities, broader tasks and greater autonomy, while the latter group with part-time or non-permanent labour contracts, in general, carries out the more repetitive and monotonous jobs with less responsibility.

12.3 The impact on labour relations

In the context of structural change, management strategies are particularly focused on the promotion of worker involvement and the introduction of team-work as two important methods of governing work processes. The following sections, therefore, explore the impact of these management strategies on labour relations and participation processes.

12.3.1 Direct participation and negotiated participation

The introduction of new forms of work organization also has an impact on labour relations at decentralized levels. In processes of organizational innovation traditional forms of company-level interest representation are increasingly exposed to the pressure deriving from the managerial techniques of direct employee involvement. Such forms of direct participation are often introduced by management, supplanting traditional forms of representative participation. As a result, certain topics regarding working conditions are not covered by the activities of the structures of interest representation. Therefore, a deterioration of the efficacy of representative participation appears evident.

Thus the problem that emerges regards the relationship between direct participation and negotiated or representative participation. Italian industrial relations are characterized by an almost non-existent institutionalization of participation rights. In the absence of legislation, the participatory experiences of workers or their representatives related to decisions about the organization of work appear in the form of direct participation or in the form of negotiated or representative participation.

All policies and techniques involving workers can be defined as direct participation. In the context of international competition, management considers workers, too, as a flexible component; there also appears to be an attempt to use the various forms of worker involvement to achieve objectives defined by management (cf. Felger et al. 2003; Harley, Hyman and Thompson 2005). In this case, the workers' concrete influence is limited to the involvement at the operational level, for example through the modalities of performance of the working tasks. According to Baglioni (2000) direct participation that does not allow the chance to modify the criteria for the implementation of the managerial prerogatives can be classified as *weak participation*.

Companies rarely offer forms of participation that go beyond direct participation. Participation in organizational choices is generally the result of requests by workers' representatives or unions and is achieved through negotiated participation. By forms of negotiated participation we mean formalized participative pathways that are generally activated through union negotiations. Negotiated participation that ranges from the right to information and consultation through economic participation to co-determination can be defined as *strong participation* (Baglioni 2000), in that it is capable of modifying the criteria for the implementation of the managerial prerogatives.

Since in Italy most significant participation experiences are based on agreements between social partners, we can speak here of a negotiated road to participation. The lack of an institutionalization of participatory rights and the differentiated approaches of the various companies to participation mean that the Italian situation, in terms of participation, is particularly fragmented. This is also true for the local production systems in Emilia-Romagna.

With regard to the regional situation, the second characteristic consists in the fact that, at the level of local production systems, processes of globalization have contributed to the dissemination of managerial strategies aimed at fostering worker involvement in the operational modalities in order to contribute to reaching the objectives defined by management (Bardi and Garibaldo 2005). The management strategies clearly tend towards expanding forms of direct participation to the detriment of forms of negotiated or representative participation. This trend leads to a neglect of the issues dealt with by traditional forms of interest representation. Trade unions, therefore, push for a stronger coordination between the two modalities of participation.

12.3.2   The diffusion of participation experiences in the context of organizational change

Direct participation

Numerous research results underline the fact that, with respect to the choices of the actors in participation processes, the involvement of the workers themselves is fundamental for guaranteeing the use of their skills and their creativity, which, in turn, is indispensable for an effective implementation of organizational innovation (Brödner 2000).[3] The sharing of the project of organizational change and, therefore, the necessary motivation during the application phase, largely depends on the possibility of achieving workers' direct participation.

In the second half of the 1990s, the EPOC report[4] examined the different experiences of direct participation in the European Union. Direct participation meant the consultation or delegation of individual or group-level functions. Three main issues were investigated: the diffusion of direct participation; its socio-economic effects; and the possible influence of the workers on the organization of work. To pursue these issues, in the autumn of 1996 an investigation was performed within the company management of ten member states of the European Union by means of an *ad hoc* questionnaire. From the conclusions it emerged that:

- direct participation has a greater likelihood of being introduced in companies in which complex and non-manual tasks are performed and in companies with team-work, a highly skilled labour force and in-house training;

- economic and qualitative performance rises as direct participation rises;
- employment cuts are likelier in workplaces without direct participation than in companies that consider its implementation.

In regard to the Italian situation it has been highlighted that, if in regard to group consultation Italy is situated more or less at average level, it is below average in the delegating responsibilities to workers (both at individual and group level).

This result is confirmed, at least with regard to manufacturing companies, by research carried out within the scope of the first Annual Report of the Institute for Labour Foundation. According to the empirical research carried out in Emilia-Romagna, the valorization of human resources in manufacturing companies comes about firstly on the basis of skilled and specialized work, but also through the demands for worker versatility and responsibilization (Capecchi and Carbone 2000). The integration of executive and control tasks, along with decision-making decentralization at the operational level and at the level of worker autonomy, are, instead, less diffused modalities.

It is also interesting to observe that according to the research cited the cases in which workers participate, the organization of work is more diffused in service companies. This higher propensity for participation regards the levels of participation of the workers in management, as well as the contents of the participation itself. In these cases, the participation does not just concern salary or professional training but also aspects linked to the organization and the working environment. In manufacturing companies, on the contrary, it seems that there are only a few experiences of worker involvement in the processes of introduction of new forms of work organization.

Overall, the results seem to indicate that the diffusion of experiences of a participative nature is rather weak. Instead, when we are faced with the involvement of the workers, it generally does not come about in the initial phase of the design of new organizational models but rather on the basis of a model already defined by management. A final important consideration concerns the fact that in the cases in which there is worker involvement in organizational change, it seems that the unions remain excluded (Capecchi and Carbone 2000).

The problems that arise when the union is excluded from the processes of organizational innovation are highlighted in the third Annual Report of the Institute for Labour Foundation (Fondazione Istituto per il Lavoro 2003). This report has analysed, among other things, the quality of working life in various sectors. An important aspect within the scope of this survey concerned the diffusion and the quality of the practices that could be classified as forms of direct participation. Empirical research has been performed through case studies distributed in the economic sectors of the automobile sub-supply industry, the building industry, the software industry, the banking and insurance sector and the public utilities.

In nearly all the cases analysed in which there was a direct worker involvement, these forms of direct participation are experienced by the workers' representatives as a threat and in some cases lead to open conflicts.

In the automotive cluster in Emilia-Romagna, forms of direct participation are often introduced in the context of the introduction of new forms of work organization. When it comes to the building of teams, new professional roles such as the team leader emerge. They can become a point of reference for the members of the teams, not only with regard to the organization of work, but also with regard to aspects regarding working conditions. As a consequence, the traditional structures of interest representation face a loss of bargaining competencies (Garibaldo and Bardi 2005). In addition, company-level structures of interest representation are loosing control over effective working conditions.

Unilateral decisions by management to introduce forms of direct participation can, therefore, undermine the relations of trust between the actors and favour attitudes of opposition on the side of the worker representatives. As a consequence, the direct participation experience nearly always remains scarcely effective. These cases indeed make evident the need to choose an integrated approach between forms of direct and representative participation. In the event of a lack of coordination between the two forms of participation, the forms of direct participation that are justifiable in theory are mostly destined to failure. As a whole, the results appear to indicate that the diffusion of successful experiences of direct participation is rather weak.

The increasing dissemination of managerial strategies aimed at fostering direct worker involvement also has an impact on the formalization of management-employee relationships. The pressure of focal firms on subsidiaries, or supply firms, to apply managerial strategies able to respond to the needs of an integrated production organization have led to more structured forms of work organization and worker involvement, also in regional SMEs. Thus in many companies that in the past were characterized by highly informal management-employee relations, the specific demands of focal firms that are often transnational enterprises have contributed to more formalized management-employee relations. In other SMEs that, in the past, were already characterized by functioning industrial relations at company-level, the introduction of forms of direct worker involvement, in many cases, has contributed to a shift of competency between competing forms of social regulation.

Negotiated participation and work organization

In Italy there has always been a preference to aim at bargaining for the defining of the criteria and the forms of participation. In the absence of legal regulation of participation, the social pact signed on 23 July 1993 represents the only institutionalized basis that can, in some way, promote the experiences of participation (Telljohann 2001). This social pact provides for the following possibilities of participation:

1. economic participation through wage increases is linked to the trend in productivity, the quality of the product and the profitability of the company. Wage increases should be correlated to the results achieved in the realization of the programmes agreed between the parties. On the basis of this formulation, agreed programmes could be hypothesized concerning the processes of organizational innovation with a consequent positive impact on the labour productivity and/or the product quality, which, for its part, should create leeway for wage increases;
2. the information and consultation procedures with regard to the social effects connected with corporate transformation, such as technological and organizational innovations, as well as processes of restructuring that affect conditions of safety, work and employment, but also in relation to the law on equal opportunity.

One may add to these possibilities participation within the scope of bilateral commissions, which, in general, is defined through collective bargaining. These commissions, which also deal with questions concerning working conditions in the company, hardly ever play a decision-making role but rather only a consultative one. As regards the possibilities of participation laid down in the social pact, it can be concluded that they represent a rather weak and insufficient basis. On the one hand, as regards economic participation, there is only a generic reference to the chance that the social partners should jointly develop programmes to establish mechanisms for the definition of wage increases at company level; on the other hand, as regards the participation within the scope of restructuring processes, the social pact of 1993 lays down a role for unitary workplace union structures (RSU) only with regard to the 'management of the social effects connected to the company transfor-mations, such as the technological and organizational innovations, and the restructuring processes'. Thus it is not an involvement *ex ante* but rather, *ex post*.

Considering that these are the only possibilities envisaged by the 1993 social pact that allow for the promotion of participation experiences at the company level, we must conclude that, in Italy, we are faced with a *low level of institutionalization* of the rights to participation. The possi-bilities for participation have proven, from the standpoint of timeliness, certainty and incisiveness, to be wholly inadequate, such that in prac-tice the experiences of participation within the scope of organizational innovation processes have remained very limited, as we try to demon-strate further on.

The fact, highlighted in the first Annual Report of the Institute for Labour Foundation, that the trend to act in favour of the autonomy of workers through group work, responsibilization and the decentraliza-tion of the decisions is wholly independent of the level of unionization and union policies, which are, in turn, independent of the level of participation of those who are involved in the management of the com-panies (Capecchi and Carbone 2000), seems to demonstrate that there is no link between union policies of company-level concertation and entrepreneurial strategies that envisage the introduction of forms of work organization capable of favouring the autonomy of employees. The issues of work organization, indeed, appear to be a matter of industrial relations at company level only in a minority of cases.

The limited presence of issues concerning the organization of work in second-tier bargaining is also confirmed by studies on company-level bargaining in Emilia-Romagna (IRES Emilia-Romagna 1999). In the bargaining rounds of 1994–7 one finds in only 15.1 per cent of the integrative agreements items concerning work organization.[5] As regards the bargaining of organization measures post-1994, there is a new item, namely quality certification. Until 1997 this item was bargained over in less than 2 per cent of the cases analysed. Moreover, the effects on the organization of work actually seem very limited.

The spread of voices concerning work organization in second-tier bargaining varies with company size. In micro-companies these issues are often informally regulated. The IRES Emilia-Romagna report indeed highlights the fact that in the companies with fewer than 20 employees bargaining in organizational change is almost non-existent.

These results are also confirmed by more recent investigations. In its conclusions the third Annual Report of the Institute for Labour

Foundation (Fondazione Istituto per il Lavoro 2003) states that no important experiences in bargaining and/or representative participation have been found in terms of work organization. In the best of cases there were well-structured experiences of industrial relations within the scope of which the union bodies act on the basis of a consolidated presence. But it seems that in no case a relatively strong position of the union bodies has led to an innovative practice of industrial relations based on experiences of bargaining and representative participation characterized by the development of autonomous projects of organizational innovation by the union. Even in the scope of direct participation the experiences carried out in the cases analysed are quite disappointing, both from the point of view of their efficacy and from the point of view of the integration between direct participation and representative participation (Telljohann 2003: 496–7). That means that, in general, the introduction of new forms of work organization is not an issue of company-level industrial relations.[6]

If at present trade unions do not seem to be involved in processes of organizational innovation, it is, however, interesting to note that at the end of the eighties the strategy of the metalworkers' unions in the Emilia-Romagna Region was focused on the negotiation of processes of organizational change and the definition of new models of employee participation (Telljohann 1991). In these cases, the trade-union strategy of *co-determination* was based on a convergence between management and union. While, on the one hand, management had to concede a part of its traditional prerogatives, the union, on the other hand, had to go beyond its traditional bargaining role and deal with the needs of the company with a cooperative attitude. Already by the nineties these experiences entered a crisis as divergences in the evaluations of management and the union movement regarding the application of traditional industrial relations and participation models considerably increased. As a consequence, most of the joint projects on organizational change were abandoned.

Economic participation

As 'industrial democracy' is linked to economic structure, it goes beyond a democracy understood in a formal way alone. In order to define the criteria for workers' economic participation, the company actors must identify a way to assess their performance in relation to the corporate organizational model. This possibility of participation should, theoretically, be the expression of a valorization of human work and the need to involve the workers and their representatives actively in the processes of organizational change.

Nevertheless, the report of IRES Emilia-Romagna (1999) shows that, in most of the cases in which forms of economic participation are applied, no procedures of bilateral confrontation are provided, which could, in theory, offer the chance of an involvement of workers in management and the assessment of models defining variable-wage proportions. We thus find ourselves faced with a traditional set-up that limits participation to economic aspects, waiving an active and accepted cooperation of the workers (Pini 2000).

By analysing company-level bargaining over the output bonuses, the report highlights how the social partners tend to use traditional forms of incentives (Auleta et al. 1999). The *participation incentive* is, instead, little used; it seems that the output bonus has been 'conceived preferably as an instrument of flexibilization and reductions of labour costs, in its incomes part, rather than as a mechanism of economic and managerial involvement of the human resources in the company's activities' (Auleta et al. 1999: 179). The link between work organization, participation and wage increases is still missing.

Further research carried out more recently reaches similar conclusions. In 2001–2, IRES Emilia-Romagna, in collaboration with the University of Ferrara, analysed organizational patterns, industrial relations and economic performances for a sample of companies in Emilia-Romagna (Monatti et al. 2003). The research results show that flexibility regarding remuneration, company organization and management (numeric, functional, temporal and organizational) constitute for management and the bodies of interest representation two distinct spheres, because they are generally dealt with separately. Furthermore, the characteristics of the bonuses analysed reveal the prevalence of 'aims linked to traditional incentive patterns and the subdivision of the company risk. This also underlines the low participative content of the mechanisms introduced' (Monatti et al. 2003: 150). The results indeed indicate the lack of a link between organizational innovation and the determination of variable salary. The bonuses seem to aim to reduce company conflicts rather than to promote workers' participation or a broader process of innovation in organizational patterns (Monatti et al. 2003).

12.3.3   The impact of restructuring processes on participation

The amount of conflict and the low level of institutionalization that have historically characterized Italian industrial relations have definitely been obstacles to the diffusion of a more participatory culture. Though in the 1990s the social partners made significant progress towards overcoming this conflict-based tradition, in the first half of the new decade, following a change in the strategy of the entrepreneurs' associations, we have witnessed a return to industrial relations increasingly based on power relations. This change in industrial relations can be noticed particularly in the subsidiaries of transnational enterprises. Within the scope of strategies based primarily on reducing labour costs, it has become widespread practice to carry forward processes of restructuring at the European level on the basis of the results of internal benchmarking. European plants are, above all, made to compete with one another in order to obtain, in the framework of restructuring processes, increases in productivity based on a reduction in labour costs through reductions in salaries, longer working time (with wages unaltered), and/or the lowering of employment levels (Telljohann 2007).

Benchmarking can be used to close down less competitive plants or simply threaten them with closure in order to then receive unilateral concessions from the workers in the name of competitiveness. However, not only transnational enterprises use the exit option. Family-owned companies also relocate or threaten to relocate their production to low-cost countries (Mercuri 2005).

One consequence of the primacy of the market rationale thus consists in the undermining of the cooperative industrial relations that in the past represented the basis for the achievement of consensual compromises and solutions. In accordance with the asymmetry of power between companies and workers today, bargaining processes generally lead to adaptations to the requests of the market. Within the scope of restructuring processes, workers' susceptibility to blackmail has now superseded the rationale of reciprocity between actors.

This type of strategy – focused on reduced labour costs – is an indicator of the deep-seated changes in the power relations between capital and labour. In this new context participation risks are becoming only a side-interest for companies, in that it is no longer functional in their changing managerial strategies. A notable consequence is the increasing marginalization of the instruments of participation.

12.3.4 The role of social partners in the context of change processes

As a whole, the processes of bargaining organizational change and the involvement of the workers in the Emilia-Romagna Region must be considered below expectation; this is, therefore, a clue to the as yet insufficient spread of a participation culture. As we have seen, this problem is posed both in quantitative and in qualitative terms.

If the unions have preferred to give up on the investment in co-determination, companies, too, have never fostered the diffusion of negotiated participation experiences. Instead, when they became aware of the increased importance of the active involvement of the workers, they preferred the application of direct participation methods, thereby excluding the unions from the processes of organizational innovation. But also in this case the companies chose a minimalist approach, avoiding the delegation of competence and limiting themselves to straightforward forms of involvement. However, in this way companies risk wasting possible improvements in performance.

On the part of trade unions we are faced with a strategy that was never invested with any conviction in a strategy of negotiated participation within the scope of processes of organizational change. The risk here is that, in the future, the unions will continue to remain excluded from the processes of organizational change, with foreseeable effects, such as the reduction in their capacity for action, and also in other issues dependent on the organization of work (for example, work-time, wages, job classification, health and safety), and an intensification of the crisis of representivity, especially when it comes to white-collar and highly skilled workers.

12.4   Conclusions and outlook

This contribution has attempted to show that in the context of the globalization processes, traditional industrial districts are going through a process of radical change. Against the background of the primacy of the market principle, the production process has become a dependent variable of market mechanisms. As a consequence in the case of the *Third Italy*, there has been a transformation of the region's production structure, including the reconfiguration of production organization at the company level.

The new dynamics of cooperation and dependency between manufacturers and suppliers has led to processes of segmentation of the labour market and negative effects on working conditions. The greater strain employees experience in work teams is one of the reasons for the deterioration of working conditions. If, on the one hand, the intensity of their work is increasing, employees have, on the other hand, gained only little added empowerment.

From the company point of view the labour force, in that it represents a part of the production costs, represents a dependent variable. The generalized application of market principles implies the implementation of a new, if indirect, method of governing work processes and working life in general: objectives to be achieved on the market are translated into production targets to be achieved. This new method of governing work processes means that each worker is directly faced with the demands of the market and clients.

By means of the orientation to flexible objectives and working hours the traditional institutional buffers between the individual and the market are broken down. Indeed, the individual management of the growing dynamic of market and customer demands is becoming increasingly important. Similar to the findings of Fichter, in the case of SMEs located in Emilia-Romagna the processes of reorganization and restructuring also tend to contribute to a stronger individualization in employee-management relations. Direct involvement, responsibilization of the individual workers and individualized wages are the most striking aspects of this tendency (cf. Fichter in this volume).

Management strategies thus attempt to promote worker involvement and team-work as two important methods of governing the work process. The innovation of production processes is often combined with the introduction of new forms of work organization that are directly controlled by management. This control is also exerted through direct worker involvement, which, in a growing number of cases, leads to competition with traditional forms of representative participation. That also means that the traditional representative structures of interest representation must face a partial loss of bargaining and participatory competence. As a result, the company-level structures of interest representation are loosing control over the actual working conditions and the determination of wages. Unilateral management decisions to introduce forms of direct participation can, therefore, undermine the relations of trust between the actors and favour attitudes of opposition.

Although in SMEs direct communication between employees and management or owner-managers is more common, there is a growing formality in the mechanisms for communicating directly with employees. This process can be explained with the need to adapt to the production systems of clients or focal firms. That means that the development of formality comes as a response to specific demands expressed by these firms. Thus in many companies where in the past there were highly informal management-employee relationships, the specific demands of focal firms, often transnational enterprises, have contributed to more formalized management-employee relationships. In other SMEs that had functioning industrial relations at company level in the past, the introduction of forms of direct worker involvement has often contributed to shifts in competence between competing forms of social regulation.

An advanced system of social regulation seems to be less necessary from the management's point of view. The management policy of unilaterally deciding over processes of change means that, in general, the introduction of new forms of work organization is not an issue of company-level industrial relations. In fact up until today in the Emilia-Romagna Region, participative experiences within the scope of organizational innovation processes have hardly been widespread. As we have seen, there are various reasons that can explain why the introduction of new forms of work organization is so infrequent. Thus, there are various challenges that must be dealt with if we wish to make headway in this field.

As we start investigating the causes of the insufficient spread of participatory experiences in the processes of organizational innovation, we have to note that since the beginning of this decade the climate of cooperation between the social partners, typical for the eighties and early nineties, has been undermined by a shift towards industrial relations that are increasingly based on the balance of power between actors. Fostering participatory experiences in the field of work organization today implies the need to return to a more cooperative industrial relations model.

In this context a particular shortcoming regards the lack of a tradition in the field of participation. The social pact of 23 July 1993, therefore, offers the chance to set down programmes agreed upon between parties whose objectives certainly are increases in productivity, quality and other elements of competitiveness. But it also provides an important instrument for promoting, at the company level, industrial relations based on bilateral talks also capable of fostering worker participation and the involvement of their representative bodies in the main choices concerning the organization of work. Nevertheless, the concrete results achieved so far are the expression of a participatory culture that is still poorly developed.

Because even the negotiated road to participation has not been able to give satisfactory results, it seems that there is a need for a more incisive regulation and legislation capable of mandating participation in the processes of organizational innovation. The limitation of the 1993 social pact lies in the fact that it only indirectly provides an incentive to participation. In the future it would thus be auspicious to have an *institutionalization of participation rights* in order to create a context more favourable to processes of organizational innovation.[7]

An initiative for institutionalization would also have to provide an effective solution with regard to the need for the integration and coordination of different forms of participation. There is thus a need to innovate on the traditional system of interest representation by developing new hypotheses capable of clarifying the relationship between direct participation and representative participation. A lack of clarity over the respective competence of and interconnections between the different levels and actors puts the experiences of participation at risk of failure. Another challenge to be faced regards the need to develop forms of interest representation along the value chain, overcoming, in this way, the effects of the segmentation of the labour market.

Because the Italian scenario is not just characterized by an almost non-existent institutionalization of participation rights in terms of participation within the scope of organizational innovation processes, but also by scarcely encouraging results and trends coming out of the few concrete experiences that have taken place in the past, we can sum up that negotiated participation in terms of organizational innovation today has produced disappointing results.

In the face of such a poorly promising balance, the initiatives of the European Parliament in favour of information and consultation will likely take on relevance as regards the rights to participation at the national level. The Community norms in terms of the rights of workers to information, consultation and participation in companies located in the European Union contained above all in the three directives 94/45/EC, 2001/86/EC and 2002/14/EC might represent a chance for a modernization of participation instruments in Italy.

Notes

1. The Institute for Labour Foundation was set up by the Government of the Emilia-Romagna Region in 1998. One of its tasks consists in drafting annual reports regarding ongoing trends in the Region in terms of changes in work and its organizational patterns, both in the industrial and the commercial, public and private services, public administration and agriculture sectors.
2. An empirical analysis of the supply industry shows the role of the so-called reverse-auctions for carrying out cost-cutting strategies. The practice of participating in online auctions is also widespread among the small and micro-companies. There are, in fact, small enterprises acquiring up to 20 per cent of their supply contracts online.

3. In regard to the importance of direct participation Brödner (2000: 8) remarks: 'Direct participation simultaneously serves as [a] discussion process of diverse perspectives and interests, as [the] integration of distributed knowledge and competence for problem solving, as a forum for negotiating and balancing interests, as motivation to act, as [a] space for collective learning, and as transparent horizontal control of events.'

4. Epoc (Employee Direct Participation in Organizational Change) is a project of the European Foundation for the Improvement of Living and Working Conditions of Dublin. The results of the project can be found in *New Forms of Work Organization. Can Europe Realize its Potential?* (Dublin: European Foundation for the Improvement of Living and Working Conditions), 1997.

5. As compared with the previous round it is, nevertheless, worthwhile observing an increase in the diffusion of these issues (1991–1993: 11.2 per cent).

6. There are similar results in other Italian regions. In 2006 the Industrial Association of Lombardy, Assolombarda (2006), published a report on trends in relation to the introduction of new forms of work organization in the area of Milan. Although the survey is not representative of the country as a whole it provides interesting information on the spread of new forms of work organization and on the ways they were introduced. According to the report, companies largely adopt unilateral action of management when it comes to the introduction of new forms of work organization. With regard to the introduction of job rotation and job enlargement, too, forms of direct involvement were found. The involvement of trade union representatives is much less frequent (Della Torre 2006).

7. On the relevance of institutions see Artus in this volume.

References

Assolombarda (2006) 'La modernizzazione del lavoro nelle imprese milanesi', *research report* (Milan: Assolombarda).

Auleta, O., R. Fabbri, M. Melotti and P. Pini (1999) 'La contrattazione aziendale del premio di risultato nelle imprese emiliano-romagnole: alcuni risultati preliminari', in Ires Emilia-Romagna (ed.), *Secondo Rapporto sulla contrattazione in Emilia-Romagna: 1994–1997. Un'indagine sull'esperienza della contrattazione aziendale dopo il 23 luglio 1993* (Milan: Franco Angeli), 165–90.

Baglioni, G. (2000) 'La partecipazione nel tempo della globalizzazione', *L'impresa al plurale. Quaderni della partecipazione*, 5, 13–43.

Bardi, A. (2007) 'Emilia-Romagna after Industrial Districts: Regional Policy Implications', *unpublished paper* (Bologna: Fondazione Istituto per il Lavoro).

Bardi, A. and F. Garibaldo (2001) 'The Economic and Social Impact of Mergers and Acquisitions in Local Productive Systems: The Automotive Cluster in the Emilia-Romagna Region', *IpL Working Paper*, 9 (Bologna: Fondazione Istituto per il Lavoro).

Bardi, A. and F. Garibaldo (eds) (2005) *Company Strategies and Organisational Evolution in the Automotive Sector: A Worldwide Perspective* (Frankfurt, Berlin, Bern, Bruxelles, New York, Oxford, Wien: Peter Lang).

Bardi, A. and F. Garibaldo (2005) 'The Automobile Filière in Emilia-Romagna: Strategic Positioning and the Consequences of the FIAT Auto Crisis', in A. Bardi and F. Garibaldo (eds), *Company Strategies and Organisational Evolution in the Automotive Sector: A Worldwide Perspective* (Frankfurt, Berlin, Bern, Bruxelles, New York, Oxford, Wien: Peter Lang), 331–75.

Becattini, G. (ed.) (1987)*Mercato e forze locali: il distretto industriale* (Bologna: Il Mulino).

Bonora, C. and F. Garibaldo (eds) (2006) *La qualità della vita lavorativa e delle condizioni di lavoro in Emilia-Romagna. V Rapporto su Salute e Sicurezza in Emilia-Romagna* (Santarcangelo di Romagna: Maggioli Editore).

Bonora, C., D. Dazzi, F. Garibaldo, E. Ribecchi and G. Rubini (2006) *Come i lavoratori percepiscono le proprie condizioni di lavoro. Indagine tra le aziende dell'Emilia-Romagna* (Santarcangelo di Romagna: Maggioli Editore).

Brödner, P. (2000) 'Organisational Learning? Beyond Continuous Improvement', paper presented at the 3rd International Conference (Euro) CINet CI 2000: From Improvement to Innovation, Aalborg, 18–19 September 2000.

Brusco, S. (1989)*Piccole imprese e distretti industriali* (Turin: Rosenberg & Sellier).

Calabrese, G. And F. Erbetta (2005) 'Factors of Performance in a Context of Market Change: The Automotive District of Turin', in A. Bardi and F. Garibaldo (eds), *Company Strategies and Organisational Evolution in the Automotive Sector: A Worldwide Perspective* (Frankfurt, Berlin, Bern, Bruxelles, New York, Oxford, Wien: Peter Lang), 213–50.

Capecchi, V. and E. Carbone (2000) 'Una sintesi degli studi di caso: le dimensioni per interpretare il cambiamento e l'innovazione nelle imprese', in Fondazione Istituto per il Lavoro (ed.), *Sviluppo, lavoro, competitività in Emilia-Romagna. Rapporto annuale dell'Istituto per il Lavoro* (Milan: Franco Angeli), 139–82.

Coletto, D. (2006) 'Comparative Study on IR in SMEs – Case of Italy', European Foundation for the Improvement of Living and Working Conditions, <http://www.eurofound.europa.eu/eiro/2006/02/word/it0511207s.doc>.

Cooke, W., D. Meyer and C. Huxley (2006) 'Il teamworking nel settore automobilistico negli U.S.A.: strategie ed effetti sulle prestazioni produttive e sui risultati dei lavoratori', in A. Bardi, F. Garibaldo and V. Telljohann (eds), *A passo d'auto. Impresa e lavoro nel settore automobilistico* (Santarcangelo di Romagna: Maggioli Editore), 315–60.

Della Torre, E. (2006) 'Increasing Use of New Work Practices in Companies', European Foundation for the Improvement of Living and Working Conditions, <http://www.eiro.eurofound.eu.int/2006/10/articles/it0610039i.html>.

European Foundation for the Improvement of Living and Working Conditions (1997) *New Forms of Work Organisation. Can Europe Realise its Potential?* (Dublin: European Foundation for the Improvement of Living and Working Conditions).

Felger, S., W. Kruse, A. Paul-Kohlhoff and S. Senft (2003) *Partizipative Arbeitsorganisation: Beteiligung jenseits von Naivität. Ergebnisse aus dem PartArt-Projekt* (Münster, Hamburg, Berlin, Wien, London: Lit Verlag).

Ferro-Camacho, J. (2005) 'The Automotive Cluster of Galicia. The Role of PSA in the Regional Dynamics', in A. Bardi and F. Garibaldo (eds), *Company Strategies and Organisational Evolution in the Automotive Sector: A Worldwide Perspective*

(Frankfurt, Berlin, Bern, Bruxelles, New York, Oxford, Wien: Peter Lang), 181–211.

Fondazione Istituto per il Lavoro (ed.) (2003) *Globalizzazione, strategie di impresa e qualità della vita lavorativa. Profili di alcuni settori italiani. Terzo rapporto annuale dell'Istituto per il lavoro* (Milan: Franco Angeli).

Fondazione Istituto per il Lavoro (ed.) (2004) *Dinamiche e prospettive di sviluppo economico nella Provincia di Bologna. I comparti del motociclo, packaging e credito,* unpublished research report (Bologna: Fondazione Istituto per il Lavoro).

Garibaldo, F. (2007) 'Democratising Change', *AI & Society,* 21(4), 515–35.

Garibaldo, F. and A. Bardi (2005) 'Introduction', in A. Bardi and F. Garibaldo (eds), *Company Strategies and Organisational Evolution in the Automotive Sector: A Worldwide Perspective* (Frankfurt, Berlin, Bern, Bruxelles, New York, Oxford, Wien: Peter Lang), 7–29.

Garibaldo, F. and E. Rebecchi (2006) 'Organizzazione del lavoro', in C. Bonora, D. Dazzi, F. Garibaldo, E. Ribecchi and G. Rubini, *Come i lavoratori percepiscono le proprie condizioni di lavoro. Indagine tra le aziende dell'Emilia-Romagna* (Santarcangelo di Romagna: Maggioli Editore), 77–106.

Harley, B., J. Hyman and P. Thompson (eds) (2005) *Participation and Democracy at Work. Essays in Honour of Harvie Ramsay* (Basingstoke: Palgrave Macmillan).

Hoffmann, J. (2006) 'The Relevance of the Exit Optino: The Challenge for European Trade Unions of Post-Fordism, Internationalisation of the Economy and Financial Market Capitalism', *Transfer,* 12(4), 609–20.

IRES Emilia-Romagna (ed.) (1999) *Secondo Rapporto sulla contrattazione in Emilia-Romagna: 1994–1997. Un'indagine sull'esperienza della contrattazione aziendale dopo il 23 luglio 1993* (Milan: Franco Angeli).

Lugli, L. and S. Tugnoli (2002) *Rapporto sui processi di 'outsourcing' e condizioni di lavoro in Emilia-Romagna,* Ires Materiali, (Bologna: Ires).

Mercuri, F. (2005) *Indagine sul sistema di relazioni industriali in Emilia-Romagna,* IpL working paper no. 16 (Bologna: Fondazione Istituto per il Lavoro).

Monatti, J., L. Lugli, M. Nosvelli, P. Pini and S. Tugnoli (2003) 'Nuovi modelli organizzativi, relazioni industriali e contrattazione nelle imprese dell'Emilia Romagna', *Economia e Lavoro,* 37(1), 129–52.

Pini, P. (ed.) (2000) *Premio di partecipazione o premio di risultato? La contrattazione aziendale in Emilia-Romagna dopo il 1993* (Bologna: Clueb).

Poma, L. (2003) *Oltre il distretto. Imprese e istituzioni nella nuova competizione territoriale* (Milano, Franco Angeli).

Telljohann, V. (1991) 'Kodetermination – ein Strategieansatz zur Überwindung der Subalternität der italienischen Gewerkschaften', *WSI Mitteilungen,* 44(1), 34–42.

Telljohann, V. (2001) 'The Italian Industrial Relations System and New forms of Participation', in D. Foden, J. Hoffmann and R. Scott (eds), *Globalisation and the Social Contract* (Brussels: ETUI), 277–94.

Telljohann, V. (2003) 'Strategie d'impresa, relazioni industriali e modelli di partecipazione', in Fondazione Istituto per il lavoro (ed.) *Globalizzazione, strategie di impresa e qualità della vita lavorativa. Profili di alcuni settori italiani. Terzo rapporto annuale dell'Istituto per il lavoro* (Milan: Franco Angeli), 485–99.

Telljohann, V. (2007) 'Interest Representation and European Identity – A Twofold Challenge for European Works Councils', in M. Whittall, H. Knudsen and

F. Huijgen (eds), *European Works Councils and the Problem of European Identity* (London: Routledge), 150–68.

Warschat, J., K. Wagner and C. Edelmann (2005) 'Automotive District Stuttgart – Evolution and Trends with the Focus on Cooperation in Virtual Clusters', in A. Bardi and F. Garibaldo (eds), *Company Strategies and Organisational Evolution in the Automotive Sector: A Worldwide Perspective* (Frankfurt, Berlin, Bern, Bruxelles, New York, Oxford, Wien: Peter Lang), 125–58.

13
Polish SMEs at a Crossroads: Market Strategies and Labour Relations in Global Competition

Ralph-Elmar Lungwitz, Manfred Wannöffel and Yvonne Rückert

13.1 Introduction

Politicians and scholars dealing with Central and Eastern Europe (CEE) apply mainly one of two perspectives: A first group stresses the ongoing convergence within the EU and presupposes that sooner or later economic efficiency and welfare in CEE countries will reach the level of the established market economies in Western and Northern Europe. This approach not only corresponds to the official view of the European Commission, but also to the hopes of the people of CEE for what was once labelled their 'return to Europe'. With respect to social policy, it includes the concept of a 'European Social Model' (Witte 2004) combining decent working conditions with social dialogue based on legally granted workers' rights.

An alternative view rests on the characterization of the CEE market economies as 'peripheral' (Bohle 2002) or 'dependent' capitalism (King 2002). It envisions tendencies towards a 'maquiladorization' of these countries (Musiolek 1999: 8). This term refers to a belt of production sites in Northern Mexico and Central America that assemble components and re-export the products to the US. Low wages, poor working conditions and the violation of worker rights are regarded as characteristic of these sites. It became a synonym for the 'low-road' model of fierce price competition among low- and medium-tech firms on the bottom-end of trans-national value chains.

Polish economic development since 1990 and after EU accession appears to encourage the first view. The Polish economy is among the most dynamic in the EU, with average annual growth of GDP during the last ten years at 5.4 per cent. After a slowdown in the years 2001 and

2002, Polish GDP grew by 6.1 per cent in 2006, and in 2007 a growth of 5.5 per cent is expected (Ost-West-Contact 2007: 26). Which of the two models is finally going to predominate, however, can hardly be predicted without taking Polish SMEs into consideration. In contrast to other former communist countries, Poland had a significant private sector already before 1990. By the end of the 1980s, about 19 per cent of GDP was produced by non-agrarian private firms (Mroczek, v. Schuttenbach, Ciurla 2000: 25). In the course of the societal transformation, the number of these firms tripled, above all as a result of newly established businesses (Ministry of Economy and Labour 2005: 25). Today, Polish SMEs make up 50 per cent of GDP and supply about 71 per cent of jobs in Poland (Lewiatan 2006: 3). The SMEs are, however, very small: 95 per cent of all Polish firms are micro-firms employing fewer than ten people; only 0.8 per cent are medium-sized (50–249 employees). Of Polish SMEs 38 per cent belong to the industrial sector (Lewiatan 2006: 3). About 10 per cent of SMEs with more than nine employees export their products; almost a half of this export goes to Germany (Ministry of Economy 2006b: 14).

In this chapter we pursue two goals. We suggest that Polish SMEs in traditional manufacturing sectors stay today at a crossroads. Which way they turn will not only influence their economic performance and the working conditions at their sites but also have an impact on the further development of the Polish welfare state and the system of labour relations. Thus, an analysis of the economic and social situation of this type of enterprise is needed to conceptualize sufficiently in which direction the Polish market economy and its institutions could develop.

In the first section of this chapter, we explore the country's labour-relation institutions and how Polish SMEs are formally integrated into this system. We search for explanations for the open hostility of Polish SMEs towards employee participation, which is strongly linked to the 'low-road' competitive strategy still widespread among them. In the second and third sections, we analyse how entrepreneurs generally react to the new challenges of globalization and European integration and how SMEs in particular react to them.

The findings are drawn from surveys of the SME sector conducted on a regular basis in Poland, and from our own qualitative studies focusing on the way entrepreneurs interpret their competitive situation, which strategy they consider successful, and what concept of labour relations they pursue. In addition to the eight in-depth interviews we conducted with manager-owners in the Polish clothing and furniture industries, we also interviewed 22 workers from the Polish clothing industry about working conditions and labour relations. In spite of the explorative status of our research we believe the findings are transferable to other industrial sectors where SMEs play a major role.[1]

13.2   Labour relations and competitive strategy

The role of trade unions and worker participation in Poland is rather weak compared to the situation in most other countries of Western and Northern Europe, where collective regulation of working conditions is agreed on between unions and employers' associations. As a rule, the concrete stipulations of labour contracts in Poland are negotiated directly between single employees and the respective employers. Nevertheless, legal regulations in the fields of labour law and workplace health and safety standards give employees and trade union organizations a number of rights that are comparable to West- and North-European standards, and in some cases even surpassing these. After 1990 Poland, like most of the other post-communist countries in Central and Eastern Europe, applied the scheme of a 'monistic' structure of worker participation in the trade unions as the only legitimate representatives of employees at the enterprise level. Trade unions rejected the idea of independent 'workers councils' (the 'dual system') as they exist, for example, in Germany and Austria, fearing a loss of influence in the firms. In addition, workers councils stood in the minds of many for the failed model of a 'third way' between capitalism and socialism (Bluhm 2007: 91).

In 2002, the European Union, however, issued a directive[2] that obliged all member countries to establish a legal framework ensuring employees' rights to information and consultation. After a process of controversial discussion between trade unions, employer associations and state authorities the Polish parliament in April 2006 adopted the 'Law on the Informing of and Consulting with Employees'. Formally this law marked the change from a monistic to a dual system of worker participation, because it stipulated the mandatory foundation of workers councils in all enterprises with more than 50 employees. Firms with more than 100 employees were obliged to set up the councils within six months; the other firms must have founded the councils by March 2008. Nevertheless, a recent study revealed that by March 2007 only 22 per cent of enterprises with more than 100 employees had a council in place. And even the owners of these firms quite often refused to supply information about the economic situation of the firm to the councils or provide the required financial resources (Partner 2007).

As in almost all CEE countries, the influence of trade unions (TUs) has decreased dramatically in Poland. While at the beginning of transformation in 1990 almost all employees were trade union members, in a survey carried out by the Public Opinion Research Centre (CBOS) in October 2006 of a representative sample of 999 adult Poles, only 14 per cent of employees declared themselves members of a trade union. The Solidarity trade union assembles 5 per cent of all employees, the Trade Union Federation OPZZ 4 per cent and the Trade Unions Forum 3 per cent. Among TU members there are more skilled than unskilled workers and trade unions face great difficulty recruiting young people. In the public sector (education, health system, public administration and so on), trade unions play a much larger role than in the private sector. The degree of unionization rises with the size of the firm: in firms with less than 50 employees only 8 per cent of the respondents declared union membership, compared to 14 per cent in firms with 50 to 249 employees, and 25 per cent and in firms with more than 250 employees (CBOS 2006). Especially private SMEs founded after 1990 tend to not have a trade union organization.

Another survey of CBOS carried out in November 2004 (Table 13.1) supplied clear evidence that in firms without a TU organization workers' rights are much more frequently violated than in firms with a TU organization.

The extremely weak position of trade unions in the SME sector may have contributed to the general tendency that in CEE the larger the

Table 13.1 The existence of TU organizations in firms and the enforcement of workers' rights (in per cent)

	With TU organization			No TU organization		
	Yes	No	Difficult to say	Yes	No	Difficult to say
Are wages regularly paid in your firm?	95	5	0	87	13	0
Are employees forced to work in conditions not in line with contracts?	18	82	0	21	78	1
Is there unpaid overtime work?	26	74	0	34	65	1

Source: CBOS 2005, BS/3/2005, n = 998

enterprises, the better the employment and working conditions are (European Commission 2004: 166).

Although the surveys of CBOS indicated a certain improvement of the situation as far as the acceptance of worker rights is concerned, also in the 2006 survey, 26 per cent of respondents contradicted the statement 'the workers have the right to found trade unions or join already existing unions' (CBOS 2006). Although these results do not reflect the size of the firms, it seems justified to assume that the violation of worker rights occurs more frequently in private SMEs than in large firms or the public sector.

Case studies and the findings of the already-mentioned analysis of the newly founded workers councils (Partner 2007) create the impression that the vast majority of private owners of firms have a hostile attitude towards worker participation based on legally granted worker rights and carried out by institutionally-backed actors, such as trade unions or workers councils. Although this attitude certainly can come from different sources (just to mention one, the experience of socialist-period 'rubber-stamp' trade unions), we assume a link between this hostility and the dominant way of integration of many Polish firms in cross-border value chains, and the fierce price competition most SMEs are exposed to. Price competition means a strong incentive for employers to cut costs including labour costs, to exceed legal limits on/to break legal rules regulating the use of the workforce, and to resist institutionally-backed participative actors who could hamper the implementation of such business practices. To a certain extent the situation, at least for a part of Polish SMEs, resembles that of the Mexican *maquiladoras* where a dependent position in cross-border value chains also involves fierce price competition, low wages and a hostile attitude of entrepreneurs towards employee participation.

An annual survey of the private employers' association 'Lewiatan' among 1,100 Polish SMEs with a maximum 250 employees indicates what firms consider to be their comparative advantage (see Figure 13.1).

Even more crucial than the mere relevance of prices to competition is the relation between the price and factors related to innovation. The importance attached to prices as a factor ensuring competitiveness rose continuously over the survey period, while the importance of the factors 'new products' and 'quality' significantly diminished.

If we focus on manufacturing only, the situation appears a little better. A survey among 629 SMEs conducted at the end of 2006 (Ministry of Economy 2007a: 22) indicated 40 per cent of SMEs in manufacturing had carried out innovation measures in 2006. Obviously those firms had

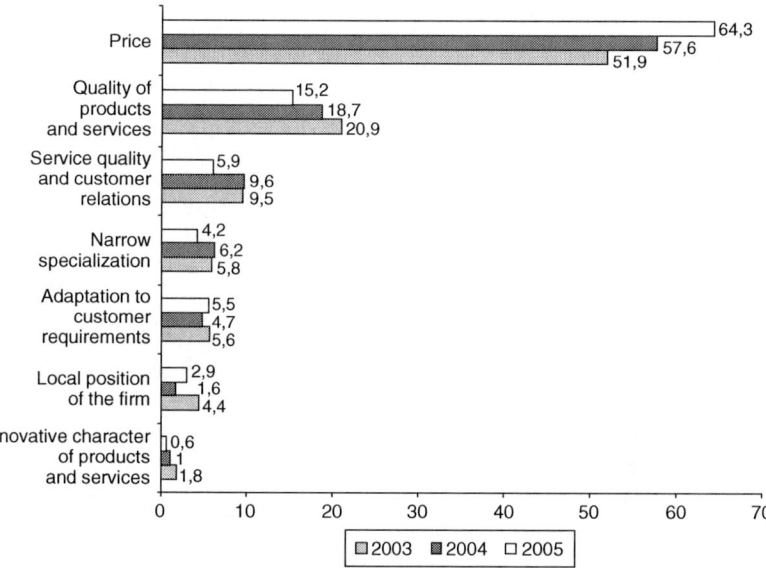

Figure 13.1 Factors crucial for competitiveness according to entrepreneurs (2003–2005)
Source: Lewiatan 2006: 23.

the motivation and the resources to do so. In another survey (Ministry of Economy 2006a: 50) the firms were asked to name the main obstacles to investment in innovation measures. The most frequent answers were:

- 'lack of financial means';
- 'the specific character of our market does not require that kind of investment';
- 'the specific character of our products and services does not require that kind of investment.'

While the first answer refers to the financial situation of Polish SMEs, the second and third answers point to the growing integration into western value chains that, so far, assigns Polish SMEs only a low-end role. Even in cases where materials and components of innovative products are assembled by Polish firms, SMEs play just a passive role in the process, because it is mainly West-European firms who are responsible for the relevant investment decisions and realization of the innovations. From the perspective of Polish firms, it is therefore appropriate to say that the specific character of their products or markets does not require investment in innovation projects.

Asked about barriers to their entrepreneurship[3] most of the SMEs asked note excessively high taxes and contributions as the major obstacle[4], while 'labour costs' play only a minor role at first glance. Since 'taxes and contributions' is an issue in all countries anyway, especially for SMEs, it might be that Polish entrepreneurs approach a study carried out by the government as simply a (rare) opportunity to convey a political message to the authorities. Yet, the picture becomes more differentiated when the size and economic sector the firms belong to is considered. SMEs in construction and manufacturing state more often than other firms that 'labour costs' are a barrier to entrepreneurship. As to size, the survey distinguished between micro-, small- and medium-sized firms. Although firms of all sizes complain of high taxes and contributions, significantly more owners of medium-sized firms (50–249 employees) state – significantly more often than owners of micro- and small firms – that 'labour costs' are the second-most important problem (Ministry of Economy 2007a: 8). In short, medium-sized manufacturing firms, in particular, regard labour costs as still too high for their markets on which they try to compete via prices.

This finding also indicates the specific pattern of involvement of Polish SMEs in the value-added chain of West-European, and in particular, German firms. Cost-cutting is an important motivation for German firms to engage themselves in Poland; for German SMEs it is even the central incentive (Bluhm 2000; Kinkel et al. 2004). Cost-cutting strategies of the predominantly western firms in the chains endanger the turnover of their Polish partners and push these to apply cost-cutting strategies themselves (Bontrup 2006). If these firms do not have the resources for that, the pressure on worker incomes will increase. Moreover, the priority of low prices set by western firms inevitably results in massive (price) competition between CEE firms for orders from western firms; this competition is waged not least via wages and labour costs. The weakness of innovation and the importance of prices and labour costs as means of competition resulted mainly from the Polish path into the market economy, but are nonetheless the basic facts of the situation from which Polish SMEs will have to rise to the challenges of ongoing globalization.

13.3   Growing pressures on SMEs and the ways they respond

The existence of an economically consolidated Polish SME segment proves that it has been possible to achieve some economic success on the above-described basis. However, there is rising pressure on this competitive strategy: China's full membership in the WTO, and the foreseeable disappearance of restrictions on certain kinds of goods imported into the European Union, is one issue here; the growing labour migration within Europe and growing interest in the Ukraine and Romania as offshore locations are others. We argue that, especially in manufacturing, Polish SMEs are facing growing pressures to change their strategy, which will not remain without consequences for labour relations within firms. This does not necessarily imply that western firms will simply shift their production further eastward. Previous studies have indicated that German SMEs, in particular, do not hasten to change existing and well functioning cooperation with CEE firms only in the vague hope that there could be a yet cheaper partner elsewhere (Lungwitz and Preusche 2002). Yet, just the awareness that a step like this could be possible enhances the pressure on Polish firms and increases price competition between CEE firms for production orders.

It is not only globalization that proves a challenge to Polish SMEs but also labour-market effects, resulting from the tremendous labour migration in recent years that expose Polish SMEs to changed business conditions. According to different estimations, between 600,000 and 4 million Poles have left their country as labour migrants since the accession to EU in 2004, with the UK, Ireland and the Scandinavian states being the favourite destination countries (Ministry of Economy 2007b). Large-scale labour migration and dynamic economic growth have resulted in a drop of unemployment and a significant lack of skilled labour in many fields. In addition the competition for skilled workers is increasing as western firms in Poland usually give skilled workers better pay and working conditions.

Many Polish firms react to this labour-market situation by enhancing wages for skilled workers to some extent. This may lead to growing wage differences between more- and less-skilled workers on the enterprise level and also in general. In our interviews with employers, it became clear that most of them felt they were in a certain dilemma: On the one hand, they were quite aware that they had to react to the labour market by increasing wages, at least for skilled workers; on the other hand, they continued to regard cheap labour costs as an indispensable precondition to successful competition. This also explains the growing criticism about taxes and social contributions – for them a solution to the dilemma would be to pass these costs on to public.

Also, labour relations at the firm level will be affected by these changes as the position of skilled workers in the power structure is strengthened.

This will probably lead to a growth of informal interest-representation, at least on the part of these groups of employees. On the other hand, employers will not change their hostile attitude much towards trade unions and formalized schemes of participation based on legally granted rights.

Our studies show that Polish SMEs react in different ways to this pressure. While some firms stick to the traditional competitive strategy, new types of SMEs have emerged that are acquiring a different position within West-European value chains. On the basis of our in-depth interviews, we identified two basic types of SME reactions to the ongoing globalization, which we would like to label 'low-road traditionalism' and 'high-road seeking'. These types are a combination of different structural characteristics, as well as different attitudes and practices of management towards employees. Nevertheless, there are no basic differences between these types of SMEs as far as formalized labour relations are concerned: trade union organizations are missing in both types, and as a rule the entrepreneurs oppose the idea of worker-representation based on legally granted workers' rights. Although labour costs remain an important issue to all types of SMEs, differences occur in the rigour of the low-cost concept applied, and in the enterprise culture. We assume that these types are widespread in CEE at this stage of development, and that further combinations of those two basic types can be expected.

13.3.1 Low-road traditionalism

Firms that follow this concept, as a rule, are either final producers of simple and easily imitated consumer goods that they sell on the domestic market, or take a low-end position in the cross-border value chains of West-European firms, performing the labour-intensive stages of production and no strategic functions, such as design or marketing. They attempt to maintain position in global competition through low labour costs, long working hours and the far-reaching subordination of workers to company flexibility needs. They do not strive to find new market segments for their products and services or advance their position within the value chain, seeing no chance of success at this because of a lack of resources necessary to upgrading – not only financial resources, but also skills, experience, image, and so on. Low profits, rather expensive bank loans and the lack of state subsidies have been obstacles for Polish SMEs to implementing necessary innovation measures.

The attitude of owners and managers of these firms towards employees is characterized as a mixture of authoritarian and patriarchal elements. Particularly in economically less-developed regions with low-skilled workers the entrepreneurs assume that employees do not have many alternatives on the regional labour market and are ready to accept almost any demands of the firm. Especially in the clothing industry, wages of the female workforce are calculated under the assumption that in most families there is a partner (husband) whose earnings ensure the survival of the family.

Low-road traditionalism is accompanied by an attitude of entrepreneurs that infringements on labour regulations and employment condition norms are necessary to keep the low-cost comparative advantage. In the previously mentioned CBOS survey (CBOS 2006), 18 per cent of all respondents declared that they were sometimes forced to work longer than stipulated in their work contract without being correspondingly paid, while for the transport and communication sector the figure was 23 per cent, and in trade and services 20 per cent. Of all respondents 10 per cent (33 per cent in construction) stated that the entrepreneur did not correctly pay taxes and social-security contributions on their wages. This illustrates the widespread practice of splitting wages into 'official' and 'unofficial' parts, the taxes and contributions being paid only on the 'official' part of the wages. Workers as a rule accept this practice, because it also means a higher net pay for them. Trade unions, however, are against this practice, because workers thereby lose on their pensions and sickness benefits. Equally popular is the practice of replacing employment contracts by works contracts regulated by civil law, a practice that effectively deprives workers of many rights granted by labour legislation. The weakness of actors and organizations, whose task it is to enforce legal norms in this field, results in a certain permissiveness in labour relations and entrepreneurial action (Bluhm 2006), which has an impact on employment conditions as well. According to a comparative survey of labour law and its practical implementation (Labour Rights Standards Index), Poland is at the end of the ranking of 25 EU member-states in this regard (Kohl et al. 2006).

In a poll among SME owners, 46 per cent stated that a strict application of legal norms would force them to close their firms. Another 44 per cent stated that they would have to restrict their business activities substantially. In a survey from 2000 and 2001, almost all owners of private firms said that they were forced by labour conditions to avoid taxes and split wages into an official and an unofficial part (Gardawski 2005).

13.3.2 High-road seeking

In our case studies, we also met Polish SMEs that proved able to react to the growing pressures and achieve economic success by complex innovation processes and means other than low prices and labour costs. Even in 'low-tech' branches, such as clothing and furniture, there seem to be cases of innovative SMEs that have become so by changing their business strategies, enterprise organization and, of course, technology (Hirsch-Kreinsen 2005). Elements of such innovation strategy can be for example:

- outsourcing labour-intensive stages of production and its relocation into low-wage countries outside of Poland, such as the Ukraine;
- upgrading the position of Polish SMEs within cross-border value chains; carrying out not only simple and labour-intensive production tasks, but also taking responsibility for more complex functions with a higher value generation (design, purchase of components and materials, logistics, financing), resulting in a greater share of these firms in the gains from globalization (Kaplinsky 2004);
- orientation of business strategy to the production of goods in high-quality, high-price market segments;
- creation of firms' own brands;
- concentration on flexible, small-batch production and efforts to benefit from the proximity to the German market and German partner firms;
- obtaining the status of process specialists, as in the mastery of specific welding technologies.

Upgrading the position of Polish SMEs in value-added chains reflects also the changed business concepts of West-European and, in particular, German firms. The motivation for this is the desire to benefit from the cost advantage in production and other business functions, as well as the integration of production with other functions, such as design or procurement of components in a single firm, which can contribute to the elimination of coordination problems. It is an open question whether this restructuring of the value chain is only connected with German firms' search for new business partners in Poland, or whether Polish firms that formerly carried out pure production tasks for German clients are now undergoing a process of upgrading.

There is, of course, no direct link between those innovation processes and labour relations on the enterprise level, but owing to their economic successes, these firms dispose of a broader range of possibilities to shape wages and other employment conditions. Although in these firms, too, formalized worker-representation bodies are almost entirely lacking, we do have the impression that enterprise culture is marked by greater openness and more mutual trust between management and workers than in other type of SMEs. And though, of course, these firms, too, are exposed to price competition, price is not the only, or at least not the main means of competition for them, since quality and flexibility also play a crucial role. Owners and managers are faced with skilled workers who are aware of their own value and have specific requirements concerning their working conditions.

In our sample we found one firm employing 400 people in the ladies' wear industry, which can be regarded as a good example of this type of SME. The firm had completely outsourced production to local subcontractors, that is, delegated out the pressure for lower costs, and concentrated its own business activities on the design of fashionable, high-quality goods, the purchase of materials through global sourcing, and setting up its own brands on the Polish, CEE and German markets. The firm possesses a network of its own shops, all in larger Polish and some East-European towns, and supplies goods to some German boutiques. It also plans to set up its own retail network on a franchise basis. The economic situation of the firm was described by its management as 'excellent'.

According to the managing director, even the lowest wages in the firm are well above the average for the clothing branch in Poland; the growth rate of wages was rather high. Such wages were regarded as necessary to keep good employees in the firm. 'The best ones are working abroad anyway', as the director put it. The management is fully aware that the success of the firm depends not least on the commitment of the workers, and they know this commitment cannot be achieved by coercion. Most of the employees know they could find a similar or even better job, if not on the regional labour market, then abroad, and this has an impact on the power relation between the firm and its employees. Management regards their wages, high in comparison to other Polish clothing companies, as an important precondition to achieving this worker commitment, but also uses other incentives to keep a high level of motivation. For example, employees are informed at regular meetings about the situation and prospects of the firm. Sales assistants in the firm network have the chance to become shop managers or franchisers.

A few innovative furniture companies also are trying to react to the challenges of globalization by elaborating their own brands for the domestic and East-European markets through product and process innovations. This strategy also includes upgrading within the western value chain in which these SMEs are integrated. An indicator of these changes is in the growing importance of the supply of complete furniture products to German trading partners, with the supplying of furniture components only losing its formerly dominant role. It remains to be seen whether these Polish SMEs can continue on the high road, since their fate strongly depends on the prospects of German firms in whose value chains they are involved. If German firms fail to cope with globalization, or if German trading firms reorganize their network of suppliers, for example by replacing Polish firms with Asian ones, the result could, in principle, be the collapse of their Polish subsidiaries or partner companies.

13.4 Conclusions

The question whether it will be possible in the foreseeable future, in economic and social regard, for Poland to open up to the established West-European market economies, or whether Poland will remain permanently in the position of a dependent country, is being decided not least through the further development of the Polish SME sector. Up to now, the principle means for many firms to keep up with the competition has been to maintain low prices. This created a strong impulse to hold wages low and a systematic non-compliance with norms regulating taxation, labour and social-system rights. For carrying out such an entrepreneurial concept, the Polish institutional, economic and social environment was quite functional for a number of years, but now the environment has begun to change, especially for industrially producing SMEs. Economic growth and a massive emigration of native labour have led to falling unemployment and an often perceptible lack of specialists on the labour market. Globalization is intensifying cost competition, particularly for industrially made mass-consumption goods. At the same time, West-European firms are further restructuring their value chains by transferring increasingly more complex, value-creating tasks to Polish firms that go beyond the direct production phase. While a few SMEs, because of lacking investment power and entrepreneurial know-how, will stay on the traditional low road, already a new developmental path is being traced out; more and more strategy-savvy SMEs are emerging, who are self-responsibly putting out products and services at home and on foreign markets, or are performing more complex functions within cross-national value chains.

Managing the challenges accompanying this also demands a different approach to labour relations. Future economic success will depend importantly on qualified and motivated employees, who will have to be not only suitably paid, but who will also expect better working conditions and a different style of management. Although the future role of unions in these enterprises will still be weak, an increase in the opportunities for employee interest-representation is foreseeable. This corresponds to the needs of qualified employees and will be consciously utilized by management to heighten identification with the firm. Higher wages and greater value-creation in SMEs will also increase tax liabilities and reduce the temptation by companies to secure their existence on the basis of avoiding tax and social-security regulations.

Notes

1. This research project was carried out by the authors in 2005–6 and was funded by the Hans-Böckler-Foundation.
2. Directive 2002/14/WE.
3. The formulation applied in the questionnaire was: 'What is the most important problem your firm is at present facing?' The respondents had to make their choice among 11 items. They could also select more than one item, but in that case they were asked to evaluate their choices (most important, less important, etc.).
4. We followed the formulation 'taxes and contributions stipulated by law' in the questionnaire submitted to the entrepreneurs. Obviously, the authors of the questionnaire assumed that from the employers' perspective, taxes and contributions that employers must pay are more or less the same, although it could be argued that, from an economic point of view, social contributions are, instead, part of labour costs, which another item in this questionnaire addressed.

References

Bluhm, K. (2000) 'East-West Integration and the Changing German Production Regime: A Firm-Centered Approach', <www.ces.fas.harvard.edu/publications/author_index.html#B/Bluhm53.pdf>.

Bluhm, K. (2006) 'Auflösung des Liberalisierungsdilemmas', *Berliner Journal für Soziologie*, 2, 173–88.

Bluhm, K. (2007) *Experimentierfeld Ostmitteleuropa?* (Wiesbaden: VS Verlag für Sozialwissenschaften).

Bohle, D. (2002) *Europas Neue Peripherie. Polens Transformation und Transnationale Integration* (Münster: Westfälisches Dampfboot).

Bontrup, H.-J. (2006) 'Markt- und Wettbewerbsideologie', Presentation on the 2nd Conference of IG Metall on SME Related Policies, Berlin.

CBOS (2005) 'The Acceptance of Workers' Rights and the "Grey Sphere" of Employment. Trade Unions in Enterprises', BS/3/2005, Warsaw.

CBOS (2006) 'Collective Work Agreements, Violation of Workers' Rights and the "Grey Sphere" of Employment', BS/167/2006, Warsaw.

European Commission (2004) *Industrial Relations in Europe*, Directorate-General for Employment and Social Affairs, Brussels.

Gardawski, J. (2005) 'Labour Relations in Private Small and Medium Sized Companies', *Polish Center for the Monitoring of Industrial Relations*, 149–151,

<http://www.isp.org.pl/files/468330794045510900112375062S.pdf?PHPSES-SID=2cfc5f259fbad88d35abd89f0d3f126f>.

Hirsch-Kreinsen, H. (2005) "'Low-Tech-Industrien": Innovationsfähigkeit und Entwicklungschancen', *WSI-Mitteilungen*, 3, 144–50.

Kaplinsky, R. (2004) 'Spreading the Gains from Globalization', *Problems of Economic Transition*, 47(2), 74–115.

King, L. (2002) 'Postcommunist Divergence: A Comparative Analysis of the Transition to Capitalism in Poland and Russia', *Studies in Comparative International Development*, 7(3), 3–34.

Kinkel, S., G. Lay and S. Maloca (2004) 'Produktionsverlagerungen ins Ausland und Rückverlagerungen', Research Report, Fraunhofer-Institut für Systemtechnik und Innovationsforschung, Karlsruhe.

Kohl, H., F. Lehndorff and S. Schief (2006) 'Industrielle Beziehungen in Europa nach der EU-Erweiterung', *WSI-Mitteilungen*, 7, 403–9.

Lewiatan (2006) Competitiveness of Small and Medium Sized Firms, 2006, author: Starczewska-Krzysztoszek, Warsaw, <http://www.prywatni.pl/upload/plik/ko-nkurencyjnosc_sektora_msp_2006_3128609.pdf>.

Lungwitz, R.-E., E. Preusche (2002) 'Kooperation zwischen Kleinen und Mittelständischen Firmen in Ostdeutschland und Firmen in Polen und der Tschechischen Republik', Research Report, WISOC, Chemnitz.

Ministry of Economy (2006a): Entrepreneurship in Poland 2006, Warsaw,<http://www.mgip.gov.pl/NR/rdonlyres/E6AAC9B0-FCD9-408F-882E-80CACE683CAE/22693/PrzedsiebiorczoscwPolsce2006druk1.pdf>.

Ministry of Economy (2006b): Trends in the SME Sector in the Evaluation of the Entrepreneurs in the Second Half of 2005, Warsaw.

Ministry of Economy (2007a) 'Trends in the SME Sector in the Evaluation of the Entrepreneurs in the Second Half of 2006', Warsaw, <http://www.mgip.gov.pl/NR/rdonlyres/B07FB5D7-8280-4372-8A13-467220A3636F/31861/msp_2006II.pdf>.

Ministry of Economy (2007b) 'The Impact of Wage Migration on the Polish Economy', Warszawa, <http://www.egospodarka.pl/pliki/migracja-zarobkowa-2007.pdf>.

Ministry of Economy and Labour (2005) 'Entrepreneurship in Poland 2005', Warsaw, <http://www.mgip.gov.pl/NR/rdonlyres/9E5F299E-66F1-4AAF-A8CC-45D03DB4644C/11405/Przedsiebiorczosc_w_Polsce_2005.pdf>.

Mroczek, E., L. v. Schuttenbach and M. Ciurla (2000) *Mittelständische Unternehmen in Polen* (Heidelberg-New York: Physica Verlag).

Musiolek, B. (1999) (ed.) *Gezähmte Modemultis; Verhaltenskodizes: Ein Modell zur Durchsetzung von Arbeitsrechten?* (Frankfurt/Main, Wien: Brandes & Apsel Verlag).

Ost-West-Contact (2007) 'Wachstum weiterhin ohne Euro', 6, 26.

Partner, S. (2007) 'Monitoring of the Law from April, 7th 2006 on Information and Consultation of Employees', paper presented at the international conference 'The Contribution of Social Partners in the Strife for Decent Work in Poland and Europe', Warsaw, 14 May.

Witte, L. (2004) 'Europäisches Sozialmodell und Sozialer Zusammenhalt: Welche Rolle spielt die EU?', *Internationale Politikanalyse Europäische Politik*, December 2004, Friedrich-Ebert-Stiftung, 1–13.

14
Unravelling Regulation: How Production Relocation to the East Impacts the German Model of Labour Relations at the Workplace

Michael Fichter

14.1 Introduction

Over the past several years, the issue of production relocation from Germany to lower cost sites in Central and Eastern Europe has repeatedly been in the news, reflecting the contentious nature of the political and economic conflicts it has generated. In an academic context as well, there has been a broad discussion of this phenomenon and its potential and existing ramifications for *Standort* Germany. While there is no doubt that there has been a steady and considerable decline in industrial employment in Germany over the past 30 years (Statistisches Bundesamt 2008), there is no data that distinctively show the extent to which this decline can be attributed to production relocation to foreign countries. In both the political and academic context, when focusing on developments in Germany, topics such as the threat of relocation, its actual planning and motives, as well as the process development have been at the forefront. For its part, research on labour relations at the relocated plant has concentrated on the issue of the extent to which a particular home country model has been transferred. In contrast, there has been virtually no discussion of the changes and developments associated with the impact of such relocation processes on labour relations at the home sites in Germany.

This chapter draws on research dealing with firms based in Germany that have relocated substantial parts, or all, of their production facilities to Central and Eastern Europe (CEE) since 1990. It focuses on the impact of such relocation processes on workplace labour relations in Germany, that is, the way in which they may be invoking or accelerating changes to the structure and working of the German model of production. This chapter argues, in the first place, that while companies usually pursue a one-to-one transfer of their production processes and know-how, labour relations are not included in the relocation package. This raises questions regarding the institutional complementarity of the German model of production. Secondly, it will show that relocation is a strategic option (and necessity) not only for large multinationals, but also for SMEs. Thirdly, it will reflect on how relocation is undermining the core of German labour relations – and thus the German model of production – through the elimination of production jobs that have been held by the core workforce, the backbone of union membership and works-council mandates.

By way of introducing the pertinent issues and laying the groundwork for the basic arguments, the following section 14.2 will present a brief explanation of the German model, as it is generally agreed that the institutional structure of labour relations is an essential element of this model. This will be followed in section 14.3 by an overview of how production relocation has spread to encompass small- and medium-sized enterprises (SMEs). Section 14.4 presents insights drawn from case studies on relocation and labour relations, which were part of two research projects in which the author was involved between 2001 and 2005. Insights drawn from these case studies provide the basis for several arguments presented in the concluding section.

14.2 The German model of labour relations and production – where do SMEs fit in?

Without going too deeply into its history (cf. Lehmbruch 2001), it is important to recognize that what came to be called the German production model in the 1980s is the result of some 30 years of cooperation and conflict, primarily involving the state, trade unions as well as the employers and their associations. The development and outcomes of this struggle are what has given the model its distinctive institutional structure. Hall and Soskice (2001) have referred to Germany as being a 'coordinated market economy', and Lehmbruch uses the term 'socially embedded capitalism' (2001: 47) to describe the model. For his part, Wolfgang Streeck (1997: 36) has provided us with an extensive analytical description of the 'highly institutionally coordinated, (...) politically negotiated and typically legally constitutionalized' German political economy. He goes on to explain the role of 'politically instituted and socially regulated' markets; firms as 'social institutions' in which labour and capital (universal banks) have institutionalized roles; the 'enabling' role of a state with 'vertically and horizontally fragmented sovereignty'; 'publicly enabled associations'; and an economic culture with a preference for quality (Streeck 1997: 37–40). Features of the institutional framework that are common to all of these characterizations are summarized succinctly by Flecker and Schulten (1999: 83):

> Accordingly, the model consists of the following main parts: 'social market economy' (*soziale Marktwirtschaft*), that is, capitalism tamed by political macro-regulation and redistribution of income by the state; long-term perspectives and a preference for productive investment on the part of capital; highly organized industrial relations combining sectoral multi-employer bargaining and cooperative labour relations within the enterprise; a vocational training system that combines on-the-job training with education in vocational schools; and diversified quality production based on highly skilled workforces.

As such, the starting point of the following discussion of current challenges is that this stylized model still exists despite pressures to change, evidenced by the shifting power relationships within its structures and signs of erosion, especially at the edges, that is, outside of the core sectors of manufacturing (cf. Artus 2001; Hassel 1999; Hoffmann et al.1998). Indeed, there are several sectors of the economy, especially in services that qualify as 'edges'. One can surely argue that there have always been limits to the reach of the model both within the core sectors – among SMEs and in outlaying regions – and in peripheral sectors.

For one, the applicability of the model may vary in detail across the various sectors of the economy, depending on such factors as the numbers and sizes of enterprises, the extent to which they are export-oriented, and the organizational density of trade unions and employers' associations. Secondly, the question has been raised as to the actual practice of the model beyond the realm of the large stock corporations, for example, whether all of the elements of the model are 'in place' and functioning in SMEs, which make up the bulk of the enterprises in Germany. As we ascertained in our project research (see below), in which our case studies comprised a number of SMEs that were generally (still) privately owned and operated, some important modifications to the model must be recognized. While SMEs operate in the overall context of a 'social market economy', political macro-regulation, in particular, financial and employment measures, tend to be predominantly influenced by large corporations. Where trade-union influence can be exerted, it is also keyed to its membership strongholds in large enterprises. In this connection, another main part of the model – highly organized labour relations – impacts differently on SMEs than on large companies. While SMEs are not absent from the membership roles of the employers' associations, which bargain over sectoral contracts with the responsible industrial union, it is difficult for them to make their voices heard in association decision-making processes when contract conflicts are focused on large enterprises. SMEs also have fewer managers, many of whom are also owners, and generally, there exists a more personalized style of human resource management and labour relations. On the employee side, the works councils usually have a weaker role, as contact and exchange between employees and management is more direct (see also Wassermann 1992). SMEs also generally depend heavily on the policies and product demands of large customers, not only for volume output but also as regards their pricing, technological standards and product development. This kind of dependency is not generally recognized as an element of the model. Yet it has a profound impact on the business strategies of such enterprises, and as such, at least indirectly on labour relations as well.

Because the role of labour relations as a determining factor for positioning SMEs within the German Model is crucial, we must take a closer look at the formal system of legally mandated works councils in SMEs. As Ellguth (2006) has recently shown, a clear majority of SMEs with 100 or more employees do have works councils. According to data from a panel survey conducted in 2003 by the research institute of the Federal Labour Office, some 65 per cent of all SMEs with 101 to 199 employees had a works council. And from 500 employees upward it is virtually certain that there is a works council in the firm, at least in Western Germany (Ellguth 2006: 48–51). In contrast, works councils are rarely to be found in enterprises with 50 or less employees and in less than one half of those enterprises with 50 to 100 employees (see more Artus in this volume; Stettes 2006).

The apparent conclusion that may be drawn from these data in regard to SMEs in the German model is that works councils, as an essential element of the model, are missing in the majority of firms with one hundred or less employees. As will be shown in the next section of this chapter, many of these employees have lost their jobs over the past few years as a result of production relocation and as such, have had to deal with this development without the benefit of an institution of collective representation.

14.3   Relocation and German SMEs

Production relocation beyond the borders of the home country has become a widespread phenomenon, even beyond the widening circle of multinational 'global players'. As such, it should be regarded and analysed as an instrument of business restructuring, most likely to be turned to as a strategic option for meeting the challenges of globalization. Of note is the fact that production relocation is no longer a strategic option open only to large enterprises, which are usually categorized as multinationals. Indeed, rapid developments in technology, transportation and (tele)communications have made relocation an affordable and viable option under certain conditions for SMEs as well.

Since 1990, the countries of Central and Eastern Europe have developed rapidly into one of those options. To be sure, prior to 1989 some investment in production facilities had taken place but on a very restricted scale. Following the collapse of the Soviet Bloc and the initialization of a 'dual' transformation process (Offe 1995) to political democracies and market economies, foreign direct investment in production and services expanded rapidly. The CEE countries, especially those closest to the European Union, which quickly became to be regarded as candidates for membership, had the advantage of geographic proximity. Moreover, for companies looking to invest in production, a low-wage workforce with basic tacit knowledge of industrial processes and exhibiting high skill and education levels was available.

According to research carried out by the German Fraunhofer Institute for Systems and Innovation Research (*Systemtechnik und Innovationsforschung*) and published by Kinkel, Lay and Maloca (2004), the CEE region and, in particular, the eight countries that joined the European Union in 2004 advanced to the top of the list for FDI. Some 45 per cent of all enterprises surveyed relocated production to the CEE region; whereas Asia, with a quota of 29 per cent, was second on the list. SMEs participated widely in this process. For example, it was found that 16.3 per cent of German manufacturing enterprises in the core sectors[1] with at least 20 but less than 100 employees had relocated production to a foreign site during the period 2001–2003; slightly less than one half (48.6 per cent) of these companies maintained a site in the CEE area. Among SMEs with 100 to 499 employees, 39.3 per cent have established a foreign production site, 39.7 per cent of which are in the CEE area (Kinkel et al. 2004: 10–14). As for the reasons behind the decision to relocate, 85 per cent of all enterprises named production costs as the primary motivation, with market entry a distant second (42.3 per cent)[2]. The need for more flexibility was considered decisive for around 35 per cent of responding SMEs, while an increase in production capacity, the opportunity to avoid home country taxes and take advantage of host country subsidies, and the need for proximity to a large customer were designated as further motives by 25–30 per cent of the respondents. (ibid. 15)

While the Fraunhofer survey provides interesting data on the structure and evolvement of production relocation to the CEE region during the past few years, it should be recognized that it does not cover the issue completely. For one, it did not include enterprises that have no production in Germany or no longer have any production in Germany. As can be seen from the case studies referred to in section 14.4, it is not unusual for SMEs to have only one main production site and to have relocated this site in full to the CEE region. Secondly, the study also covers relocation activities only during the three year period 2001–2003. To be sure, the results are indicative of the relevance of relocation as a strategic restructuring option for SMEs. However, the percentages do not indicate how many SMEs have relocated production to the CEE area since 1990.

14.4   Relocation and labour relations in SMEs – insights from case studies

Having established the relevance of production relocation to the CEE region for German based SMEs, the following section will present findings from empirical research on the impact of such relocations on labour relations (Dörrenbächer et al. 2000). The research involved case studies of production relocation to Hungary, a leading recipient of German FDI in the 1990s. After a first wave of interviews at some 15 enterprises – 11 of which were SMEs – in-depth case studies at 5 enterprises (4 of which were SMEs) were conducted. Data from two of the in-depth case studies will be used to illustrate the arguments in this chapter. One of the companies (ALPHA) is family owned but no longer family managed. It manufactures electronic components for customers primarily in the packaging and automotive industries. In 1988, prior to production relocation, the company had some 800 employees at a single site in Germany. Of the employees 600 were production workers. The other company (BETA) is from the auto supply sector and manufactures cables and heating elements. In 1998, the owner, who had withdrawn from management a few years prior, decided to go public with the company. Prior to the relocation of production from Germany to Hungary, around 120 of the 200 persons employed at the main site in Germany were directly involved in production.

In regard to the policies of the sample firms in transferring the German production model (in its company-specific forms) to their Hungarian subsidiaries, we found no verification for our hypothesis that labour relations are an integral element of the German production model. Indeed, apart from labour relations, all of the essential elements of the production process (including company-specific know-how) were included in a virtually complete one-to-one transfer. As such, our case studies showed that the production model functions even when the German regulatory framework and culture of negotiated employee-relations is absent, as is the case in Hungary. Basically, the enterprises refrained from pursuing exogenous influence (from corporate headquarters in Germany) and instead found it advantageous to adapt their policies on employee relations to the endogenous conditions (Dörrenbächer et al. 2003).

The transfer of the German Model was one sided; product and processes transfer was not coupled with the societal control of consensual decision-making with workers' representatives in any of the cases we researched. Relocation was thus incomplete inasmuch as it excluded all elements of formal collective labour relations. Labour relations, training and wage determination at the Hungarian subsidiary showed little resemblance to their counterpart in Germany. Indeed, management made no effort to transfer, assuming that its production system would function without attempting to replicate the home-country labour relationships. A further assumption was that employee relationships and personnel issues were delicate matters best regulated in the local environment. As such, management involved its personnel departments in the transfer process only in cases of special training programmes. Works councils in Germany showed a disinterest in labour and working conditions at the subsidiary resulting from their own plant-specific range of operation and their lack of a legal basis to influence the transfer. To put it more bluntly, German companies escaped from the highly institutionalized environment of labour relations and happily accommodated themselves to the comparatively unregulated Hungarian environment.

Several other studies on production relocation and employment relations in the CEE countries have also found corroborating evidence for this phenomenon. While the case study research conducted by Kluge and Voss (2003) showed that it could not be taken for granted that German multinationals would take their company culture of labour relations with them to other countries, there is some evidence that 'in terms of labour relations and policies', at least large corporations and stock companies are 'bound to the institutions that shaped the German "production regime"' (Bluhm 2001: 170). Still, more recent research has shown that even this binding may not be found in large German enterprises if they are highly internationalized (Fichter et al. 2005: 13).

14.4.1   Effects on employment at the home country site

Up to this point, this chapter has focused on the issue of the 'forward diffusion' (Ferner and Varul 2000) of the company-specific modes of the German production model to Hungary via FDI, that is, the practices and strategies used to implement production relocation. But what is also of interest is the impact of relocation on the subsequent practice of the German production model at those home country sites directly affected by the process. In comparison to the large body of literature on forward diffusion and impact of home-country practices on foreign subsidiaries, there is virtually no research available on post-relocation developments in the home country. In his study of 'reverse diffusion', that is, the practice of introducing employment practices from foreign operations to home country sites, Edwards (2000) touched partly on this issue while seeking to determine the kind of multi-national corporation where reverse diffusion was likely to occur. Using data from ten enterprises, he found evidence of such a practice in only two cases, both of which he categorized as being 'globally integrated firms' (Edwards 2000: 120).[3] Edwards also addresses the question of the potential challenge reverse diffusion may pose for worker representatives in regard to established labour practices (ibid. 126). However, his concern is limited to the actual transfer of practices from subsidiaries and, as such, he does not deal with the key issues of this paper, that is, the overall impact of changes wrought by the relocation process itself, which are not limited to those that fall under the heading of 'reverse diffusion'.

14.4.2   Loss of production jobs – creation of white-collar employment

The most immediate and noticeable impact of production transfer is the loss of employment 'on the shop floor'. Depending on the actual product, the kind of jobs lost varied to some extent in our sample cases. For the most part, unskilled and semi-skilled positions, mostly held by women, were eliminated. This can be illustrated by using data from the two companies described above. In 1989, the electronics component company ALPHA employed 800 persons at its sole production site in Germany. The first wave of production relocation eliminated 250 jobs. By 1998, all manufacturing processes, except for a small production unit for proto-types and special orders, had been relocated to Hungary. In this 10 year period, nearly 600 production jobs were eliminated. At the automotive supply company BETA, relocation began in 1998. At the time of completion in 2001, all of the 120 production workers employed in 1997 were gone. In both of these cases, as well as in all other cases from the project sample, company works-councils were able to negotiate severance pay along with some retraining[4].

It is interesting, however, that as production jobs were eliminated, new positions were created, so that after completion of relocation, employment at the German site of these and many of the other companies in our sample returned to the pre-transfer level or even increased. In 2001, the ALPHA company had 630 employees at its German site; while at the automotive supply company BETA, total employment was back to 204 by 2002. Skilled white-collar employees, such as engineers, technicians, commercial staff and IT specialists, had been hired to support the new production arrangement, bolster the marketing strategy and control the increased complexity of internationalized production. Even into later stages of the Hungarian investment, when the subsidiary had taken on responsibilities only indirectly related to production, the home country site did not experience a new wave of job losses similar to that which had taken place in production. In the sample as a whole, when employment cutbacks did occur in Germany, they were the direct consequence of a poor economic performance by that company (Dörrenbächer et al. 2003).

14.4.3 Increasing reliance on team-work

A second observation is in regard to effects of the relocation on work processes. We found strong evidence that team-work at the German site was intensified, both within the site and – necessarily – with the new production subsidiary. The introduction of such German-Hungarian teams proved to be an experiment in intercultural cooperation, in which the Germans had the advantage of language as well as the initial privilege of greater company-specific and product-related knowledge. However, they also had to deal with the uncertainty of the future of their positions in respect to the further growth and development of the subsidiary. Many of them expressed their worries to us that by working together with the Hungarians they were in effect training their replacements. Their uneasiness over this situation was mitigated, however, by the strength of their skill and knowledge level, both in general and in regard to company-specific processes. What came across was a certain feeling of being indispensable to the company and, therefore, not easily replaceable, supplemented by a strong dose of confidence in their ability to easily find a new job if necessary.

14.4.4 Erosion of the system of workplace labour relations

A third observation concerns the status of industrial relations and the role of the works council at the German site from which production was relocated. The 'delocalization' of production as a strategic response to competition (Abraham and Konings 1999: 591) is the process we were studying in this research; in our sample cases it entails the relocation of the routine and standardized processes to Hungary and the retention of high value-adding activities in Germany. In all cases of relocation, the result was the removal of the core of labour relations at the German site. The organizational density of union membership declined proportional to the loss of production workers. Also, the backbone of support for the role of the works council as the representative of workers' interests was eliminated. With the disappearance of a sizeable contingent of production workers, the workforce became inevitably almost fully white-collar. In its new composition, the workforce was more non-union and characterized by strong individual career interests. As a consequence, the coordinates of management-workforce relations were redrawn. New topics appeared on the agenda of the works councils at these sites and at election time. They went through membership shake-ups that reflected this extensive shift from a low-skilled, blue-collar workforce to a high-skilled, heterogeneous white-collar workforce. This did not necessarily mean that works councils became generally irrelevant. Although this was the case at some enterprises, at others their role was not questioned but rather was launched on the path of redefinition.

14.5 Arguments – hypotheses – conclusions

This chapter has sought to direct attention to developments in employment and employment relations at home country sites of SMEs – an aspect of the process of production relocation that has not been the focus of research previously. To be sure, the data and arguments presented do not provide a solid foundation for generalized conclusions. Nevertheless, they do give an indication of one type of change affecting the German model of production and labour relations that should be considered in conjunction with future research. The main arguments, in summary, are as follows:

Relocation targets mainly core production processes, eliminating production jobs of which most are low-skilled or unskilled, even in so-called technologically 'high road' (Soskice 1999; Turner et al. 2001) processes. While these jobs were generally held by women, skilled male workers – the backbone of union membership and core mandate of works-council representation in manufacturing – also lost their jobs. As such, union presence on the shop floor and a strong and rather homogeneous interest representation disappeared from the context of workplace labour-relations.

Relocation beyond core production processes is not as straight forward, being much more contingent on particular product developments, specific production processes, customer relations and employee qualifications. While companies may decide to relocate certain aspects of production-related processes (that is, back-office support, product distribution, warehouse management and so on), the quantitative impact on employment will be considerably less than in the case of production relocation.

Relocation serves as a catalyst for a general restructuring of the workplace environment at the home-country site to include a greater emphasis on individual goal-oriented work and pay schemes. The existence of a new company site has a discernable impact on employee interaction and between employees and management.

Relocation is a management decision taken without works-council participation. Despite more informal and personal interaction between management and employee representatives in many SMEs, relocation is a decision often taken without even informing the works council beforehand.

For its part, the works council remained glued to its site mandate. Once informed, works councils concentrate on dealing with the employment consequences for employees facing job loss. Although some of the works councillors whom we interviewed recognized the strategic importance of developing a company-wide (cross-border) approach, there was very little or no interest in taking concrete steps toward developing contacts or policies with employees, workplace representatives at the new subsidiary, or even with the responsible sectoral trade union in the other country. An important cause of this reticence was the language barrier that existed on both ends of the line.

Nevertheless, relocation initiated both a change in membership on the works council and a radical shift in the agenda. In general, the role of the works council as a collective voice of the employees decreased in importance.

In all of the cases we researched there was no strategic involvement of the responsible trade union regarding the future prospects of collective employee representation throughout the company. Trade unions seem to be overextended and overtaxed by the widespread incidence of relocation and restructuring, thus concentrating their limited resources on dealing with such cases at large enterprises. As complementary research shows, the impact of such processes on attitudes of union members, whether direct or indirect, can foster right extremist attitudes (Fichter 2008).

The European Works Council is not considered to be a strategic option in most SMEs because such enterprises do not reach the employment threshold required by law. Where it is an option, employees in SMEs face such problems as a lack of interest (which may be indicative of an underlying element of internal competitiveness) at the subsidiary level in coordinating and cooperating with employee representatives from the headquarters; the difficulty of initiating and establishing representative selection procedures; a general lack of resources to develop an infrastructure of representation; and, on top of all this, reluctance and even opposition on the part of management.

Beyond this immediate focus on employment and employment relations there is a further insight that addresses the broader issue of restructuring and strategic management issues in SMEs. Delocalization of core production processes represented a substantial qualitative organizational change even in enterprises with sales subsidiaries and some modest production facilities in various regions of the world. New and affordable information technology systems (for example, SAP) presented both an opportunity and satisfied a need to control this process in such a way that the previously acceptable independence of far-flung subsidiaries could be overcome, their operations harnessed in the interest of an holistic enterprise strategy.

Within the enterprises of our sample, there were ongoing struggles in management over the dimensions of restructuring and the advantages of a centrally-steered course of operation as a control framework for the overall coherence of the enterprise. The introduction of new IT-systems presented both a chance for the subsidiaries to use central data to improve their operations and for headquarters management to keep an up-to-date eye on the external operating units. The overarching capabilities of such instruments thus dovetailed with the new productive capacities resulting from the transfer process to generate potentially dynamic and innovative approaches. How each of the enterprises was actually meeting this challenge differed markedly and will presumably lead to a variance in the outcomes on this level.

In sum, the issue of relocation as presented in this chapter highlights a development that contributes to the overall long-term decrease in industrial manufacturing employment and corresponding increase in white-collar employment. Many SMEs are no less caught up in the whirlwind of restructuring than multinationals; at the same time, relocation as an element of that process appears to have a more dramatic impact on the workplace system of labour relations at SMEs. While the evidence presented in this paper is far from being sufficient to allow for generalizations regarding the impact of relocation on the system of workplace labour-relations at SMEs, it does add to the empirical mosaic of elemental changes impacting the German model. Using this as a starting point, further research on this topic could help to clarify the extent to which such relocation processes have contributed to the development of right extremist attitudes among trade union members in Germany. Taking a different approach, the problem of institutional erosion in Germany, as evidenced by the elimination of the core of workplace labour relations in SMEs, could be studied in the context of the current debate on the varieties of capitalism (VoC). VoC emphasis on the importance of institutional complementarities would seem to provide an analytical framework for addressing the potentially dysfunctional impact of relocation on the status and input of works councils.

Notes

1. The survey covered manufacturers in chemicals, rubber and plastics, metalworking, machine tools, office equipment, automobiles and trucks, optics, medical equipment, electronics and electrical equipment.
2. The corresponding figure for SMEs with less than 100 employees was 35 per cent, for SMEs with 100–499 employees 45 per cent.
3. This would seem to complement the above cited findings of Fichter et al. 2005.
4. In neither of these two companies, nor in any of the other companies in our sample, did the layoffs lead to labour disputes.

References

Abraham, F. and J. Konings (1999) 'Does the Opening of Central and Eastern Europe Threaten Employment in the West?', *The World Economy*, 22(4), 585–601.

Artus, I. (2001) *Krise des deutschen Tarifsystems. Die Erosion des Flächentarifvertrags in Ost und West* (Wiesbaden: Westdeutscher Verlag).

Bluhm, K. (2001) 'Exporting or Abandoning the "German Model"?: Labour Policies of German Manufacturing Firms in Central Europe', *European Journal of Industrial Relations*, 7(2), 153–73.

Dörrenbächer, C., M. Fichter, L. Neumann, A. Tóth and M. Wortmann (2000) 'Transformation and Foreign Direct Investment: Observations on Path Dependency, Hybridisation, and Model Transfer at the Enterprise Level', *Transfer*, 6(3), 434–49.

Dörrenbächer, C., M. Fichter, L. Neumann, A. Tóth (2003) 'Exogenous Influences in Path Dependent Transformation Processes – The Effects of German Foreign Direct Investment on Work Organization and Labor Relations in Hungary'. Final Report. Berlin. <http://www.polwiss.fu-berlin.de/tu/english/research.html>.

Edwards, T. (2000) 'Multinationals, International Integration and Employment Practice in Domestic Plants', *Industrial Relations Journal*, 31(2), 115–29.

Ellguth, P. (2006) 'Betriebe ohne Betriebsrat – Verbreitung, Entwicklung und Charakteristika – unter Berücksichtigung betriebsspezifischer Formen der Mitarbeitervertretung', in I. Artus, S. Böhm, S. Lücking and R. Trinczek (eds), *Betriebe ohne Betriebsrat: Informelle Interessenvertretung in Unternehmen* (Frankfurt/Main, New York: Campus Verlag), 43–80.

Ferner, A. and M. Varul (2000) ' "Vanguard" Subsidiaries and the Diffusion of New Practices: A Case Study of German Multinationals', *British Journal of Industrial Relations*, 38(1), 115–40.

Fichter, M. (2008) 'German Trade Unions and Right Extremism: Understanding Membership Attitudes', *European Journal of Industrial Relations*, 14(1), 65–84.

Fichter, M., M. Frybes, G. Meardi, P. Marginson, M. Stanojević and A. Tóth (2005) 'Varieties of Multinationals. Embedding Foreign Investors in Central Europe', Paper for the 7th ESA Conference, Toruń, 9–12 September 2005.

Flecker, J. and T. Schulten (1999) 'The End of Institutional Stability: What Future for the "German Model"?', *Economic and Industrial Democracy*, 20(1), 81–115.

Hall, P. A. and D. Soskice (2001) 'An Introduction to Varieties of Capitalism', in P. A. Hall and D. Soskice (eds), *Varieties of Capitalism. The Institutional Foundations of Comparative Advantage*, (Oxford: Oxford University Press), 1–68.

Hassel, A. (1999) 'The Erosion of the German System of Industrial Relations', *British Journal of Industrial Relations*, 37(3), 483–505.

Hoffmann, R., O. Jacobi, B. Keller and M. Weiss (eds) (1998) *The German Model of Industrial Relations between Adaption and Erosion*, Graue Reihe 145, (Düsseldorf: Hans-Böckler-Stiftung).

Kinkel, S., G. Lay and S. Maloca (2004) 'Produktionsverlagerungen ins Ausland und Rückverlagerungen. Ergebnisse aus der Erhebung "Innovationen in der Produktion" des Fraunhofer-Instituts für Systemtechnik und Innovationsforschung'. Bericht zum Forschungsauftrag Nr. 8/04 an das Bundesministerium der Finanzen, Karlsruhe.

Kluge, N. and E. Voss (2003) 'Managementstile und Arbeitnehmerbeteiligung bei ausländischen Unternehmen in Polen, Tschechien und Ungarn', *WSI-Mitteilungen*, 56(1), 66–9.

Lehmbruch, G. (2001) 'The Institutional Embedding of Market Economies: The German "Model"and Its Impact on Japan', in W. Streeck and K. Yamamura (eds), *The Origins of Nonliberal Capitalism. Germany and Japan in Comparison* (Ithaca, London: Cornell University Press), 39–93.

Offe, C. (1995) 'Designing Institutions for East European Transitions', in J. Hausner, B. Jessop and K. Nielsen (eds), *Strategic Choice and Path-Dependency in Post-Socialism. Institutional Dynamics in the Transformation Process*, (Aldershot: Elgar), 47–66.

Soskice, D. (1999) 'Divergent Production Regimes: Coordinated and Uncoordinated Market Economies in the 1980s and 1990s', in H. Kitschelt, P. Lange, G. Marks and J. D. Stephens (eds), *Continuity and Change in Contemporary Capitalism* (Cambridge: Cambridge University Press), 101–34.

Statistisches Bundesamt (2008) 'Employment (national concept) by industries. Germany', <http://www.destatis.de/jetspeed/portal/cms/Sites/destatis/Internet/EN/Content/Statistics/TimeSeries/LongTermSeries/LabourMarket/Content75/lrerw13a.templateId=renderPrint.psml>.

Stettes, O. (2006) 'Comparative Study on IR in SMEs – the Case of Germany', Study prepared for EIRO Report on Employment Relations in SMEs, <http://www.eurofound.europa.eu/eiro/2006/02/study/index.html>, downloaded July 24, 2007.

Streeck, W. (1997) 'German Capitalism: Does it Exist? Can it Survive?', in C. Crouch and W. Streeck (eds), *Political Economy of Modern Capitalism: Mapping Convergence & Diversity* (London: Sage), 33–54.

Turner, L., K. Wever and M. Fichter (2001) 'Perils of the High and Low Roads', in K. Wever (ed.), *Labor, Business, and Change in Germany and the United States* (Kalamazoo: W. E. Upjohn), 123–56.

Wassermann, W. (1992) *Arbeiten im Kleinbetrieb: Interessenvertretung im Deutschen Alltag*, HBS-Praxis 4 (Cologne: Bund-Verlag).

15
Irregular Forms of Employee Interest Representation in SMEs: A German-French Comparison

Ingrid Artus

15.1   Introduction

The idea of 'irregular forms of employee interest representation' assumes that employee interest can also be represented using 'regular', general norms or rules. In the following discussion, these are equated with the existing legal norms. Thus, this chapter deals with enterprises in which the legally foreseen institutions of workplace interest-representation are partly or completely missing: in Germany, these workplaces have no works councils. In France, they have only a partial set of the legal institutions of workplace representation. Such workplaces are found particularly often among small- and medium-sized enterprises (SMEs).

This research breaks with the institutionalist approach widespread in comparative studies that focus on differences between national systems only. To differentiate 'varieties of capitalism', Hall and Soskice (2001), for example, focus mainly on the sets of different formal rules and regulations, which they link to large corporation strategies. In contrast to this, I argue that we need not only take sectoral differences (including those between large corporations and SMEs) seriously, because they challenge the concept of a 'national model'; I will also show that formal institutions do not always play such a crucial role as institutionalist approaches normally suppose. The analysis of institutional *practices* in German and French SMEs with irregular forms of interest representation helps us to understand that the real importance a formal institution depends on its internal structure (its quality), as well as on the interpretation of the actors within a specific cultural context.

This chapter will proceed as follows: in section 15.2 I will review legal standards of workplace interest-representation in Germany and France, that is, the regular, country-specific forms of representation. In section 15.3 I will describe the 'representation gap' in Germany and France in general, and in SMEs in particular. In section 15.4 I will analyse and compare the institutional practices of a German (15.4.1) and a French SME (15.4.2) with 'irregular' forms of workplace representation. I will conclude this chapter with a brief discussion of what this comparison implies for the relevance of institutions.

15.2 The formal rules of workplace representation in Germany and France

In both Germany and France there is a dual system of interest representation, consisting of workplace representation and unions. Yet, the national systems are constructed differently: in Germany, the *works council* forms the sole body of employee representative at the company level; it is elected directly by the employees and formally independent of the trade unions.

Besides having the right to be informed and consulted, the German works council has a relatively strong voice in workplace decisions – the so-called Right of Co-Determination (*Mitbestimmung*). However, German works councils do not have the right to initiate strikes – a right exclusively reserved for trade unions, which in turn, however, have no legally guaranteed presence in the workplace (cf. Schmidt and Trinczek 1991; Müller-Jentsch 1995; Addison et al. 2000).

In any workplace with more than five employees, a works council can be elected. Yet this is optional, not mandatory: employees must actively implement this right in order to have a voice in decision-making. The new German 'Workplace-Constitution Law' (*Betriebsverfassungsgesetz*) of 2001 contains amendments designed to encourage co-determination, especially in smaller workplaces. According to this new law, a workplace with at least 200 employees (prior to the reform 300) can now free at least one employee from work to assume works-council duties. For companies with fewer than 50 employees (and, with consent of the employer, even for those with up to 100 employees), the quite complicated works-council election process was simplified. Expectations among trade unions and Social Democrats of increased co-determination in SMEs, however, appear to be disappointed, as first empirical estimates show that through these amendments the number of works councils in SMEs has hardly increased (Ellguth 2006: 53; Rudolph and Wassermann 2006: 99; Behrens 2003).

France has a considerably more complex set of various worker-representation structures called 'personnel-representation institutions' (*institutions représentatives du personnel, IRP*). The three most important institutions (cf. Lecher 1994; Tschobanian 1995; Dufour and Hege 2006) are the following:

- *Délégués du Personnel* (Personnel Delegates, DP) are mainly responsible for transmission of individual grievances to management and have the right to question management.
- *Comité d'Entreprise* (Enterprise Committee, CE) is responsible for the employee social fund[1] and is, thereby often primarily occupied with social and cultural matters. The committee is also charged with collective interest representation, has relatively comprehensive access to information and must be consulted by management in several matters. In contrast to German works councils, the committees have no significant co-determination and veto rights. The formal chairmanship of the CE is held by company management.
- *Délégués Syndicaux* (Union Delegates, DS) are the '*responsables*', or formal office-holders of union sections among workplace employees. Only DS may actually bargain with management. While union pluralism in France means that an enterprise can have DS from several unions, and all DS have the right to bargain contracts with company management. Any agreements that they reach are binding for all the firm's employees. Therefore, management chooses its bargaining partner strategically, taking into account the different unions' influences and strike capabilities.

The personnel delegates (DPs) and the enterprise committee (CE) are elected by all employees, whereby, in principle, two ballots are foreseen: in the first round, there are only union-proposed candidates. Only when these are not present in sufficient number, or do not receive the necessary quorum, does a second ballot follow, in which non-union candidates may also participate. In France, the election of DPs is obligatory in companies with 10 or more employees; a CE must be chosen in companies with at least 50 employees. In companies with fewer than 200 employees, both institutions can merge into a *Délégation Unique* (single delegation, DU).

In contrast to the German works council, the election of DPs and CEs is mandated by law, and management, rather than employees, are responsible for complying with the regulation. This procedure is monitored by the state labour inspectorate (*Inspecteurs du Travail*) with the power to punish non-compliance. Only a lack of candidates can justify the absence of the legally mandated institutions. The DS (union delegates) are company employees who are not elected to the position but rather chosen by each union.

Since in France there is an individual right to strike – strike activities are not under the direct control of unions or other workplace representatives – and co-determination and veto rights are lacking, strikes and work-actions play a crucial role in the establishment of a *rapport de force* (power relationship) with management.

15.3 Extent of coverage of interest-representation structures – the representation gap

15.3.1 The representation gap in Germany

The representation gap in Germany can be measured by the percentage of enterprises and employees who are not represented by works councils. The data indicate that this gap is sizable. In 2003, 89 per cent of all private-sector workplaces with five or more employees in Germany as a whole (52 per cent of West-German and 61 per cent of East-German workplaces) had no works council. This means that only about five out of ten employees in the West, and about four out of ten employees in the East, are represented by a works council (see Tables 15.1 and 15.2).

Tables 15.1 and 15.2 reveal a strong correlation between the presence of works councils and company size. In workplaces with up to 50 employees, the existence of a works council can be considered an exception: they represent only about every tenth employee. And even workplaces with 50 to 100 employees have usually no works council. Only when approximately 100 employees and more are present, do workplaces gradually realize the 'standard' legal provision of a works council.

An analysis of IAB panel-data by economic sectors shows that in construction, sales and services the representation gap is especially large. Only in the manufacturing industry, the primary sector and the insurance sector is co-determination widespread (Ellguth 2006: 52). Statistically, 'the typical workplace without a works council is a (...) small, young, new and privately-owned start-up enterprise, a single operation, not bound to collective-bargaining systems, and has rather few qualified workers and proportionally many women' (Ellguth 2002: 11, translation by author).

To sum up, the German representation gap has been significant and constant since the mid-1990s. At least no clear tendency can be observed in one direction or the other. Regular forms of interest representation,

Table 15.1   German companies without a works council according to company size, 2003 (in per cent)

Company size	5–50 employees	51–100 empl.	101–199 empl.	200–500 empl.	>500 empl.	Total
Western Germany	93	53	32	18	9	89
Eastern Germany	93	58	32	25	21	89

Source: *IAB-Betriebspanel*; author's calculation and table after Ellguth and Kohaut (2004: 452)
Basis: Social-security-paying employees in private enterprises of 5 or more employees

Table 15.2   German employees in workplaces without a works council according to company size, 2003 (in per cent)

Company size	5–50 employees	51–100 empl.	101–199 empl.	200–500 empl.	>500 empl.	Total
Western Germany	89	53	32	17	6	52
Eastern Germany	88	58	30	26	18	61

Source: *IAB-Betriebspanel*; author's calculation and table after Ellguth and Kohaut (2004: 452)
Basis: Social-security-paying employees in private enterprises of 5 or more employees

that is, workplaces with works councils, are found above all in larger operations, while in German SMEs other, irregular forms of interest representation are the rule.[2]

15.3.2   The representation gap in France

As Table 15.3 shows, the 'absolute representation gap' – the extent to which no workplace representation exists – is in France significantly smaller than in Germany; this is true even when we consider that French statistics do not include workplaces of fewer than 20 employees. Only 12 per cent of all French employees (in private companies with 20 or more workers) are not represented by any workplace-representation body.

In France too, a strong link exists between the degree of interest representation (IRP presence) and company size. However, a complete lack of representation is unusual, even in small enterprises of 20–50 employees. Around two-thirds of these small firms have some kind of representative structure, most often *délégués du personnel* (DP), which is legally required in workplaces with ten or more employees. For workplaces with 50 workers or more, the presence of DPs and the other IRPs is the rule.

Table 15.3 French companies and employees without any workplace structures of employee representation (IRPs), according to company size, 1998–99 (in per cent)

Company size	20–49 employees	50–99 employees	>100 employees	Total
Share of companies	35	13	4	25
Share of employees	33	12	2	12

Source: *Enquête Réponse* 1998–99; author's calculation and table after Dufour and Hege (2006: 340)
Basis: private enterprises of 20 or more employees

Table 15.4 French companies and workers with the complete system of workplace interest-representation

	Share of all companies (in per cent)	Share of all employees (in per cent)	Company size (average number of employees)
DP + CE + DS	16	41	203
Délégation Unique + DS	5	6	89
Total	21	47	–

Source: *Enquête Réponse* 1998–99; author's calculation and table after Dufour and Hege (2006: 341)
Basis: private enterprises of 20 or more employees

Thus, French SMEs are not typically institution-free. Yet seldom are *all institutions* of interest representation foreseen by law actually implemented. Table 15.4 shows that the complete set of standard interest-representation forms is mainly present only in larger companies. Therefore, in the French context, as in Germany, irregular forms of interest representation also often exist, especially in SMEs.

The share of French workers covered by the complete institutional model approximates the coverage of West-German workers by works-council representation; in both countries, slightly less than half of all employees work within the official institutional framework of interest representation. Similar in Germany and France is that the regular institutional forms of workplace representation are more often found in large companies. In both German and French SMEs, irregular forms of interest representation are the rule.

In most cases of irregular interest representation in France, the union-delegate structure is lacking (cf. Dufour and Hege 2006: 341). This means that, because local union sections are missing, there is no one present who is able to bargain valid contracts with management[3]. Since DPs and the CEs have only limited representation rights, the absence of a collective union voice usually means limited bargaining power for the elected representatives.

In summary, as in Germany, irregular forms of interest-representation can also be observed in relatively small, young and non-subsidiary French enterprises operating in new industries (cf. Dufour and Hege 2006: 343). The French institutional system, however, is capable of assuring (limited) representation rights in a large number of workplaces outside the core of large, well-organized union workplaces. While in German SMEs irregular interest representation is typically that which takes place in the absence of a works council – thus lacking any formalized institution of interest representation – in French SMEs the typical irregular forms of representation are those which simply do not involve unions.

Overall, the German system tends to require a higher level of 'critical effort' on the part of employees to establish some formal representation – a level which often cannot be attained, especially in SMEs. The French system, by contrast, seems to offer more legal possibilities to implement something that could be called 'low-level participation structures'. From a formal and statistical point of view, the institutional regulation clearly makes a difference in theory – but does it also in practice?

15.4 Irregular forms of employee representation in German and French SMEs in practice

If we look beyond the formal structure of interest representation, several questions come to mind: how do the quite widespread forms of irregular worker representation in German and French SMEs actually work in practice? How do the different institutional situations affect the employees' possibilities for realizing their interests in the workplace? Does, for example, the higher level of coverage by French representational bodies also mean a greater efficiency of representation? In short, do the institutions matter – and in what way?

As an approach to these questions, I will briefly describe two SME case studies. The German example stems from a research project on companies without works councils carried out in 2003–06 at the Technical University of Munich. The second case study is from the project 'Institutional gaps in workplace interest-representation in Germany and France' conducted from autumn 2005 to spring 2006 at the IRES in Paris.[4]

15.4.1 Village Machine Company: a German SME without a works council

The Village Machine Company (VMC) was founded in 1986 as a rural subsidiary of a South-German specialty-machine manufacturer. The company produces tailor-made, high-quality steel parts with CNC-controlled tool machines.

Decisive for the success of the company are quality and on-time delivery, while production costs play a lesser role. The personality of the managing director strongly influences company management culture. In spite of his clear claim to authority, he does not lack a sense of social responsibility. Among the employees he enjoys the reputation of a 'fair boss'.

The 120 employees are mainly highly qualified male workers with strong bonds to the region. A few are part-time farmers. Most have spent the greater part of their occupational life in the company. Employee turnover, regardless of initiator, is very low. Besides the regional bonds, the job security assured by the company is crucial for the workers' obvious loyalty. The managing director and workers agree on a solid common interest, according to the motto: 'What's good for the company is good for us' (employee statement). Yet there is also an awareness of a permanent need to balance differing interests and potential conflicts in a robust culture of informal communication and negotiation. For example, the great number of individualized work plans indicates that personal needs of employees are taken seriously.

More precarious, however, are the compromises on the issue of wages. The company is not a member of an employers' association and, therefore, not bound to collective wage-agreements. As a result, overall wages are somewhat lower than – though roughly oriented to – collective wage-agreement levels of big industry. 'Everybody complains about it', said one employee interviewed. The rather egalitarian, yet still below average, wages caused repeated dissatisfaction in the past. As the dissent began to have an obvious effect on the workplace environment, the director attempted to steer the informal criticism into more formal channels by arranging the election of so-called 'employee spokespersons'. He saw to it that 'the most talkative' employees were elected, who could voice informal criticism and disarm any discontent threatening the work-climate. The spokespersons, however, have no co-determination or any other legally guaranteed rights, and turned out to be comparatively 'tame' in direct dialogue with the manager (the word he used). While the position continues to exist, it only maintains a low-level intensity of representation. It is 'above all for those who don't have the nerve to speak to the supervisors' and resolves 'about once a year some minor problem' (employee statement).

Because of a company culture that is generally perceived as open and direct in terms of communication – also vertically – in everyday operations, problems and conflicts are, overall, quickly resolved bilaterally. However, there is no policy of collective employee inclusion in, or information about, company matters, no form of collective interest articulation or anything resembling power-oriented, collective negotiation. From the perspective of the employees, they possessed 'no means to power at all' over management (employee statement). In spite of intensive informal or semi-structured communication, the social arrangement in this workplace is far from a relationship of direct democracy. Rather, it could be called 'legitimate domination'. The company manager exercises his directive power in a comparatively socially responsible, yet unilateral manner – a process that has never been questioned.

The lack of a works council at VMC is, above all, the result of the director's rejection of the institution and his fear of complications and slow-downs in market adjustments related to work-time flexibility. Since works councils have quite strong rights to co-determination in this area, and the company's main strategy versus competitors is a flexible reaction to customer needs, this is a very sensitive issue. Also, the director simply does not want others interfering with his heretofore unlimited freedom of disposition, nor does he want to justify his decision-making to third parties. While he made his position rather clear, employees are less certain of how they feel about the possible benefits of a works council. In the words of one employee: 'We would have liked to try out a works council once, to see what it's like, but we just weren't at the point yet to actually do it.'

Overall, the situation at the VMC is similar to that found by Rudolph and Wassermann (2006: 83) in comprehensive empirical studies: if employees display no interest in having a works council, it is not because of a 'fundamental rejection of formal co-determination', but rather because of the 'satisfaction with the dominant, informal form of dialogue. (...). They fear that, through installing a works council things could became complicated, that room for manoeuvre and the status quo could be lost through a polarization of employers and employees' (author's translation). The 'lack of interest' in, or scepticism towards, the election of a works council is also 'an indirect result of the situation of dominance in the company' (ibid.: 84).

Rudolph and Wassermann also argue that SMEs reject works councils because they 'count as the trap-door to union influence on a company's development' (ibid.: 83). This view cannot be confirmed in the case of the VMC. Unions are just not an issue here. Employees and management display similar attitudes: unions are important, in principle at least, as representation of 'the other party', a counterweight to managerial power. But current union politics, criticized as estranged from reality, seem to have no advocates in this workplace.

15.4.2 The Recycling Company: a French SME with non-union employee representation

The Recycling Company (RC) has a total of three locations, two of which are located in a medium-sized French manufacturing city and the third in a distant rural area. The firm evolved out of a non-profit environmental association in 1999. In the context of a state reorganization of the public waste sector, it was transformed into a private enterprise. The main activity of the firm is sorting household waste, which takes place in two sorting centres.

A kind of secondary service is the occupational re-insertion of unemployed people: of the total 105 employees, almost half are employed on a (maximum 18-month) re-insertion contract. Thus, RC employees, on the one hand, consist of such 'marginals' – contracted, formerly unemployed persons with, as a group, frequent turnover – and on the other, include a nucleus of permanent workers. Particularly the latter make up the *maitrises*: the team and group leaders in production. The criterion for attaining this position is the verification of having been a 'good worker' in some other industrial workplace, as well as the possession of leadership qualities. Since its founding, the company has grown continually and has almost no competitors in the regional market.

The most decisive figure in the interaction taking place concerning workplace labour relations is the managing director, who was recruited outside of the firm at the time of its founding. Her great competence and professionalism in business, but also her sense of social responsibility, is attested to on both sides. Her dialogue-oriented philosophy of leadership advocates horizontal hierarchies, direct communication and individual responsibility. She finds great value in ensuring that 'the place can run even without me'. However, it has also been said that she 'does have her hardened positions, especially when it comes to wages.' Another important leadership function is filled by the production manager. According to employee representatives, 'a real dialogue' is possible with him, as well.

Unlike the German VMC, the French RC is bound to a collective wage agreement and has a workplace interest-representation body, which, however, does not involve unions. In 2001, a *délégation unique* (DU) of five members was elected for the first time. This body combines the function of the *délégués du personnel* and the *comité d'entreprise*. Three of the members are *titulaires* (officeholders), and two are *suppléants* (substitute representatives). This number represents fewer than legally required. However, only these five employees were willing to candidate for the office. In terms of persons and firm politics, the DU is clearly dominated by supervisors from the production line.

The DU delegates 'never' take the legally possible 20-hour-per-month allowance of duty time 'because they're very busy at their jobs. They have trouble taking this time off, perhaps also because it's a small enterprise' (manager's statement). The secretary of the DU carries out bureaucratic tasks, such as protocoling the mandatory monthly meetings of management and employee representatives, which is normally the responsibility of the *délégués du personnel*. The DU treasurer is occupied, above all, with the use of the social-event budget: she arranges employee perquisites, such as shopping coupons, entertainment discounts and the distribution of refreshments and snacks. The third officeholder, or *titulaire*, represents the employees in the rural production location. Although the DU does facilitate information and communication between management and employees to some extent, the body is mainly occupied with the 'little extras', that is, perquisites that make working at RC 'nice' (DU treasurer's statement).

The body does not, however, have the function of collective interest-representation and has very little influence on internal interaction processes, though this does not mean that potential conflicts to be solved are absent. For example, a shift-work system was recently implemented due to a broadening of production, causing relatively inconvenient working hours for some employees. The DU's activity on this issue was limited to 'inquiring' and communicating employee dissatisfaction. For most workers, wages at RC – in spite of the good financial situation – are around (or slightly above) the legal minimum wage.[5] The production manager admits: 'If the employee representatives were a bit more aggressive, they would demand higher wages. They've never tried to, but they should.' The same is true for the precarious heating and ventilation conditions: workplace temperatures may rise to over 40°C in the summer and sink to 3°–4°C in the winter. On a particularly cold day, this led to a collective, employee-initiated work stoppage that lasted around three quarters of an hour and ended when the production manager promised to arrange additional heating, to which he promptly attended. The DU and its representatives had no part at all in this incident.

Despite the underlying dissatisfactions, the actors interviewed at RC perceive the workplace conditions – as in the German firm – as 'unproblematic'. The production manager explains this as follows: 'The company seeks the necessary solutions in case of problems. We don't hold fast to routine positions, insisting for example: the law says such and such. If it's necessary, if there is some demand, then we go a little further to avoid a conflict.'

In his perspective, it is always the managing director who, in case of conflict situations, presents solutions without delay – and to which the employee representatives 'consistently agree'. In an atmosphere of 'little criticism', the relationship between management and the employee representatives is, essentially, one of accepting management decisions.

In short, the relationships at RC are similar to those described as typical for smaller French enterprises by Dufour et al. (2006): 'The logic of exchange and negotiation are also not lacking in such small workplaces that have no representation structures whatever. Although it is true the dominance of the *patron* is rarely questioned' (ibid.: 64; author's translation). These authors believe that, because of the low number of employees in SMEs, it may be generally difficult to legitimate representation processes. For RC employees, the question of what actually justifies particular workers being separated from the collective and claiming the right to represent all may retain some virulence. The legally mandated elections may not provide sufficient legitimacy where a permanent culture of informal communication tends to make formal representation seem unessential. Often it is, therefore, even the elected representatives themselves who 'in general try to balance the weight of the structures, as well as the significance and status of persons [holding the functions]: "In fact, it doesn't change very much"' (ibid.: 72).

French IRPs, not being based on union organizing and, thus, not able to count on collective mobilization and support of the employees, are very weak institutions. Due to the absence of 'hard' co-determination or veto rights, they do little more than serve as an information and communication body and take care of the 'little extras'.

This situation can change only by IRPs becoming credible collective-representation entities and claiming a certain bargaining power through the threat of collective action; it is usually only the presence of unions as well as collective conflicts that plays the decisive role in establishing a *rapport de force*, a real power-sharing relationship with management. The production manager at RC probably had this in mind when asked why there was no union present: 'Perhaps just because there is no big conflict, or because I have my antennae, we can intervene before the problems and conflicts get started.'

Again, Dufour et al. (2006: 74) is instructive. According to them, recent representation structures are seldom union-organized. This reticence is explained not only by the attitude of the *patron*; the employees and their representatives (*élus*) for their part fear a destabilizing effect of union intervention which may threaten the social or even economic equilibrium of the workplace. (Ibid.: 74.)

15.5   A comparative summary: the relevance of institutions

The comparison of the German and French companies addresses first the constants in the social constitution of small- and medium-sized workplaces: Both display a well-established informal workplace negotiation culture, with multiple possibilities for direct reconciliation between employees and superiors. The existence of everyday, case-specific 'this-for-that' exchanges guarantees 'more or less fair' compromises – from the employee perspective as well as from that of the management. In this way, a formal and effective interest-representation seems for them to be unnecessary.

Quite similar in both cases is also that such informal compromises leave management's unilateral directive rights untouched. In this respect, the German workplace, while lacking a works council and commitments to industry-wide agreements, hardly differs from the French workplace with its non-unionized representation and somewhat stronger orientation to the standards of collective contracts. The 'little extras' in the form of information, communication and social benefits that the French IRPs (*institutions représentatives du personnel*) arrange for the workers are far from negligible advantages. However, the same effect could also be achieved through non-mandatory forms of worker representation or specific human-resource strategies of management, as we have seen in the German case.

The strong similarities in institutional *practice* in spite of different formal institutional settings are not only an effect of the size of the companies; the two companies also display quite similar management cultures. In both cases, management takes employee interests into account – at least to a certain extent. Each management pursues a conflict-avoidance strategy and in no way lacks social responsibility. This may be one substantial reason for the far-reaching 'irrelevance' of formal institutions in both companies. Conversely, it is also true that in (for example) larger companies with more professional employee-representation structures, as well as in cases of more repressive management, the institutional effects of workplace interest-representation likely play a different role.

In any case, the comparison shows the necessity of distinguishing between formal institutional coverage and institutional practice: The stronger legal mandate and state surveillance of the French system of worker representation insures greater institutional coverage, but this is not equal to greater employee influence and power. The French IRPs show a sometimes limited effectiveness – particularly when not enforced by union presence.

This does not justify, however, the assumption of a generally weaker employee representational power in French workplaces. The level of empowerment of a given representation structure depends heavily on the capacity of local actors to use the liberal right to strike (Artus 2007). Hence, a comparison of institutions is insufficient in that it merely determines the existence or non-existence of institutions and the degree of their coverage. A comprehensive study must also examine what power the given institutions – under specific sets of conditions – possess *in practice*. Consequently, the question is not so much 'Do institutions matter?', but rather 'Which institutions *do* matter, in which ways and in what contexts?'

The above comparison has shown that, in some contexts, the formal implementation or non-implementation of institutions makes no difference. In the same way, it can be assumed that identical institutional rules, in different contexts, have different effects (cf. Artus 2002). Comparisons of institutions – in a generalizing way limited to comparing specific countries' institutional rules or specific countries' models of industrial relations as a whole – are, therefore, insufficient or represent perhaps even a methodological dead-end (Dufour and Hege 2002: 17).

It seems essential, instead, to examine the specific institutional *practices* in comparable sectors of the economy. Such a methodological approach may detect similarities in practice beyond national institutional differences. Such a procedure would also do justice to the realization that specific institutional practices do not result deterministically from certain institutional rules, but also always obey logics of action that have been historically learnt and are, therefore, embedded in culture.

Notes

1. In French workplaces the CE is usually given a social-fund budget of 1–2 per cent of the total wage to be used for supplemental employee perquisites.
2. However, the reverse (that is, that the majority of all German works-council delegates are employed in large enterprises) is not true. Data from the *IG Metall* union show that almost half (49.5 per cent) of the works-council delegates in the metal industry are employed in companies with less than 100 employees (Wassermann and Rohde 2004: 86).
3. This situation was a particular problem for the application of the legal work-time reduction to 35 hours per week in SMEs – a reason for which the new institution of the *salarié(e) mandaté(e)* (mandated salaried employee) was created in the year 1995. 'These are employees given temporary negotiating powers by a union for a specific negotiation purpose. They are obligated to answer to the union.' (Dufour and Hege 2006: 356, author's translation). In practice this new institution proved to be an efficient instrument for realizing legal regulations in the workplace. Usually, however, the naming of the *mandaté(e)s* was strongly related to specific cases and did not have the character of an innovative, sustainable or legitimate representative institution. Therefore, union hopes for better access to workplaces in the area of SMEs were disappointed (Dufour et al. 2000).
4. The following persons were involved in the project: Sabine Böhm, Stefan Lücking, Rainer Trinczek and the author. See http://www.wi.tum/sociology/research/bob and Artus et al. 2006. The research in France was supported by the *Maison des Sciences de l'Homme*. For the French cases, see http://www.wi.tum/sociology/research/sirp.
5. The legal minimum wage in France is currently €8.27 per hour.

References

Addison, J. T., C. Schnabel and J. Wagner (2000) 'Nonunion Representation in Germany', in B. Kaufman and D. G. Taras (eds), *Nonunion Employee Representation: History, Contemporary Practice and Policy* (London: Armonk), 365–85.

Artus, I. (2002) 'Le transfert du système (ouest)allemand de relations professionnelles à l'Est: des rôles différents pour des institutions identiques', *Revue de l'IRES*, 39, 33–59.

Artus, I. (2007) 'Prekäre Interessenvertretung. Ein deutsch-französischer Vergleich von Beschäftigtenrepräsentation im niedrig entlohnten Dienstleistungsbereich', *Industrielle Beziehungen*, 1, 5–29.

Artus, I., S. Böhm, S. Lücking and R. Trinczek (eds) (2006) *Betriebe ohne Betriebsrat. Informelle Interessenvertretung in Unternehmen* (Frankfurt, New York: Campus).

Behrens, M. (2003) 'Wie gut kehren neue Besen? Das neue Betriebsverfassungsgesetz in der Praxis', *WSI Mitteilungen*, 3, 167–75.

Dufour, C. and A. Hege (2002) *L'Europe syndicale au quotidien. La représentation des salariés en France, Allemagne, Grande-Bretagne et Italie* (Bruxelles, Bern, Frankfurt, New York, Oxford, Wien: P.I.E.-Peter Lang).

Dufour, C. and A. Hege (2006) 'Akteure und Sozialbeziehungen in französischen Betrieben mit und ohne institutionalisierte Interessenvertretung', in I. Artus, S. Böhm, S. Lücking and R. Trinczek (eds), *Betriebe ohne Betriebsrat. Informelle Interessenvertretung in Unternehmen* (Frankfurt/Main, New York: Campus), 333–62.

Dufour, C., A. Hege, S. Murhem, W. Rudolph and W. Wassermann (2006) *Les relations sociales dans les petites entreprises. Une comparaison France, Suède, Allemagne* (Bruxelles, Bern, Frankfurt, New York, Oxford, Wien: P.I.E.-Peter Lang).

Dufour, C., A. Hege, C. Vincent and M. Viprey (2000) 'Le mandatement en question', *Travail et Emploi*, 82 (April), 25–36.

Ellguth, P. (2002) 'Betriebsräte in Kleinbetrieben – ein bislang eher seltenes Phänomen', *IAB Materialien*, 1, 10–11.

Ellguth, P. (2006) 'Betriebe ohne Betriebsrat – Verbreitung, Entwicklung und Charakteristika – unter Berücksichtigung betriebsspezifischer Formen der Mitarbeitervertretung', in I. Artus, S. Böhm, S. Lücking and R. Trinczek (eds), *Betriebe ohne Betriebsrat. Informelle Interessenvertretung in Unternehmen* (Frankfurt/Main, New York: Campus), 43–80.

Ellguth, P. and S. Kohaut (2004) 'Tarifbindung und betriebliche Interessenvertretung : Ergebnisse des IAB-Betriebspanels 2003', *WSI Mitteilungen*, 8, 450–54.

Hall, P. A. and D. Soskice (eds) (2001) *Varieties of Capitalism. The Institutional Foundations of Comparative Advantage* (New York: Oxford University Press).

Lecher, W. (1994) 'Betriebliche Funktionsfähigkeit der französischen und deutschen Arbeitnehmerinteressenvertretung – ein empirisch gestützter Vergleich', *Industrielle Beziehungen*, 2, 179–202.

Müller-Jentsch, W. (1995) 'Germany: From Collective Voice to Co-management', in J. Rogers and W. Streeck (eds), *Works Councils: Consultation, Representation, and Cooperation in Industrial Relations* (Chicago: University of Chicago Press), 53–78.

Rudolph, W. and W. Wassermann (2006) 'Übergänge zwischen Betriebsratslosigkeit und Betriebsratsgründung: Neue Betriebsratsgründungen im Bereich kleiner Betriebe und Reform der Betriebsverfassung 2001', in I. Artus, S. Böhm, S. Lücking and R. Trinczek (eds), *Betriebe ohne Betriebsrat. Informelle Interessenvertretung in Unternehmen* (Frankfurt/Main, New York: Campus), 81–105.

Schmidt, R. and R. Trinczek (1991) 'Duales System: Tarifliche und betriebliche Interessenvertretung', in W. Müller-Jentsch (ed.), *Konfliktpartnerschaft. Akteure und Institutionen der industriellen Beziehungen* (Munich, Mering: Hampp), 167–199.

Tschobanian, R. (1995) 'France: From Conflict to Social Dialogue?', in J. Rogers and W. Streeck (eds), *Works Councils: Consultation, Representation, and Cooperation in Industrial Relations* (Chicago: University of Chicago Press), 115–152.

Wassermann, W. and W. Rohde (2004) *Konfliktfeld Kleinbetrieb. Mittelstand zwischen Alleinherrschaft und Mitbestimmung* (Frankfurt/Main: Bund).

16
Social Relationships in German SMEs: An East-West Comparison

Rudi Schmidt

16.1 Introduction

Social relationships in German firms are structurally shaped by institutions of co-determination (*Mitbestimmung*). This is an essential element of 'Rhine Capitalism' (*Rheinischer Kapitalismus*) or the 'coordinated market economy' and, as part of the societal order going beyond the economy, is not exposed to direct market influence. As far as the consistency of this system goes, the question is all the more interesting whether indirect effects on German co-determination are observable through market change, liberalization and globalization – in a certain sense as proof of the repeatedly expressed assumption of a convergence of the coordinated market economy towards the Anglo-Saxon type of capitalism. There are indeed some indications for this. A systematic overview and evaluation of the now quite extensive research on this aspect of the socioeconomic order cannot, however, be undertaken in this short contribution. I limit myself here to the analysis of selected themes of the social relationships in workplaces and examine, in particular, the influence of management on employee co-determination, works councils and unions from an East-West comparative perspective with a focus on East-German manufacturing SMEs.

As a result of the empirical research presented in this chapter, I will examine the idea that the transfer of the entire system of industrial relations from the West to the East did not guarantee the functioning of these institutions in the originally intended manner. Instead, the East German actors, works councillors and managers agreed to do everything possible to strengthen the competitiveness of their respective companies, including tolerating weaker practices of co-determination and falling short of labour law regulations.

This chapter will proceed as follows: section 16.2 outlines the differences in the institutionalization of the German labour relations system according to enterprise size and addresses the pressure exerted by the different enterprise types. In section 16.3 I investigate how East and West German SME managing directors assess co-determination. Finally, the reasons for persisting East-West differences will be explored in section 16.4.

The empirical basis for this chapter consists of, among other things, panel data from two study waves conducted in 2002 and 2005 among circa 750 enterprises and managing directors in the East and West of Germany.[1] In addition to these data, material was used from parallel qualitative studies and other University of Jena investigations.

16.2 Labour relations and size differences

The basis of worker co-determination in German enterprises was laid out in the 'Works Constitution Act' (*Betriebsräte-Gesetz*) of 1920, which was suspended in 1933 by the Nazi regime and newly legislated in 1952 in modified form as the 'Law on Workplace Constitutions' (*Betriebsverfassungs-Gesetz* or *BetrVG*)). This law stipulates that in all enterprises and plants with more than five employees a works council can be elected upon the formal request of employees or a union represented by an employee; however, this is not legally obligatory. The German works council has comprehensive rights to information and a voice in all questions of employment, output, work and wage conditions and must be consulted in all matters of basic workplace changes (organization, production, job relocation and the like). As a rule, works councils cooperate closely with unions, which makes them an important source of union support in gaining new members and in conflicts of interest with opposing parties. The unions, for their part, take on consultation and coordination functions. Therefore, loosening union bonds, as a rule, also weakens works councils. Because of the institutional separation of both – nonetheless interacting – levels of actors, we speak of the German 'dual system of industrial relations' (see Schmidt and Trinczek 1993; Müller-Jentsch 2007). On the other hand, however, works councils are obliged by law to cooperate and not initiate labour conflicts with employers (*Friedenspflicht*).

The long conflict-laden process of its creation and historical establishment made of workplace co-determination in Germany a pillar of social emancipation towards an 'industrial' or 'economic democracy'.

Though the unions desire from time to time a broadening of co-determination rights – and entrepreneurs their limitation – the core of co-determination law is uncontested among all German political parties.[2] That is not equally true of the co-determination that is mandatory in larger enterprises and foresees a role for works-council members and union representatives in decisions of the supervisory board. The latter facet of co-determination is omitted from this chapter, which is dedicated, above all, to social relations in East-German SMEs, because it plays – following the de-industrialization in the wake of the political transformation – only a minor role; in East Germany there are only few firms with more than 2000 employees – the legal limit for the above mentioned type of enterprise co-determination.

From the general political acceptance of co-determination in enterprises, however, one cannot infer a similar level of assent among entrepreneurs. Although the creation of a works council in private enterprises with over 500 employees is practically a matter of course – 88 per cent of these firms in West Germany have a works council and 82 per cent in East Germany (Ellguth and Kohaut 2007: 513) – the level of acceptance declines constantly with diminishing firm size and reaches, in the large segment of SMEs employing five to 50 people, only about 6 per cent. This group lowers the average so much that in the East as in the West of Germany only 10 per cent of all firms with more than five employees (not counting the public-service sector) have works councils. However, because of the higher works-council density in large enterprises, this figure represents 46 per cent of employees in the West and 38 per cent in the East (ibid.). From the enterprises included in our study, 58 per cent had a works council. However, there was a clear East-West difference: in the West-German firms 68 per cent had a works council; in those firms managed by West Germans in the East 62 per cent; but in those managed by East Germans only 46 per cent (see Table 16.1)

In large enterprises, particularly in subsidiaries headed by managers of large stock companies, the works council often functions as a branch of the personnel department, as in the highly unionized auto industry, for which Volkswagen serves as an excellent example. The purpose of this close collaboration is to allow works councils the opportunity to help reduce social complexity in a firm's daily business and, subsequently, contribute to relieving the managerial load. This is not the case in owner-led small- and often also in middle-sized enterprises, whose growth is typically not accompanied by adequate adjustments in organizational structures.

Table 16.1 Enterprises with works council in East- and West-German manufacturing SMEs

Does your workplace have a works council?		West-German managers in the West	East-German managers in the East	West-German managers in the East	Total
Yes	Number	201	119	83	403
	Per cent	67.7	45.9	61.5	58.3
No	Number	96	140	52	288
	Per cent	32.3	54.1	38.5	41.7
	Total	297	259	135	691

The public critique of employee co-determination in enterprises also receives international support by, above all, Anglo-Saxon investors, which may, in the long run, weaken this form of co-determination. This is particularly true if the tendency to choose the legal form of a 'Societas Europaea' (SE) increases in Germany. The SE provides multinational enterprises with the option to operate throughout the EU with one set of regulations and a choice regarding employee co-determination, possibly leading to weaker interest representations. Another insidiously progressing development appears even more serious and could undermine the still relatively stable plant-level co-determination in the sense of the *BetrVG*. This is the almost complete absence of legally and externally defined co-determination in start-ups in the high-tech industries and in innovative service branches. The mostly highly qualified employees of such firms strongly believe in their own individual bargaining powers and prefer to avoid the help of interest-representatives except in, at the most, crisis situations.

In general, the founders of new enterprises have no genuine interest in establishing a 'parallel-government', especially if it is perceived as being controlled from afar by the unions. Typical for SMEs is a firm-centred, more or less autocephalous management with short information and decision paths that corresponds with flat hierarchies and flexible, highly reactive organization structures. Hence, a differentiated employee interest-representation with its own state-mandated legal structure is like a foreign body that slows down, blocks or disrupts decision-making processes whenever its representatives are not *de facto* fully and affirmatively integrated into the enterprise culture and motivationally committed to its management philosophy.

16.3   East-West-Differences: assessments regarding co-determination and unions

At its core the concept of employee *co-determination* describes the installation and co-work of the legally legitimated works council in plants. However, it also broadly denotes every form of interest representation, including also, for example, union 'shop stewards' in workplaces and even direct participation. When we ask managers about their relationship to co-determination, we gather rather general opinions about the influence of employees and their interest representation (works councils and unions) on plant-level decision-making, which usually also provides information about their attitudes towards cooperation and power-sharing.

In our manager interviews we obtained only a very reserved assent on the subject of co-determination, whereby the East-German managing directors expressed themselves more positively (see Table 16.2). Interviewees were asked to assign a value – on a scale ranging from strong agreement (1) to strong rejection (5) – to prepared statements. As expected, they gave the most positive judgement to the statement 'Co-determination has a high value for employees' (mean = 2.42). More closely positioned to the respondents' personal opinions was the statement 'Co-determination is a necessary element in a pluralistic society'. Here one can remain assentingly neutral, even when one does not share the premise of a pluralistically constituted society. However, because most would agree with this premise, the implicit request for a normative judgement is probably stronger. A weak assent dominated: the average value was 2.62 but worsened somewhat in comparison to the survey in 2002 (mean = 2.44).

Perhaps the closest to personal convictions were the valuations of the statement about co-determination being 'disturbing' for an enterprise. The mean value of 3.33 showed no difference worthy of mention for the different manager groups and expressed only a slight rejection: exceeding the indifference threshold marked by a median of 3 only slightly. The managers viewed somewhat more positively the function of co-determination in helping to enact decisions (mean = 2.70); here the West Germans had slightly lower scores than the East Germans (mean = 2.86/2.51, median = 3/2, respectively). As we shall see, an ambivalent, practical alliance between East-German management and works councils is thereby expressed, for 'enacting decisions' always means enforcing them against the employees' will and, perhaps, also their resistance.

Table 16.2 Assessment of worker co-determination and union influence

	West-German managers in the West				East-German managers in the East				West-German managers in the East			
	No.	Mean	Standard deviation	Median	No.	Mean	Standard deviation	Median	No.	Mean	Standard deviation	Median
'Co-determination is a disturbance in the enterprise'	284	3.31	1.2	3.00	256	3.31	1.1	3.0	133	3.39	1.3	3.0
'Co-determination helps to enforce decisions'	284	2.86	1.1	3.00	256	2.51	1.0	2.0	131	2.73	1.2	2.0
'Co-determination is highly valued by employees'	286	2.45	1.0	2.00	249	2.36	1.0	2.0	133	2.46	1.0	2.0
'Co-determination is an essential element in a pluralistic society'	283	2.69	1.1	3.00	257	2.52	1.0	2.0	129	2.68	1.3	2.0
'Unions are unnecessary'	294	3.1	1.307	3.00	256	2.34	1.309	2.0	134	2.91	1.438	3.0

If we differentiate the respondent managers according to status, it becomes clear that the owner-managers are more critical with regard to co-determination than employed managers. When one is the 'head of the house' for only a specified time, one apparently tends to favour discursive decision-making processes, even in the context of opposing interest structures. Thus, entrepreneurs are less convinced that co-determination is a necessary element in a pluralistic society (mean = 3.07/2.48, respectively) and are also indifferent to the statement about its potential for disturbance. Employed managers, on the other hand, tend rather to reject such a thesis (mean = 3.12/3.53, respectively – no Table).

This sceptical-indifferent to moderately-positive image of co-determination contrasts with the clearly positive evaluation of the works council (see Table 16.3). Circa 87 per cent of those interviewed reported – without greater internal differentiation – having a positive relationship with a works council; barely 17 per cent considered the works council superfluous. Noticeable is the marked difference between East- and West-German company managers in the estimation of the active role of the works council in management processes. One-third of the West-German entrepreneurs and managers ascribed an important role to the works council ('takes over important tasks from business management'); among the East Germans, only half as many held this opinion.

Relevant in this context are also the differences between owner-managers and employed managers, with the latter being very prominent

Table 16.3   Management's relationship to the works council

	West-German managers in the West	East-German managers in the East	West-German managers in the East
'Relationship to works council is one of trust'	87.1%	84.0%	89.2%
'Relationship to works council is tense and conflictive'	8.0%	10.9%	7.2%
'Cooperation with works council is generally unproblematic'	85.1%	87.4%	91.6%
'Works council is unnecessary'	18.4%	17.6%	10.8%
'Works council takes over important tasks from management'	32.3%	17.6%	36.1%

among the group of West-German managers working in East-German enterprises. Present in great numbers are managers of West-German subsidiaries who are long familiar with works councils and influenced by a firm-wide, outspoken culture of western-style co-determination. In addition, 'corporate works councils' (*Konzernbetriebsräte*) responsible for all dependent firms in Germany belonging to the corporation place great value, at least within Germany, on subsidiaries and units having work and benefit standards similar to those of the parent enterprise, if possible. The assumption that these different preconditions must have an effect on the relationship to co-determination and works councils was confirmed. In East-German enterprises run by West-German *employed* managers, the works council density is distinctly greater (66.7 per cent) than in East-German enterprises (50 per cent) run by a West-German owner, which also have fewer employees in average. Of the employed managers, 91.7 per cent said that they had a relationship of trust to the works council, but only 81.8 per cent of the entrepreneurs did. With the suggestion that works councils might be superfluous, 22.7 per cent of the West German owner-managers in the East, but only 6.7 per cent of managers, agreed. This tense relationship between West German entrepreneurs and works councils in their East German enterprises is also the result of often being forced to conduct conflict-laden arbitration proceedings (22.7 per cent of the West German entrepreneurs as compared to 11.7 per cent West German employed managers in the East – no Table).

Besides works councils, the externally-acting *unions*, through their norm-setting function and close cooperation with the works councils, are a regulative factor with which every manager must operate. It can be assumed that managers do not care for them; at the least they treat them with a critical distance. All the more surprising is that West-German SME managers, known for their particular aversion to unions, maintain a stance of thoughtful neutrality towards them (see Table 16.2, final row). East-German managers, by contrast, show their aversion more clearly. With an average value of 2.34, a majority of these managers consider unions unnecessary. This corresponds to the significantly lower level of commitment to collective bargaining of the East-German enterprises. Only one-forth of them are subject to collective or company agreements; by contrast, 40 per cent of West-German plants are (Ellguth and Kohaut 2007: 512). Though many collective-bargaining-bound firms are oriented to sector-wide agreements so that their norms remain critical for the great majority of dependent workers, a further drop in the low level of collective-agreement commitment in East Germany is foreseeable in the long run, which is also expressed in lower wage levels.

In workplace labour and social relationships, as in industrial relations overall, even after 17 years of German unity, clear differences still exist between the country's two parts. In the following, we will discuss the causes of this more closely with reference to the themes focused on here.[3]

When one surveys the countless reports of workplace changes, one will notice that *works councils* – among the main actors in co-determination and social relationships in workplaces – currently face exceptional challenges. The liberalization of markets in the wake of EU integration and globalization have intensified competitive conditions for enterprises, who frequently react defensively by lengthening labour hours and enacting wage cuts, outsourcing, relocation of operations and so on. Collective bargaining norms are undermined and workplace agreements frequently cancelled. Many works councils have their hands full just trying to halt the further erosion of standards of labour and income they achieved over long years of hard struggle. Parallel to this growing pressure, the most important allies of works councils, the unions, are losing their regulative power. Thus, works councils in East and West Germany are in a comparatively similar situation. However, they do differ in a few important aspects, which can be traced back to structural and historical causes.

16.4   East-West differences – structural and historical reasons

Works councils have existed in the West of Germany at least since 1952, in the East only since 1990. In West Germany there are considerably more large plants than in East Germany. Therefore, the dispositional or work-exempt type of works council (possible in firms with 200 or more employees, after the last change in the *BetrVG*) is more frequent in the West than in the East. The exemption of council members permits a more intensive occupation with the core assignments of the works council and, therefore, represents an important opportunity for increased professionalization. By far not all East-German works councils who could exempt themselves from work for their duties actually do so. They renounce this right, rather, because they are more sensitive to entrepreneurs' argument of the cost burden. For the same reason, training courses on labour law and the like during work time are relatively seldom attended by East-German works-council members. Though, in truth, there are also great differences in this respect – works councils in the steel industry are hardly behind their West-German colleagues in regard to professionalism and conflict experience – but, in general, East-German works councils exhibit a lower level of professionalism (cf. Artus et al. 2000; Hinke et al. 2002).

However, this lack of professionalism is not perceived so much as a deficiency in East Germany. This has to do, in part, with the history of the German transformation since 1989, but also with the East-German economy. In the period of privatization by the 'trust foundation' (*Treuhandanstalt or THA*), many East-German works councils struggled for the survival of their firms, investment concepts and jobs. For the most part they could not hinder the radical downsizing or the liquidation of their enterprises. Yet, many of them built the core group of the so-called 'Notgemeinschaft' – a community of survivors of the industrial decline whose collective message was self-assertion in the new, aggressive market society. Often standing together with management against the THA or new investors during the THA privatization period, many East-German works councils were strongly focused on preserving workplaces. All other matters, even the unions, were secondary. The struggle was against outside forces, the THA and false promises of investors, and for survival in the marketplace. Internally, consensus dominated. Among the 'community of survivors' common interests outweighed individual ones. These plant-centred relationships, unmarred by conflict, were continued in second and third generations of works councils. They found their complement in the labour policy of the managers who preferred simple wage-for-worktime models, flexibility via working time and governed motivation through bonuses and job security. In manager-employee relations direct, personal communication and a chummy, first-name workplace culture dominated. But at the same time, an authoritarian, patriarchal, supervisory and order-giving style of management was common. While this style has, meanwhile, slowly converged with the more distant and participative-delegatory type of management of West Germany, it persists in some areas, at least in the older generations (see Martens and Michailow 2003: 29). In the past, such a self-confident policy of interest representation in a works council, faced with such authoritarian-patriarchal management practice, would have had little chance of success.

Just as East-German managers – who are predominantly socialized in natural- and engineering-science environments – had to learn that buying and selling is not a rational process ending with the victory of better arguments (cf. Gergs 2002), but is based rather much more on power, trust, speed and risk-taking, so too did East-German works councils have to learn that the interests of the employers are anything but identical with those of the employees and may even be completely contradictory.

While many in the East have indeed learned this in the meantime, their methods of interest representation is, all the same, still more moderate than in the West. In addition, they also still have a greater understanding of the economic and market constraints of their firms. This also applies to their perception of the costly rights and duties spelled out in the *BetrVG* – not only the right to work exemption or training during work time for works councillors, but also the mandatory quarterly plant assemblies. These are taken seriously only by a minority of works councils; most make do with one or two assemblies per year without in some way compensating for the rest (Artus et al. 2000).

In the sphere of corporate interest-representation where domination and exploitation for the benefit of political and economic elites run rampant, labour laws like the *BetrVG* are not automatically valid, but rather must be invoked by employees and those representing their interests, sometimes even by risking workplace conflicts. This was a long learning process in East Germany, which is explainable in the light of the GDR experience, where the sole directly functioning power was the state and the party apparatus that was *de facto* identical to it. That legal norms are based on power and, thus, politically negotiable, is a fact that the works councils in the East first had to internalize as basic knowledge essential to action. This was also the case with the much more basic realization that, following the system transformation, there was no longer a simple duality of state and individuals or the employed (*Werktätige*). Instead, these were essentially reconstituted in an intermediary sphere, where partially autonomous groups mediate between the two levels.[4]

Among these groups are the economic special-interest associations, which possess autonomous norm-setting privileges, the validity of which depends, in part, on the numbers of their members and followers. Union members and works councils in the East at first expected the member-unions of the DGB (*Deutscher Gewerkschaftsbund*, the western 'German Union Federation') to be very close to state power (making a structural analogy to the FDGB, the *Freier Deutscher Gewerkschaftsbund*, the GDR's 'Free German Union Federation'), for they expected from them nothing less than absolute job security. This notion was lost in the radical industrial decline during the THA privatization, with a corresponding loss of prestige for the unions. Only very slowly did the East German union members and works councils gain understanding for the fact that in an open democracy the power of interest groups results, above all, from the numerical strength of their memberships.

This explains why East-German works councils have a relatively distant relation to the unions of their branch, as do their counterparts in management, as well, despite taking on a different form and rationale. As interest-representation organizations beyond the level of the single company, unions must be interested in norms and standards in labour relations – the precondition to sectoral collective agreements – which also makes negotiation easier for works councils. However, their firm-centred orientation and the corresponding ease when dealing with wage norms either keeps the works councils at a distance to the unions or strengthens them. The University of Jena Sociology Institute's 2001 empirical study of the East-German metalworking industry showed that those plants bound to collective wage agreements, in part, operate below standards both in terms of work-time as well as pay (Hinke et al. 2002); the obligation to norms, that is, commitment to collectively-agreed pay-levels, has thus decreased over the course of recent years. Whether out of weakness or a conviction of the works councils, their acceptance of such deviation is, in any case, an indication of their practice of distancing themselves from the unions.

In the same study researchers found that not even half of all employees worked the 38-hour week prescribed for East-German wage regions; for these employees the typical work week was much longer. Against the backdrop of consensus-oriented labour relations and diminutive experience in strikes or conflicts, it was, therefore, a risky step in 2003 to force a gradual introduction of the 35-hour work-week, since in plants not even the 38-hour week had been strongly established as the norm. The strike – the first in 50 years and a turning-point in the long post-war period of successful labour and wage conflicts led by this industrial union – was lost (see Schmidt 2003b). Because a lost strike disadvantageously affects the freedom of action for unions and works councils over the course of many years, the latter will be able to react even less to increasing pressure for differentiation and flexibility in wage norms in the future. This strengthens decentralization and in-house regulation and shifts other responsibilities for taking action onto works councils, who lack a corresponding increase in their potential for action. Agreements advantageous for employees can be achieved by works councils, however, only through the active support of the unions. If support is lacking, in-house solutions will probably be accompanied by a wage decrease.

16.5   Conclusion

Labour- and social relationships in East-German industrial workplaces, in contrast to those in West-Germany, are characterized by several peculiarities that, in the intervening years following the transformation of the planned economy and its integration into the capitalist market, have persisted or taken the form of specific adaptation phenomena. Considered formally, all institutions of the West-German system as well as the collective actors (unions and employer federations) and labour laws have been transplanted in the East. However, in areas where official norms are not imposed by the state itself, but rather are worked out together by intermediary actors and the power of the market, they remain deficient in comparison to the West-German level. The circa 30 per cent lower economic capacity in the East (GDP per capita) leads to correspondingly lower wages and, therefore, intensifies tensions with unions – whose wage policies are intent on equalling income- and living-standards in Germany. Correspondingly, only half as many enterprises in the East are employer-federation members and, with that, bound to wage-standard agreements as in the West.

The formally adapted but in workplaces only weakly integrated unions in East Germany are able to act much less in the establishment of norms. In the East they are more strongly perceived by both workplace parties (works council and management) as external agencies than in West Germany. Particularly owner-managers of East-German SMEs emphasize the differences and maintain more distance towards works councils. The works councils are, for their part, less conflict- and interest-oriented and more concerned with consensus and cooperation than those in West Germany. The resulting freedom of action possessed by Eastern managers has thereby been often used to establish efficient, highly flexible production regimes that, in this respect, are at least on a par with West-German competitors.

There is one point, however, over which East-German entrepreneurs and works councils are in agreement: the attempt to form a productive balance between the maintenance of a competitive cost advantage on the market and the commitment to keeping the sought-after specialist labour force in East-German workplaces through market-level wages. The demand for uniform living-standard and income conditions or uniform Germany-wide and branch-wide wage levels is, in contrast, for most East-German works councils secondary. Therefore, the East does not function as a 'deregulation laboratory' for West-German downsizing strategies; rather, an 'elevator effect' is to be presumed. Downsizing in the West evokes corresponding effects in the East, for East-German companies cannot afford to do without such competitive advantages. Such policies are accepted – if with pursed lips – by most East-German works councils.

Meanwhile the integration of East-German managers into the capitalist market economy has progressed so far that a kind of over-identification with the rules of the new system has appeared. While as managers in state socialism they were obligated to the collective welfare, the majority now declare their normative preference to profit-maximizing competitive capitalism in a radical abstraction of market reality. In contrast one finds proponents of the moderately capitalist concept of the 'social market-economy' among West-German managers (see Martens and Michailow 2003; Martens 2007). Despite the capitalistic message stressed by some East-German managers, concepts such as finance-market-driven shareholder-value encounter little resonance among owner-led or personality-oriented SMEs because of their distant relation to the stock market. To the extent, however, that the weaker co-determination-oriented social relationships in East-German enterprises do indeed give their managers more autonomy than is the rule in the West, investors with their aggressive interest in value could, if they get the upper hand, more easily overcome possible employee resistance in trying to sell restructured enterprises for profit on the stock market.

Notes

1. The project has run since 2001 at the Friedrich Schiller University of Jena's Sociology Institute in the framework of the DFG-financed 'SFB 580' under the title *Generationswechsel im Management. Persistenz oder Wandel der Managementstrategien in Ost- und Westdeutschland* (Generation Shift in Management: Persistence or Change of Management Strategies in East and West Germany). The project team is made up of Katharina Bluhm, Robert Hinke, Bernd Martens und Rudi Schmidt. For the project concept see Gergs and Schmidt (2002); for an overview of the results see Martens and Michailow (2003). In addition, see also the contribution from Bluhm and Martens in this book. The summary reference to managers in this paper always denotes both entrepreneurs and employed managers.
2. For more on the state of the co-determination discussion, see Bertelsmann Stiftung and Hans-Böckler-Stiftung (1998) and Streeck and Kluge (1999).
3. The tendencies described here are extensively discussed in Artus et al. (2000), Artus (2001), Artus et al. (2001), Hinke et al. (2002), Fichter (1997), Schmidt and Artus (1998) and Schmidt (2003a), Schroeder (2000), Turner (1998: 48) and Upchurch (1995).
4. According to our Jena study, the number of cases of arbitration proceedings with a works council at 8.4 per cent in East-German firms managed by East-Germans is only half as high as in West-German workplaces (16.7 per cent).

References

Artus, I. (2001) *Krise des deutschen Tarifsystems. Die Erosion des Flächentarifvertrags in Ost und West* (Wiesbaden: Westdeutscher Verlag).

Artus, I., R. Schmidt and G. Sterkel (2000) *Brüchige Tarifrealität. Der schleichende Bedeutungsverlust tariflicher Normen in der ostdeutschen Industrie* (Berlin: Edition Sigma).

Artus, I., R. Liebold, K. Lohr, E. Schmidt, R. Schmidt and U. Strohwald (2001) *Betriebliches Interessenhandeln. Zur politischen Kultur der Austauschbeziehungen zwischen Management und Betriebsrat in der ostdeutschen Industrie* Vol. 2 (Opladen: Leske + Budrich).

Bertelsmann Stiftung and Hans-Böckler-Stiftung (eds) (1998) 'Mitbestimmung und neue Unternehmenskulturen – Bilanz und Perspektiven', Report from the Commission for Co-determination (gütersloh: Kommission der Mitbestimmung).

Ellguth, P. and S. Kohaut (2007) 'Tarifbindung und betriebliche Interessenvertretung – Aktuelle Ergebnisse aus dem IAB-Betriebspanel 2006', *WSI-Mitteilungen*, 60(9), 511–14.

Fichter, M. (1997) 'Unions in the New Länder: Evidence for the Urgency of Reform', in L. Turner (ed.), *Negotiating the New Germany. Can Social Partnership Survive?* (Ithaca, London: Cornell), 113–38.

Gergs, H. (2002) *Manager und Märkte. Eine soziologische Untersuchung der Markterschließungslogiken im osteutschen Management* (Munich, Mering: Hampp).

Gergs, H.-J. and R. Schmidt (2002) 'Generationswechsel im Management ost- und westdeutscher Unternehmen. Kommt es zu einer Amerikanisierung des deutschen Managementmodells?', *Kölner Zeitschrift für Soziologie und Sozialpsychologie*, 54, 553–78.

Hinke, R., S. Röbenack and R. Schmidt (2002) *Diesseits und jenseits des Tarifvertrags. Die Gestaltung der Lohn- und Leistungsbedingungen in der ostdeutschen Metall- und Elektroindustrie*, second edition (Berlin, Jena: Otto-Brenner-Stiftung).

Martens, B. (2007) 'Orthodoxie der Proselyten – Einstellungsmuster ökonomischer Funktionseliten im Ost/West-Vergleich', *Zeitschrift für Soziologie*, 36, 118–30.

Martens, B. and M. Michailow (2003) 'Konvergenzen und Divergenzen zwischen dem ost- und dem westdeutschen Management', in B. Martens, M. Michailow and R. Schmidt (eds), *Managementkulturen im Umbruch, SFB 580 Mitteilungen*, 10 (Jena: SFB), 13–55.

Müller-Jentsch, W. (2007) *Strukturwandel der industriellen Beziehungen. Industrial Citizenship zwischen Markt und Regulierung* (Wiesbaden: VS Verlag).

Rudolph, W. and W. Wassermann (2007) 'Gestärkte Betriebsräte. Trendreport Betriebsrätewahlen 2006. Ergebnisse der erweiterten Analyse', *Working Paper* (Kassel: Büro für Sozialforschung).

Schmidt, R. and I. Artus (1998) *Mitbestimmung in Ostdeutschland: Expertise für das Projekt, 'Mitbestimmung und neue Unternehmenskulturen' der Bertelsmann-Stiftung und Hans-Böckler-Stiftung* (Gütersloh: Bertelsmann-Stiftung).

Schmidt, R. (2003a) 'The Rebuilding of Industrial Relations in Eastern Germany', in W. Müller-Jentsch and H. Weitbrecht (eds), *The Changing Contours of German Industrial Relations* (Munich, Mering: Hampp), 81–102.

Schmidt, R. (2003b) 'Der gescheiterte Streik in der ostdeutschen Metallindustrie', *PROKLA*, 33, 493–509.

Schmidt, R. and R. Trinczek (1993) 'Duales System: Tarifliche und betriebliche Interessenvertretung', in Müller-Jentsch, W. (ed.), *Konfliktpartnerschaft*, second edition (Munich, Mering: Hampp), 135–46.

Schroeder, W. (2000) *Das Modell Deutschland auf dem Prüfstand. Zur Entwicklung der industriellen Beziehungen in Ostdeutschland (1990–2000)* (Wiesbaden: Westdeutscher Verlag).

Streeck, W. and N. Kluge (eds) (1999) *Mitbestimmung in Deutschland. Tradition und Effizienz. Expertenberichte für die Kommission Mitbestimmung Bertelsmann Stiftung/Hans-Böckler-Stiftung* (Frankfurt/Main, New York: Campus).

Turner, L. (1998) *Fighting for Partnership. Labor and Politics in Unified Germany* (Ithaca, London: Cornell University Press).

Upchurch, M. (1995) 'After Unification: Trade Unions and Industrial Relations in Eastern Germany', *Industrial Relations Journal*, 26(4), 280–92.

Index

Note: 'n.' after a page reference indicates the number of a note on that page.

accounting systems
  Anglo-German comparison   67
  German SMEs   9, 46–8
  large firms' influence   8–9
Ackermann, Josef   42, 54n.6
acquisitions *see* mergers and
  acquisitions
age factors, French owner-managers
  105, 106, 112
Altana   119
ambiguity
  governance of   167
  role, OEM–suppliers   160, 167
  scale   161, 167
anticipated entry, family businesses
  128
architectural innovation strategies
  174
'Asian way', Polish SME development
  191–2
Australian family businesses   125–6,
  130
automobile industry
  collaboration   159
  Germany   276
  large firms' influence   8
  the new 'local'   161
  vertical disintegration   154, 155
automotive supply industry,
  Emilia-Romagna   8, 205–10,
  220–3
  labour relations   210–20
Aventis   26, 27

Bangladesh, clothing industry   145
bank-based financial systems   4–5
Bank for International Settlement
  (BIS), Basel II *see* Basel II
banking systems
  Anglo-German comparison   62–7
  Finland   54n.8

Germany   31, 39–40
  restructuring   43–9
  Poland   190, 195–6
bank loans   4
  'dictatorship of lenders'   29–31
  German SMEs   42
bankruptcy
  Anglo-German comparison   63
  Poland   188
Basel II   5
  financial markets, power of   29
  Germany   5, 9, 31, 44
  Poland   195–6
  UK   5
Bayer Group   26
benchmarking   162, 163
  Illinois Tool Works   164
  restructuring based on results
    of   219
BMW   27
bonuses (output), Emilia-Romagna
  218
Borg Warner   154
branding, clothing industry   139,
  140, 141, 148
bribery, Poland   187
  see also corruption, Poland
'Buddenbrooks syndrome'   119, 122
Business Angels in Poland   195
Business Process Outsourcing (BPO)
  centres, Poland   194

Cambodia, clothing industry   145
capital scarcity, Poland   194–6
career paths, French SMEs   109–13
Central and Eastern Europe (CEE)
  clothing industry   143, 145
  competition   234
  entrepreneurship   77
  German production relocated to
    243–55

Central and Eastern Europe (CEE) –
    continued
    perspectives   228
    trade unions   231
    worker participation   230
    see also specific countries
chimney careers, German SMEs   52
China
    clothing industry   145
    WTO membership   235
Cisco Systems   164
clothing industry see textile and
    clothing industry
clusters, Emilia-Romagna   206–7
co-determination
    Germany (*Mitbestimmung*)   70,
        259, 261, 274
    East-West comparison   276–87
    Italy   217, 220
collectivization, Poland   187
commissions, social impact,
    Emilia-Romagna   215
community orientation, East
    Germany   80, 83, 85, 87–8,
    92, 94
competition
    Anglo-German comparison   71
    Central and Eastern Europe   234
    Poland   190, 191, 230–4
    manufacturing sector   157
competitive capitalism   79, 94
continuous development innovation
    strategy   172–3, 175, 177, 178,
    180
cooperation   152–3, 154, 156–9
    Emilia-Romagna   204, 209–10, 222
    governance of fluidity,
        contradiction and ambiguity
        161, 166–7
    lacking in Polish SMEs   196–7
cooperative banks, Germany   39, 43,
    62, 64
cooperative Polish SMEs   186
coordinated market economies
    (CMEs)   58, 59
    Germany   40, 58, 244, 274
corporate financing, Anglo-German
    comparison   58–61, 62–7, 71–3
corporate governance

Anglo-German comparison   62,
    68–9

Germany   39–40
    bank restructuring   43, 45
    insider corporate governance
        system   40, 41, 44, 50–1
    professionalization   46–8, 51, 53
    institutional 'embeddedness'   4
    professionalization   9
        Anglo-German comparison   62
            68–9
        Germany   46–8, 51, 53
    regional level   165–8
    rethinking   152–3
        fluidity, contradiction and
            ambiguity   161–8
        vertical disintegration   154,
            155–7
corporate social responsibility (CSR),
    East Germany   86–91, 94
corruption, Poland   185, 187, 190,
    197–8
craftsmen's workshops, Poland   186,
    187
credit ratings
    Anglo-German comparison   64–6
    Basel II   44
    financial markets, power of   29
    German SMEs   44–5
cultural capital, family businesses
    124
cultural issues, transforming societies
    79, 81
customer-oriented innovation
    strategy   173, 174, 175, 176–7,
    179
Cut-Make-and-Trim (CMT) sourcing,
    clothing industry   142, 143, 145

Daimler Benz   155, 157
daughter-succession, family
    businesses   129–30, 131
debt capital culture, German SMEs
    40, 43
Dell Computers   194
demographic changes, France   100,
    106

deregulation, UK 61, 69
Deutscher Gewerkschaftsbund (DGB) 284
development perspectives of non-research-intensive SMEs 181–2
diffusion of new technologies 180
Direct Buying strategy, clothing industry 142, 143
direct participation, Emilia-Romagna 211–15, 222
distributed knowledge base, non-research-intensive SMEs 175, 179
division of labour
inter-firm 161–2
Poland 198n.5
Dresdner Bank 44
dynasties 11, 119, 120, 124
patriarchalism, erosion of 127, 128, 129
social dynamics of business families 125, 126

economic development, Poland 228–9
economic institutionalization, transforming societies 78
economic participation, Emilia-Romagna 215, 217–18
Economic Value Added (EVA) 21
education and training
Anglo-German comparison 68–70
Central and Eastern Europe 247
clothing industry 139, 147
Emilia-Romagna, Italy 209
family businesses 124, 126–7
French SMEs 99, 107–9, 113–14
German SMEs 51–2, 245
clothing industry 139
East Germany 84, 88, 89, 90
production relocation to Hungary 249, 251
innovation strategies of non-research-intensive SMEs 177–9, 181
Polish SMEs 187–8, 189, 193, 194
social background of SMEs 10–11
see also qualifications

Emilia-Romagna region 8, 203–5, 220–3
automotive supply industry 8, 205–10
labour relations 210–20
employee social fund, France 260
employee spokespersons, Germany 265–6
employers' associations
Germany 246
Poland 230
employment contracts, Poland 237
Employment Retirement Investment Security Act (ERISA) 20–1
engineering sector, Germany 30, 31
engineer managers 104
French SMEs 109–13
Enterprise Committee, France (CE) 260–1, 263, 264, 268
entrepreneurs 104
financial markets, power of 23
French SMEs 106–13, 114
German SMEs 40
careers and value preferences 77–94
succession 50–1
new economy 49
Polish SMEs 187–9, 197–8
see also owner-managers/managing directors
EQUA-Foundation 118
equity based finance, 25–6
German SMEs 41–2, 43, 49
equity ratios
Anglo-German comparison 64–5
Basel II 44
German SMEs 39–40, 46, 49
ERISA 20–1
Esser, Klaus 42, 54n.6
Estonia, transforming society 93
ethnicity issues, UK clothing SMEs 138, 144
European Parliament 223
European Union (EU)
bank restructuring 43–4
Central and Eastern Europe 247
direct participation 212–13
information and consultation, employees' rights to 223, 230

European Union (EU) – *continued*
   Poland   191, 192, 197
   'Societas Europaea'   277
executives, France   107–8
exports
   clothing SMEs, British and German
      140, 141
   French SMEs   106
   Polish SMEs   191, 229

failed businesses, Anglo-German
      comparison   63
family businesses   104, 118–19
   generational change of families in
      119–27
   Germany   11–12, 41, 127, 128
      clothing industry   138
      succession   49–50, 52
   patriarchalism, erosion of   127–31
   Poland   186, 187
   social change   11
family shareholders, conflict between
      active and non-active   125, 126
family shares, market for   126
filial obligation, family businesses
      128–9
financial markets
   Anglo-German comparison   71
   German SMEs   41–3
   institutional 'embeddedness'   4–5
   Poland   190, 195–6
   power   17–24, 33–5
      companies and 'dictatorship of
         lenders'   28–31
      financialization and innovation
         31–3
      listed companies and shareholder
         influence   24–8
Fischer Body   154
fixed-term employment contracts,
      Emilia-Romagna   209
flexible production systems   152–3,
      156–61
   German production relocation to
      Hungary   248
   governance   161–8
Fordism
   financial markets   17

'long shadow' of   1
foreign direct investment (FDI)
   Central and Eastern Europe   247
   Poland   190, 194, 197
   clothing industry   143, 144
formalization
   in governance   153, 161–8
   of labour relations
      Emilia-Romagna   214–15,
         221–2
      Poland   236
founder managers   104
founding dates of SMEs,
      Anglo-German comparison   61
France   99–101, 113–14
   bank-based financing   4
   entrepreneurs, emergence of new
      106–13
   innovation   10
   labour relations   5
      formal rules of workplace
         reputation   259–61
      irregular forms, German-French
         comparison   258–71
   owner-managers of SMEs   103–6
   quantitative data on SMEs   101–2
   role and importance of SMEs
      102–3
   social background of SMEs   10–11
Freier Deutscher Gewerkschaftsbund
      (FDGB)   284
Full Package (FP) sourcing, clothing
      industry   142, 143, 145
furniture industry, Poland   239–40

'gazelles', French SMEs   100, 103, 106
gender factors
   family businesses   125, 126,
      129–30, 131
      Hohner   122
   job losses, production relocation
      from Germany to Hungary   250,
      253
   wage levels, Poland   237
General Motors   154
German production model   244–6,
   255
   relocation to the east   249

Germany
  accounting systems 9, 46–8
  bank-based financing 4, 5
  Central and Eastern European firms,
    cooperation with 235
  change within traditional channels
    39–41, 53–4
    bank restructuring and SMEs'
      proactive strategies 43–9
    limited influence of new financial
      investors 41–3
    succession 49–53
  corporate financing, management
    and organization 58–73
  East and West compared 6, 274–87
  family businesses 11–12, 41, 127,
    128
    clothing industry 138
    succession 49–50, 52
  financial markets, power of 20, 24,
    34, 35
    'dictatorship of lenders' 30–1
    shareholder value 24
    stock exchange capitalization
      25, 26
  institutional embeddedness 6
  labour relations 5, 8
    East-West comparison of social
      relationships 274–87
    formal rules of workplace
      representation 259–61
    irregular forms, German-French
      comparison 258–71
    production relocation to Hungary
      243–55
  large firms' influence 6–7, 9
  Polish SMEs 234, 238, 240
  qualification deficits 178
  regional production systems 2
  social background of SMEs 11–12,
    49–53
    East Germany 10, 79
  stakeholder versus shareholder
    orientation (East Germany)
    77–94
  textile and clothing industry 6–7
  and UK SMEs, comparison between
    58–73
    clothing firms 135–49

global commodity chains (GCCs)
  136–7
global isomorphism 58, 73
globalization
  Anglo-German comparison 71
  Emilia-Romagna 206
  financial markets 29–30
  French SMEs 99, 107
  German production relocation
    247
  labour relations 212
  non-research-intensive SMEs 181
  Polish SMEs 235, 236, 239–40
  regional production networks 208
globalized production networks
  flexibility and formalization
    152–68
  German and British clothing firms
    135–49
  innovation strategies of
    non-research-intensive SMEs
    171–82
  large firms' influence 3, 6–9,
    12–13
  Polish SMEs 185–98
goals, German SMEs 51
Goodrich Company 198n.4
Google Company 194
governance *see* corporate governance

heir(ess) managers 104
hierarchies in SMEs 154–5
  Anglo-German comparison 68
  break-ups 156
high-road seeking, Poland 236,
  237–40
HMS 198n.4
Hohner 121–3, 124
Hohner, Anna 122
Hohner, Ernst 123
Hohner, Hans 122
Hohner, Matthias 121–2
Hohner family 121–3, 124
hostile takeovers
  financial markets, power of 25, 26,
    27
  Germany 42, 54n.6
Hungary, German production
  relocation to 248–52

IG Metall 166–7, 272n.2
Illinois Tool Works (ITW) 163–4
imitation approach, business start-ups 99
incremental innovation strategies 174
Indian family businesses 128–30
individualism, Poles 196–7
industrial districts, Italy 203, 204, 220
industrial relations *see* labour-relations systems
information technology, and production relocation 254
infrastructure, Poland 196
in-house careers, German SMEs 52
innovation
  business start-ups 99
  Emilia-Romagna 204, 206, 209
  labour relations 211, 212, 213–14, 217, 222–3
  financial markets, power of 31–3
  French SMEs 99–100, 103, 108–9, 114
  owner-managers 103, 104, 105
  intra-firm relations 162–3, 164
  non-research-intensive SMEs 171–2
  companies and inter-company relationships 174–7
  developmental perspectives 181–2
  societal and institutional conditions 177–81
  strategies 172–4
  Polish SMEs 191, 192–6, 197, 232–4, 236, 237
  regional level governance 167
  social background of SMEs 10
  see also research and development
insider corporate-governance system, German SMEs 40, 41
  Basel II 44
  succession 50–1
institutional 'embeddedness' 2–6, 12
  innovation strategies of non-research-intensive SMEs 179–80, 181
institutional investors 19–24

insurance companies 20
inter-company relations, non-research-intensive SMEs 174–7
intra-firm relations 162–4
Ireland, qualification deficits 178
irregular forms of employee interest representation, German-French comparison 258–9
  formal rules of workplace representation 259–61
  institutions, relevance of 270–1
  in practice 264–70
  representation gap 261–4
ISO standards 8, 197
Italy
  banks 4
  clothing SMEs 140
  Emilia-Romagna region 8, 203–5, 220–3
    automotive supply industry 8, 205–10
    labour relations 210–20
  industrial districts 203, 204, 220
  labour-relation system 8
  regional production systems 2, 7–8
  social background of SMEs 10

job creation, French SMEs 102–3, 106
job market
  Emilia-Romagna 208–9
  France 107–8, 113–14
  innovation strategies of non-research-intensive SMEs 177–8
  Poland 190
  production relocation from Germany to Hungary 250–1
joint ventures, clothing industry 143

Kenya, Indian family businesses in 129
knowledge base, non-research-intensive SMEs 174–5, 179
knowledge organization and management

Emilia-Romagna 209
non-research-intensive SMEs
175–7

labour, division of
inter-firm 161–2
Poland 198n.5
labour contracts
Emilia-Romagna 210
Poland 230
labour costs
Central and Eastern Europe 234
Poland 234, 235, 236, 237
reducing 219
see also wages
labour-relations systems
Anglo-German comparison 70
East-West German comparison
274–87
German-French comparison
258–71
German production relocation to
Hungary 243–55
institutional 'embeddedness' 5–6
Italy 210–23
large firms' influence 8
Poland 228–41
labour supply problems, Poland 191,
192, 197, 235
large firms
family businesses 119
influence on political
macro-regulation 246
influence within globalized
production networks 3, 6–9,
12–13
regional production networks,
importance of 208
restructuring based on
benchmarking 219
trickle-down effects 8, 46
labour market *see* job market
leadership, East German
entrepreneurs 80–1, 83, 92, 93
learning processes
Anglo-German comparison 65–6
collaboration 158
East German entrepreneurs 94

German SMEs 47
'new pragmatic disciplines' 162
leasing, German SMEs 49
lenders, 'dictatorship of' 28–31
life cycle of the family 121–5
liquidity, German SMEs 51
listed companies and shareholder
influence 24–8
loans, 'dictatorship of lenders' 28–31
local production systems, Italy 203,
206
fragmented participation 212
low- and medium-technology (LMT)
companies, innovation in 171–2
companies and inter-company
relationships 174–7
developmental perspectives 181–2
societal and institutional conditions
177–81
strategies 172–4
low-road traditionalism, Poland
236–7

management
Anglo-German comparison 58–61,
67–73
financial market, power of 25, 26,
27–8
German SMEs 52–3
East Germany 80–1, 84–94
payment 27
Anglo-German comparison 70
Germany 42
replacement 25, 26, 27
routes to 104
values, East Germany 80–1, 84–94
see also owner-managers/managing
directors
management buy-ins (MBIs), family
businesses 125, 128, 131
management buy-outs (MBOs)
family businesses 125, 128, 131
UK clothing SMEs 138, 146
management–employee relationships
direct worker involvement
214–15, 221–2
production relocation from
Germany to Hungary 252, 253

managing directors *see*
   owner-managers/managing
   directors
mandated salaried employees, France
   272n.3
Mannesmann   26, 54n.6
manufacturing sector
   Anglo-German comparison   63, 64,
      67, 69, 71
   Germany   39–54
   production relocation to Hungary
      247, 248
   non-research-intensive SMEs
      171–2
   Poland   229, 232–4, 235–7, 239
   rethinking space and governance
      152–3
      fluidity, contradiction and
         ambiguity, governance of
         161–8
      vertical disintegration, ambiguity
         and new relations of proximity
         and distance   153–61
   worker participation   213
maquiladorization   228, 232
market-based financial systems   4, 5
market concentration, clothing SMEs
   140
market for corporate control   25, 26,
   27
market strategy, clothing SMEs
   139–41
Marks & Spencer (M&S)   144, 145,
   147
Mauritius, clothing industry   145
media, and power of financial markets
   21
mergers and acquisitions
   banking sector   43
   Cisco Systems   164
   German SMEs   43
   Poland   188
Mexico, maquiladoras   228, 232
mezzanine capital   42, 54n.5
   family businesses   126
migrant workers
   innovation strategies of
      non-research-intensive SMEs
      178

Poles   191, 192, 197, 235
Mittelstand   71
   clothing industry   138, 140, 144,
      148, 149
   financial markets, power of   30–1,
      34, 35
modernization theory, transforming
   societies   78
modularization, Italian automotive
   supply industry   209
Module Assembly Units, Italian
   automotive supply industry   209
Moody's   29
motives
   East German entrepreneurs   83,
      91–2, 94
   French entrepreneurs   111
mutually-owned banks, Germany
   39, 43, 62, 64

National Economy Bank, Poland
   198n.8
negotiated participation,
   Emilia-Romagna   211–12,
   215–17, 220, 223
'New Economy'
   'bubble'   22, 26, 40
   entrepreneurs   49
   financial markets, power of   20
   stock exchange capitalization   26
'new managerialism', UK   68
'new pragmatic disciplines'   153,
   161–2, 163
'Notgemeinschaft'   283

non-research-intensive SMEs,
   innovation in   171–2
   companies and inter-company
      relationships   174–7
   developmental perspectives   181–2
   societal and institutional conditions
      177–81
   strategies   172–4

off-shoring
   clothing industry   141
   locations   235

Organisation for Economic
Co-operation and Development
(OECD) 171
organization in SMEs, Anglo-German
comparison 58–61, 67–73
original equipment manufacturers *see*
supplier–OEM relationships
output bonuses, Emilia-Romagna
218
outsourcing
automobile industry 207
clothing industry 141, 142, 143,
144–7
Poland 194, 238, 239
Outward Processing Trade (OPT)
sourcing, clothing industry 142,
143, 145
overdrafts 4
Anglo-German comparison 63
overtime, Emilia-Romagna 209
owner-managers/managing directors
French SMEs 100, 103–6, 114
entrepreneurs, emergence of
106–13
German SMEs 41, 49–51
East Germany 81, 84–5, 87,
88–94
social background of SMEs 9–10,
11
see also entrepreneurs

participation
Emilia-Romagna 211–20, 222–3
Poland 230, 236
restructuring processes' impact on
218–19
patent applications
EU acceding countries 192
Poland 196
patriarchalism 11, 124
erosion of 127–31
Poland 236
pension funds 19, 20–1
performance-related payment,
Anglo-German comparison 70
Personnel Delegates, France (DP)
260, 262–3, 264, 268

personnel-representation institutions,
France (IRPs) 260, 262–3, 269,
270, 271
pharmaceutical sector, innovation
33
Poland 185, 228–30, 240–1
bank-based financing 4
challenges and pathologies in SME
sector 196–8
development of SMEs after 1989
189–92
economic development 228–9
growing pressures on and responses
of SMEs 234–40
innovation gap in SMEs 192–6
labour relations and competitive
strategy 6, 230–4
large firms' influence 7
origins of SMEs 186–9
works councils 6, 230
PolBAN 195
Porsche 27
portfolio theory 21
pricing issues, clothing industry
147, 148
principle-agent governance 154, 156
private equity firms
family businesses 118, 126
UK clothing SMEs 138
private Polish SMEs 186, 187
privatization
East Germany 84, 87, 89, 90, 91,
94
trust foundations 283, 284
Poland 187, 188
process specialization innovation
strategy 173, 175, 176
production networks
globalized *see* globalized production
networks
regional variations 2
product strategy, clothing SMEs
139–41
professionalization
corporate governance 9
Anglo-German comparison 62
68–9
Germany 46–8, 51, 53
family businesses 126–7, 131

professionalization – *continued*
  innovation in
    non-research-intensive SMEs
    176
  transforming societies 82
profitability
  automobile industry 207
  family businesses 125
  German SMEs 51
    clothing industry 138
    Polish SMEs 187
    UK clothing SMEs 138
property-rights theory 78
proximity effects 103, 115n.9
  non-research-intensive SMEs
  180–1
public opinion, power of financial
  markets 21, 24

qualifications
  France 107, 108–9
  Germany 51–2
    East Germany 88
  hybrid 178
  innovation strategies of
    non-research-intensive SMEs
    178
  Poland 193–4
  see also education and training
quality certification 216
quality issues
  clothing industry 147
  Poland 191, 197
quality standards 8, 197
Quandt, Herbert 119
Quandt family 119, 120

radical innovation strategies 174
raider managers 104
ratings *see* credit ratings
recruitment, Emilia-Romagna 208
regional level
  erosion of regional ties,
    non-research-intensive SMEs
    180–1
  governance at the 165–8
regional policy, large firms' influence
  7–8

regulation theory 17
relationship banking, Anglo-German
  comparison 62–3, 66
representation group
  France 262–4
  Germany 261–2
representative participation,
  Emilia-Romagna 211–12,
  215–17, 220, 223
'reproducers', French SME
  owner-managers 103, 104–5,
  109, 113
reproduction approach, business
  start-ups 99
reputation networks
  Anglo-German comparison 65, 66
  German SMEs 40, 48
research and development (R&D)
  expenditure 171
  French SMEs 106
  Poland 193–4, 195, 197
  see also innovation
research institutes 179
resource-dependency theory 62
reverse-auctions, automotive supply
  industry 223n.2
risk assessment
  Anglo-German comparison 64
  financial markets, power of 29, 31
  German SMEs 44
Robert Bosch 154
role ambiguity, OEM–suppliers 160,
  167
Romania
  as offshoring location 235
  transforming society 93
rule enforcement by third parties 2

Sanofi Syntélab 27
savings banks, Germany 31, 39
  Anglo-German comparison 62, 64
  restructuring 43–5
scale ambiguity, for products and
  regions 161, 167
Schering 26
Schwarz 119
Schwarz, Patrick 119
Schwarz, Rolf 119

service sector
  German production model 245
  worker participation 213
share buy-back programmes 26
shareholder value
  Anglo-German comparison 58–9
  financial markets, power of 21–3,
    24–8, 43
  Germany 9, 10, 24, 42, 53
    East 77–94
  profit orientation 47
short-termism 59
  East German entrepreneurs 85, 87,
    91, 93
single delegation, France (DU) 260,
  263, 268
size of companies
  Anglo-German comparison 60
  and bargaining, Emilia-Romagna
    216
  Central and Eastern European
    SMEs, working conditions 23
  French SMEs 102, 103
    representation gap 262
  German SMEs 275–7
    works councils 246, 261–2
  and innovation 103
  Polish SMEs 229
    barriers to entrepreneurship 234
    unionization 231
size of industrial sectors
  Anglo-German comparison 61
  clothing industries 138
skydiver careers, German SMEs 52–3
social background of SMEs 3, 9–12,
  13
  Germany 11–12, 49–53
    East Germany 10, 79
social dynamics of business families
  121, 125–7
socially embedded capitalism,
  Germany 244
social fund, France 260
social pact, Italy 215–16, 222
social relationships in German SMEs
  274–5, 285–7
  East-West differences
    co-determination and unions
      278–82

structural and historical reasons
  282–5
labour relations and size differences
  275–7
'Societas Europaea' (SE) 277
socio-institutional conditions,
  innovation strategies of
  non-research-intensive SMEs
  177–81
Solidarity 231
Sommer, Ron 42, 54n.7
sourcing strategies and modes,
  clothing industry 142–5
space
  erosion of regional ties,
    non-research-intensive SMEs
    180–1
  rethinking 152–3
  arm's length contracting 155–6
  governance 167–8
  vertical disintegration 158,
    159–61
Spain, family businesses 127
specialized research institutes 179
spokespersons, employee (Germany)
  265–6
Sri Lanka, clothing industry 145
STACO network 198n.4
stakeholder orientation, East
  Germany 77–94
stakeholder theory 80
Standard & Poor's 29
state central banks, Germany 31,
  55n.10
state-owned Polish SMEs 186
Steilmann 119–20
Steilmann, Britta 119–20
Steilmann, Klaus 119
Steilmann, Ute 120
step-by-step product development
  172–3, 175, 177, 178, 180
stewards' committees, UK 70
stock exchange capitalization 25–6
strategic company goals, German
  SMEs 51
strategic management theory 135–6
strikes
  France 261, 271
  Germany 259, 285

strong participation 211
succession
   family businesses 120, 121, 123,
      124, 125
   patriarchalism, erosion of
      127–31
   social dynamics 125, 126
   French SMEs 105–6
   German SMEs 49–53
supplier–OEM relationships
   Emilia-Romagna 206–8
   governance 165–6
   large firms' influence 7, 8
   role ambiguity 160, 167
   vertical disintegration 154–60
supply chain management
   automotive supply industry 207
   clothing industry 143
   manufacturing industries 152
Switzerland, family businesses 127–8

takeovers *see* hostile takeovers;
   mergers and acquisitions
taxation, Poland 195, 234, 235, 237
team-work, Italian automotive
   supply industry 209–10,
   214, 221
Technological Credit Fund, Poland
   194
technological loan, Poland 194
temporary agency workers,
   Emilia-Romagna 208–9
textile and clothing industry 6–7
   Anglo-German comparison
      135–49
   Poland 237, 239
Thatcher government, UK
   deregulation policies 61
   'new managerialism' 68
'Third Italy' 203, 220
   see also Emilia-Romagna region
Timken 154
Trade Union Federation OPZZ 231
trade unions
   Anglo-German comparison 70
   Central and Eastern Europe 231
   direct and negotiated participation
      211, 212, 213

France 260–1, 263–4, 269–70
Germany 246, 259, 267, 275–6
   East-West comparison 278–86
   production relocation to Hungary
      252, 253, 254
   right extremism 255
   IG Metall 166–7, 272n.2
   Italy 216
   Emilia-Romagna 205, 217, 220,
      221
   Poland 230, 231–2, 236, 237
Trade Unions Forum 231
training *see* education and training
transaction banking 63
transformation theory 81, 93
transmission of businesses 105–6
   see also succession
transparency
   Anglo-German comparison 65–6,
      67
   German SMEs 44, 48
trickle-down effects 8, 46
trust foundations, East Germany
   (*Treuhandanstalt, THA*) 283, 284
Turkey, clothing industry 145
turnover
   clothing SMEs 138, 146
   German SMEs 51, 138, 146
   UK SMEs 138, 146

Ukraine
   as offshoring location 235
   Polish SMEs outsourcing to 238
unanticipated entry, family businesses
   129, 131
unemployment
   France 107, 114
   Poland 186, 189, 190
Union Delegates, France (DS) 260–1,
   263–4
unions *see* trade unions
United Kingdom
   bank-based financing 4, 5
   corporate financing, management
      and organization 58–73
   deregulation 61, 69
   financial markets, power of 19
   and German SMEs, comparison
      between 58–73

clothing firms   135–49
Indian family businesses   129
social background of SMEs   10
textile and clothing industry   6–7
Anglo-German comparison
   135–49
Thatcher government   61, 68
United States of America
clothing industry   140, 141
family businesses   129, 130
financial markets, power of   19, 20,
   24
automotive industry   27
stock flotations   25–6
Indian family businesses   129

value chains
automotive supply industry, Italy
   210
clothing   139
innovation strategies in
   non-research-intensive SMEs
   179
Polish SMEs   234, 238, 239–40
value-oriented management   21–3,
   26
values
East German employees   92–3
East German entrepreneurs   80–1,
   83, 84–91, 94
Varieties of Capitalism (VoC)
approach   1–2, 39
clothing industry   136, 137, 141,
   144, 147, 148
institutional erosion in Germany
   255
large firms' influence within
   globalized production networks
   6–7
vertical disintegration   153–61, 165
vocational training *see* education and
   training
Vodafone   54n.6
Volkswagen   276

wage levels
Central and Eastern Europe   247

Emilia-Romagna   215
irregular forms of employee interest
   representation
France   267, 268
Germany   265
Polish SMEs   235, 237, 239
see also labour costs
weak participation   211
white-collar employment, production
   relocation from Germany to
   Hungary   250, 252
WIETPOL   198n.4
wife's role, family businesses   124
Hohner   122
Wisconsin Manufacturers'
   Development Consortium
   (WMDC)   165–7
working conditions, Emilia-Romagna
   210, 214
work organization, Emilia-Romagna
   209–10, 214, 215–17, 221, 222
Workplace Constitution Laws
   (Germany)
1952, 275
2001, 259
Works Constitution Act (Germany
   1920)   275
works contracts, Poland   237
works councils
Germany   70, 246, 259, 266–7,
   275–6
East-West comparison   276–8,
   280–6
production relocation to Hungary
   249, 251, 252, 253–4
representation gaps   261, 262
rejected in Poland   230
workshops, Poland   186, 187
World Trade Organization (WTO),
   China's membership of   235

Zahnradfabrik Friedrichshafen   154